MW01697906

BRAVURA

BRAVURA

Virtuosity and Ambition in Early Modern European Painting

NICOLA SUTHOR

Princeton University Press

Princeton and Oxford

Copyright © 2021 by Nicola Suthor

Requests for permission to reproduce material from this work
should be sent to permissions@press.princeton.edu

Published by Princeton University Press,
41 William Street, Princeton, New Jersey 08540
In the United Kingdom: Princeton University Press,
6 Oxford Street, Woodstock, Oxfordshire OX20 1TR
press.princeton.edu

Front cover: Peter Paul Rubens, *The Fall of Phaeton* (detail), ca. 1604–1605.
Oil on canvas, 98.4 × 131.2 cm. National Gallery, Washington, DC.
Back cover: Jean-Honoré Fragonard, *Abbé Claude Richard de Saint-Non*, 1769.
Oil on canvas, 80 × 65 cm. Musée du Louvre, Paris.

All Rights Reserved

ISBN 978-0-691-20458-1
ISBN (e-book) 978-0-691-21343-9
Library of Congress Control Number: 2020946307

British Library Cataloging-in-Publication Data is available

Published in part with the generous support of the Publications Fund
of the Department of the History of Art, Yale University.

Designed by Julie Fry
Composed in Baskerville
Printed on acid-free paper ∞
Printed in Italy

10 9 8 7 6 5 4 3 2 1

Contents

CHAPTER ONE

Celebrations of Violence

THE ARTIST AS EXECUTIONER

The artist who wishes to garner the reward of applause must make a personal appearance in their artwork. One of the most common and simple ways of achieving this is to sign the work, which not only guarantees remembrance but can also "signpost ambition," as the art historian Patricia Rubin has pointed out.[1] This ambition becomes more transparent when the inscribed name interacts with what is represented and thus participates in the artwork's meaning.[2] Another strategem is for the artist to insert their own image. Both practices were already well established by the seventeenth century; however, they were being used now with a forcefulness that announced a new narrative: rather than merely petitioning the beholder, they were meant to strike a blow.

The painter Mattia Preti (1613–1699) from Calabria, praised by his colleague Luigi Scaramuccia (1616–1680) as *molto bravo disinvolto* (very recklessly bold),[3] inserted his own likeness in a most extraordinary manner on an altarpiece he donated to the church of his hometown (fig. 1). The artist has placed himself in a prominent position in the foreground of the image. With his left hand, he touches his chest and proudly indicates the large Maltese cross emblazoned on his robe that identifies him as a knight of the Order of Hospitallers, while with his right hand he grasps a paintbrush and a sword.[4] The pairing of these two instruments, one placed above the other to form a vertical axis, is remarkable for there is no conceivable task that could require their use in concert. Preti holds the brush poised as if painting, but the instrument is inverted. Aligned with the sword grip and terminating in a white, sharp brushstroke, the pointed end of the brush handle points downward like the analogous tip of the sword.

1 (FACING)
Mattia Preti, *John the Baptist Preaching*, c. 1672. Oil on canvas, 290 × 202 cm. Church of San Domenico, Taverna.

The narrative of the altarpiece into which Preti has inserted his self-portrait provides a motivation for these mismatched attributes. In the center of the canvas, John the Baptist, the patron saint of the Order of the Hospitallers, delivers a sermon. His bent right arm directs our attention to the undulating banner held by a putto, on which *POENIT* (repent) is clearly legible. This single word discloses the sermon's message: "You viper's brood! Who warned you to flee from the wrath

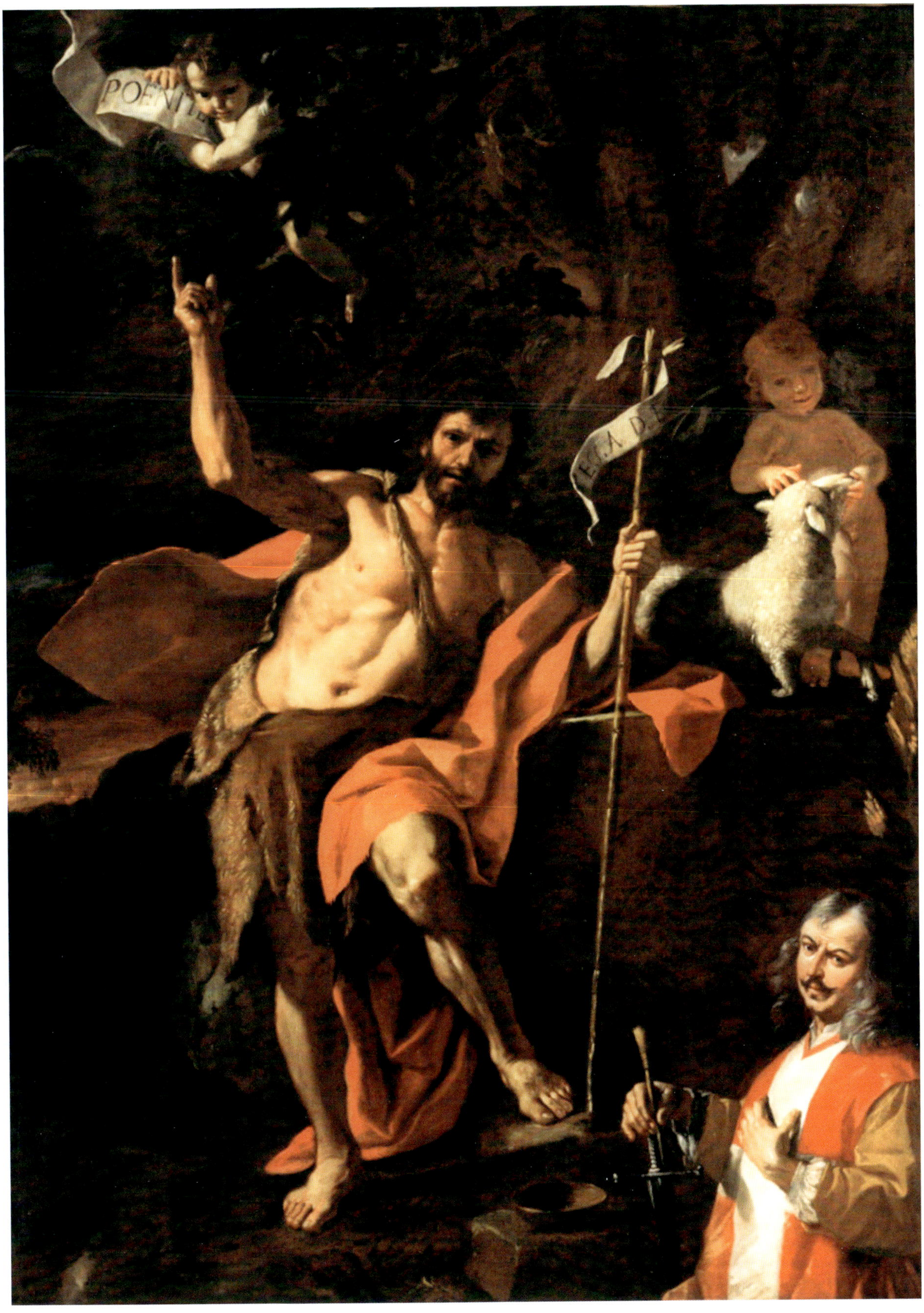

to come? Therefore bear fruits worthy of repentance."[5] Although Preti positions his image in the foreground of the depicted event, spatially he seems to stand in front of his work. As an intermediary between beholder and saint, his gestures and facial expression communicate his empathetic participation in the painting's theme of sin and redemption. Ostentatiously, but undeniably, he has borne fruit worthy of repentance in the form of this altarpiece that he has created and donated to the church.

In a panegyric to *Il Cavalier Calabrese famosissimo Pittore* by the notable Jesuit playwright Andrea Perrucci (1651–1704), Preti accrues prestige for the religious role he performs through his art: "When you allure souls and deceive the eye, Eternity has chosen her brush to fill the oblivion of blasphemies and harms, while Fame has discovered winged pens to shed light on your excellent paintings."[6] In a second poem, Perrucci again cites Preti's duty as a Maltese knight battling heresy through his painting. Preti "defends the saintly Heroes of the sublime Religion"; the "terrifying traces imprinted by his brush" bring him not only "applause and acclaim" but also glory, in the same way that "iron" makes "the candid cross on his breast blaze." By comparing the blood shed in the name of the cross with the sweat of Preti's labor, both substances decorating the "eternal Crown,"[7] Perrucci endows the act of painting with stark martial overtones: the paintbrush is no longer just an artist's implement; it has become a weapon that will be used to fight religious contests.

Several decades later, Giambattista Piazzetta (1682–1754) will amplify the identification between painting and violence when he renders himself as none other than Herod's executioner in an altarpiece featuring the beheading of John the Baptist. He is not only the main protagonist, but also the scene's most malign figure (fig. 2).[8] The work was commissioned for the Church of San Antonio in Padua, along with a number of other pieces painted by the most important artists of the time.[9] Piazzetta's response to this competitive challenge was a self-portrayal hardly to be outdone in its audacity. Charles-Nicolas Cochin the Younger (1715–1790), the French engraver and member of the Royal Academy, reviewed the painting on a trip to Italy thirteen years after it was first displayed in 1745. Although praising the work's composition as "ingenious," he found fault with the portrayal of the villain: "There is too much action in the figure of the executioner, who rolls up his sleeves."[10] He concludes by commending the painterly style as "generous, rich, and tasteful, and having something quite grand" (*large, grasse, pleine de goût et a quelque chose d'assez grand*) but criticizes the mannerism of the colors; for him, the shadows are too black, the areas of light too white.[11] Cochin's critique was soon repudiated by G. B. Rossetti in his guide to the paintings of Padua, published in 1765: "No one but Cochin would perceive these defects, for the action is not forced; the color is as natural as could be."[12] Rossetti goes on to explain the extreme chiaroscuro as expressive of the scene's particular setting: it suggests an opening in the ceiling of the prison cell, through which light falls dramatically onto the saint.

Paolo Faccio, writing in 1818, considered this painting "one of the best ever brought forth by Giambattista Piazzetta's brush; neither the evening light nor mottling used by the painter ever came together so well as in this representation."[13] The historiographer Luigi Lanzi, however, in his *Storia pittorica della Italia* (1795) criticizes Piazzetta's brushwork in the altarpiece: "Such rapidity of the brush that some

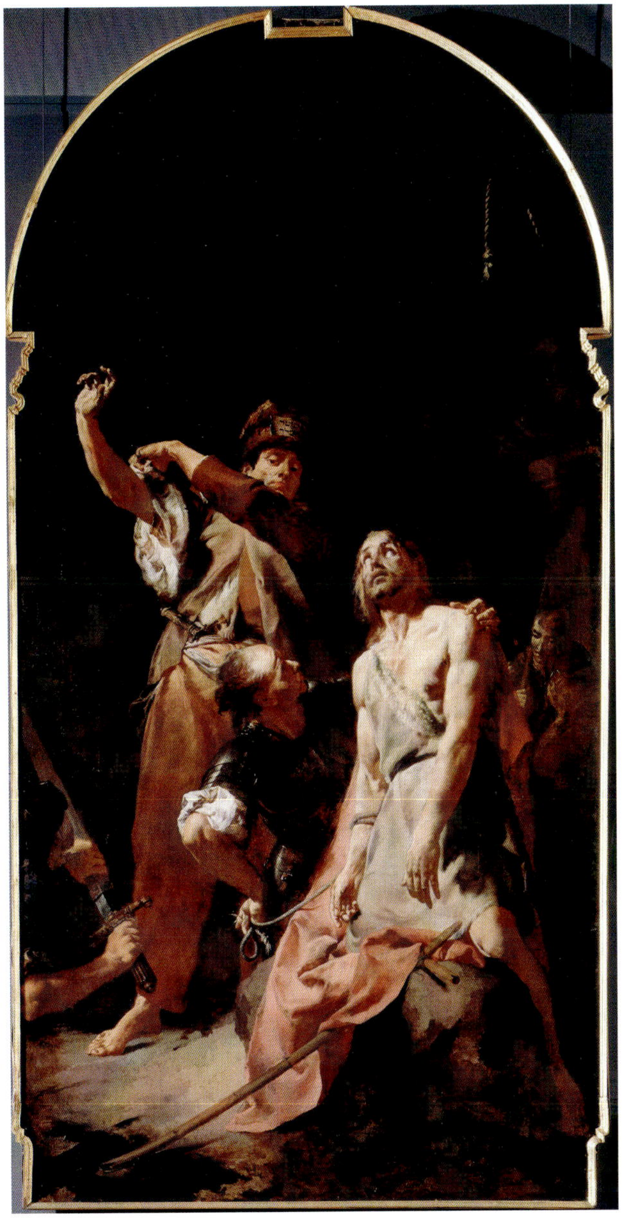

2
Giambattista Piazzetta, *The Beheading of John the Baptist*, 1744. Oil on canvas, 318 × 183 cm. Museo Antoniano, Padua.

call bravura, to others sometimes seems like neglect [*incuria*], which abandons the work prematurely."[14]

In the picture Piazzetta wears a fur hat, so typical a feature in artists' self-portraits, bearing a legend in Hebrew that underscores, although in encrypted fashion, the surrogate nature of the violence about to take place. Styled as the "constable of the king" (*shotar ha melekh*), Herod's henchman acts with supreme confidence. He raises his bared arm, which, parallel to the weapon proffered from below, hovers menacingly over the head of the saint.

A series of contrasting juxtapositions between the saint and the executioner reinforces the painting's theme. The powerful agency of the executioner's raised arms opposed to those of the saint drooping passively, and his intense facial expression, his lips tightly closed, contrast with John's detached countenance and slightly

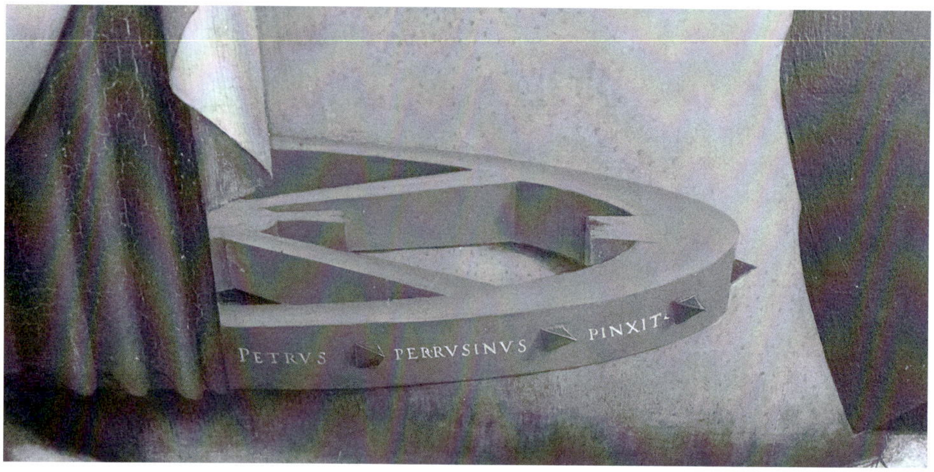

3
Pietro Perugino, *Madonna and Child in Glory with the Saints John the Evangelist, Apollonia, Catherine of Alexandria, and Michael the Archangel* (*Scarani Altarpiece*), c. 1500. Oil on wood, 273 × 211 cm. Pinacoteca Nationale, Bologna.

opened mouth; John's skyward gaze counters that of the executioner, who looks downward from an elevated position and fixes his eyes on the beholder. The actual *beheading* of John the Baptist, the decisive act of martyrdom the painting was commissioned to depict, has yet to occur.[15] Piazzetta is not poised to strike, which is the usual motific posture of Herod's henchman, but instead is caught in an earlier moment in the chain of events leading up to the sacrifice.

The executioner is accompanied by a soldier who leans forward and gazes intently up at John's face. He holds a restraining rope in his right hand and with his left reaches around the saint's back, encircling him from behind and touching John's powerful shoulder with his fingertips. John's upturned eyes communicate a state of rapture, which the soldier seeks to comprehend. The soldier seems to be waiting for a sign that is portended solely by means of the lighting effects Cochin deemed exaggerated. His figure is cast in shadow, in contrast to John who radiates a supernatural glow. This opposition of shadow and artificial light could be theologically motivated by Christ's teaching on the eyes as luminous lamps of the body: "Your eye is the lamp of your body. If your eye is healthy, your whole body is full of light; but if it is not healthy your body is full of darkness" (Luke 11:34; NRSV). The soldier's desire to witness a miracle, conveyed by his searching eyes, is rooted in disbelief, whereas John's heavenward gaze speaks of religious faith and devotion. The expectancy that accompanies this witness's ignorance may likewise mirror a desire in the beholder for the sensational.

As the executioner raises his arm and rolls up his sleeve, a sword is held out to him by a servant almost entirely cut off by the left edge of the picture and reduced to his hands and lost profile. This servant is balanced on the right side of the scene by two of John's followers, positioned behind the saint. One covers his face with both hands, powerless and in despair. Whereas these two remain in the background, the servant acts as a link between the viewer and the figure of the executioner. Does Piazzetta mean to imply that it is we who are responsible for uttering the execution command?

Whatever the beholder's complicity may be, Piazzetta's self-incrimination explicitly addresses the notion that the pictorial representation of martyrdom acts as a spiritual reenactment of the sacrifice, but it is done here in a manner far more striking than the more subtle peripheral implication of the artist's complicity in the crime as staged in other works of art. At least as far back as the early Renaissance we can find many examples of covert allusions to the painter as executioner. For instance, Pietro Perugino (1445–1525) affixed his name in golden letters to the broken wheel of St. Catherine in his altarpiece (Bologna, Pinacoteca Nationale; fig. 3), and even more strikingly, on a wounding arrow in his bust-length *Saint Sebastian* (St. Petersburg, Hermitage). According to the art historian Alfredo Bellandi, this self-inscription expresses Perugino's Christian piety, which led him to develop a new and highly successful "expressive register" of sacred art calculated to solicit an emotive response by tempering the "iconography of pain," "sweetening" the martyr's facial expression, and "softening" the body's anatomy.[16] This devotional rendition of martyrdom, which reached its zenith in the work of Perugino's student Raphael, invested the alliance of martyrdom and painterly execution with a new significance and became a compelling alternative to representations that primarily sought to arouse disgust or horror.

Raphael's fierce opponent Sebastiano del Piombo, who instigated the open rivalry between Raphael and Michelangelo, took a different approach to the illustration of suffering. In his 1520 *Martyrdom of Saint Agatha*, a knife is shown lying on a stone parapet that separates the pictorial space from the beholder (fig. 4).

4
Sebastiano del Piombo, *Martyrdom of Saint Agatha*, 1520. Oil on wood, 132 × 178 cm. Galleria Palatina, Palazzo Pitti, Florence.

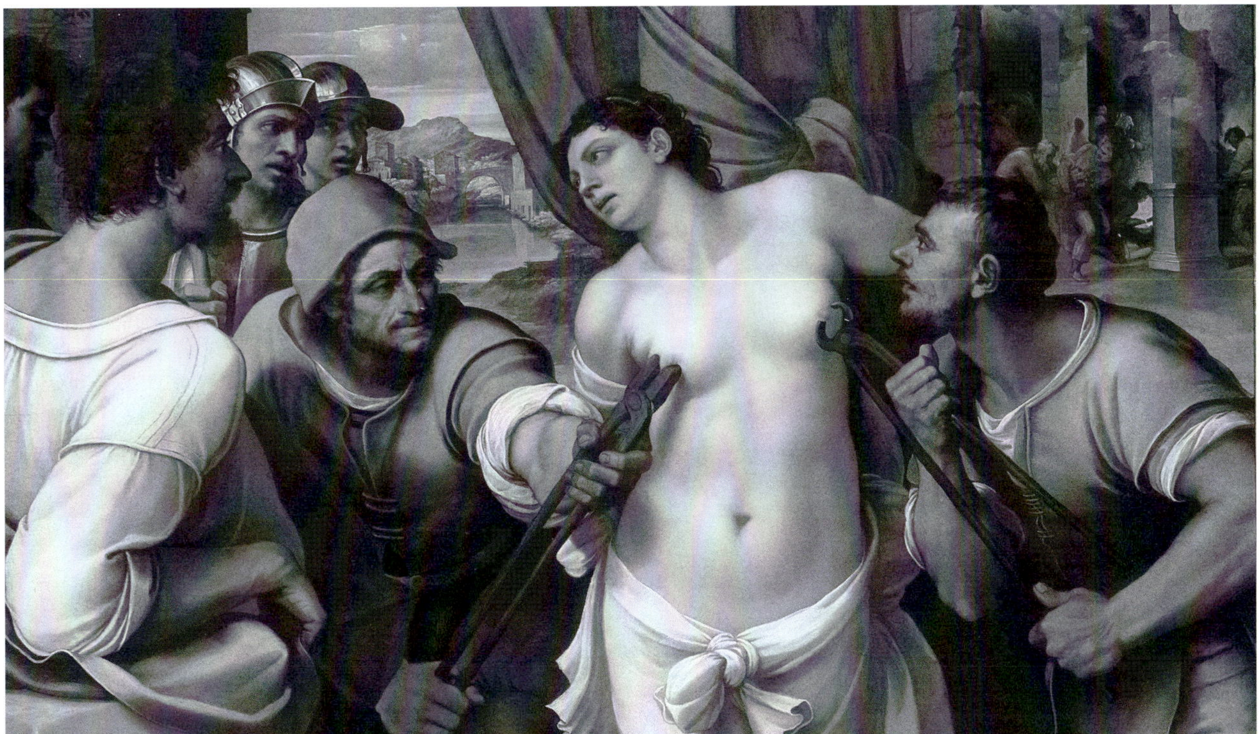

The blade, projecting beyond the wall's edge as it points to the chiseled inscription "SEBASTIANUS VENETUS FACIEBAT ROME MDXX," constitutes, in Jill Burke's words "a bravura exhibition of the painter's skill."[17] The scene takes place before St. Agatha's death as she is being tortured with tongs. Only the attention-grabbing knife in the foremost picture plane, suggesting the future prospect of her breasts being cut off, evokes the means of her eventual martyrdom. The beholder's gaze is met not only by the proffered body of the saint, but by the sharp tip of the jutting blade; the same weapon that will kill the saint therefore forcefully incites the viewer to imagine an image substantially different, and thus "severed," from the one depicted. By awakening the viewer's awareness of what is to come, the knife also makes us participants in the future act of violence.

The most famous and radical example of a similar self-referential gesture is Michelangelo Merisi da Caravaggio's *Beheading of John the Baptist* (1608) for the Oratory of San Giovanni Decollato in Malta, the only painting he ever signed (fig. 5).[18] The inscription of his signature, "f michel Ang.," seems to play an active part in the scene. The letters, drawn as if by a finger dipped in the adjacent pool of John's blood,[19] form an encrypted message. The art historian Karin Gludovatz compares this motif to St. Peter Martyr using his finger to inscribe the Credo in the earth as he was expiring.[20] In Caravaggio, however, the signature seems like a confession of the artist's responsibility. He has caused the biblical story to take place once again. Paradoxically, none of the execution implements are bloody,

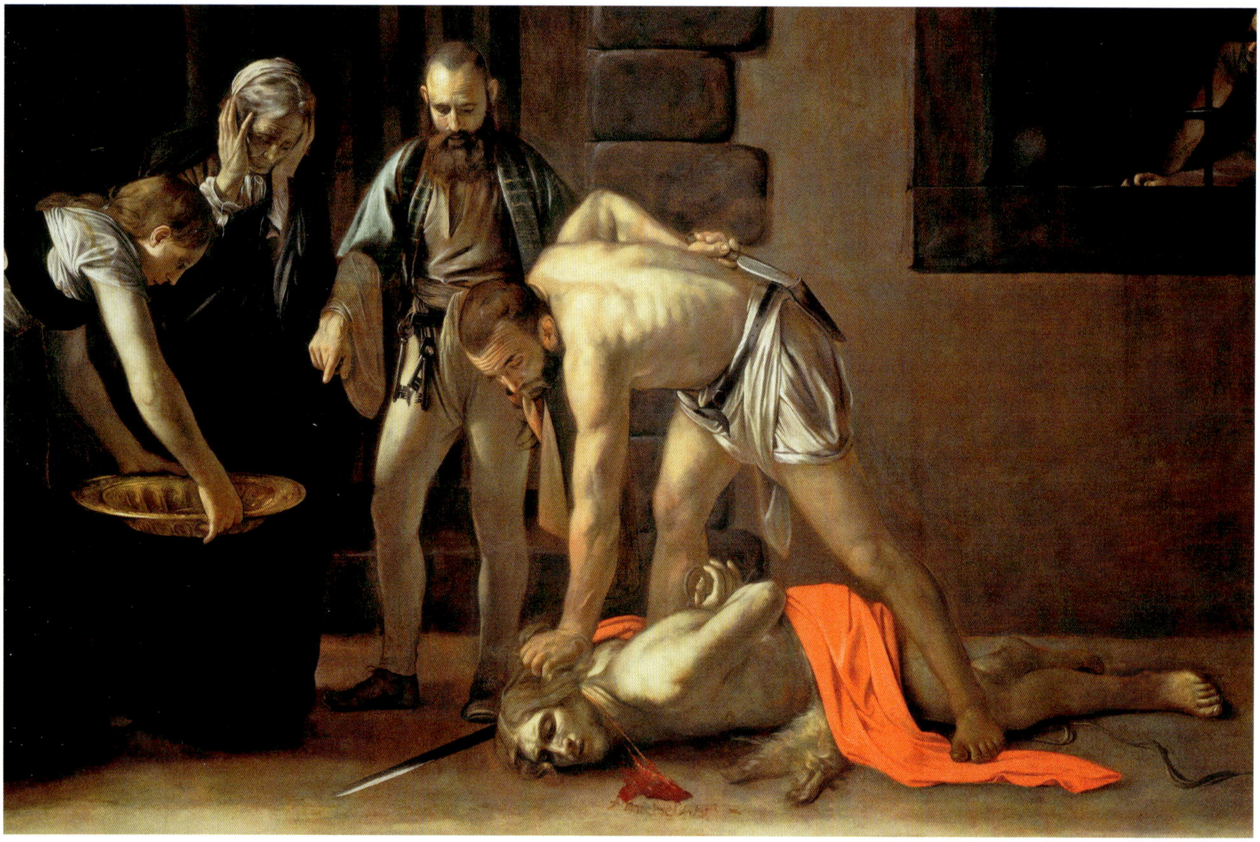

5
Michelangelo Merisi da Caravaggio, *Beheading of John the Baptist*, 1608. Oil on canvas, 361 × 520 cm. St. John's Museum, La Valetta.

neither the sword with gleaming tip nor the knife which, according to the painter and art biographer Giovan Pietro Bellori (1613–1696), the decapitator is about to draw from its sheath to sever the uncleanly struck head that he grasps tightly by the hair.[21] The head appears to be still well attached to the torso, its separation not yet realized. John's face does not express a death already transpired, but rather the moment of breathing one's last. The body of the saint, pressed to the ground like a sacrificial animal, blends with the tangible presence of the lambskin that girds him, the legs of the pelt extending out from under a bright red cloth.[22] By focusing his composition on the spurting blood spilling from the fresh neck wound, Caravaggio conforms to a Eucharistic prototype: he offers up the hemorrhage as a sacrificial libation. As a result, the horror of the actual decapitation has been removed from the act itself, displaced to the narrative surroundings, to the red of the mantle that covers the body, and chromatically resonates with the artist's signature.[23]

Such self-reflexive devices hint at the painter's dubious complicity in the execution they reenact and produce as well a powerful and uncanny alliance between painter and spectator. They will be prolifically employed in the years to come. Jusepe de Ribera (1591–1652), a native of Valencia who soon moved to Naples and was praised by Joachim von Sandrart for his "superb manner of painting" (*fürtrefliche Manier zu mahlen*), gained a reputation for "horrible subjects" (*e tanto si stabilì negli orrori*).[24] He was strongly influenced by Caravaggio's realism and chiaroscuro,[25] for which he was "highly esteemed" (*grosse stima*) in Naples.[26] In the *Abecedario pittorico* (1763), the Bolognese writer and art historian Pellegrino Antonio Orlandi (1660–1727) explained Ribera's adoption of "Caravaggio's style and colors" as aimed at equipping himself with the artistic means to surpass his rival, the Bolognese painter Domenico Zampieri, called Domenichino (1581–1641), who had been recruited to decorate the Cappella del Tesoro di San Gennaro in Ribera's hometown. The Neapolitan painter Bernardo de' Dominici (1683–1759) in his biography of Ribera condemns the artist's aggressive and arrogant behavior, which caused the "unrivaled Domenichino" so much distress (in the end, Domenichino was poisoned by yet another of his jealous Neapolitan adversaries). But God castigated Ribera for his aggression with the loss of honor (*perdita dell'onore*), which according to De' Dominici is the most sensitive part of the human heart.[27]

Ribera's showpiece issued a challenge to Domenichino by outdoing his rival's exemplary *Head of John the Baptist* (fig. 6).[28] The drama in Domenichino's composition, a painting otherwise reminiscent of a still life in its stasis, consists in foregrounding the perspectival distortion of the golden plate from which the severed head, surrounded by the perfect circle of an undistorted halo, seems to eerily raise up and speak to the beholder. Ribera's work instead features his painterly execution (fig. 7).[29] The head of the saint lies on a shallow golden platter, resting on its right cheek. The face shows signs of death, darkly discolored lips and firmly closed eyes, but these hardly detract from an overall expression of calm. A blood-smeared cloth lies in front of the head next to the platter. From the area marking the edge of the severed neck, fine rivulets of blood flow into the platter. Traces of blood on the white linen seem to come from wiping the blade of a sword that extends underneath the platter (as does a cross-staff in miniature on the other side), subtly recalling the act of martyrdom. The sword grip projects beyond the edge of the table and

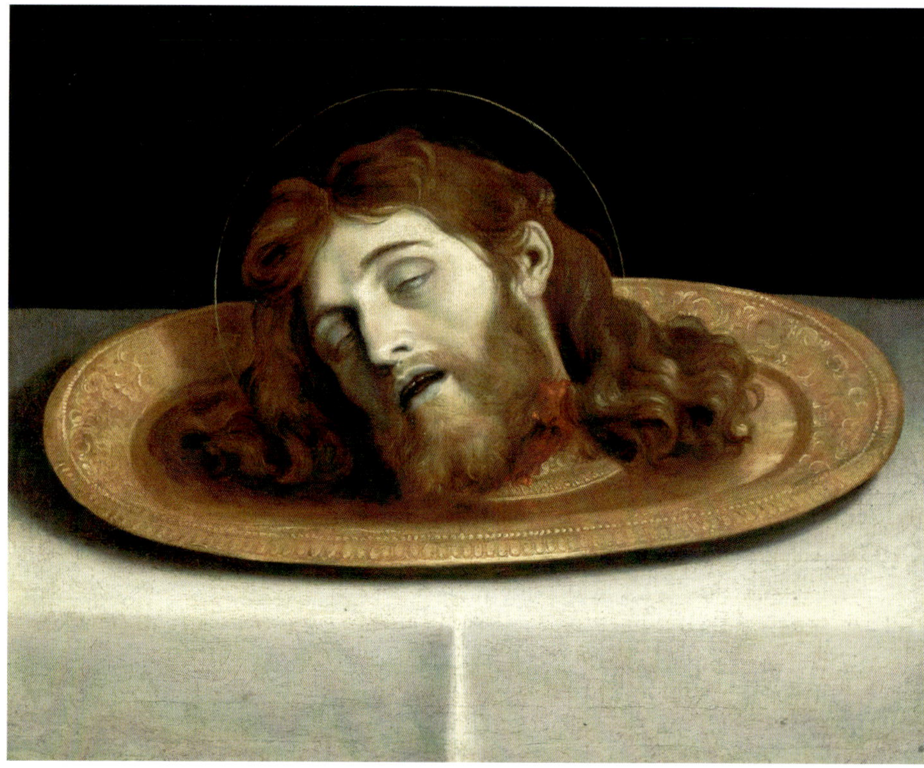

6
Domenico Zampieri, known as Domenichino, *Head of John the Baptist*, 1630–1634. Oil on canvas, 49 × 60 cm. Academia de San Fernando, Madrid.

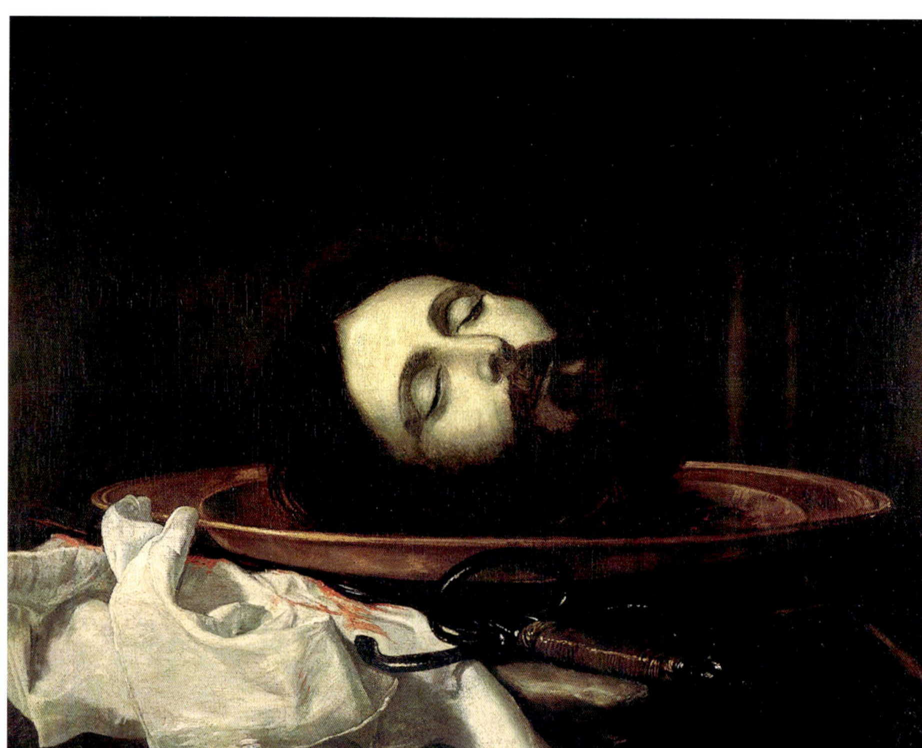

7
Jusepe de Ribera, *Head of John the Baptist*, 1644. Oil on canvas, 62 × 73 cm. Academia de San Fernando, Madrid.

alarmingly into the space of the beholder, pointing to the artist's signature inscribed on a shaded lateral face of the stone (today nearly illegible): "Jusepe Ribera Español/1644." It claims authorship of the execution of a head of captivating beauty, peaceful in and of itself, almost unaffected by the brutality of decapitation.

The artist's perplexing association of the creative act with the malice of execution addresses the oddity of the human response to the representation of gruesome subjects, a topic discussed many centuries earlier in Aristotle's treatise on *Poetics*: "Objects which in themselves we view with pain, we delight to contemplate when reproduced with minute fidelity: such as the forms of the most ignoble animals and of dead bodies."[30] Aristotle goes on to explain this *surplus* as the human desire to learn, which can reverse our emotional response and stimulate "the liveliest pleasure." The requirement of "minute fidelity" may therefore respond to a quest for deeper insight, or more importantly, it may also express the potential of the fascination born of curiosity to shift from the motif to the manner of its execution: "The pleasure will be due not to the imitation as such, but to the execution, the coloring, or some such other cause."[31] The careful rendering of detail elicits a mixed reaction of repulsion and attraction, an emotional double bind that draws and holds the beholder's interest in the painting. The identification of painting with murderous execution (which Piazzetta will later push to an extreme) breaks down the affective barriers separating the realms of art and life—and art and death—by provoking an immediate response, namely, the beholder's compassion. And that compassion becomes the spark that grants life to the subject and guarantees the stunning illusion. The artist's threatening gesture thus mesmerizes the beholder in order to seize their imagination.

Recent research has looked at the occurrence of horripilation—automatic physical reactions to psychologically unpleasant or painful stimuli—when gruesome or otherwise evocative artworks are viewed. One study argues that when the same tears and goosebumps that real-life threats manifest in the safe realm of artistic fiction, they are evidence of a "pleasurable emotional state of being moved."[32] The stimulation of an almost perverse pleasure creates a strong bond of empathy that, while able to override the rational distinction between fact and fiction, ultimately spurs a heightened awareness of artifice as a safe refuge from perceived danger.

BEAUTIFUL HORROR: *THE MASSACRE OF THE INNOCENTS* BY MARINO, RUBENS, AND POUSSIN

Depictions of martyrdom in the works discussed thus far reveal the artist's increasingly explicit identification with the role of the executioner, an attitude we can find reflected in seventeenth-century panegyric literature. A prime example is Giambattista Marino's widely read *Galeria* (1619), a collection of poems dedicated to specific artworks and addressed to their creators. Marino (1569–1625) had initially planned to collect original drawings commissioned for this purpose from the most important artists of his time—fantastic little inventions of mythological subjects "drawn with pen, pencil, or bister" (*fantasietta ... tirata di penna o di lapis o di chiaroscuro*).[33] To these he added his own "poetic capriccios"[34] praising the authors of the works. This ambitious plan did not work out. Instead, Marino ended up drawing

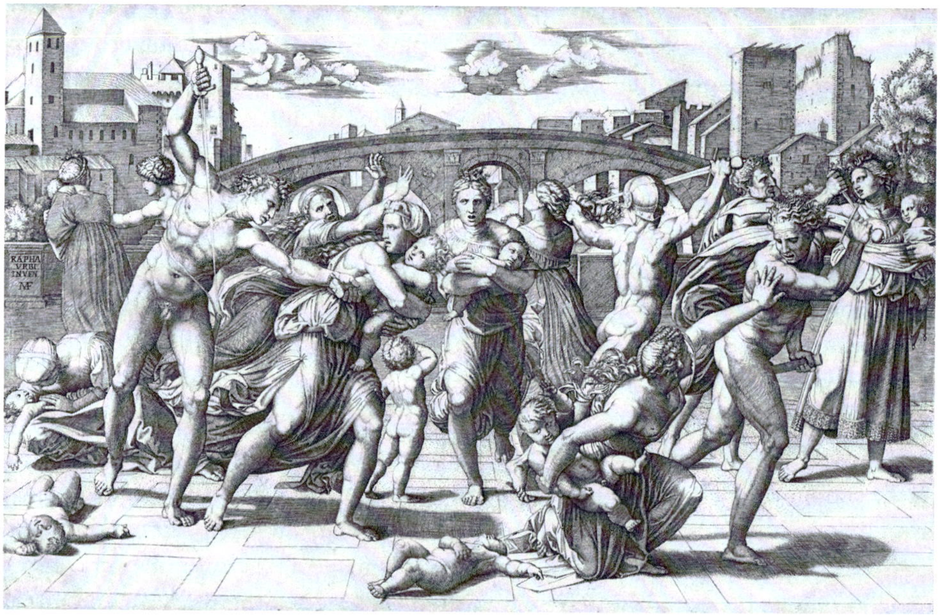

8
Marcantonio Raimondi, after Raphael, *Massacre of the Innocents*, ca. 1512–13. Engraving, 28.1 × 43.0 cm. Metropolitan Museum of Art, New York.

in the reorientation of the iconography of the Massacre of the Innocents indicates that around 1630, painters and their patrons were ready to accept his audacious handling of horror as an ingredient in a bravura art based on extreme oppositions and conceived in order to create 'meraviglia.'"[45]

The extraordinary impact of Marino's poetry was in large part due to the subject of the Massacre of the Innocents having already a well-established reputation in the visual arts as a bravura piece, its most successful and widespread iteration being Raphael's influential image made widely accessible through Marcantonio Raimondi's engraving (ca. 1511; fig. 8). Art historians Elizabeth Cropper and Charles Dempsey stress the conventionality of the elements of Raphael's composition, which reflects a long-standing literary tradition that expanded and embellished the brief report in the Bible.[46] Yet the many prints and paintings that drew on Raphael's example, as well as on its underlying written sources, stimulated in turn a literary response that greatly encouraged further use of the Massacre to demonstrate artistic skill. Likewise Ekaterini Kepetzis, in an article on the visual tradition of the Massacre of the Innocents, has pointed out that the detailed ekphrasis of this theme in art literature played a major role in the theoretical conceptualization of artistic bravura, and that for painters this gruesome subject became a prime vehicle for "grandstanding" in the elevated genre of history painting.[47] Vasari, Lomazzo, and Carel Van Mander valued it as a showcase for a variety of technical challenges: the arrangement of intense interaction among a diversity of protagonists; the mastery of anatomy and movement; the correct and abundant use of foreshortening; the rendition of mimetic expression and gesture in the actions of a single figure; and, last but not least (and in line with Leon Battista Alberti's axiom), the exhibition of *copia, varietas,* and *difficultas.*[48] The referencing of exemplary models creates a secondary level of information in the artwork that not only invites the beholder to take a step back from personal emotional involvement in order to enjoy the art itself, but also provides meaningful clarification of individual moments in the scene. Recollected images (triggered by visual allusions) allow for reflection on a particular artwork's representational density, and so remove the viewer some distance from intimacy with the depicted horror.

In the seventeenth century, the Massacre of the Innocents as an artistic subject took one of two opposing modes of expression: one staged the massacre as an onslaught of movement, the other as a complex figural constellation focusing on one particular moment. A work by Peter Paul Rubens (1577–1640) demonstrates the former trend, one by Nicolas Poussin (1594–1665) the latter.

Rubens's *Massacre* conveys the quintessence of what the Flemish artist learned during his eight years in Italy (fig. 9). As the art historian David Jaffé has noted, Rubens took the most renowned painted versions of the Massacre of the Innocents, as well as certain antique sculptures, and assimilated and reshaped them so as to create a ghastly scene whose drama is heightened by these references. Each recognizable image is swept into a tempestuous, all-encompassing momentum that is entirely Rubens's own. Jaffé describes how the interacting "clusters" of figures at first appear to be one "circular mass of tightly bound figures," until one notices

9
Peter Paul Rubens, *Massacre of the Innocents*, 1611–1612. Oil on panel, 142 × 182 cm. Art Gallery of Ontario, Toronto.

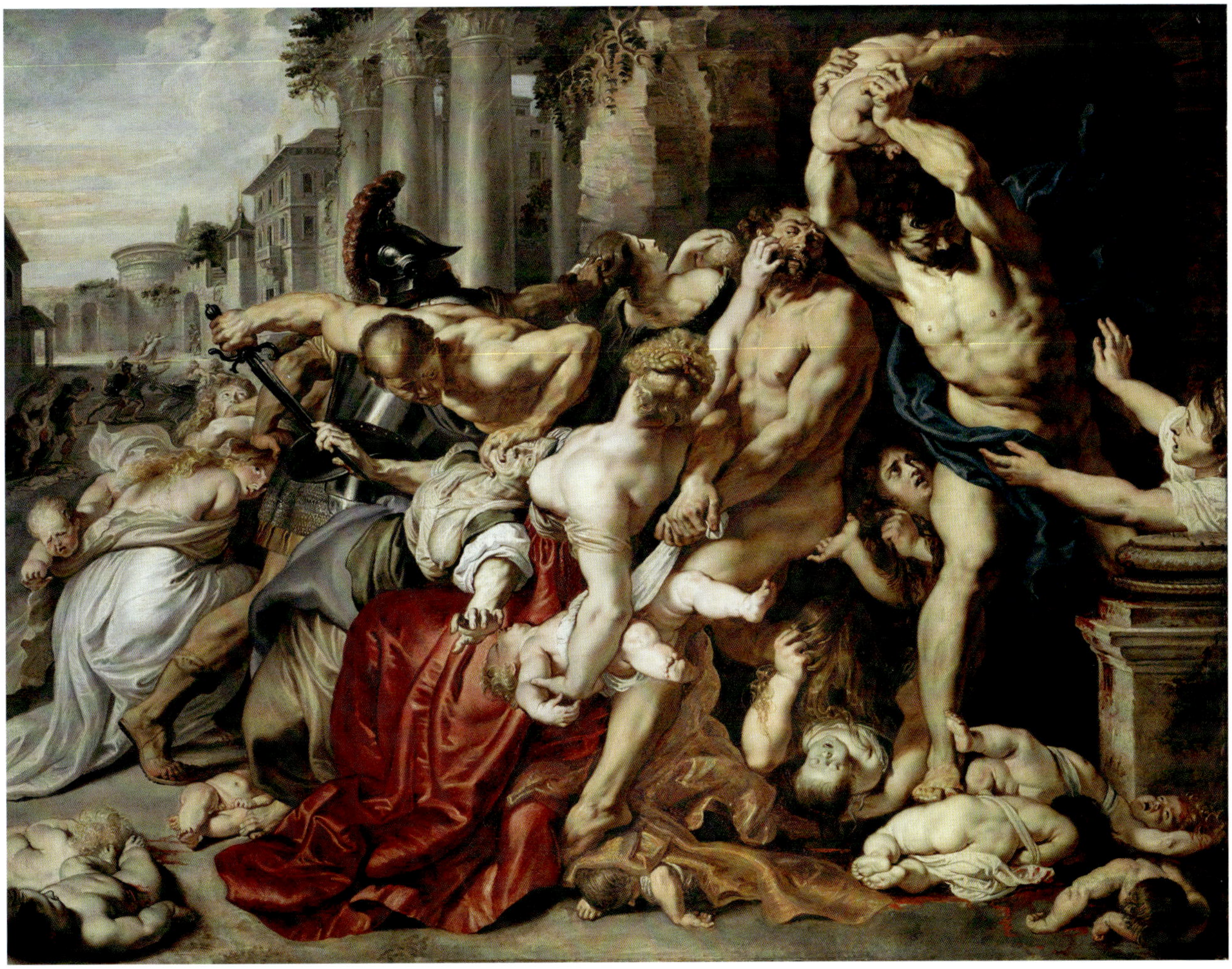

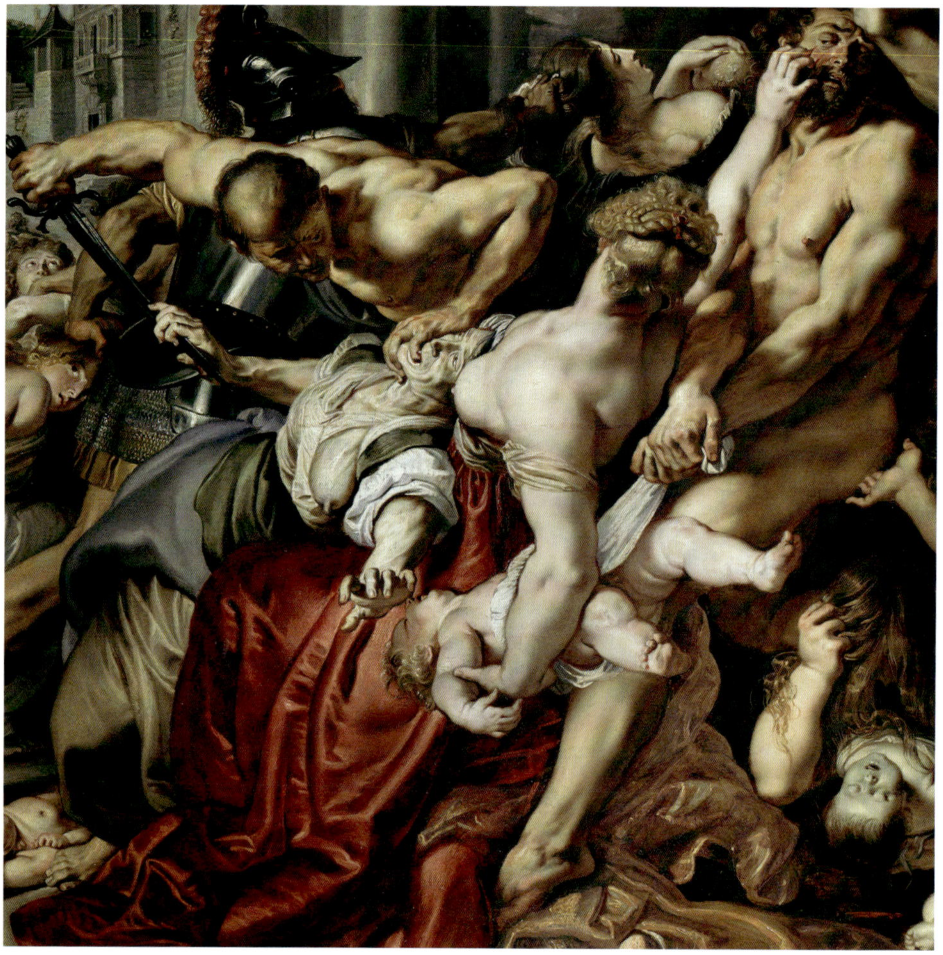

10
Detail of fig. 9
[*Massacre of the Innocents*].

the composition's diagonal axes that link the protagonists "together in a series of violent, contrasting gestures," and propel them toward the uppermost motif of an infant held aloft by an assailant who prepares to dash it against a stone plinth. "The rhythm of these interacting groups leads the eye back and forth and in and out through pose and gesture, creating the overall effect of a writhing knot of destruction which flings dead and dying infants into the furthest corners of the panel."[49]

The foremost rising diagonal, culminating in the explosive moment described above of an infant being hurled to its death, begins with a grandmother using her body to shield her daughter (fig. 10). The old woman is dressed in muted greenish-gray colors, while her daughter shines in a brilliant red garment. The embarrassing detail of the elderly mother's large, pendulous breast emerging from her virtually transparent blouse echoes, in a distorted fashion, the naked bosom of her daughter. The grandmother's right hand grabs the sword of a murderer attacking the women from the side and brings the blade's point toward her chest in an act of self-sacrifice. Underscored by the diagonal of the sword, her right hand aligns with her left, which hovers over the head of her grandchild who is being held back by the daughter. It seems no coincidence that this outstretched hand is shading, and thus protecting, the little infant who seems to have fallen innocently asleep—a foreshadowing of its approaching death. The daughter's exposed breast reveals that she is still breastfeeding, a motif clearly set out in Marino's poem ("With her beautiful breast and beautiful face, she makes a shield for her beloved"),[50] which in turn can be traced back to the literary model for Marino's work, Pietro Aretino's *L'humanità di Christo* (Venice, 1535).[51]

But in Rubens's version, the shield is formed by the sagging breasts of the intervening grandmother, not by the beautiful bosom of her daughter. Along the profile of the daughter's left side, we mainly see her shoulder whose mass counterbalances the shoulder of the assailant attacking her mother. Her response is as fierce as his aggression: while one hand holds her infant behind her back, she extends the other to dig her fingernails into the cheek of a second assailant who tries to pull her child away by grabbing its diaper cloth. This man exhibits the facial features of the *Laocöon*, a template, as Jaffé has pointed out, for the representation of human pain. But his pose, with hands crossed in front of his lap, also disconcertingly recalls the *Ecce Homo* posture. The combination of these two elements deepens the expression of physical pain and makes it more problematic (figs. 11, 12). Unlike the antique sculpture, the man in his torment does not look upward but directs his eyes down and toward the woman dressed in red, whose face is withdrawn from our sight. The beholder, looking at the back of her head and her tidily plaited hair, is spared the expression of her despair and fury that seems so deeply to affect her aggressor. If we take into account the semantic import of Rubens's reference to the *Ecce Homo*, it appears as if

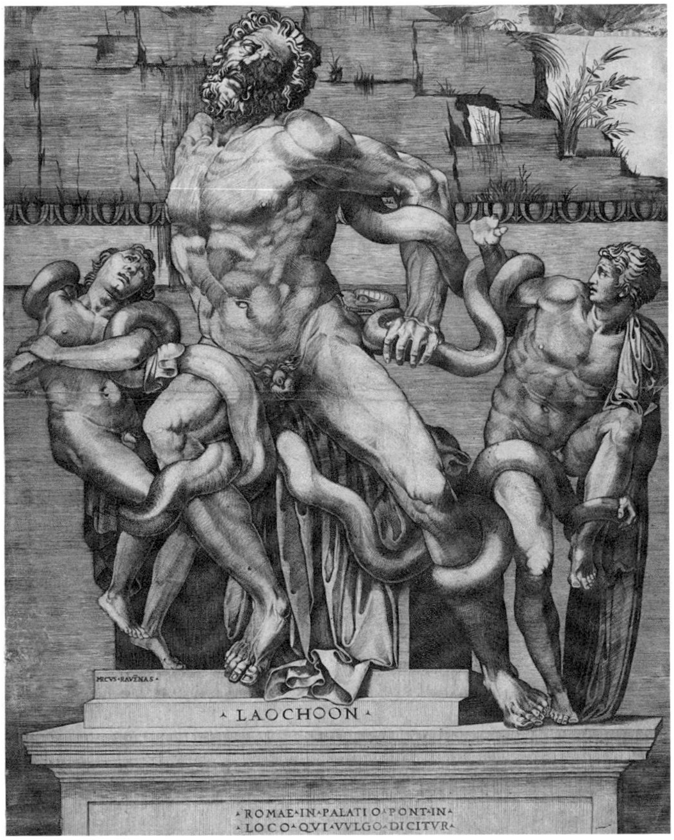

11
Marco Dente, *Laocöon*, in *Speculum Romanae Magnificentia*. Engraving, 41 × 32.5 cm. Metropolitan Museum of Art, New York.

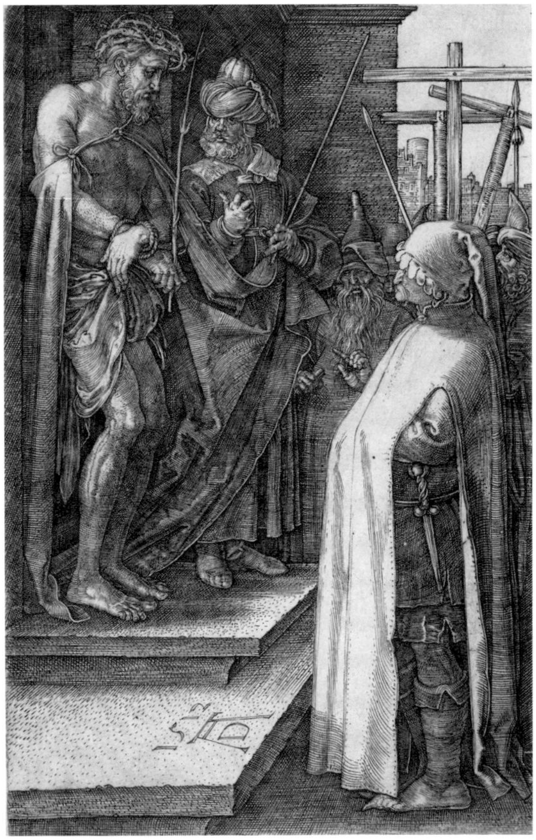

12
Albrecht Dürer, *Ecce Homo*, 1512. Engraving, 11.8 × 7.5 cm. Metropolitan Museum of Art, New York.

his villain responds with compassion to the woman's beauty and pain. Marino repeatedly envisaged this possibility in his poem, but only to intensify the opposing sentiments of inhumanity and unbearable disgust that arise as the massacre continues and becomes increasingly brutal. Rubens's image works in much the same way.

Although the outstretched arms of the woman whose body is cut off at the lower right edge of the picture will probably never be able to save the infant, her imploring gesture runs counter to the momentum of the action and holds the final act in temporary suspension.[52] The turning away of the attacking mother's face, a thematization of ineffable pain, is repeated in the woman positioned below the buttocks of the naked aggressor; her loose hair covers her face as in deep agony she bends over the dead child in her arms. The blond lustrous hair that so beautifully adorns both of these women shields their faces from view, while the disfiguring aspect of pain and despair is appropriately reserved for the old crone who sacrifices the few teeth she has left to protect her offspring.

A second rising diagonal begins at the far left of the scene, where a screaming child frantically gesticulates toward a group of dead infants lying in the foreground. The child is held back by its crouching mother, whose body turns away from the horrifying scene but looks fearfully back over her shoulder at the beholder. A soldier in full armor, his heavy hand on her head, pushes her down while striding toward another matron, whose hair he forcefully grabs as he pulls her back to keep her from fleeing (fig. 13). The discourse on beauty that began with the foremost diagonal is embodied in this squatting female figure, for according to Jaffé she echoes the famous antique sculpture of the so-called *Crouching Venus*. This figure appears widely in art of the period, as evidenced in a work by Raimondi in which cupid stands on a plinth towering over his mother (fig. 14). The Venus pose helps to establish the crouching woman's terrible situation if we recall that Rubens used the same posture in another of his paintings, where it is interpreted as visualizing "freezing" according to Terence's proverb: *Sine Cerere et Libero friget Venus*.[53]

Rubens avoids rendering the fourth assassin in the second row as a nude, and his garb signifies that the slaughter is a military campaign. But more important, this armored figure reinforces the crouching woman's association with Venus due to his resemblance to the goddess's counterpart, Mars Ultor or "Mars the Avenger" (fig. 15).[54] Most representations of Venus and Mars are imbued with the joyful domination of Venus, but here the goddess of Love is subjugated to Mars, who faces away from her in order to carry out his cruel mission. The barbarity of war symbolized by Mars Ultor is evoked in the scattered bodies of the infants that mimic the foreground of battle paintings. As Jaffé has also noted, they are likewise a variation on the famous group of three sleeping putti on a tondo plate from the Galleria Borghese (fig. 16).[55] By recasting the mothers' struggle, flight, and agony, Rubens has reinterpreted Raphael's *Massacre* (see fig. 8). With his allusions to antiquities, moreover, Rubens adds an important second layer of reference that adds yet another symbolic dimension of the story—the battle of the sexes. Theological literature and other pictorial renditions had hinted at this basic conflict, but it had never before been made so explicit.

It is the unstable position of each figure that turns the vigorous movement of the scene into a vertiginous lurch. Rubens shows just one leg of each body, and only

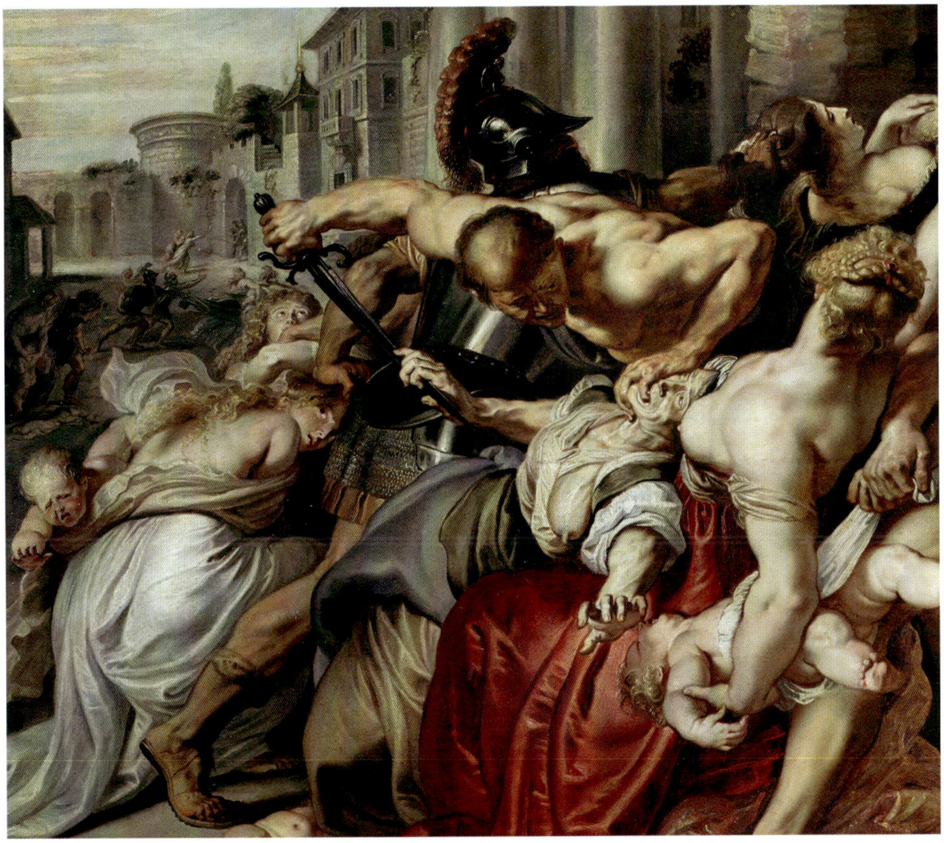

13
Detail of fig. 9
[*Massacre of the Innocents*].

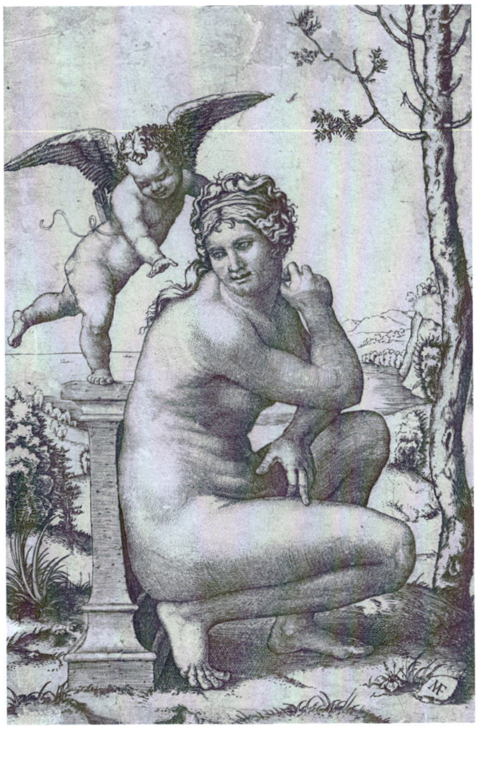

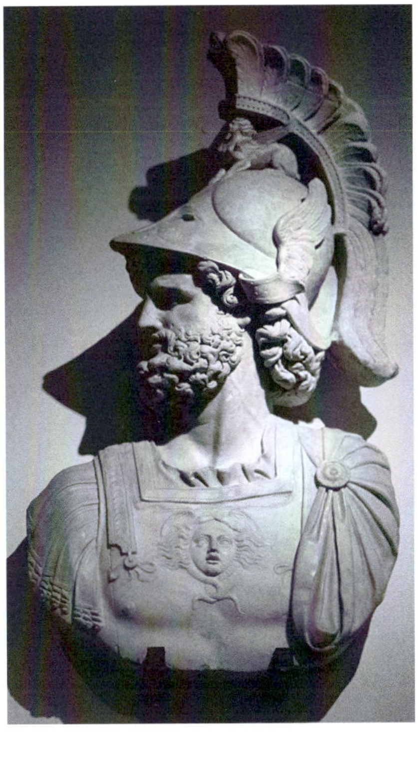

14
Marcantonio Raimondi, after Francesco Francia, *Venus and Cupid*, ca. 1510–1527. Engraving, 21.7 × 14.2 cm. Metropolitan Museum of Art, New York.

15
Bust of Mars Ultor, 2nd century CE. Marble sculpture. Palazzo Altemps, Rome.

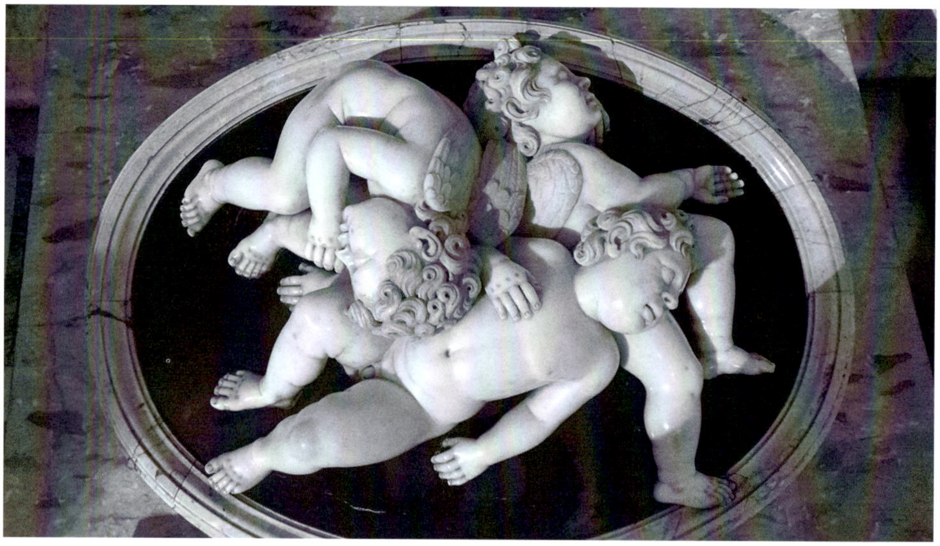

16
Anonymous, *Three Sleeping Putti*, 1609. Marble sculpture. Galleria Borghese, Rome.

the figure hurling the infant has a visible foothold, although a precarious one balanced, it seems, on the bodies of dead children. The foot of his companion seen in profile reinforces this impression of instability. It forces its way into the scene between the red skirt of the furious mother and a piece of orange clothing he must have lost in the struggle, and tramples an infant corpse lying below the cloth.

Rubens's prominent foreground motifs—the female breast as protecting shield, the treading of infants underfoot, and the hurling of one infant against a plinth (evidently a repeated action as evidenced by the bloodstain on the stone)—most likely derive from his reading of Pietro Aretino's *Humanità di Cristo* (1535).[56] They appear as well in Marino's poem. Rubens's use of these numerous literary allusions in the painting seems a concerted attempt to overwhelm the human imagination, "to blow the beholder's mind," if you will. This intense play for compassion proves overtaxing and cruel, and it brings into focus another element of the narrative. The massacre is performed exclusively for Herod's gaze; the inhumane pleasure he experiences while watching the atrocity as if it were a "delightful scene [*dilettosa scena*]"[57] leaps out from the canvas and infiltrates the beholder's view,[58] creating in us the mixed emotional reaction of revulsion and attraction. The (con)fusion of the work's artifice and Rubens's efforts to accentuate its delightful horror is apparent in his rendition of the two infants occupying the lower corners of the image. As Jaffé has noted, they are painted "with virtuoso economy" in a sketch-like fashion,[59] thus drawing our attention to their painterly "execution."

Whereas Rubens fulfilled the demands of *copia* in a most exuberant way, Poussin in his treatment of the subject expressed artistic competency by reducing the scene to a few essential elements that highlight its tragic aspect (fig. 17). Instead of staging the battle between the infants' mothers and the assassins in many discrete episodes, he condenses the whole scope of the massacre into one act and a single group of figures. His exemplary constellation is reminiscent of the one found in the right foreground of Raphael, where a man strides forward while turning his head back to look at a kneeling woman who holds her son behind her back and raises her right hand to fend off the attacker (fig. 18).[60] Poussin redefines her gesture as an expression of pleading, giving it a significantly different emotional meaning. The brutal pulling of her hair by her assailant, a motif Poussin (like Rubens) also adopted from Raphael's more densely populated scene, forcefully lifts the mother's face. This action adds to her pain by preventing the mother from looking at her child, an intensification strikingly displayed in the expression on her face which, according to Rudolf Wittkower, resembles an antique mask of tragedy.[61]

On the stage in the middle ground, a woman flees the scene of horror. Turned away from the arcing leftward movement of the struggle in the foreground, she counterbalances the agony of the mourning mothers. Only at second glance do we realize that she carries her deathly pale infant, of whom we only see a bleeding head and dangling arm. She has thrown her head back sharply at the neck and strikes herself with her clenched fist;[62] her mouth is wide open. This highly expressive supporting actor incorporates two powerful pathos figures: Oskar Bätschmann sees a resemblance to the older dying daughter of Niobe. James Thompson compares

17
Nicolas Poussin, *Massacre of the Innocents*, ca. 1632. Oil on canvas, 147 × 171 cm. Musée Condé, Chantilly.

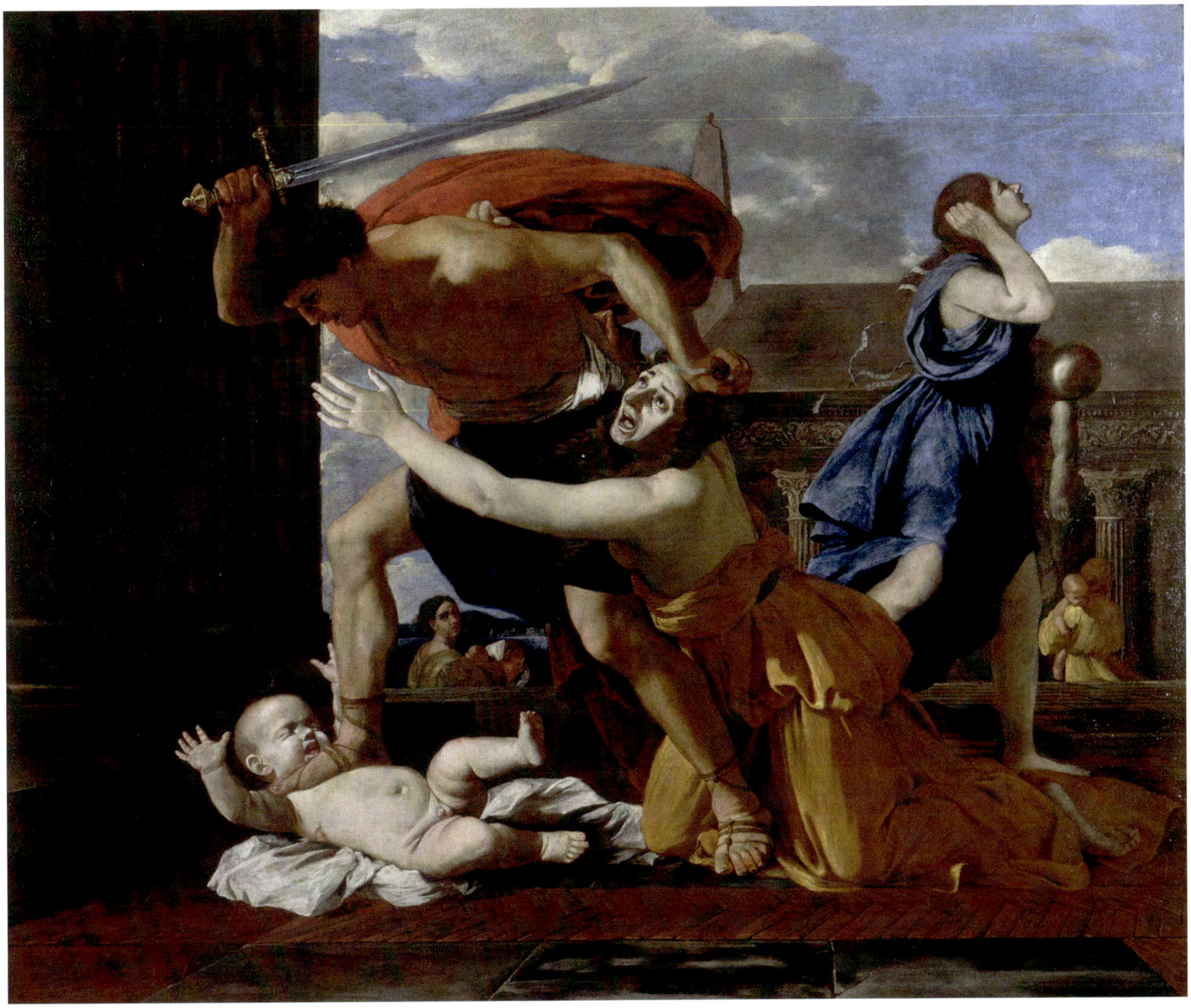

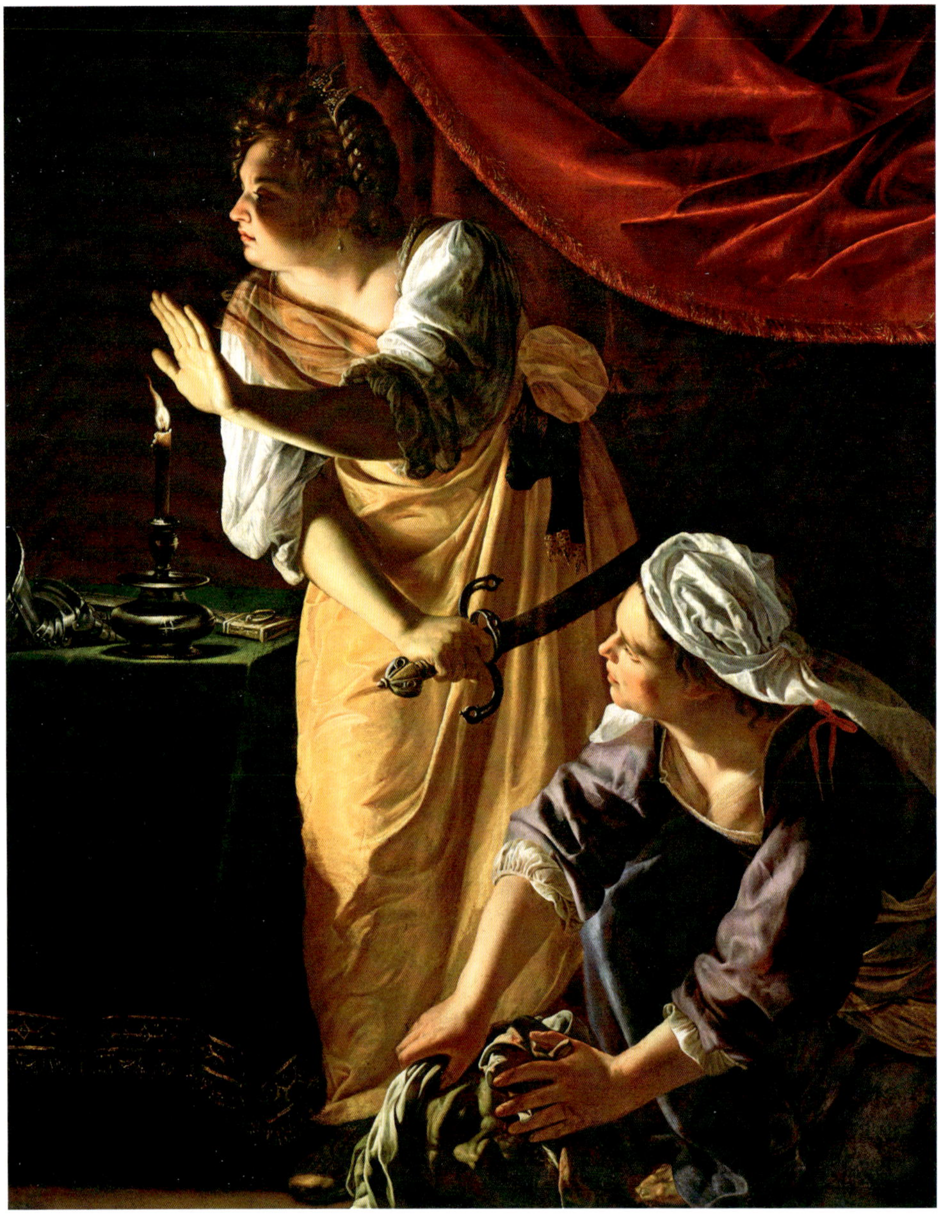

22

Artemisia Gentileschi, *Judith and Maidservant with the Head of Holofernes*, 1623–1625. Oil on canvas, 184 × 141.6 cm. Detroit Institute of Arts, Detroit.

repentant Mary Magdalene Artemisia had painted several years earlier. But in contrast to the introspective quality of the Magdalene clutching her bosom, Lucretia's self-referential touch is aggressive, as if in her anguish she is reenacting the rapist's attack on her flesh. She grips the dagger with the tip uppermost, its blade running parallel to her upward line of sight. The art historian Mary Garrard has noted that the reorientation of the blade is highly unusual, signifying Lucretia's revolt against her expected role: "Artemisia's Lucretia, with sword rhetorically poised, seems to be questioning whether she *should* commit suicide."[71]

If we take a more comprehensive look at Artemisia's oeuvre, it is perhaps not the suffering Lucretia but Judith, the defiant biblical heroine, with whom she most readily identified as a kindred spirit whose daring was a match for her own artistic bravura. Artemisia's shockingly realistic rendition of bloodshed in *Judith Slaying Holofernes*, extant in two versions, has been repeatedly construed in art-historical literature as Judith's revenge for a supposed rape perpetrated by Holofernes. But, setting aside the implicit biographical projection of this interpretation, the work is also, in Garrard's opinion, clearly a vehicle for Artemisia's "demonstration of artistic prowess," a deliberate effort on her part to surpass the bravura feats of her artist colleagues and rivals.[72] The later version's much-discussed decapitation moment is backed by rivulets of blood streaming down a stack of mattresses, where we find on one of their uncovered ends in the shaded area at the lower right an enormous inscription stitched onto the ticking: "EGO ARTEMISIA LOMI FEC." These are Artemisia's best-known paintings, but there is another that shows a subsequent episode in the Judith narrative (fig. 22). And in this work Artemisia again subtly thematizes her own masterful handling of the subject.

We see Judith and her maidservant preparing for their departure from the scene of the crime in the murder's aftermath. Alba crouches down in the immediate foreground packing the head of Holofernes, whose face is unsparingly turned toward the viewer, into a bloodstained white linen sack. She has interrupted her activity and looks up at her mistress. Judith still wields Holofernes's sword in her lowered right hand; blood dripping from its blade reveals that the killing must have just taken place. She holds up her left hand as if warning Alba to be still and silent, and her servant obeys, mirroring the tilt and direction of her mistress's head as she seems to listen carefully. Judith looks over her right shoulder and gazes into the light streaming in from the left. The dark shadow on her face, cast by her raised hand, covers one of her eyes and an ear. According to Garrard, the position of Judith's arms recalls the *Venus Pudica*, and thus visualizes Judith's unmolested state: she, the beautiful widow, was never touched by Holofernes. The odd coincidence that the sword hilt clenched in her hand is held just in front of her groin—at first glance she appears to be sheathing the weapon, until we see the scabbard resting on the table—may suggest that she prevented her violation by killing him. Her arms can further be seen to evoke the pathos figure of the fleeing person (see, for example, fig. 23). These two references create a layering of different narrative moments (the first points to the past, the second to the future), but in the composition's instant, nothing is happening; time has come to a standstill.

Several authors have pointed to the effect of the artificial lighting produced by the candle at the table's edge as evidence that Artemisia must have studied Gerrit van Honthorst's *Mocking of Christ*, where Christ's illuminated body is surrounded by a group of figures ridiculing him. One kneels in a parody of reverence and another gives Christ a staff. A third grasps a torch in his left hand as he holds his right out toward Christ, its palm lit by the torch's glare. The strong light that shines on this man's open mouth, while the upper part of his face remains in shadow, renders his act of speaking tangible to the viewer. We can see his verbal taunts. In Artemisia's painting, the strong chiaroscuro cast on Judith's face by her illuminated raised hand has the opposite effect. Instead of evoking speech in a mute picture, here the intense light strikes the heroine's closed mouth and her silencing gesture. And most important, the shadowing of her eye and ear articulates a "pricking up of the ears": Judith seems to hear something out of earshot and offstage from the viewer,

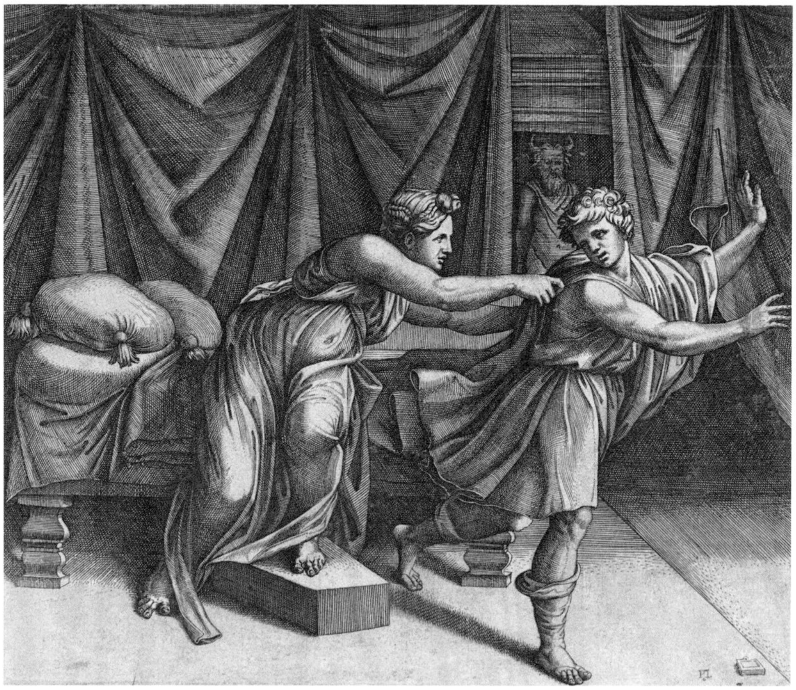

23
Marcantonio Raimondi, after Raphael, *Joseph Fleeing from Potiphar's Wife*, ca. 1515–1525. Engraving, 20.7 × 24.1 cm. Metropolitan Museum of Art, New York.

as the art historian Elena Ciletti has pointed out.[73] Her internal mental process and concentration are made palpable. (This visual embodiment of a perception is also impressively staged in Artemisia's first dated painting, which portrays the naked Susanna exposed to the whispered threats of the old men tormenting her, and in the aforementioned Magdalene, whose ear is prominently reflected in a mirror). Just as Judith's maidservant echoes her mistress's listening, we, too, begin to wonder what it is that she hears. We become "undepicted co-conspirators," if you will, concerned for the women's safe escape from the enemy's tent.

Keith Christiansen has pointed out that the position of Judith's hand mirrors that of the armored gauntlet cast aside on the table next to the scabbard, which "becomes emblematic of Judith's successful challenge to the Assyrian general."[74] Likewise, in an article on "Artemisia's hand," Garrard interprets the emptiness of the gauntlet and its removal from Holofernes as seeming to "mock his power and flaunt [Judith's] gain of it."[75] However, it is the left hand that is foregrounded here, and it is this hand that expresses, according to Garrard, "not women's power, but their vulnerability."[76] Though this may seem at first unlikely, it is quite possible that this prominent left hand is in fact the motif that Artemesia has chosen to affirm her claim to bravura. It is worth remembering that the elegance of Artemisia's physical hand was, in fact, praised by her contemporaries as a *pars pro toto* of her artistic excellence: Pierre Dumonstrier in 1635 made a drawing of her right hand holding a brush with the inscription: "The worthy hand of the excellent and learned Artemisia, Roman Gentlewoman."[77] In her painting it seems Artemisia has ingeniously substituted the left for the right, and so shifted the pictorial focus from *mano* to *ingegno*. In the scene, the left hand expresses alertness, staging the virtue of circumspection and the intelligence that overcomes brute force, and on a self-referential level, expressing pictorial mastery in the most explicit sense. By means of Judith's illuminated hand, Artemisia freezes the picture's action, and from it the fundamental stillness and silence of the image unfolds.[78]

During her many years in Rome, Artemisia became acquainted with the various strategies of pictorial rhetoric by which artists theatrically claimed to be bravura painters. One of these, self-portraiture as a *bravo*, was used successfully by a number of her male colleagues, among them her good friend the French painter Simon Vouet (who painted a beautiful portrait of her). A work by Artemisia's father, Orazio Gentileschi, the curious *Executioner with the Head of John the Baptist*, is perhaps an ironic take on this particular modus (fig. 24). Oddly, Orazio has made it almost impossible for the beholder to pay reverent attention to the head of the saint because the painting does not seem to be about John, but rather about the executioner, and particularly about his striking ugliness, produced by two physical defects: a cleft lip and squint in his left eye. Although on second glance one may detect some similarities between the features of the saint and his executioner, such

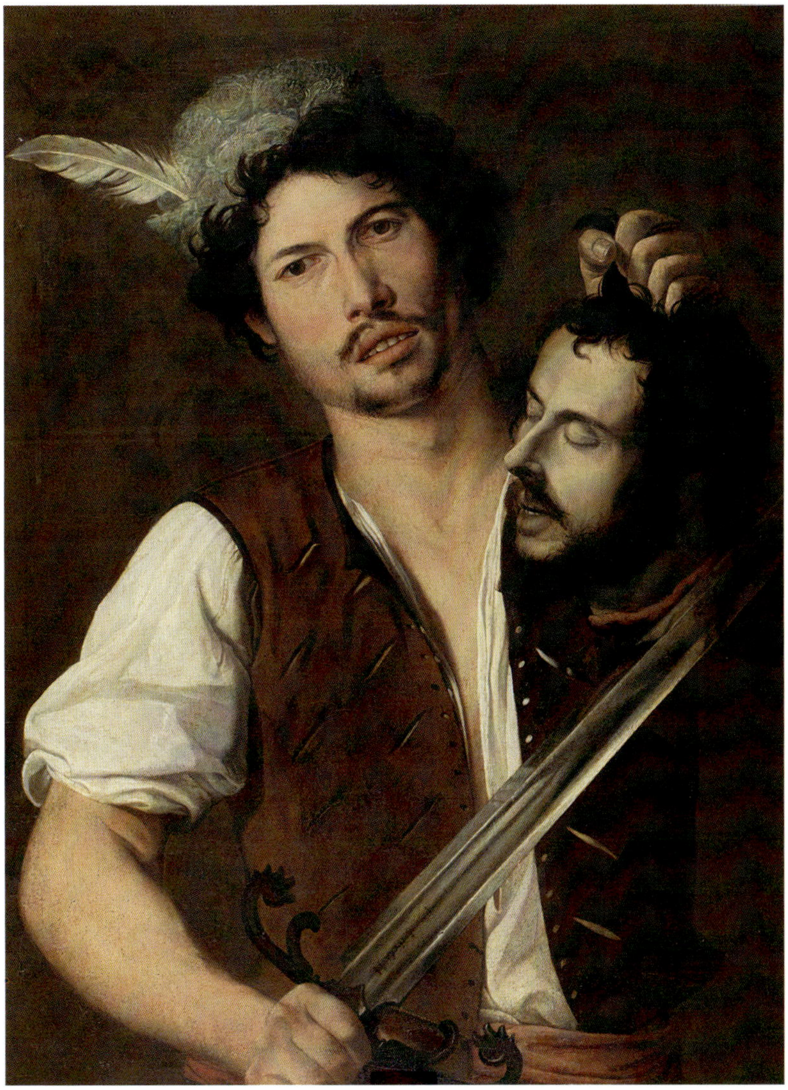

24
Orazio Gentileschi, *Executioner with the Head of Saint John the Baptist*, ca. 1612–1613. Oil on panel transferred to canvas, 82 × 61 cm. Museo Nacional del Prado, Madrid.

as the full lower lip, long straight nose, and long arcs of the eyebrows, John's much higher forehead marks a clear difference. The saint's severed head turned in a three-quarter view that "distorts" its shape, and the bloody stump of his severed neck juxtaposed with his ashen complexion also appear deliberately to provoke disgust. Thus, Orazio here sets up an intriguing negotiation between the beautiful and the grotesque. The saint's head, presented to the viewer but pushed to the side, is reduced to an attribute that attests to the character of the picture's main protagonist, on whose gleaming sword blade the letters HOR.S.LOMI are prominently displayed (Lomi is Orazio Gentileschi's father's name). Artists' inscription of their names on instruments of martyrdom had been, as we have discussed, a common device in paintings of this genre since the Renaissance (see fig. 3). But the repulsiveness of such scenes of violence, earlier hinted at by Perugino's golden inscription, is brought valiantly to the fore in Orazio's work to give horror its proper face.

In his treatise titled *If the Executioner Be Infamous* (1608), Alessandro Tassoni assigns to executioners a rank directly below that of the prince, whose authority, the author points out, would have little weight if it were not for the one who enforces his orders with his own hands. Tassoni compares the executioner with an army commander who shares in the king's military victory honors;[79] he etymologically derives the term *boia* (Italian, "executioner") from *bravo*.[80]

SWASHBUCKLING AND WARCRAFT

In the seventeenth century, artists' personal identification with the dubious figures of the hitman becomes a central topos of their self-presentation. Caravaggio undoubtedly had the greatest influence on this fashion, both for his own and subsequent generations. In his prominent commission for the Cappella Contarelli, he portrays himself as the accomplice of a foppish murderer dressed as a *bravo* in the *Martyrdom of Saint Matthew*. Caravaggio at first masks his person as a marginal figure who steals away into the background. He seems uninvolved in the action taking place, but as the perplexing *historia* unfolds, he moves to the center of events. Caravaggio's theatrical staging now makes plain his participation in the execution, even if his facial expression of sympathy reveals, as the art historian Rudolf Preimesberger points out, a degree of mental reflection and thus distance from what is taking place.[81]

The frontispiece of Giovan Pietro Bellori's *Life of Caravaggio* is unique among the illustrations in his *Vite* in that it shows the painter with a dagger grip in his hand (fig. 25). The weapon is certainly less an indication of his aristocratic right to bear arms than an allusion to his reputation as a homicide, a stigma that needless to say had far-reaching repercussions for his artistic career. As the art historian Philip Sohm has pointed out, Bellori (1615–1696) exaggerated Caravaggio's facial characteristics to give him a signature sinister physiognomy that amounts to a revelation of his art and destiny.[82] A biographer of seventeenth-century artists working in Rome, Bellori relates Caravaggio's murder of a friend to a dispute over a ball game, but he pins the ultimate blame on the painter's daily habits: each day after working on his paintings, he released his tension with weapons exercises.[83] Bellori also links

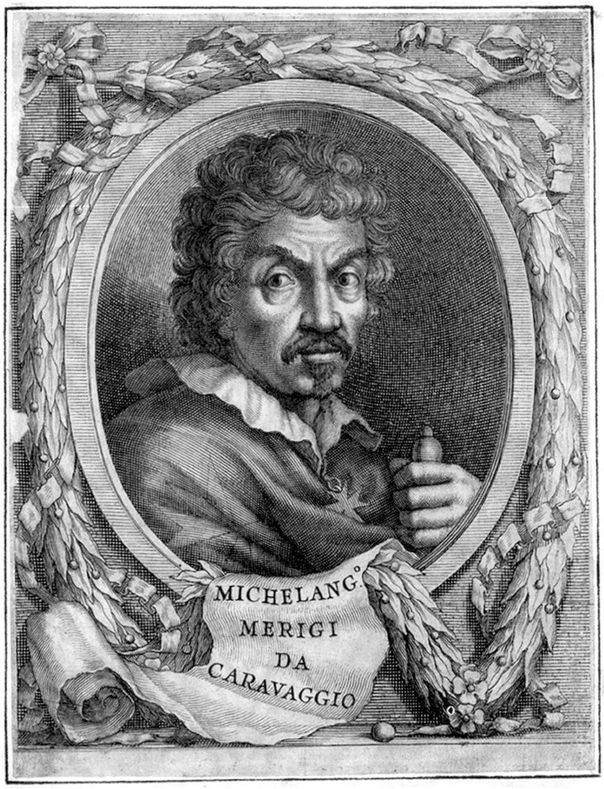

25
Giovan Pietro Bellori, *Vite dei pittori, scultori ed architetti moderni*, 1672. Frontispiece for the *Vita di Caravaggio*.

Caravaggio's dark character and criminal energy to his revolutionary chiaroscuro technique.[84]

Bellori's colleague Filippo Baldinucci (1624–1697), curator of Leopoldo de' Medici's collection of graphic works, agreed with Bellori and derisively ascribed Caravaggio's "art-degrading" painting style to the truism that "every painter depicts himself" (*ogni pittore dipinge se stesso*).[85] In other words, Caravaggio divulges his true pedigree in his paintings. They are an involuntary revelation of his ignobility and belie his concerted efforts to gain social standing. Caravaggio was, however, eventually successful in the latter pursuit and was granted the rank of Knight of the Order of Malta—an award that his enormous *Beheading of John the Baptist* (see fig. 5) was meant to justify.

The vita of *cavaliere* Mattia Preti as authored by De' Dominici, whose father was Preti's pupil,[86] echoes several central motifs of Caravaggio's biography.[87] Preti began fencing at a young age, but at seventeen he abandoned his training in order to focus on drawing and prove himself a *valente pittore*. Sadly, according to De' Dominici's legendary account, a fateful chain of events soon overtook him. After Preti was invested with the title of Knight of the Order of Malta by Pope Urban VIII in 1642, he was challenged by a well-known swordsman and champion at the papal court. In a brutal exhibition held in front of Roman society, Preti, wounded and raging, finally managed to severely injure his opponent. The pope then allegedly shipped the knightly painter off to Malta to shield him from legal prosecution. After a long and successful stay there, a simmering feud with a rival painter came

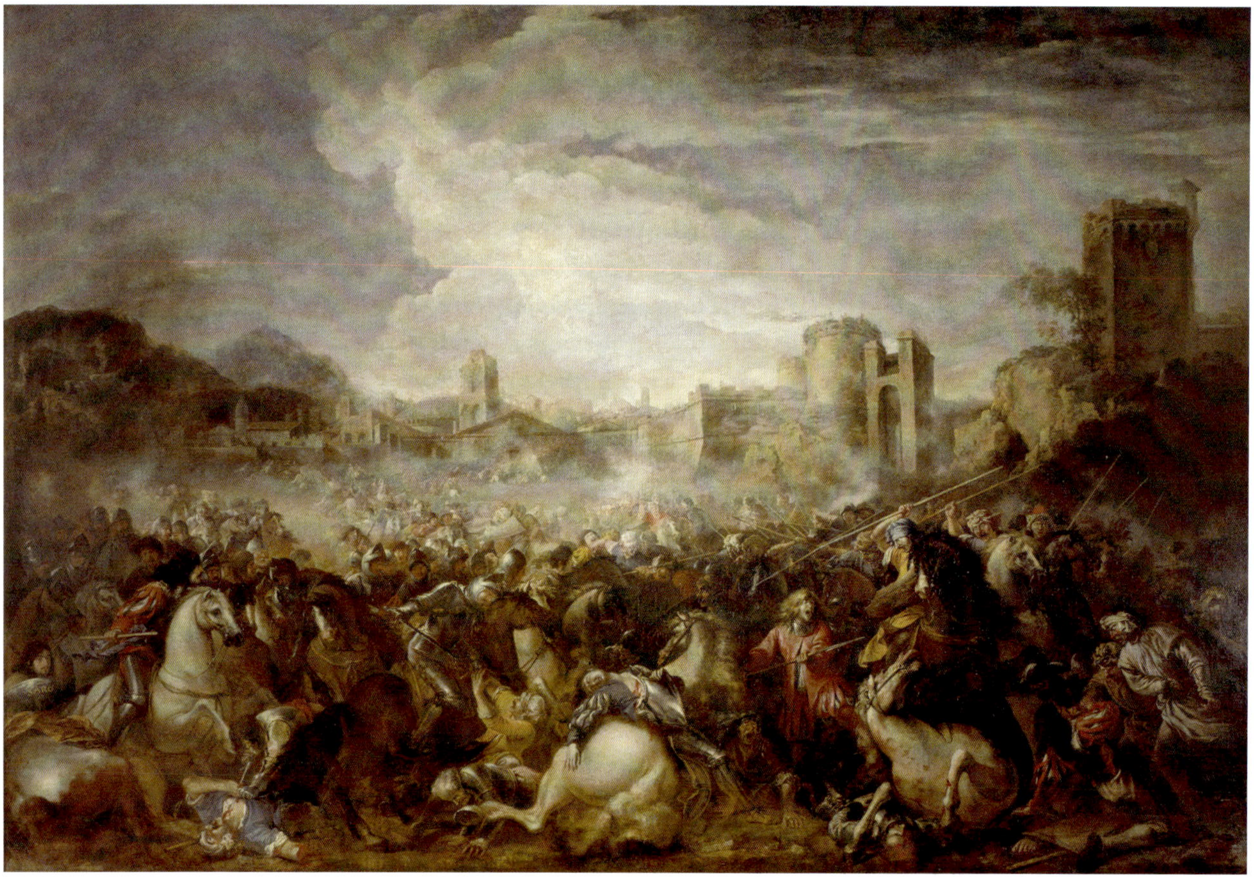

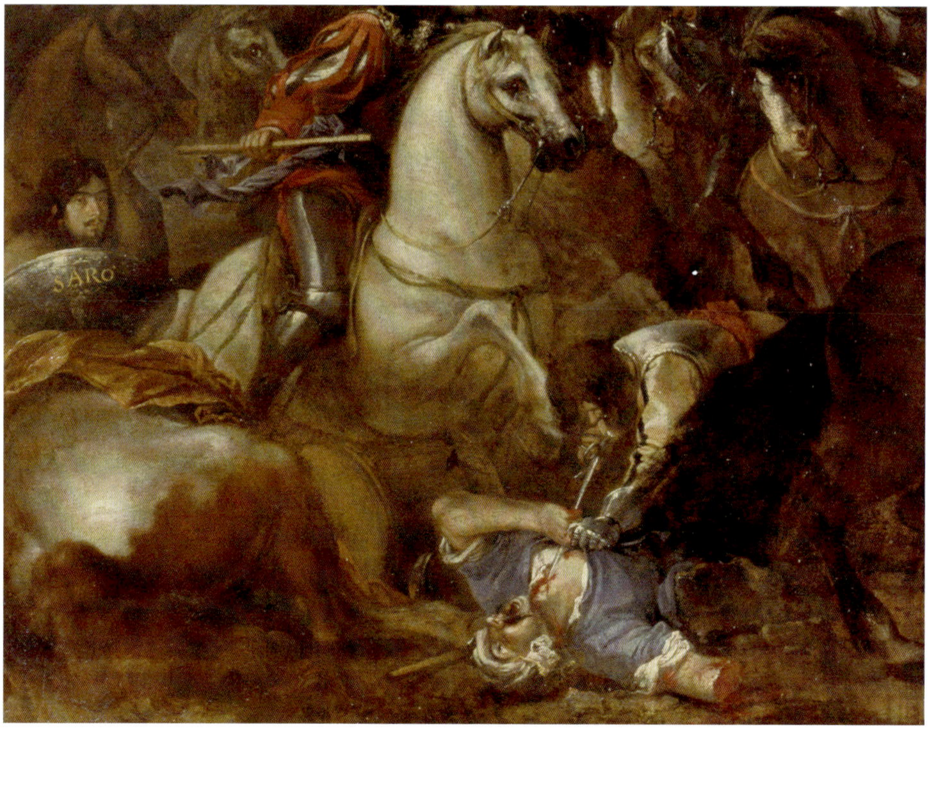

26
Salvator Rosa, *Great Battle of the Christians against the Turks.* Oil on canvas, 234 × 350 cm. Palazzo Pitti, Florence.

27
Detail of fig. 26 [*Great Battle of the Christians against the Turks*].

by the latter's shaded coat. Rosa's gaze, turned intently toward the beholder, does not boil over in battle rage; neither are his eyes bloodshot. As the composer of the scene, his role is to keep apart at a safe distance, and yet he manifests his artistic brutality, his *terrore*, in the immediate foreground of the picture where, as the art historian Elena Fumagalli has aptly observed, the arm of an impaled Turk appears to be cut off by the lower edge of the painting.[108]

Perhaps the most influential model for Rosa's work was Giuseppe Cesari d'Arpino's immense fresco in the Sala Grande of the Palazzo Conservatori illustrating the battle of Tullus Hostilius, the third king of Rome, against the Etruscan cities of Veii and Fidenae (fig. 28). The art historian Federico Zeri singles out this painting as formative for the entire battle genre.[109] We see the collision of two armies spurred on by the fanfare of trumpets. In the background the ferocity of the troops is generalized; we see only opposing rows of cavalry and their lowered spears. The full scope of the cruel spectacle, all the details of the atrocities, is manifest in the foreground. There the scene progressively develops toward the left, with a quarter of the right side taken up by reinforcements surging forward. A horseman with a billowing red cape turns toward them and gives a signal with his outstretched left hand. He forms the right margin of the main action. A fallen soldier dramatically and beautifully outstretched across the back of his horse occupies the center in the foreground. Above him and in between the two battle lines, Cesari has placed a young soldier on horseback who leaps toward the beholder, his spear held triumphantly in his outstretched arm. He must have just pierced the victim in the foreground, for his combative stance no longer has a clear target. The spear-like crown worn by his furious, rearing horse suggests that he is King Tullus.

Cesari furnishes this densely populated scene with an array of stock poses borrowed from Raphael's and Leonardo's exemplary battle paintings and from antique works. A figure in the immediate foreground recalls the famous sculpture of the so-called "Dying Gaul" (figs. 29, 30); a stream of blood pouring from his side portends imminent death as in the original, but its red color here marks the injury much more dramatically. His pale face speaks of a severe loss of blood, but its grayish tone also seeps into his hair, thus visualizing the figure's metamorphosis into white marble—indeed he appears to revert back to the stone of his model. This cunning reference is disturbed by an odd figure nearby: a white horse's pose and expression parallels the soldier's agony.

The dying man lying across the back of his horse in the center of the foreground, fully exposed to the beholder's gaze, is the emotional center of the fresco, and is not the only motif that Rosa may have taken from Cesari. The art historian Viviana Farina points out that the young Cesari has inserted his self-portrait into the combat scene, just as Rosa later would (fig. 31).[110] His attentive gaze is turned toward a mounted soldier who, stylishly dressed in a billowing orange cloak and plumed helmet, enters the scene from the left with his arm raised ready to strike a foot soldier who tries to grab the bit of his horse. It looks like the aggressor's hand has already been injured by a horse's bite. Cesari, unlike Rosa, holds up a bloodstained sword in front of his shield, thus proving himself an active participant.

Whereas Giuseppe Cesari and Salvator Rosa position themselves discreetly at the margins of the battle scene and among the common soldiers, the today almost

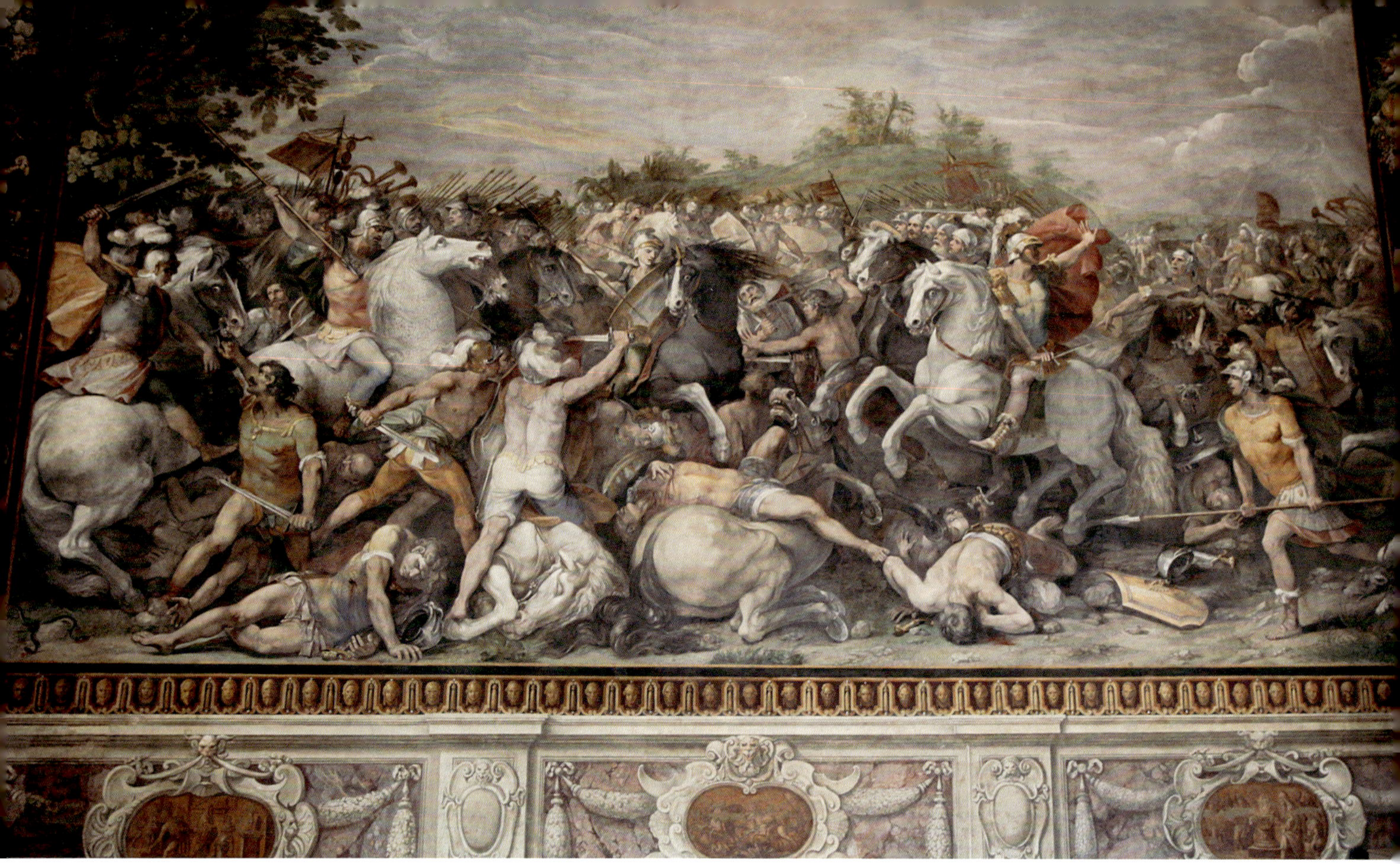

forgotten painter Giovanni Contarini (1549–1605) stages himself with utmost self-confidence as a commander at the *Battle of Verona.* (The painting is in the Palazzo Ducale's Salla delle Quattro Porte in Venice). The Venetian artist and art dealer Antonio Maria Zanetti, in his *Della pittura veneziana* (1771), was the first to point out "a soldier in the middle of the picture with a staff in hand and bared arms, which is in the likeness of Giovanni Contarini,"[111] and the identification is confirmed when we compare the soldier with a self-portrait of Contarini from the Uffizi.[112] In all of these examples, we see that the legendary template that casts the painter as a military mercenary and which De' Dominici highlights in several of his biographies, is actually the artists' choice of role for themselves in their own works. The literary legends come true in the fiction of these staged self-portraits.

Rosa not only inscribed his own person into his battle painting, but also depicted himself as a soldier and field commander in several self-portraits carried out during his Florentine interlude.[113] And he was not the only one who partook of such a masquerade. On the contrary, Rosa seems in his works to reference a type of staged self-portrait especially popular in sixteenth-century Venice and seventeenth-century Rome,[114] in which the artist self-stylizes his image as a fighter-for-hire. Many such images are listed in various museum collections under the unassuming title "Portrait of a Young Man."[115] The original prototype is undoubtedly Giorgione's *Self-Portrait as David with the Head of Goliath,* widely distributed in the seventeenth century via prints and highly influential beyond the borders of Italy (fig. 32).[116]

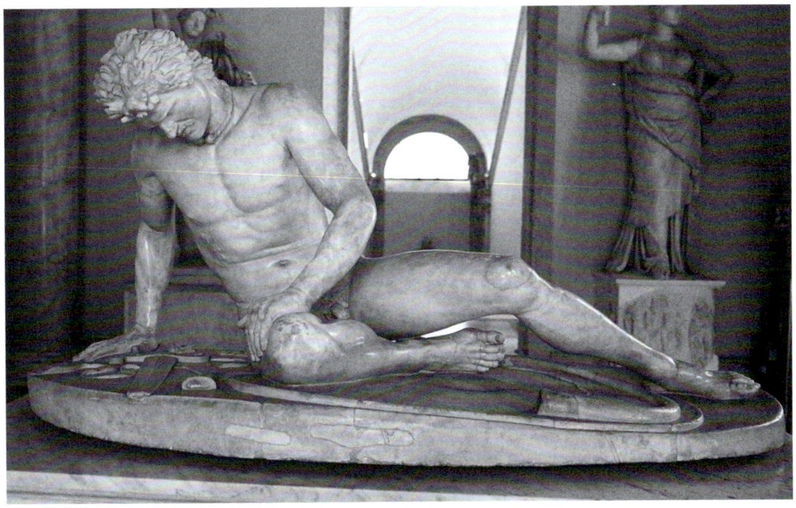

28 (FACING)
Giuseppe Cesari, *The Battle of Tullus Hostilius, Third King of Rome, against the Etruscan cities of Veii and Fidenae*, 1597–1601. Fresco, 10 × 14 m. Sala Grande of the Palazzo Conservatori, Rome.

29
The Dying Gaul or *The Dying Gladiator*. Ancient Roman marble copy of a lost Hellenistic sculpture of the late 3rd century BC. Capitoline Museums, Rome.

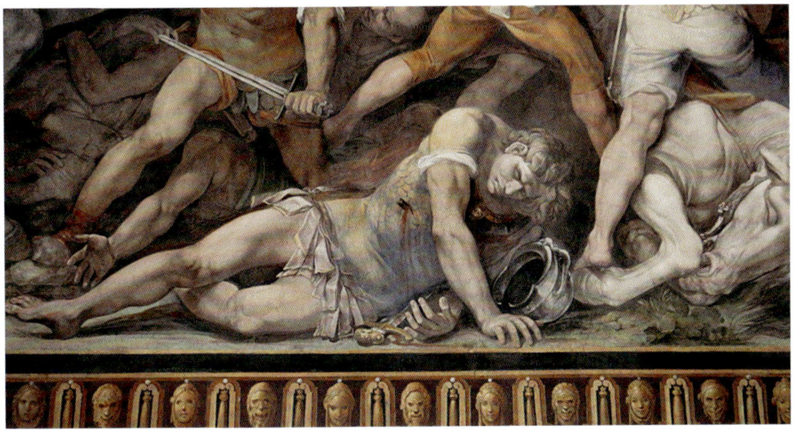

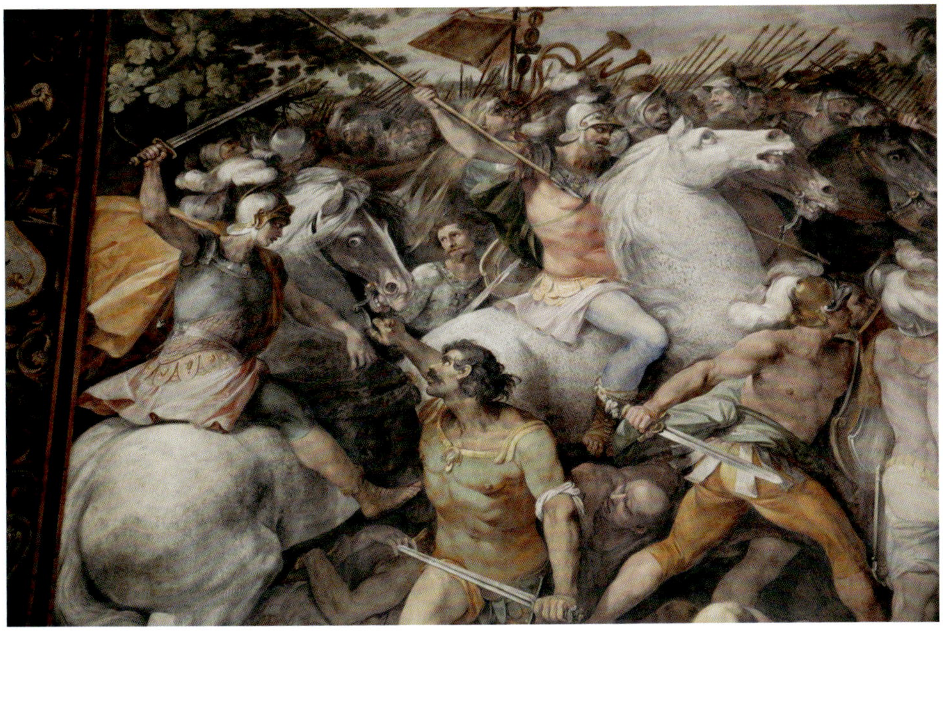

30–31
Details of fig. 28 [*Battle of Tullus Hostilius*].

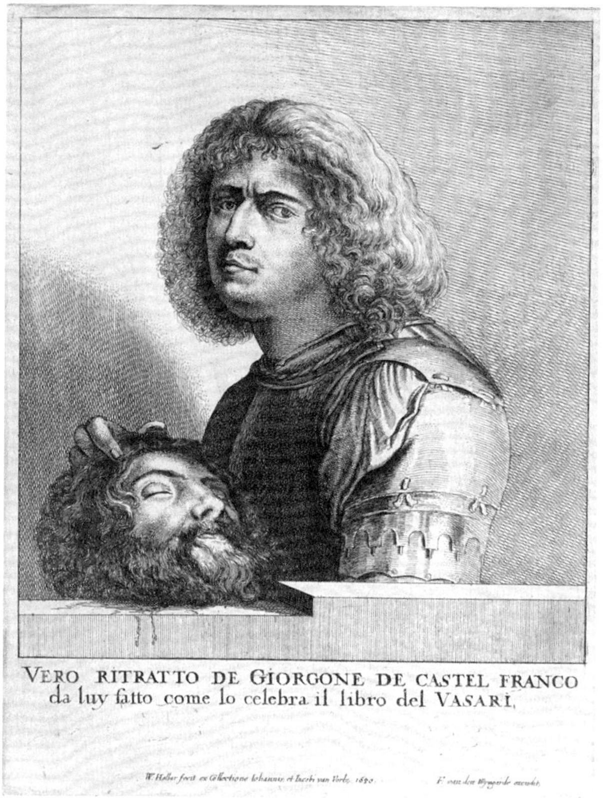

32
Wenceslaus Hollar, after Giorgione's *Self-Portrait as David with the Head of Goliath*, 1650. Etching, 25.9 × 19.3 cm. Rijksmuseum, Amsterdam.

In Giorgione's assumption of the role of the triumphant David, the synthesis of painter and executioner takes on an emphatically positive meaning, which Caravaggio famously subverted a century later when he projected his own visage onto the severed head of the giant villain in his *David with the Head of Goliath*.

The main attraction of a purported self-portrait by Simon Vouet, made around 1620 during his time in Rome, is the dagger that betokens his social ambitions (fig. 33). The elegant swept hilt of his dress rapier—with precise highlights on the grip, cross guard, and knuckle guard—stands out against the broad brushstrokes of the brown underpainting that surround it. While the fine white lines on the ornamentally coiled hilt inscribe cursive ridges of light, rough brushwork merely suggests the sleeves rather than attempting full-bodied mimesis. The viewer in fact sees the very coarse structure of the canvas coming through. Instead of astonishing the beholder by the illusionistic power of singular brushstrokes, Vouet displays a variety of the brush ductus that gives primacy to the painting's lighting conditions and color masses (fig. 34).

In doing so, the artist demonstrates the proficiency of the very hand we see represented in the painting, spotlighted with fine modeling and positioned next to the rapier hilt. Slight abrasion of the uppermost layer of paint allows us to see clearly that the hilt was originally held at a more angled position above the outstretched index finger. The correction of the composition now evident underneath the overpainting (also observable on the right shoulder) confirms the overall impression of an *alla prima* technique, which the work's sketchiness intensifies. Vouet's association of the relaxed right hand with the rapier, polished by the power of a less rapid and more precise brush, is highly programmatic. What we have in the juxtaposition of *manus* and *spada* is a class-conscious staging of the artist as *cavaliere* that while it veils the subject's profession as a painter more importantly seems quite explicitly to correlate swordsmanship with painterly *maniera*.

The painting's common title, *The Swashbuckler* (*Le Spadassin*), belies the fact that it is a self-portrait, and with good reason, for Vouet plays the character of the *bravo* literally "to the hilt" by illuminating the hand and the weapon handle while his foppish headgear casts a shadow that obscures his face. His demeanor seems indeed more fitting for a representation of a certain type than for a self-portrait. The casual, slight inclination of the body communicates a boastful nonchalance and at the same time, a readiness to swing into action in an instant. In the same time period Vouet painted a second picture of a young man with a thin face and the first growth of a beard that is considered to be either another self-portrait or a portrait of his younger brother Aubin Vouet (1595–1641), also a painter who in his early years fell under the spell of Caravaggio's chiaroscuro. The subject's physiognomy—his small mouth with full lips, rather big nose with a fleshy tip, round eyes, and prominent eyelids—is similar to those in the self-portrait examined above (fig. 35). But here the focus instead is on the face with its strong illumination. Shining eyes and lustrous skin, which in some places is faintly reddened and in others has a sheen of perspiration (alluded to by points of light on the end of the nose and above the lip), convey a lifelike quality.

The pronounced rotation of the head indicates that the subject has suddenly turned toward the viewer. The spontaneity of the moment is rendered in paint by the few "prompt" brushstrokes that mark out the clothing, establishing a ground against which the finely modeled facial features can stand out. A sophisticated painterly interplay emerges between the conceptional aspects of portrayal and the visible materiality of the medium. The young man's garment is crudely executed with thick, highly abbreviated brushstrokes on a brown-colored imprimatura, which in its visual solidity directly confronts the beholder's gaze (fig. 36). The roughly but nonetheless skillfully painted cutwork collar casts a strong shadow on the coat. The prominent profile of the coat's shoulder wing is given form solely by means of a broad band of ocher-hued brushstrokes. Below these, black strokes marking the beginning of the sleeves create a shadowed area underneath the wing. A pointed shape constructed from several coarse brushstrokes of white paint, rapidly executed directly onto the imprimatura, may suggest the bulge of an undergarment coming through the slit sleeves, but here the brushwork becomes more puzzling to read. In both paintings, Vouet's rudimentary method of applying paint with a very thick brush seems to transfer the responsibility for "realizing" what is being mimetically represented from the painter to the viewer. By means of bravura strokes the artist compels the viewer to engage their imagination, and thus are we ensnared by the daring of those strokes. Vouet has armed himself (or his brother) once again not with the tools of his profession, but, as in the painting of the swashbuckler, with a weapon. Its pommel is designated by a black round form and white squiggled highlight at the lower edge of the painting. As with the *Swashbuckler*, Vouet here avoids any realistic representation of fabric in order to better show off his bravura.

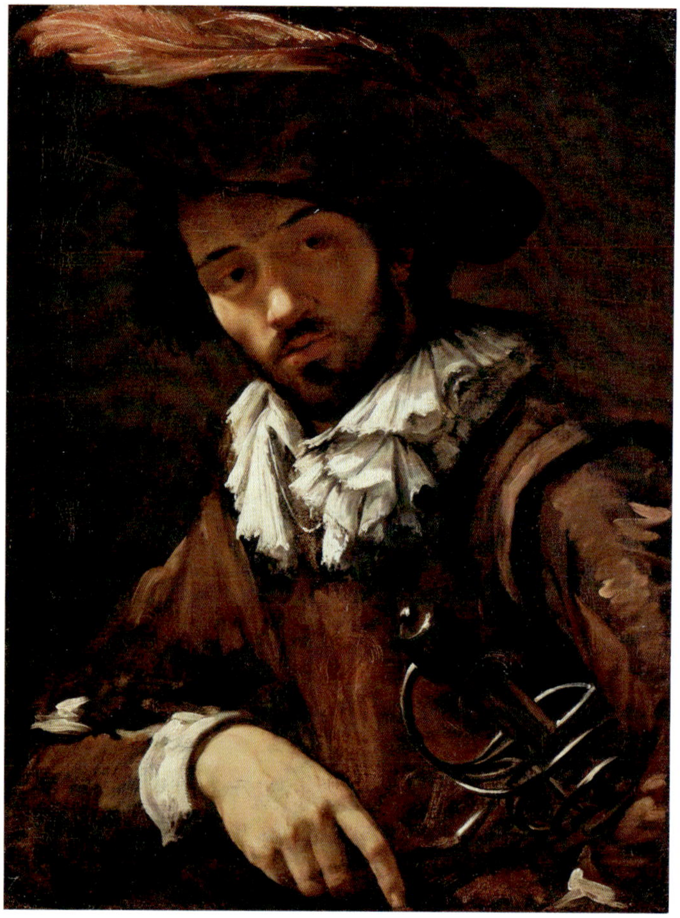

33
Simon Vouet, *The Swashbuckler* (*Le Spadassin*), ca. 1620. Oil on canvas, 74.5 × 58 cm. Herzog Anton Ulrich Museum, Braunschweig.

34
Detail of fig. 33 [*The Swashbuckler*].

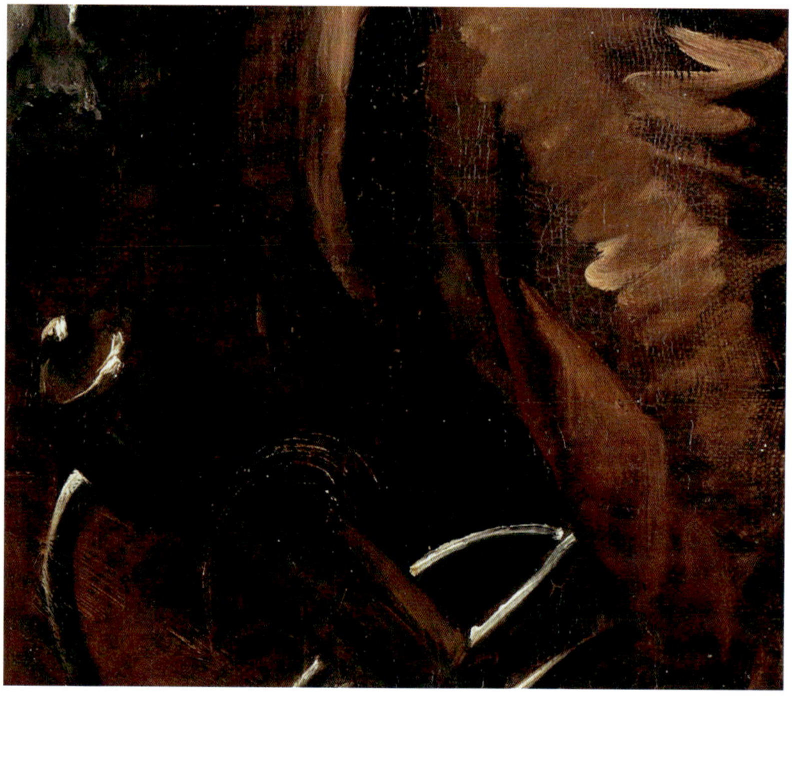

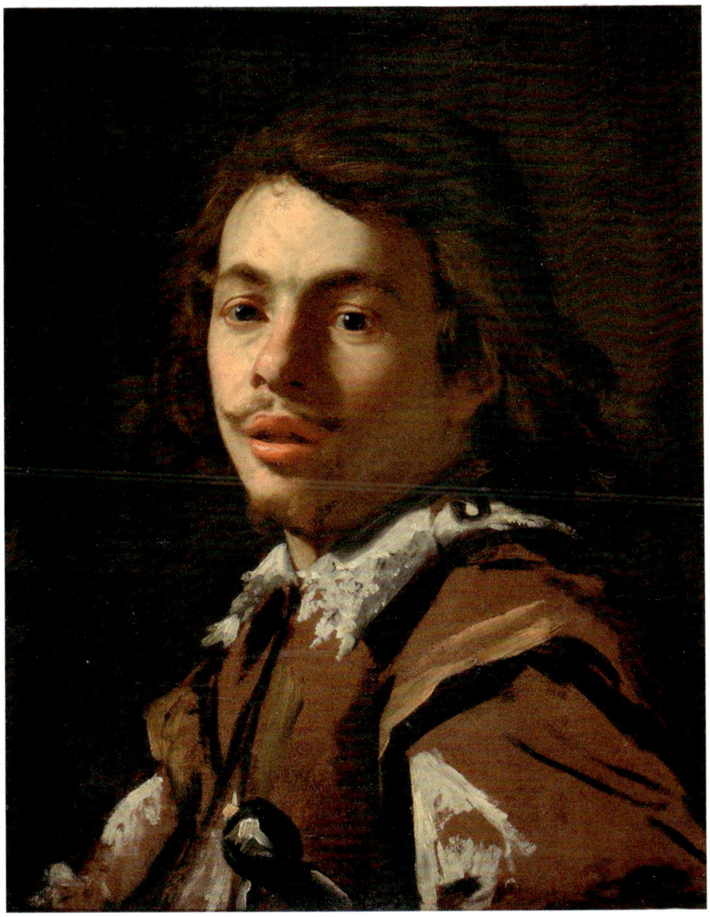

35
Simon Vouet, *Self-Portrait* (or *Portrait of Aubin Vouet*), ca. 1620. Oil on canvas, 64×48 cm. Musée Réattu, Arles.

36
Detail of fig. 35 [*Self-Portrait*].

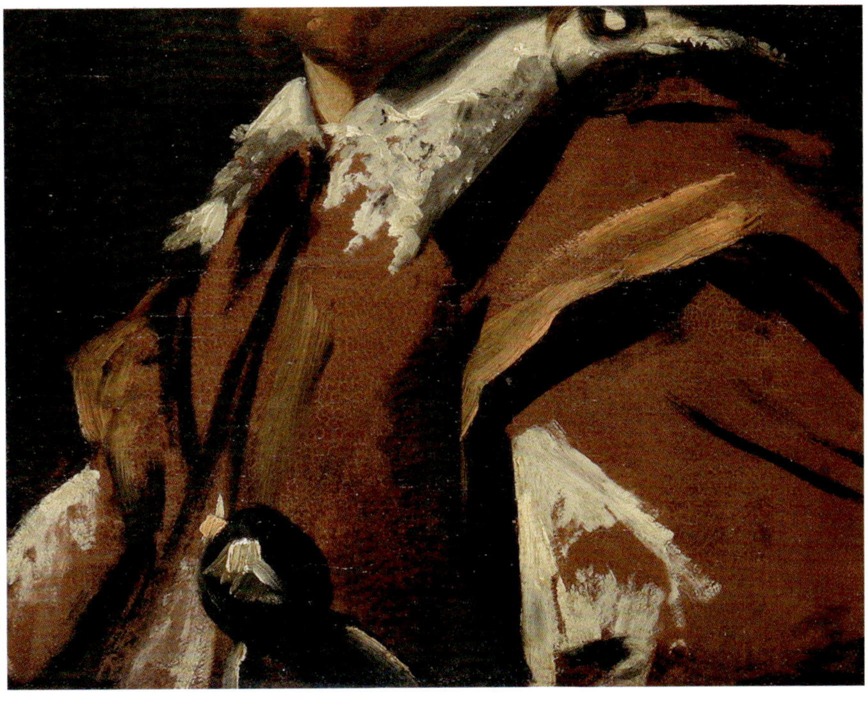

a fold of drapery or a nude contour with facility; indeed, this is seldom compatible with the continual study that kept him away from practice and from that daring liberty which permits itself everything in painting and admires itself for its own brushstrokes."[127] Domenichino's plodding and rather timid approach stands in sharp contrast to March, who required fencing as a warm-up exercise and martial music to thrill his spirit and ready him physically for the coming "battle"; that is for bravura painting. Domenichino had his share of jitters also, but in his case they helped clarify an emotional response—the compassionate empathy that is essential for the visual representation of martyrdom, but which painterly bravura cannot express. For Esteban March, the ritual stimulation of his imagination went beyond frenzied inspiration; it actually, physically loosened his hand for battle.

According to Baldinucci, it was precisely the performance of simulated battle sounds that made the battle painter Jacques Courtois (1621–1676), called Il Borgognone, greater even than the antique paragon Apelles, who was known for his marvelous representations of phenomena that are notoriously difficult to recreate visually, such as lightning, air, and fog. Courtois's imaginary battles excelled in depicting "the cries of the soldiers in combat, the moaning of the wounded and the mournful murmuring of the dying, the noise of the bombs, as well as the shuddering of the mines, as if they were real and not invented; even if none of this was heard with the ear, yet with terror it was apprehended in the mind."[128]

Courtois's ability to conjure such pictorial immediacy grew out of his own life experience. The son of a painter, in his early youth he served several years as a mercenary soldier in Spain, before starting his own artistic career. His specialization as a battle painter can be traced to his encounter with Giulio Romano's famous *Battle of the Milvian Bridge* (fig. 38). In this large fresco, we see the brutality of a fierce battle unfold before us. Romano creates an overwhelming storm of chaos that churns its way through an enormous crowd of fighters and draws the spectator in to study every clearly rendered detail of the combat. Constantine, seated upright in his saddle, radiant in his antique golden yellow garments, seems unaffected by the muddle of fighting bodies around him. The power of this victorious image is so visually disrupting that it seems to bring the atrocity of the battle to a kind of halt.

Lione Pascoli (1674–1744) reports that when the young Courtois visited the Vatican he was so taken by the *celebre battaglia di Costantino* (the famous battle of Constantine) that he studied it every day and decided from then on to paint only battle pieces.[129] Interestingly, Pascoli names Giulio Romano as the sole author of the work (*dipinta da Giulio Romano*) and fails to mention Raphael, his own master who first conceived of the fresco. Pascoli follows Vasari (*dipinse Giulio*), who, before addressing the fresco itself, noted the difference between Romano's preliminary sketches, produced in one hour and full of *vivacità, fierezza et affetto*, and the final paintings. The latter had, in Vasari's view, lost these vital qualities over the many months and years of their execution. Vasari however pronounced Giulio Romano a great master of invention and recognized the historical status of the fresco: thanks to the "maniera" of Giulio, this work became "a great light [*gran lume*] for all those who did similar things after him."[130]

We can perhaps explain why Giulio Romano received such admiration for this work by having a look at Raphael's famous double portrait representing himself

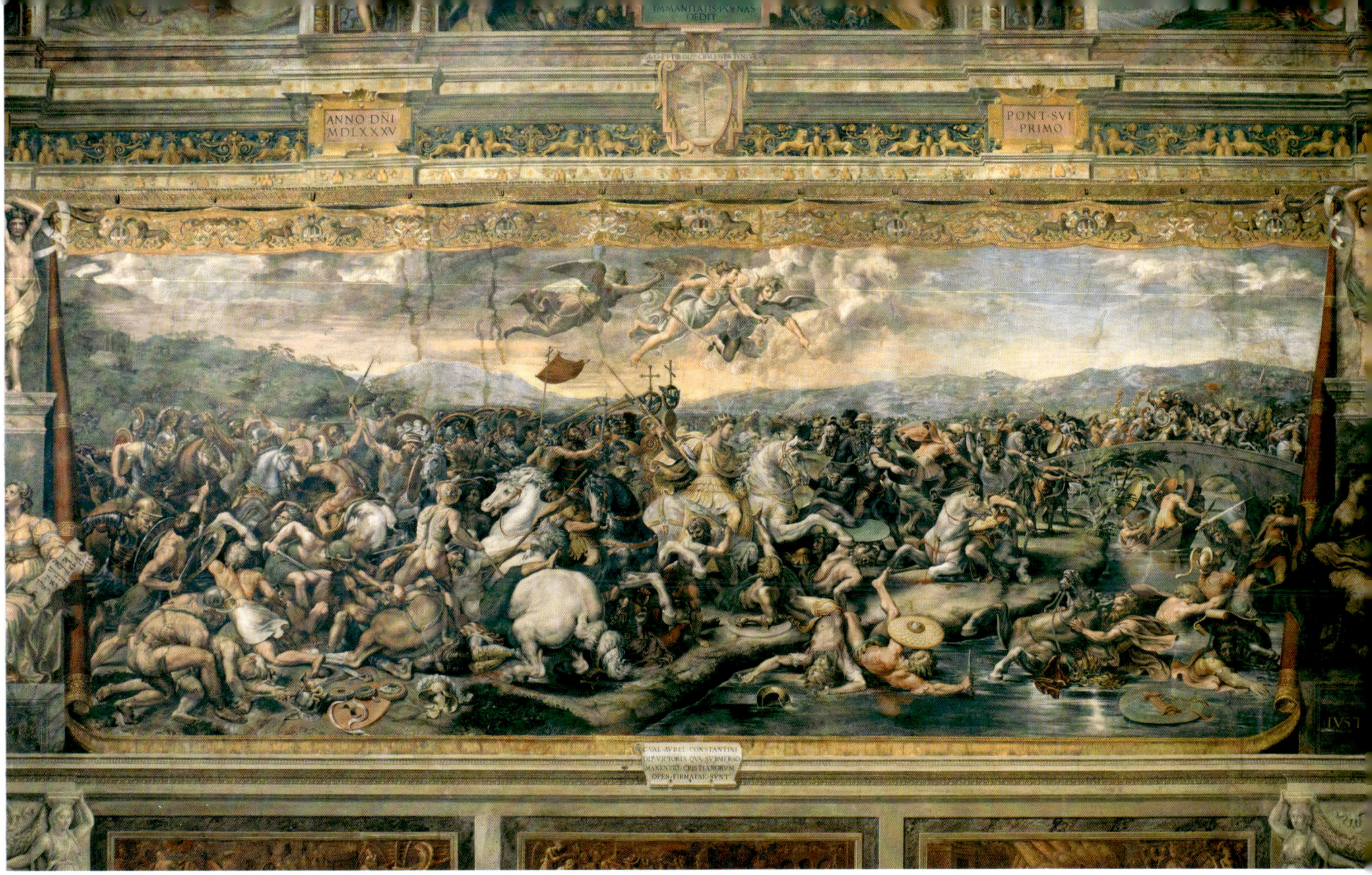

38
Giulio Romano, *Battle of the Milvian Bridge*, 1520–1524. Fresco. Apostolic Palace, Vatican City.

with a student, most likely Giulio Romano (fig. 39). Vasari begins Giulio's biography by stating that among all of Raphael's numerous pupils, it was Giulio, the "most sound, proud, certain, imaginative, versatile, prolific, and universal" (*fondato, fiero, sicuro, capriccioso, vario, abondante et universale*), whom he loved like a son. He assisted Raphael with all of his most important works.[131]

In his analysis of this work, the art historian Norbert Gramaccini did not identify the student by name, but he saw the portrait as giving insight into the distribution of work in Raphael's studio and the creative leeway allowed to his apprentices.[132] Raphael's self-portrait unflinchingly takes on the fundamental criticism leveled at his workshop, namely that he himself did not execute his own works. In a paternal gesture, Raphael rests his left hand on the shoulder of his student. His right hand touches the young man's waist, but this point of bodily contact is obscured by the darkness of their black clothing; here Raphael's arm dissolves into the second figure's body. His embrace seems to indicate that Giulio Romano is being taken under the wing of his master. This aspect of the self-portrait is not insignificant; it guides the viewer to see in the two figures a "power duo."

Whereas Giulio's clothing overlays Raphael's right hand, his own right hand is prominently displayed. Masterfully foreshortened and brightly illuminated, it seems to project into the beholder's space, while his left hand, retracted in shadow, grasps the handle of a dagger gleaming with golden highlights. This feature led

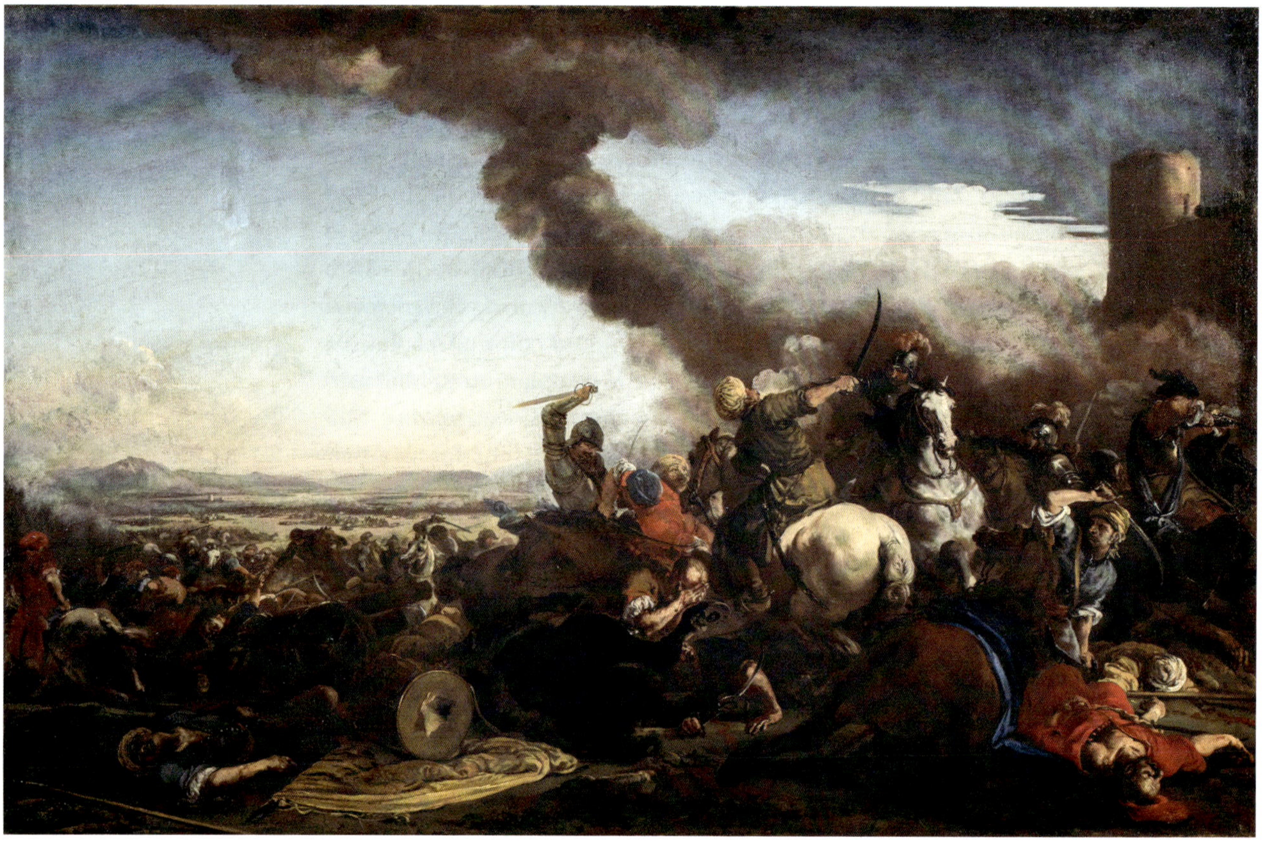

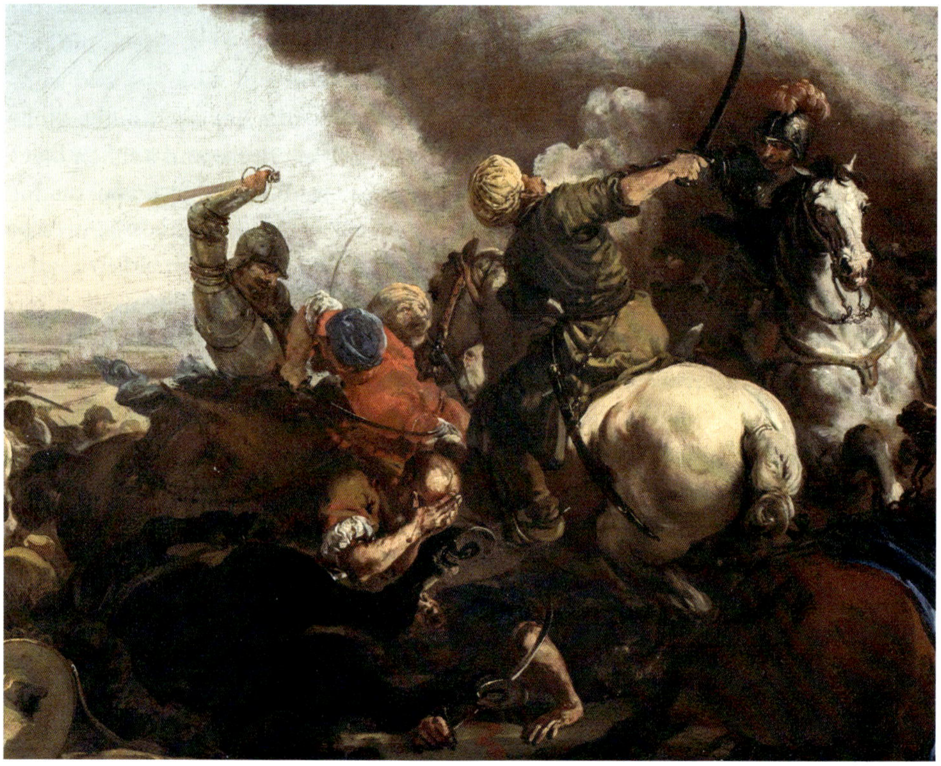

40
Jacques Courtois, called Il Borgognone, *Battle between Christians and Turks*. Oil on canvas, 98 × 148 cm. Galleria Nazionale d'Arte Antica, Palazzo Corsini, Rome.

41
Detail of fig. 40 [*Battle between Christians and Turks*].

pictorially the frightening weakening of the sense of sight overwhelmed by the chaos of war—a loss that would in turn cause heightened acoustic perception.

While Courtois was painting his battle scenes, Leonardo's earlier treatise on painting, which contained ideas related to this genre, was finally edited and belatedly published in 1651.[146] The master's instructions and advice became available to the public centuries after he had written them down, yet at a most opportune moment, for his thoughts were quite relevant to the cutting-edge techniques in use at the time of publication. Instead of providing details on how to scenically intensify a conflict in the most dramatic way or how to distinguish between victor and vanquished—in other words, instead of specifying how to make the narrative course of events visible with the greatest possible clarity, Leonardo describes confusion, a scene of archaic slaughter that threatens to be swallowed up by the churning of lowly dust and mud. He begins with a discussion of how to artistically "make" (*farai prima*) mixtures of artillery smoke and cavalry dust, then explains the optical qualities of smoke and dust, before finally taking up the figures, "which should be made as if powdered with dust on their hair and eyelashes." After discussing how to make (*farai*) furious horses and shouting or dead soldiers lying in the mud, Leonardo switches from the "making" to the imagining of (*potrebbesi vedere, potriarsi vedere, vedransi*) disarmed soldiers, fleeing or tumbling horses, and victorious soldiers wiping away the mud from their faces.[147] Dust as a substance engulfing the figures does more than just suggest an agglutination of bodies; it is the material condensation of the battle narrative. Dust becomes the "stuff" of imagination from which individual figures are then drawn forth.

CHAPTER TWO

The Figural Tour de Force

THE ART OF (FORE)SHORTENING: REPERTOIRE AND *SCORCIO* IN BATTLE PAINTINGS

In one of Esteban March's best-known paintings, showing a *Clash of Two Cavalries*, the color of the exposed imprimatura engenders a mood of falling twilight (fig. 42).[1] A squall-laden sky and hilly terrain, rendered with broad strokes of the brush, lower gloomily over a melee of mounted soldiers charging through one another's collapsed ranks. Horses, in various iterations of set poses and viewed from several perspectives, rear or rush forward in more or less full gallop.

These equine postures were certainly not studied *in natura*, but rather plainly copied from Antonio Tempesta's graphic templates (1555–1630), as several art historians have observed (fig. 43).[2] The conceit of the leaping horse as a vehicle for the display of an artist's talent, is mentioned many times in Vasari's *Vite* and condensed into handy formulae in the widely distributed prints by Tempesta, an artist praised for his "most spirited horses."[3] March singled out one horse and rider as a *pars pro toto* demonstration of expertise and a worthy tribute to this well-defined artistic device. The horse's *levade*, acting to shield his rider and threaten an opponent, is in itself a challenging and highly sophisticated equestrian maneuver that forces the horse into a physically strenuous and unnatural position. The remarkable depiction here is especially impressive because the horse's leap brilliantly conveys the force of the animal's body as it seems to break free of the picture plane and emerge into full plasticity.[4]

This insertion of highly codified figures representing different aspects of combat is a regular feature of battle paintings, especially in the seventeenth century as the genre gradually lost its heroic appeal and large format. Drawing from the reservoir of motifs offered by Leonardo and Michelangelo's legendary cartoons (see figs. 59, 60), Titian's *Battle of Cadore*, Giulio Romano's *Battle of the Milvian Bridge* (see fig. 38), and Cesari's *The Battle of Tullus Hostilius against the Etruscan Cities of Veii and Fidenae* (see fig. 28), battle painters of the seventeenth century shifted their attention from single figures to the overall composition, from the historical moment to the mundane event, and generally scaled down the scope of

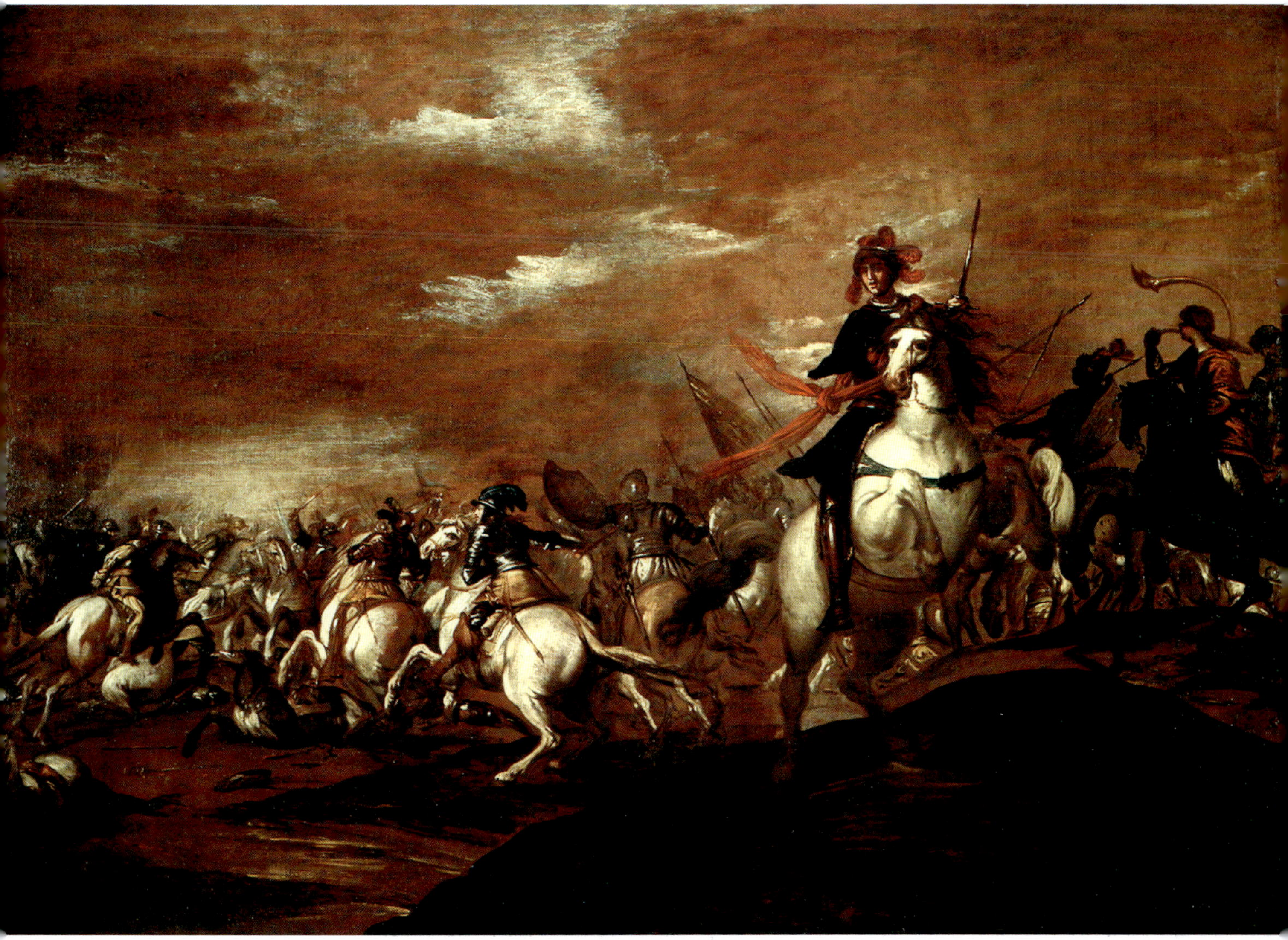

42
Esteban March, *Clash of Two Cavalries*. Oil on canvas, 136 × 193 cm. Museo de Bellas Artes, Valencia.

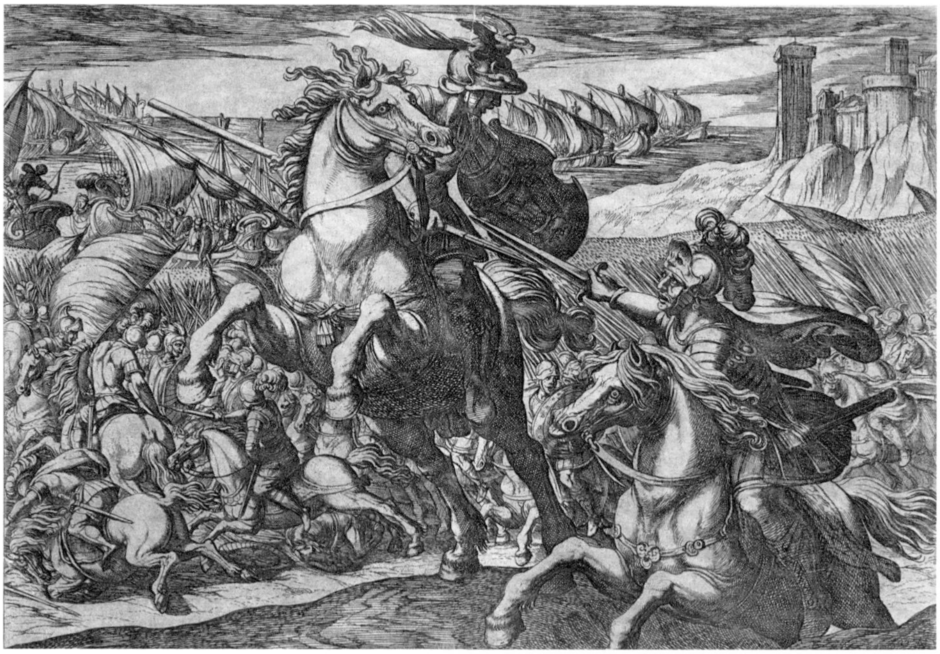

43
Antonio Tempesta, *Battle Scene* (series: cavalry battles), 1601. Etching, 23.8 × 32.6 cm. Rijksmuseum, Amsterdam.

44 (FACING)
Andrea Schiavone, *Military Triumph*. Oil on canvas, 180 cm in diameter. Biblioteca Marciana, Venice.

their scenes.[5] Even exceptions, such as the massive battles of Salvator Rosa, challenged the former heroic model with their new focus on compositional perspective. It is worth noting that the *alla prima* method of this generation diverges from Caravaggio's example insofar as he was said to work always in the presence of live models (which, as the critique goes, he turned into still lifes). The action-based genre of the battle painting must unavoidably rely more on the imagination than on models, as Leonardo incisively argued. But just as every real-life battle is carried out according to a set stratagem, the depiction of violent combat between divisions of soldiers seems also to require rich reserves of models performing a variety of actions. Undoubtedly, March's ability to execute his battle paintings with speed and self-confidence—evinced in the legendary description of his creative furor and his volatile working methods—was due in part to his adoption of such a repertory, one that he put to his own uses with so great a flourish of timbal and trumpet.

An aside found in Vasari's vita of the Venetian painter Battista Franco is an early testament to the battle painting as perfectly suited to virtuoso displays of *copia*, *varietà*, and *difficoltà*, precisely because these are the quintessential compositional ingredients of every battle representation.[6] After a passage briefly describing his colleague Andrea Schiavone's figure of a woman nursing her baby, in which he characterizes its painting style as "unfinished" (*senza esser finta punto*), Vasari mentions that he had commissioned a work from Schiavone in 1540, which he praises as very beautiful and one of the painter's best.[7] His patronage of a colleague was unusual, especially considering he rather disapproved of Schiavone's *macchie overo bozze* (blotchy or sketchy style). This renders the specific type of commission all the more meaningful: Vasari had requested a *battaglia*.[8]

The painting is no longer extant, but a similar demonstration of Schiavone's art can be witnessed in his *Military Triumph* of 1556 (fig. 44). The tondo is one of three

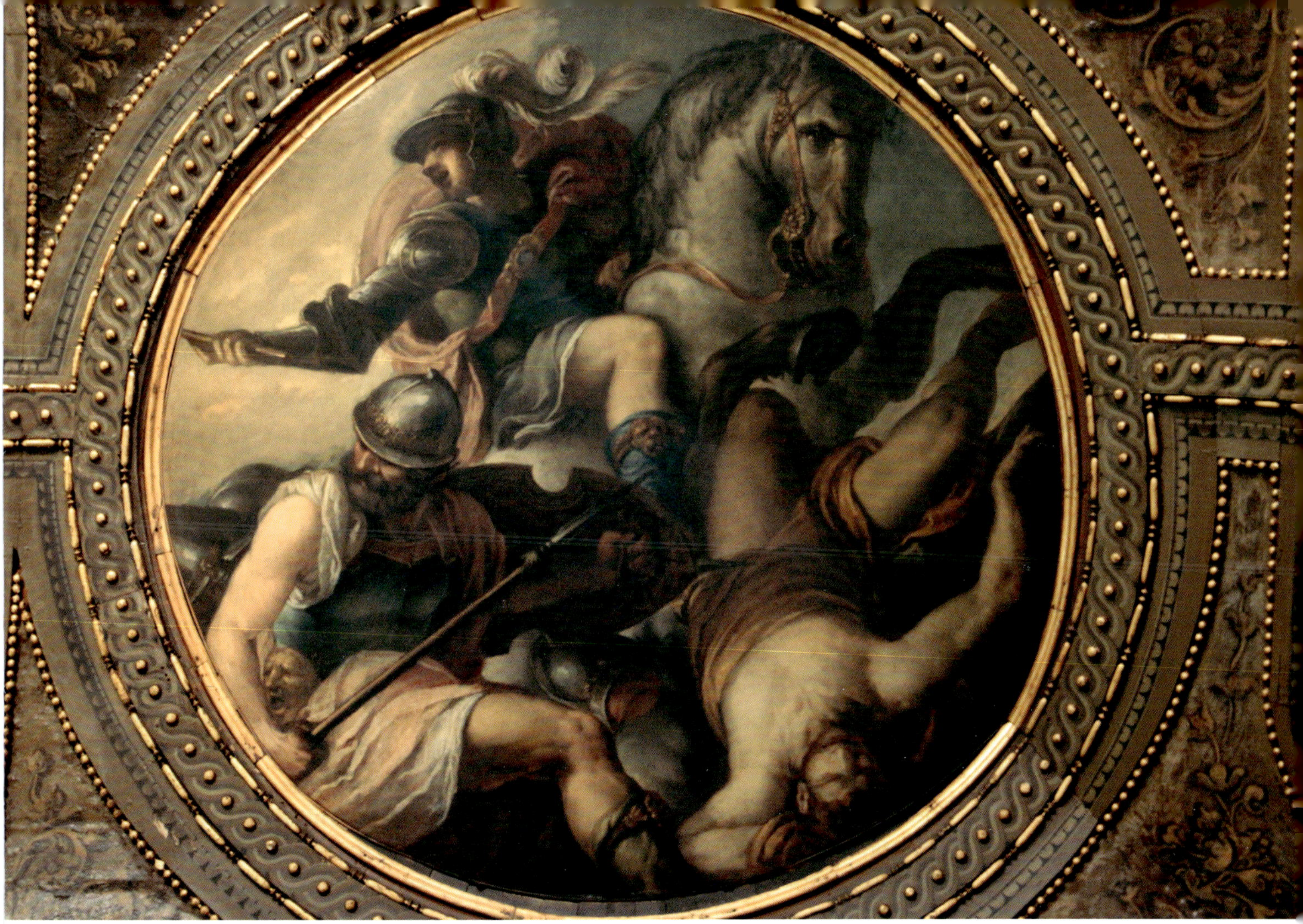

works Schiavone contributed to the decorative program of the Biblioteca Marciana, a commission that, thanks to Titian's intercession, raised the Dalmatian artist to the ranks of the most distinguished painters of his time.[9] His response to the challenge of painting a battle in a corner compartment of the ceiling was a violent figural composition that appears to burst apart so as to create distance between figures viewed from a space-contracting low-angle position.[10] Schiavone also had to deal with the ceiling's uneven ground: a slight shift in the slope of the surface produces a ridge that cuts across the tondo and results in two differently illuminated sides. Schiavone responded to this difficulty by integrating the axis of the ridge into the figural composition so that the affected figures' bodies are oriented toward it and arranging the chiaroscuro accordingly. The work in fact displays several highly divergent, nonintersecting diagonal and horizontal axes, the most dominant of these being the horizontal axis of the lance that separates the scene into victors and vanquished. Bent legs and arms produce V-shaped angles that give the composition a propulsive force, while the bodies' blurred contours and the choreographed interplay between pronounced areas of light and shadow generate a strong atmospheric effect that lends dynamic power to the rushing charge.[11]

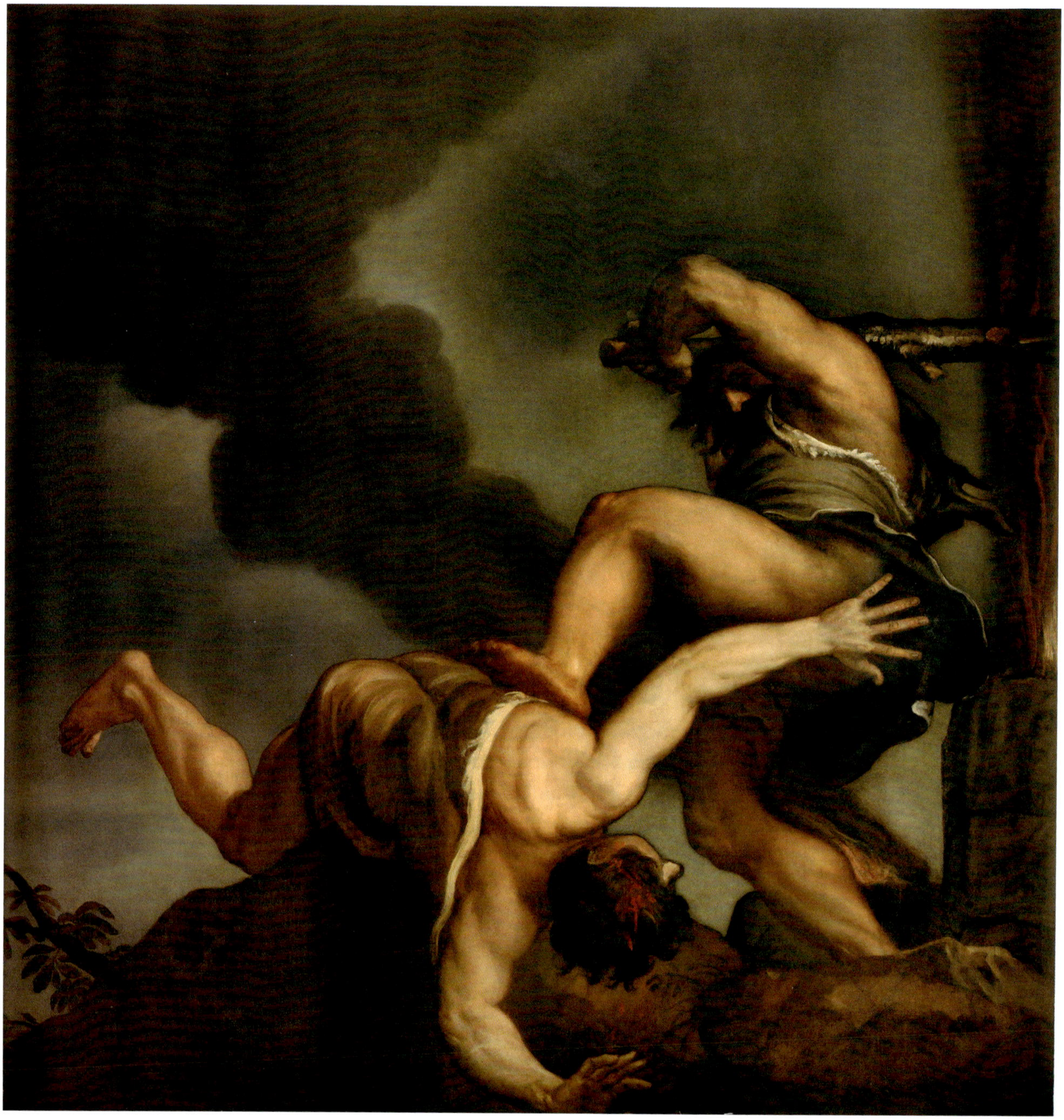

to its place and occasion.[20] The Venetian painter and art dealer Marco Boschini (1602–1681) exclaims: "What design, what *colorito!*... What agitation in the foreshortening, so life-like, so daring!"

46
Titian, *Cain and Abel*, 1544. Oil on canvas, 280 × 280 cm. Church of Santa Maria della Salute, Venice.

Because of the authoritative achievement of *Cain and Abel*, the ceiling paintings in this Venice church became a school for artists. According to Boschini, Anthony van Dyck studied the three works there very closely, which is to say, he copied "the anatomy of this painting, this design, and this bravura," specifically for the ambitious purpose of becoming famous ("E dir: sta volta me fazzo famoso").[21]

SACRIFICIAL BODIES

In keeping with Theodor Adorno's observation cited in the introduction, we could say that we witness in these works the human body sacrificially slaughtered by means of extreme foreshortening in order to hold the community of the Early Modern art world in thrall. And it therefore seems more than fitting that the complex artifice of the foreshortened nude is most often found in battle paintings and scenes of martyrdom. A spectacular example can be seen at the right margin of Correggio's *Martyrdom of Four Saints* from ca. 1524 (fig. 47). The much-admired contrived pose of the executioner, whose billowing sleeve at the small of his back together with the sharp turn of his head creates an artificial serpentine line,[22] counterbalances the outcome of his violence. The mutilation of an outstretched body—its arresting severed head is held up by a bare arm cut off by the edge of the painting, confronting the beholder in Gorgonesque fashion—is most impressively visualized by the

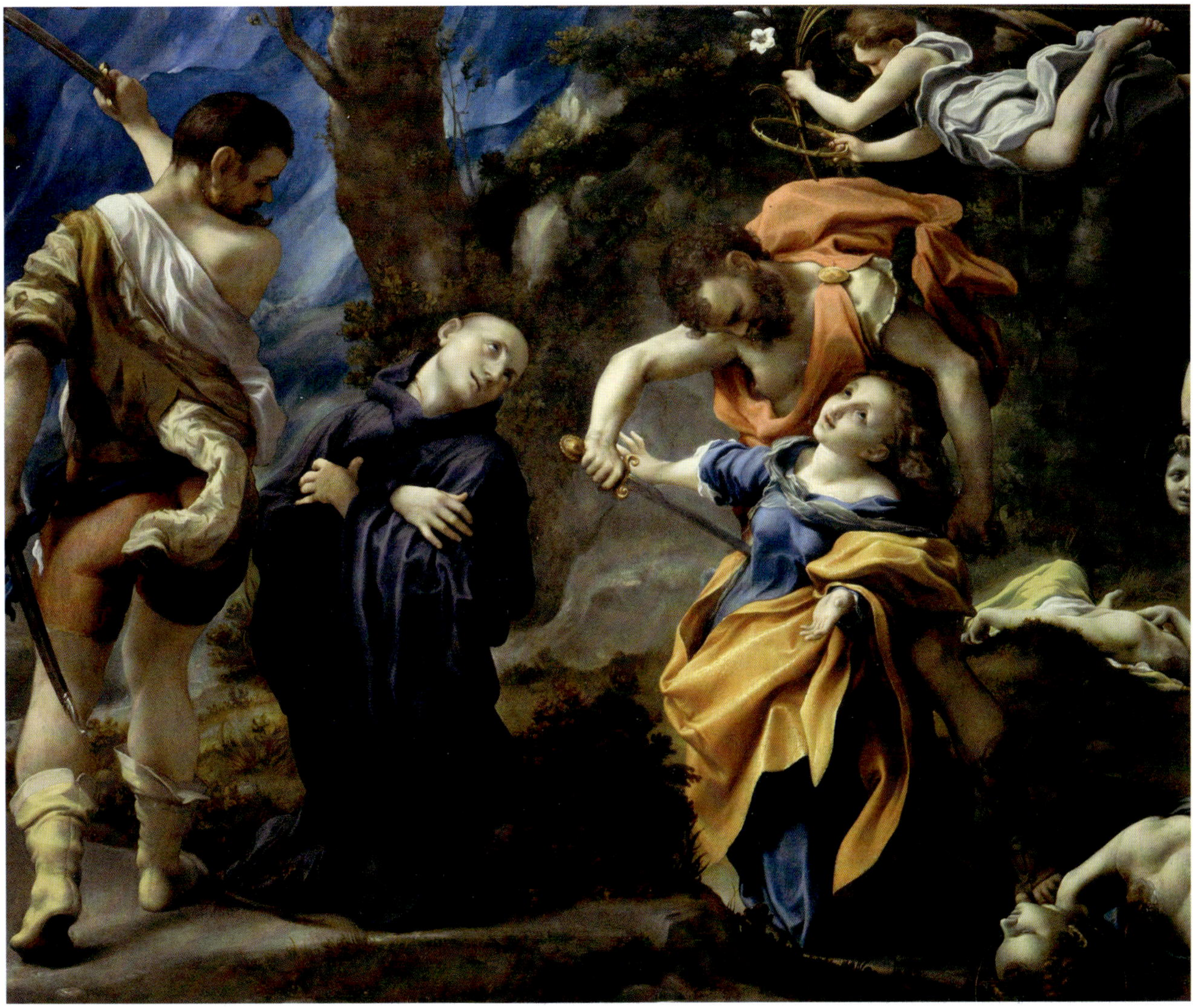

47
Antonio da Correggio, *Martyrdom of Four Saints*, 1524. Oil on canvas, 160 × 185 cm. Galleria Nazionale, Parma.

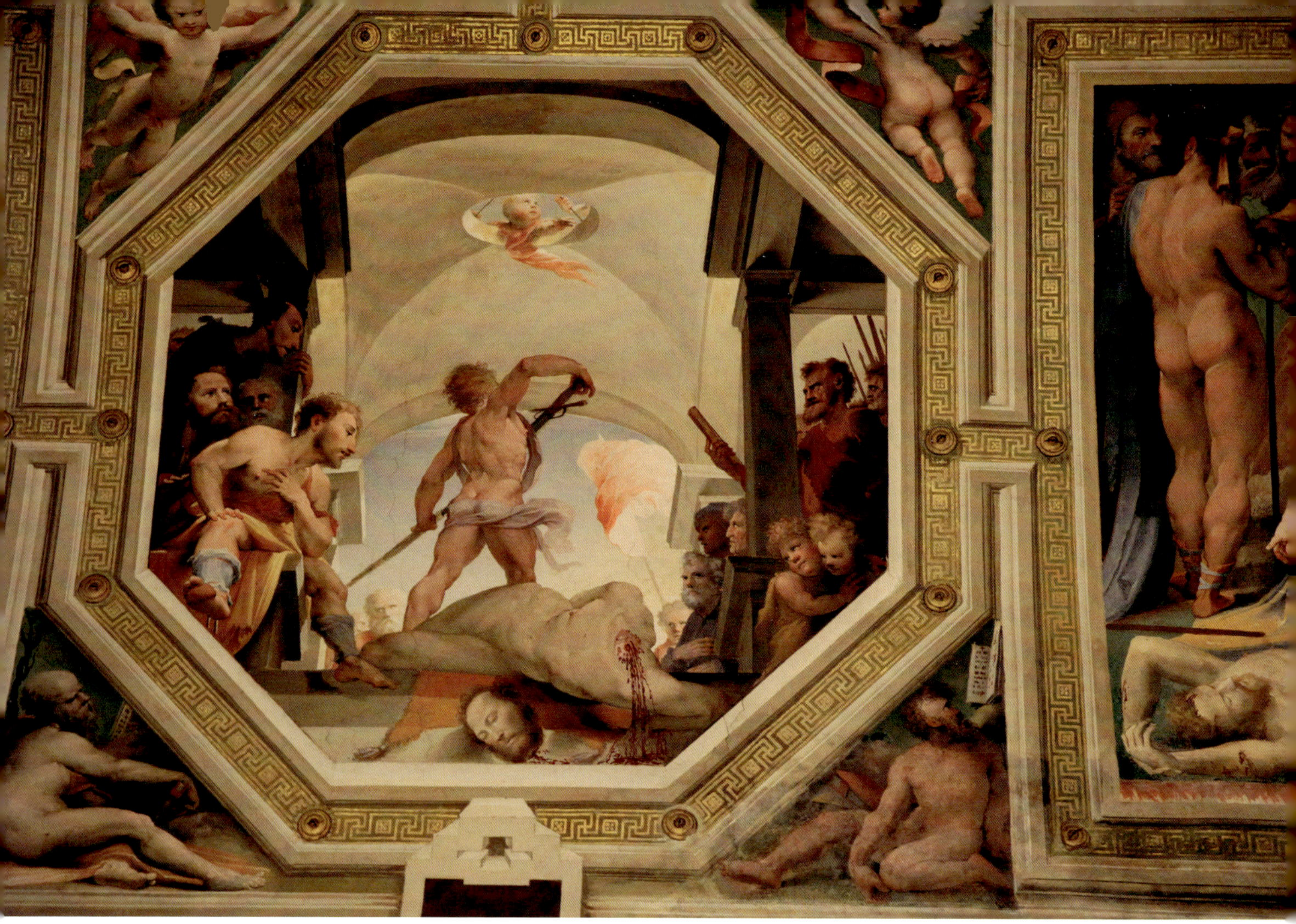

body's extreme foreshortening, which brings the shoulder close to the knee and the right foot to the level of the right hand. This deformation optically mediates the slaughter and captures the gaze of the beholder, whose imagination is called upon to mentally fill in the extension of the body.

Such pronounced foreshortening becomes most crucial in the perspectival scheme known as *al di sotto in sù*. A work by Correggio's contemporary, Domenico Beccafumi (1486–1551), illustrates the mixture of brutality and grace, a mixture that was, during this time period, both fashionable and essential to the mastery of the foreshortened body. In a ceiling painting depicting the decapitation of the Roman consul Spurius Cassius Viscellinus, the body of the victim, rolling down the stairs leading away from the domed courtyard where the murder took place, seems to be on the verge of falling into the space of the beholder below (fig. 48). The violence of the consul's twisted contrapposto is made explicit by its subtle reflection in the counterimage of the standing executioner, who ostentatiously sheathes his sword. Both figures constitute the main axes of the octagonal tondo. The horizontal position of the fallen body on the steps reinforces its lateral slide toward the spectator and mitigates perspectival distortion. Beccafumi moreover spares the viewer the deformations of a foreshortened head (he also turns the face of the executioner away from us) by having it roll away from the body; a spurt of spilled blood underlines the connection between the two and dramatizes the head's momentum. The right foot of an emotional witness sitting in the immediate foreground is suspended in the air adjacent to the victim's head, thus enhancing the impression that the head is falling into our space. The other foot casts a shadow across two of the steps, creating a spatial orientation that makes both feet appear to be the same distance from the plinth. Separated from the tormented body, the dignified features of the consul's face express a stoicism toward his fate that recalls idealized portrayals of John the Baptist.

In his vita of Beccafumi, Vasari praises the head and foreshortened body (*in iscorto*) as "very beautiful" and then elucidates the specific means used to create that beauty by referencing another piece in the same ceiling program: the central tondo with a personification of Justice, positioned adjacent to and, in the illusion of the depicted space, seemingly above the decapitation scene (fig. 49). After praising the *scorcio* in this work as "so daring that it is a miracle" (*gagliardamente che è una maraviglia*), Vasari describes how the *colorito* and chiaroscuro of its drawing are methodically elaborated from toe to head: the dark zone of the feet brightens somewhat toward the knees, progressing in this way "via the torso, shoulders, and arms" until the head is bathed in a "celestial splendor," appearing to dissolve away into nothingness (*a poco a poco se ne vada in fumo*). Vasari concludes that he has never seen a figure foreshortened "al di sotto in sù" with more discernment and art.[23]

48 (FACING)
Domenico Beccafumi, *The Decapitation of the Roman Consul Spurius Cassius Viscellinus*, ca 1535. Fresco. Sala del Concistoro, Palazzo Publico, Siena.

The painter and art-theorist Giovanni Battista Armenini (1533?–1609) defines the *scorcio* as extremely difficult (he speaks of a *difficoltà gravissima*) and as a showcase for the *forza dell' arte*.[24] Interestingly, Armenini relativizes the use of foreshortening based solely on *disegno*: the admirable talent that can make an object protrude or disappear from view on the flat surface (*sporgere contro la vista o per l'opposito sfuggirsi indietro*)[25] is not solely reliant on the rules of perspective. Armenini praises the contouring involved as difficult and extraordinary, but *disegno* is not, in his view, the unique solution to the problem posed by the *scorcio*; the distribution of chiaroscuro plays a most important part as well. [26] Calculating the exact proportions necessary for a successful *scorcio* is a creative endeavor that must take into account the whole complexity of visual reality. Its proper execution must go beyond simply applying a fixed system of perspectival laws, for the feat involves, and indeed demands, the artist's inventive effort to overcome its great difficulties. In this regard, Armenini mentions the small wax models Michelangelo made in order to better understand and study the visual effects of the foreshortened view.[27]

Armenini praises in particular Giulio Romano's *Fall of the Giants* in the Palazzo del Te (Mantua), calling the fresco completely covering the walls and ceiling of one room a *capriccio bellissimo*. Even the transitional spaces at the junctures between wall and vault are seamlessly filled to create an enormous, continuous image. The beholder who enters the room feels both immersed in the scene, and disquieted. As Armenini puts it: being "varied and novel, it is horrible and frightening to look at."[28] The bold innovation of the composition, portraying giants struggling to free themselves from beneath boulders that tumble loose and are heaped in mountainous piles, consists in its ostentatious display of the monstrous *scorcio*. The giants'

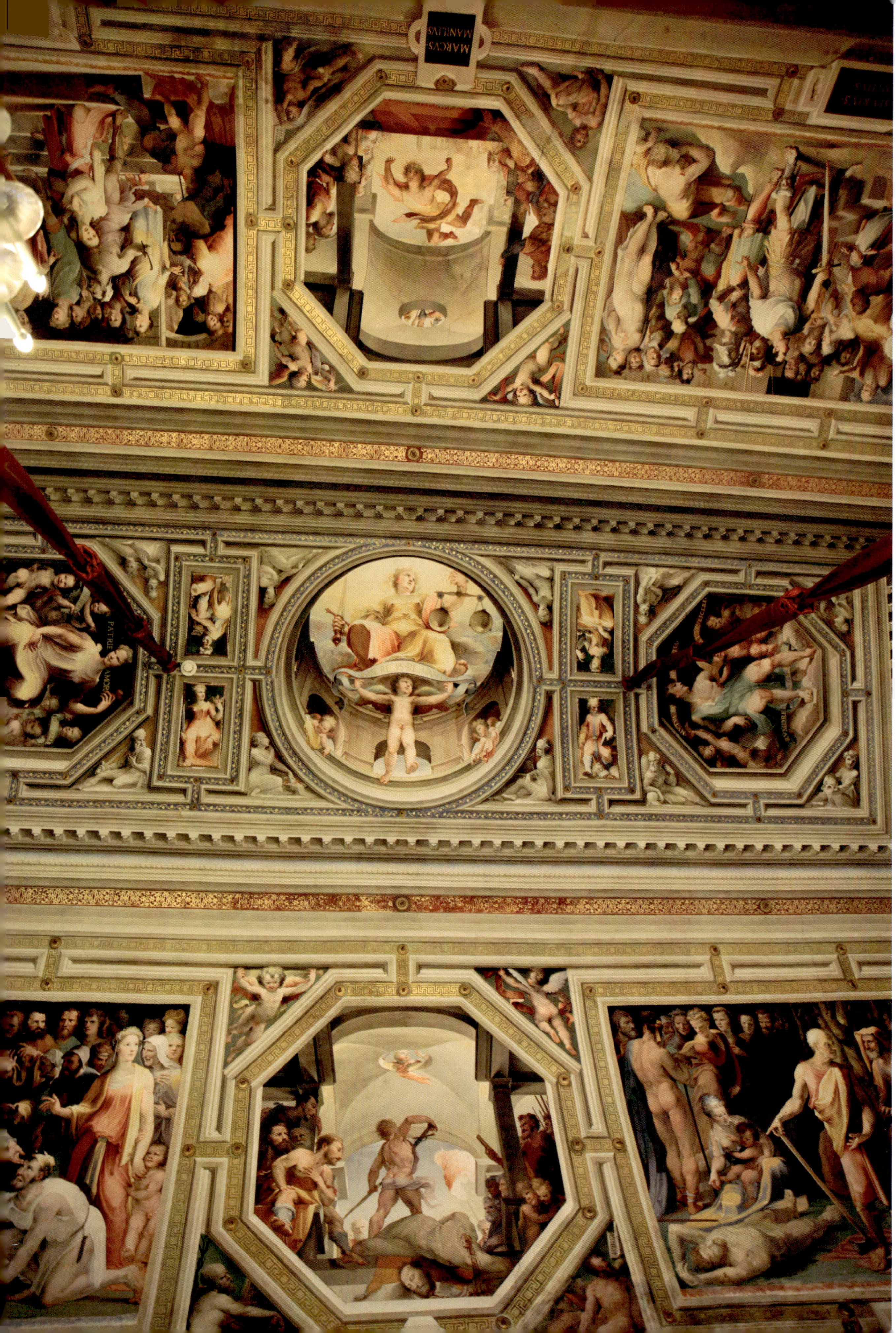
MARCVS MANLIVS
PATRIE AMOR

bodies, everywhere forcefully weighted down and contorted by the force of the stones, form along one wall a concatenation of the fallen, while on the opposite wall, a cascade of entangled and writhing bodies is pushed into the corner by the broken column that has caused their temple to fall in on them. The collapsing building depicted above and surrounding the beholder causes us to feel terror, and then we are confronted also by the strong foreshortening of the giants' massive limbs, which lends visual credence to the futility of their attempt, according to the myth, to liberate themselves (figs. 50, 51). Their deformed bodies are echoed in the malformations and obstructions of eyesight that afflict a group of three giants. In one corner of the room, a Cyclops is accompanied by a giant with a squint, while a third positioned nearby, where the ceiling curvature meets a Cyclopean masonry of massive unworked boulders, covers his eyes with his hands, wittily mirroring our distorted perspective of these scenes (fig. 52).[29]

In Lodovico Dolce's *Dialogo della pittura* (1557), Aretino and the Florentine humanist Giovanni Francesco Fabrini debate how often such a technically demanding element, which requires considerable erudition on the part of the artist, should properly be used. Fabrini's argument countering Aretino's insistence on moderation revolves around the importance of fame: "I understand that these foreshortenings are one of the principal difficulties in art. I would therefore believe that those who utilize them more often would be more deserving of praise." In response to Aretino's objection that an excessive use of foreshortening elicits "fastidio" instead of "dilettatione," Fabrini answers: "If I were a painter, I would not use them always, but as often as possible with the hope of garnering more fame than if I only seldom employed them."[30] In his *Dialogo di pittura* (1548), the Venetian painter and art writer Paolo Pino describes the *scorcio* as "the most noble part" of painting[31] and counsels artists to impress art connoisseurs by incorporating in their works at least one figure that is "*tutta sforciata*, mysterious, and difficult" due to its optical distortion.[32] Likewise, Vasari claims one may achieve *terribilissima arte* by means of this daring feat.[33]

49 (FACING)
Domenico Beccafumi, *Justice*, 1532–1533. Fresco. Sala del Concistoro, Palazzo Publico, Siena.

Armenini reports that Michelangelo, according to him the best in *scorti*, used wax figurines to study the modeling of contour lines and chiaroscuro, thereby learning how to create plasticity and relief not from theory but from visual evidence.[34] Tintoretto and others adopted his method, replacing the Early Renaissance practice of using perspective lines to produce the foreshortened view, which was now criticized as visually unconvincing and, according to Vasari, openly dismissed by many artists. Science was replaced by bravura techniques.[35] Tintoretto—who according to Ridolfi had written the motto "*Il disegno di Michelangelo, e il colorito di Tiziano*" on the wall of his workshop in hopes that, in accord with Paolo Pino's prophecy, he would thus acquire divine status as a "god of painting"[36]—intensely scrutinized some of Michelangelo's most exemplary sculptures, such as those in the Medici Chapel of the San Lorenzo Basilica in Florence, in order to achieve his own daring foreshortenings (figs. 53, 54). It is likely that miniaturized copies mediated between Michelangelo's originals and Tintoretto's sketches,[37] permitting him access to viewpoints, such as the backside of the figure, which were not visible to the viewer from the sculpture's fixed position in the Medici tomb. Far more drastic than Tintoretto's choice of surprising viewing angles in these drawings is the effect he achieves by dissolving the

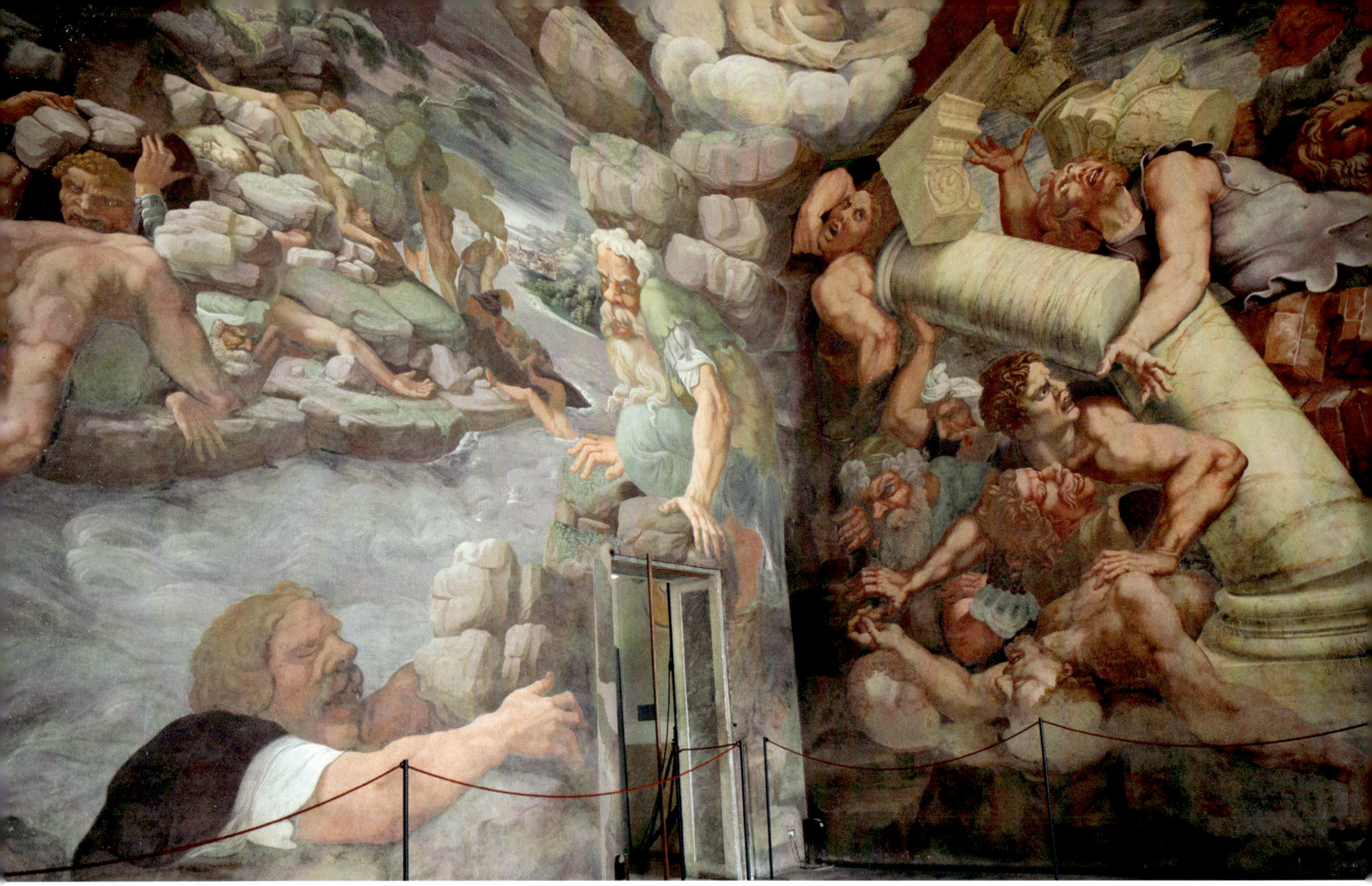

contours in favor of a mottled chiaroscuro. It turns the once coherent figure into a patchwork of light and shadow. The forcefulness with which the features of the face are deleted reflects the sculpture's *non finito* quality and adds to the drawing an aspect of painterly bravura.[38] It seems that from these studies of *disegno* Tintoretto was indeed able to acquire "the lance of Michelangelo."[39]

50–52 (ABOVE AND FACING)
Giulio Romano, *Sala dei Giganti*, 1532–1535. Fresco. Palazzo del Te, Mantua.

Portuguese painter Francisco de Hollanda (1517–1585), whose art-historical significance rests on the written record of his discussions with Michelangelo Buonarroti in Rome in the years 1538–1541, declares in his treatise *Da pintura antiga* (1548) that only the "very expert and judicious man" should be allowed to employ "foreshortening in painting" because it is "something that many mean to do, and very few actually do." This "monstrous" device, he observes, can make part of a figure seem as if it "emerges from the picture and comes straight at us; or conversely, another part of the figure or thing recede backward, which we want to look as if retreating from our sight and losing size and diminishing, like for instance, painting a bull or horse completely from the front, as if it is coming toward me from within the picture.... And with this method it is possible to paint a lance twenty *palmos* long from the front, foreshortened to a *cavado* in size, and which appears to be twenty *palmos*."[40]

Michelangelo's most exemplary demonstrations of foreshortening are found in his *Last Judgment*, a work in which, according to Michelangelo's biographer Ascanio

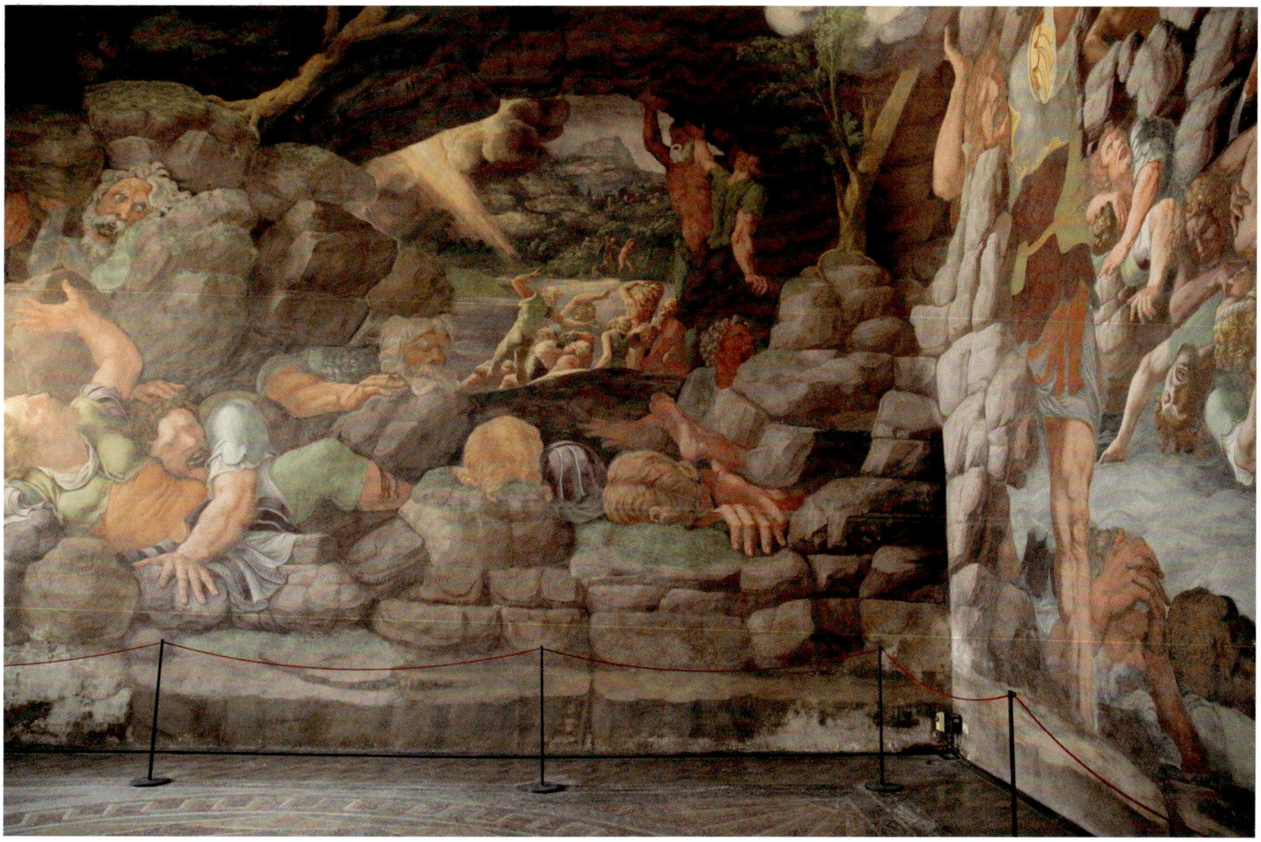

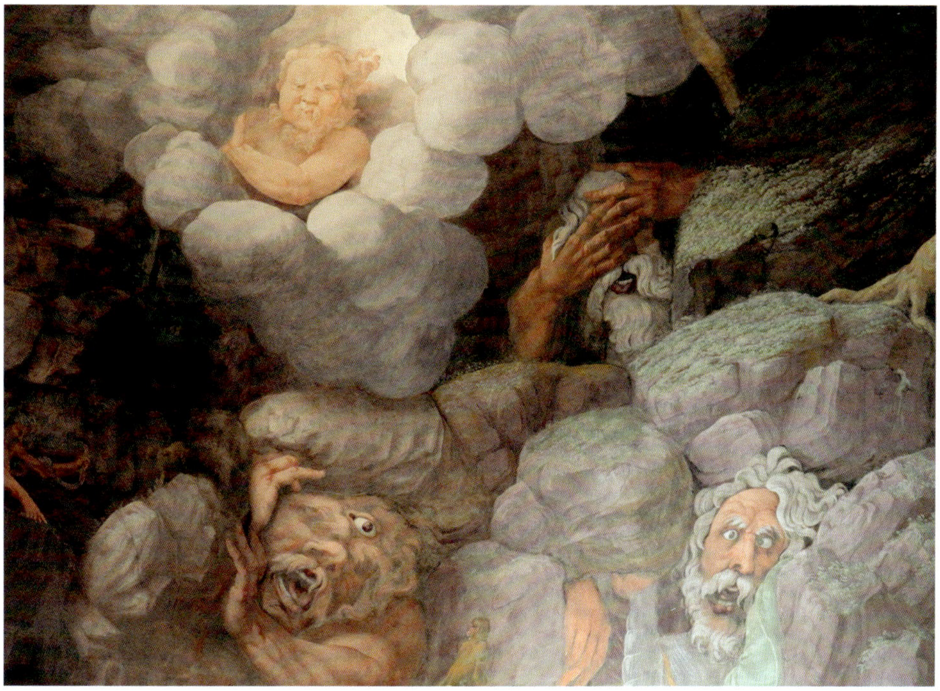

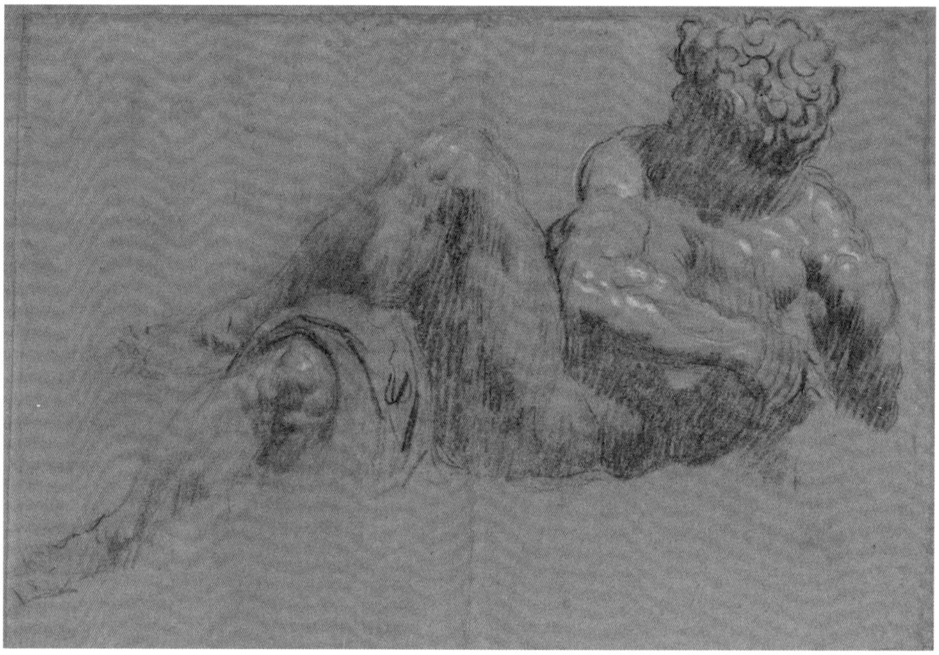

53
Jacopo Tintoretto, drawing after Michelangelo's *Il Giorno*, ca. 1550–1555. Black and white chalk on blue paper, 35×50.5 cm. Metropolitan Museum of Art, New York.

Condivi, he "expressed all that the art of painting can do with the human figure, leaving out no attitude or gesture whatever" (fig. 55).[41] For Vasari, the unparalleled achievement of the work sets the bar unattainably high for others and ultimately instigates a "last judgment" within the realm of art:

> This work leads like bound captives all those who are convinced they understand the art of painting, and in seeing the strokes he drew in the outlines of all his figures, every magnificent spirit is fearful and trembles, however knowledgeable he may be in the art of design. And in studying his labors, the senses are confused solely at the thought of how other paintings, both those that have been executed and those to come, would compare to this one.[42]

In the same vein, Armenini will later put words of condemnation such as the supreme judge himself might utter into the artist's own mouth. When Michelangelo entered the Sistine Chapel and saw numbers of other painters gathered there to copy his work, he reportedly uttered: "Oh, how many men this work of mine will expose as clumsy fools" (*O quanti quest' opera mia ne vuole ingoffire*).[43]

Art historians have pointed out an interesting detail in one scene: Michelangelo projected his own facial features onto the empty skin of St. Bartholomew (fig. 56). Missing the bone and muscle structure so intensively studied by Michelangelo, the sagging skin with crumpled facial features not only evokes pity (mixed with disgust),[44] but also seems on the point of being discarded by the resurrected saint and falling into the abyss of hell. This puzzling motif may be an attempt at self-deprecating humor addressed to Michelangelo's patron Pope Paul III, who also figures in the work as the arisen St. Bartholomew. In his vita of Michelangelo, Vasari recognizes the great benefit that accrued to Paul III from Michelangelo's work of self-sacrifice in decorating the Sistine Chapel: "And how truly happy are those

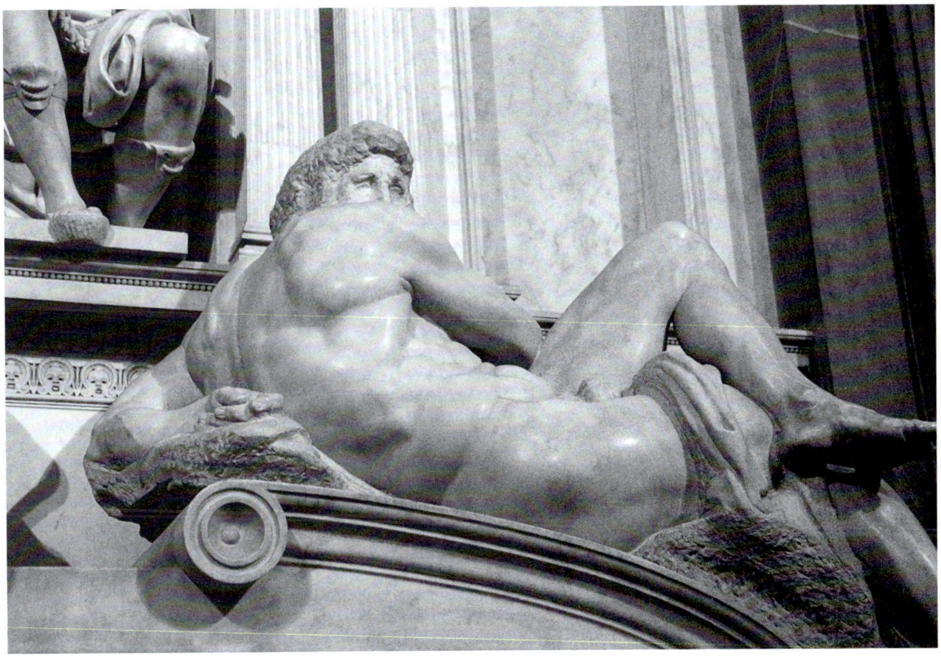

54
Michelangelo, *Il Giorno*, 1626–1631. Marble sculpture, 160 × 150 cm. Church of San Lorenzo, La Sagrestia Nuova, Florence.

who have seen this truly stupendous wonder of our century, and how happy their memories must be! Most happy and fortunate Paul III, for God granted that under *his* patronage the glory that the writers' pens will accord to *his* memory and to your own would find shelter! How greatly will [Michelangelo's] merits enhance [Paul's] own worth!"[45]

Substituting both his own features and those of Paul III for those of the same saint was a bold move. Although, admittedly, almost none of his contemporaries mention the saint's resemblance to the patron or painter, one reproduction of this detail placed Michelangelo's signature next to the distorted portrait, evidently because the printmaker was unable to convey the artist's likeness and wanted to call attention to the identification (fig. 57).[46] The obvious incongruence between the flayed skin and the resurrected body, possibly intended as a subtle joke, was considered an artistic travesty. In a letter to Giorgio Vasari, his friend Don Miniato Pitti objects: "There are a thousand heresies, especially in the beardless skin of St. Bartholomew, while the flayed one has a beard, which demonstrates that the skin is not his own."[47] This "heresy" adds to the many *capricci* in the *Last Judgment* that are criticized by one M. Ruggiero, the conservative cleric in Giovanni Andrea Gilio's *Dialogue on the Errors and Abuses of Painters* (1564). According to Ruggiero, Michelangelo's ostentations[48] and desire for glory unmask the deeper motivation behind his many violations of decorum. All five participants in the dialogue, some fervently supporting Michelangelo, agree on one point: Michelangelo has "embellished his brush and satisfied the art."[49] With his overwhelming artistic display of all movements possible by the human body, they aver, he seized the opportunity to leave a record for posterity of his extraordinary creativity (*ingegno*) and artistic skill (*arte*).[50]

We could further understand Michelangelo's *Last Judgment* as a successful attempt to outdo *himself*. As is evident in his preliminary sketches, Michelangelo

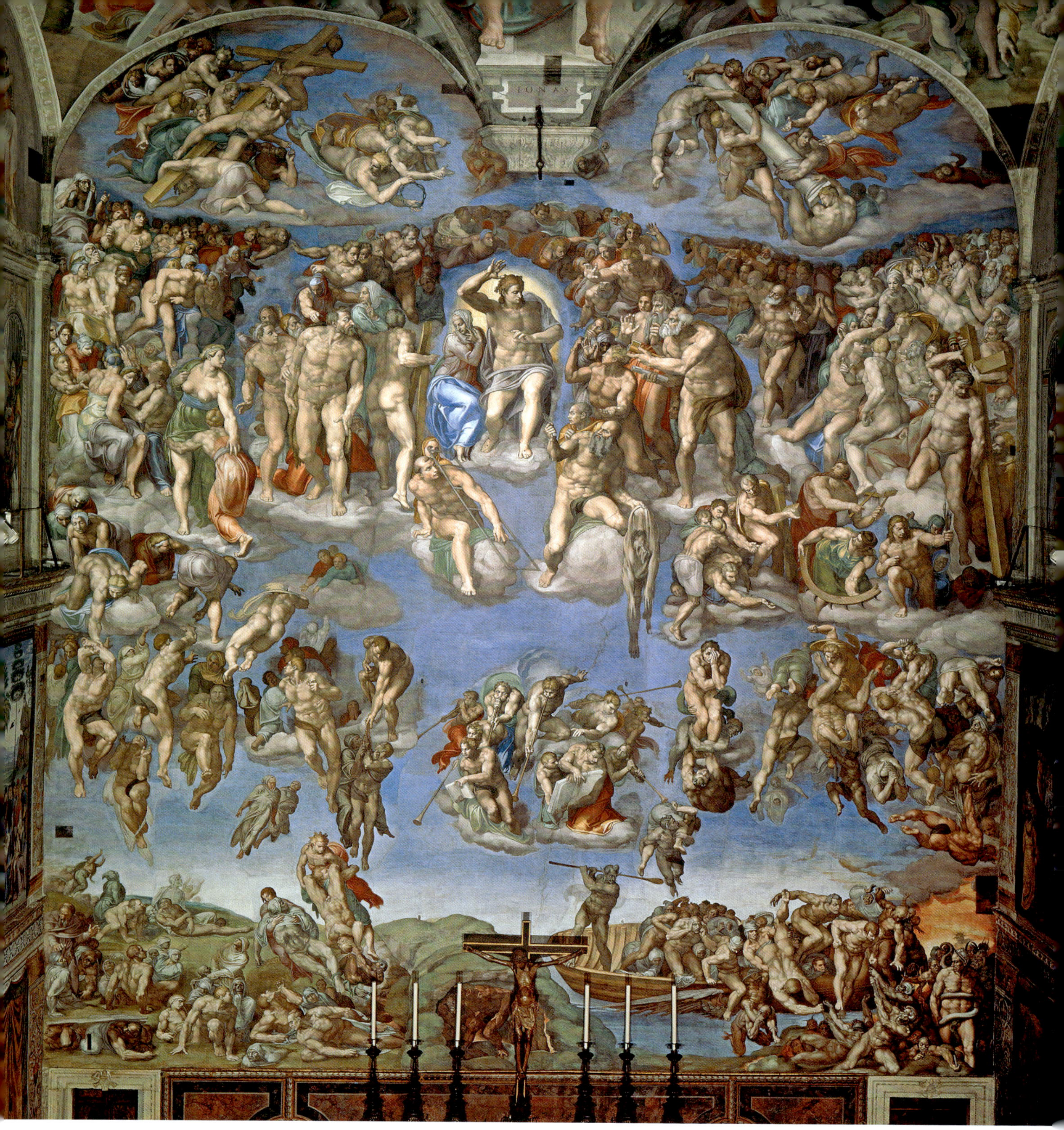

55
Michelangelo, *The Last Judgment*, 1536–1541. Fresco, 13.7 × 12 m, Sistine Chapel, Vatican City.

paid close attention to how the numerous foreshortened bodies in the composition would be linked together. In the final work their corporeal chains and knots create a succession of spatially explosive and figuratively complex incidents that open different realms within the scene. This stands in stark contrast to the scattered figures that people Michelangelo's early masterpiece, *The Battle of Cascina*. As only copies after his cartoon are extant today, however, we must bear in mind that the lack of bonding devices between the figures may not reflect the original plan.

In one of these copies we see a cohort of soldiers seeming to move past one another as they prepare for combat, each carrying out a different activity (fig. 58). The clear outlines of the figures suggest that Michelangelo was focused on the *disegno* of their foreshortening. He appears to intentionally impart a sense of disassociation among members of the troop by staging this rather fragmented composition as a pivotal moment in the immediate foreground of the work: two hands reach out from the surface of the water, but because the body below them is being swept away by the current, they have already passed out of range of the man who bends forward and extends his arm in a rescue attempt; a second man echoing the

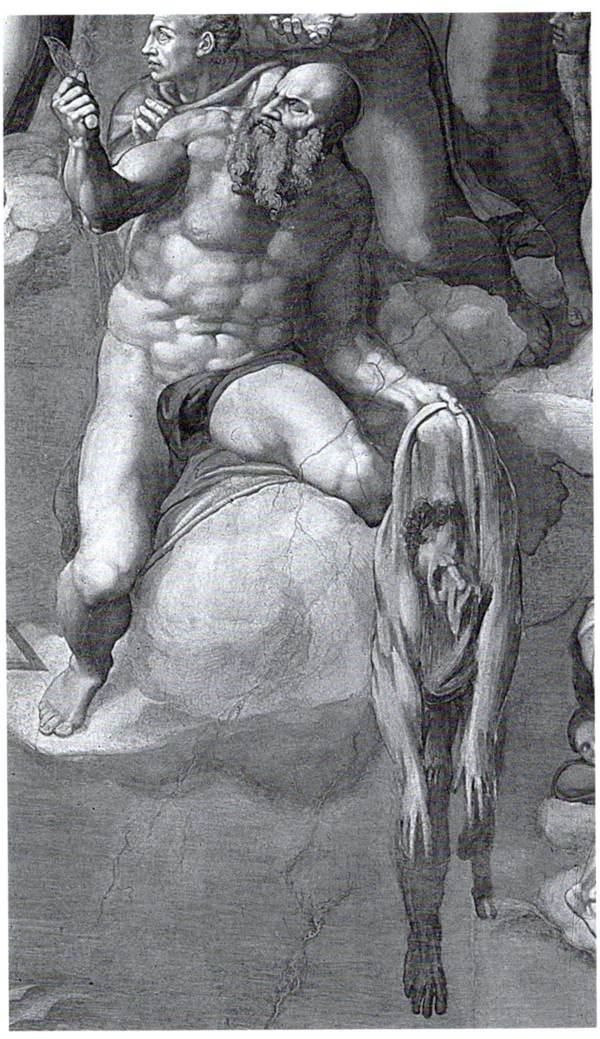

56
Detail of fig. 55 [*The Last Judgment*: *St. Bartholomew*].

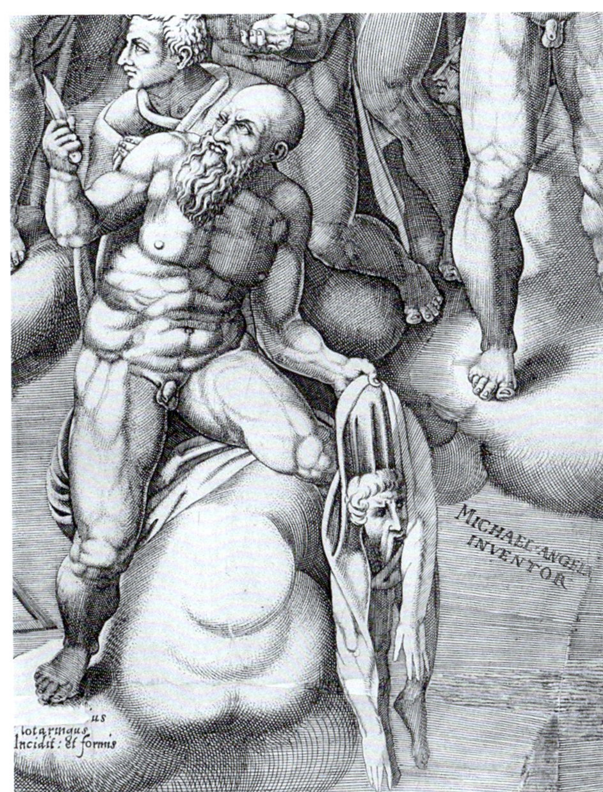

57
Nicolas Beatrizet, after Michelangelo, *The Last Judgment*, 1562. Engraving. Metropolitan Museum of Art, New York.

bent posture seems alerted to the life-threatening situation but is not yet ready to step in and save the drowning man.

Vasari reports that after hearing of Michelangelo's cartoon for the *Battle of Cascina*, the young Raphael immediately departed from Siena where he was employed and moved to Florence. And it is possible that Raphael once undertook to upstage Michelangelo's famously unsurpassable renditions of the human figure. In one of his cartoons for tapestries meant to decorate the walls of the Sistine Chapel, he addressed the *Battle of Cascina*'s theme of imminent loss by transforming it into the depiction of a successful miracle (fig. 59). The posture of two bent figures with bared torsos exposes their muscular backs in a way that resonates with Michelangelo's two nudes. But in Raphael's rendering their strong brawny arms, which he has exaggerated even further than his model, reach out to grasp "the miraculous draft of fish." That the content of this catch pertains less to the provision of food by successful fishing than to the fishing of men to which Christ called the disciples (a prior event recalled in the grouping of Jesus, Peter, and Andrew on a second boat in the same scene)[51] is clearly evoked in the reflection on the water's surface. The outstretched hands of the fishermen successfully grab at their own mirror image that has been caught in the net, signifying their belief in the miracle that has saved their lives. Raphael transforms Michelangelo's *capriccio* into a key moment: instead of diverting the beholder's attention away from the scene to its artifice (Michelangelo's fault, according to his critics), the art conveyed by the extreme foreshortening of the fishermen's focuses instead on the deeper intent of the representation, which is to grant the viewer access to a deeper level of understanding.

58
Bastiano da Sangallo, called Aristotile, copy after the central scene of the bathers in Michelangelo's *Battle of Cascina*, 1542. Oil on wood panel, 76.5 × 129 cm. Holkam Estate, England.

59 (FACING)
Raphael, *The Miraculous Draught of the Fishes*, 1514–1515. Black chalk and tempera on several sheets of paper glued one on top of the other and mounted on canvas, 319 × 399 cm. Victoria and Albert Museum, London.

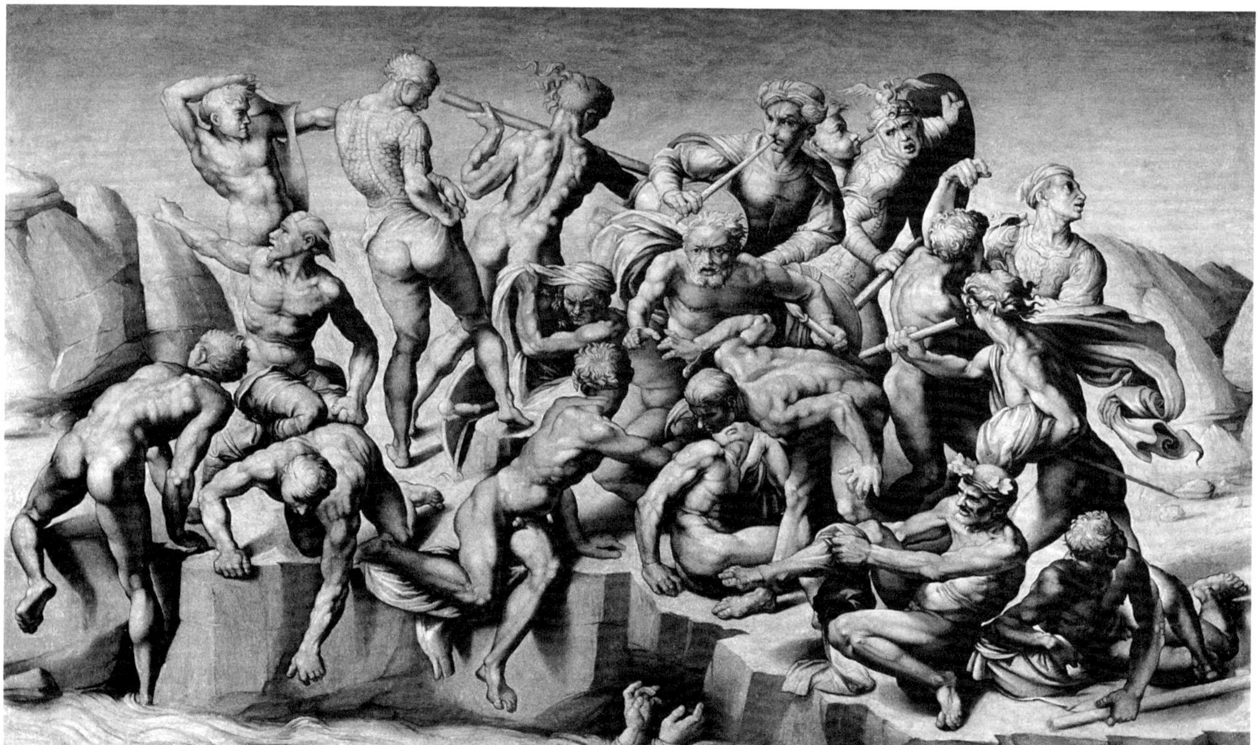

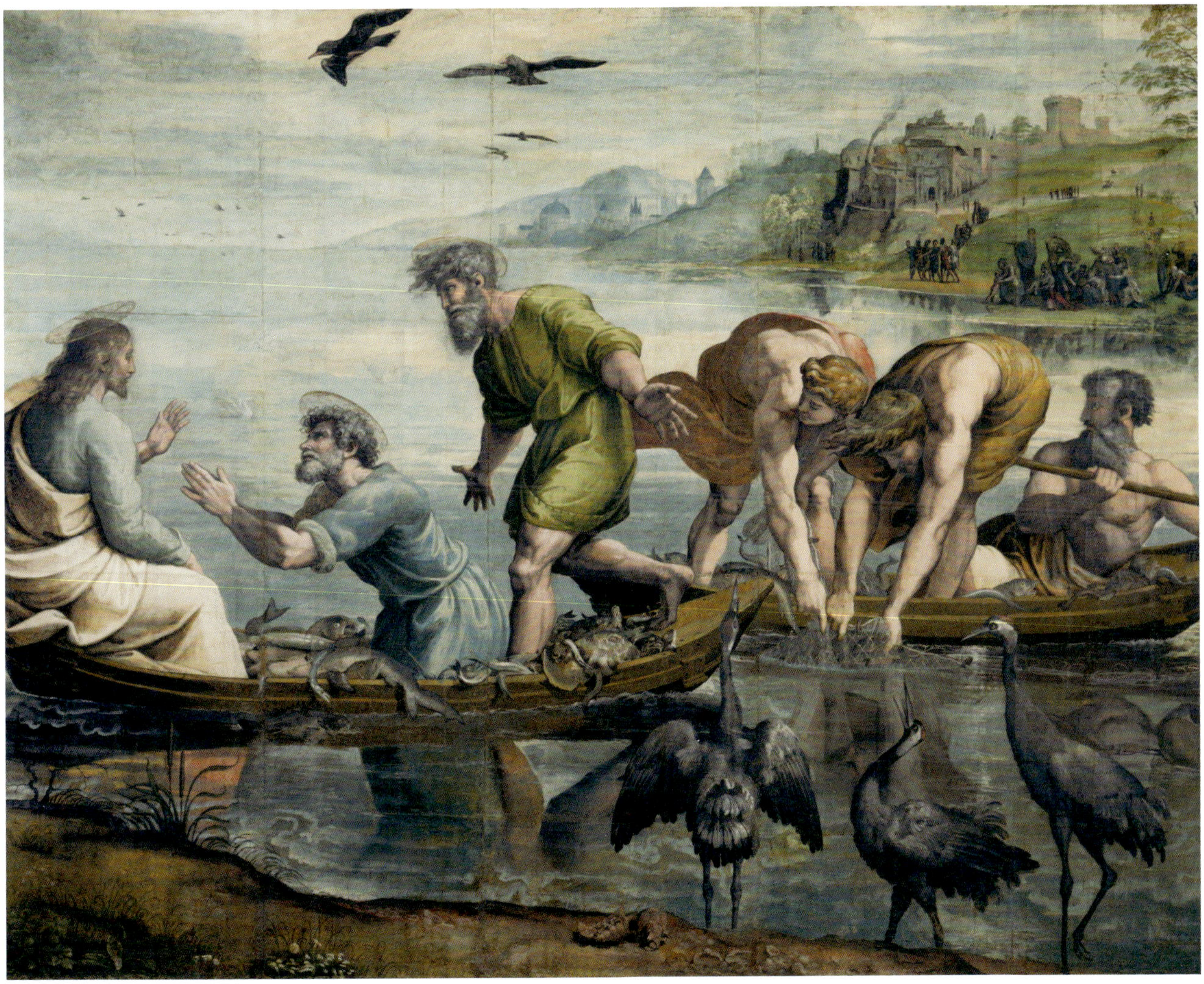

PAZZIA BESTIALISSIMA: RUBENS'S COPY AFTER LEONARDO'S *BATTLE OF THE STANDARD*

The *fama* associated with the highest achievements in art accrued not only to Michelangelo's cartoon, but also to the work he attempted to outshine, Leonardo's *Battle of the Standard.* Leonardo and Michelangelo were commissioned to decorate the Sala del Gran Consiglio Maggiore of the Palazzo Vecchio, a prestigious honor for Leonardo after a twenty-year absence from Florence. However, the hoped for staging of an epic contest between the two artists, initiated and encouraged by the city officials of Florence, never progressed far beyond the design stage. Leonardo produced a cartoon and began a wall painting but left it unfinished, possibly due to displeasure at the competitive atmosphere that developed after he began the work or, more likely, on account of the failure of his new mixed-media technique. Michelangelo moved to Rome shortly after he submitted his cartoon for the *Battle of Cascina* and evidently never developed it further.

in art, most notably by using foreshortening and unaccommodating perspectives, which he thought as difficult to execute as they were to look at. Despite good design and flawless execution, the works of this earlier epoch lacked, he thought, a crucial quality—the spirit of *prontezza*,[64] which could not be achieved by careful precision, but rather by strategies of withholding visual specificity.

The modern style, which according to Vasari originated in the works of Leonardo, is based on the ability to manifest something in the painting that—as Vasari's famous formulation puts it—oscillates between seeing and not-seeing.[65] Benedetto Varchi in his essay *Della maggioranza delle arti* (1546) judged the use of chiaroscuro in foreshortening as the most compelling means of creating the illusion of plasticity. The artistic difficulty here (*cosa difficilissima*) consisted in making something "appear that does not exist," so that the beholder is able to fathom the effort and infinite artistic skill (*fatica et artifizio infinito*) involved.[66] Vasari connects this effect to the technique of *sfumato*, and identifies it with Leonardo and with the Venetian painter Giorgione.

61 (FACING)
Rubens, *The Fall of Phaeton*, ca. 1604–1605. Oil on canvas, 98.4 × 131.2 cm. National Gallery, Washington, DC.

In this regard, it is worth noting that although Rubens in his reworking of the drawing made several completions and corrections of the figural composition, he devoted most of his effort to strengthening the chiaroscuro. The art historian Frank Zöllner, whose analysis mainly focuses on questions of attribution, described the underlying pen drawing on black chalk as "timid" of line and identified Rubens's additions as the firm, confident brush drawing done in bister and white lead.[67] Anne-Marie Logan was able to determine in her research that Rubens's retouching consisted in several places of preliminary sketch marks made with black chalk that were then elaborated in a second step with pen and bister. The plasticity of the bodies was emphasized by means of a layer of bluish-gray gouache that served to indicate the ambient. White heightening underscores the undulation of manes, the thickness of horses' necks, the fluttering of garments, the shine of armor, and the firmness of clenched hands. It also weakens contours, corrects lineal course, and adds volumetric loft. The application of bister creates depth through shadow, especially noticeable in the immediate foreground in the figure who crouches behind a shield held up for protection and appears almost to crawl into the beholder's space, while dark shadow on the back of another soldier stretched out on the ground pushes him deeper into the melee.[68]

The genre-appropriate combination of extremely foreshortened figures with a pointed and cutting chiaroscuro offsets the isolation of the *scorcio* without weakening it. In this way Rubens emphatically supplements Leonardo's model, whose *sfumato* primarily acts to soften the sharpness of the drawn lines. Rubens's intensification of the chiaroscuro not only embeds the bodies and blurs their outlines, but also heightens the powerful visual impact of the foreshortening so that it comes close to achieving the "impossible in art."[69]

RUBENS STORMS THE RAMPARTS: *THE FALL OF PHAETON*

Rubens's alterations to the famous model helped him to appropriate and emulate Leonardo's capacity to create pictorial space. The lessons he learned during this process would later coalesce in a sensational piece that can be measured stylistically

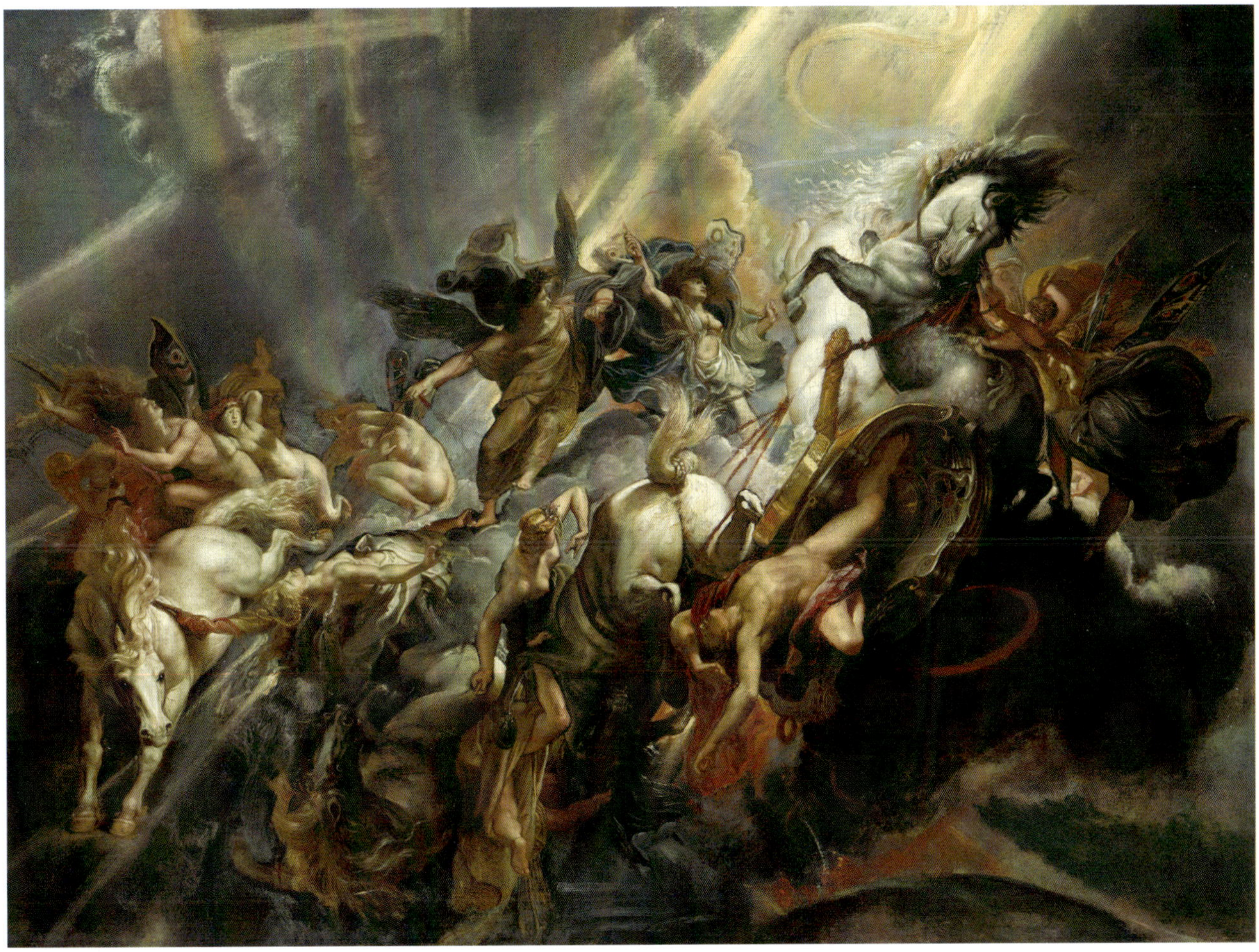

against the most glorious battle paintings in all the history of art,[70] and this despite the fact that it does not actually portray a battle, but is rather an image of such revolutionary potential and creative daring that it transcends genre boundaries.[71]

The Fall of Phaeton was created in two stages: a first concept was executed in Italy around 1605, then a few years later, perhaps after his return to the Netherlands, Rubens significantly reworked the picture. Numerous clearly visible *pentimenti* reveal the alterations (fig. 61).[72] Rubens apparently kept the painting in his possession for a long time. It was most likely not a commission, but a work that can be understood best on a more intimate level as the quintessence of Rubens's engagement with Italian art and a personal benchmark that would set the course for his unique artistic path.[73] Rubens's choice of theme draws inspiration from another heroic model of Italian art: Michelangelo's *Fall of Phaeton*—also a very personal work because it was addressed to a young beloved. It was known to him most likely via an engraved copy by Nicolas Beatrizet (fig. 62).[74] Rubens (and Michelangelo before him) may have also studied, when traveling to Rome via Florence in 1601, an antique relief showing Phaeton falling headlong from his chariot with outstretched arms into the river Eridanus.[75]

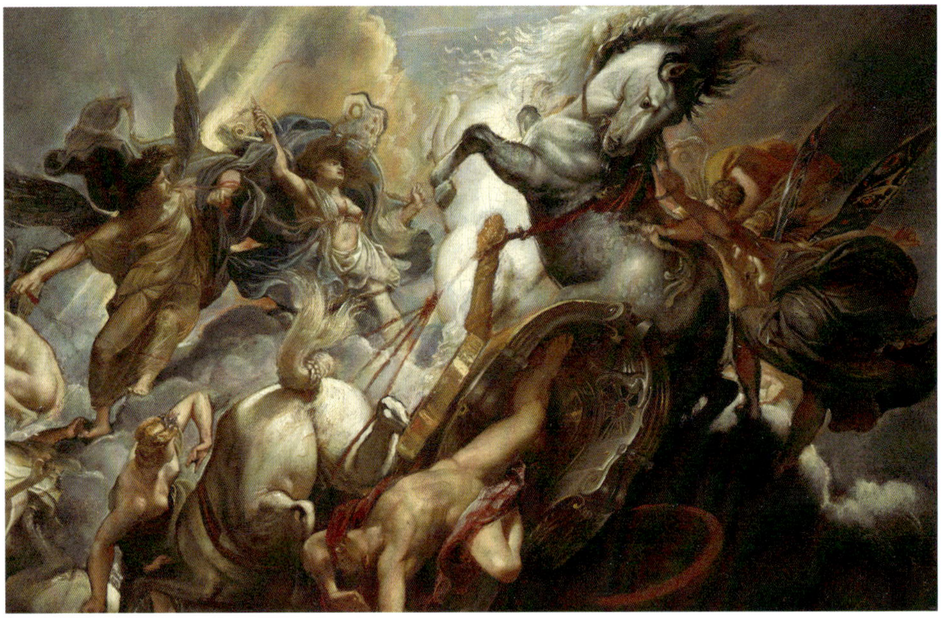

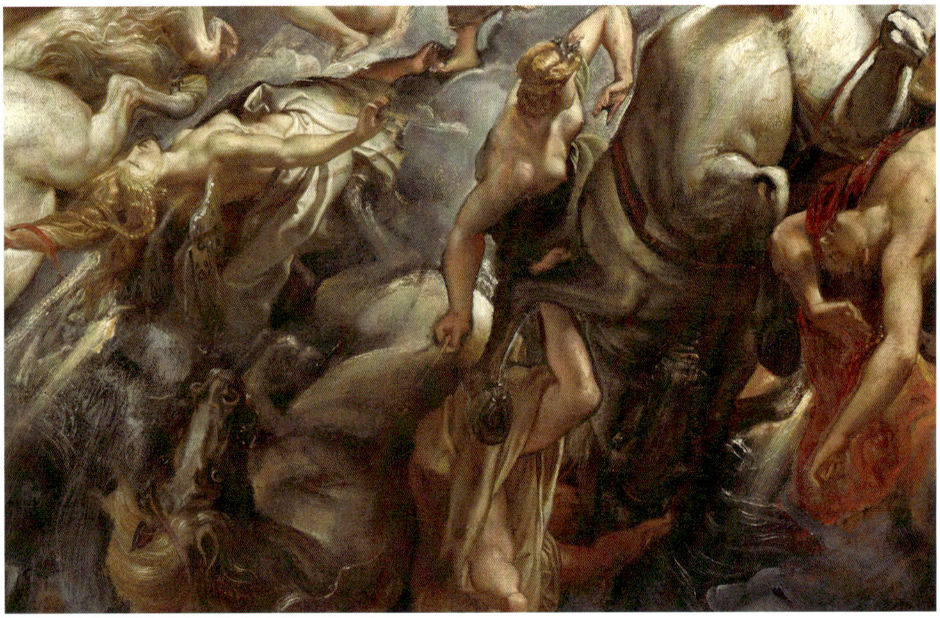

64–65
Details of fig. 61
[*The Fall of Phaeton*].

entangled with the glowing red bridle, binds her to the horse that charges in the direction of the beholder.

While Michelangelo's central event is Phaeton struck down and plummeting headfirst with the horses, Rubens arranges the situation with more nuance, extending the moment without, however, losing its precipitousness. The radiance of his strongly animated figures escalates the drama of the scene, and although their movement explodes in all directions, numerous figural resonances form strong bonds between them. The Horae subtly mirror the dispositions of the horses' bodies, thereby making it possible to sort out familiar motifs within the diversity of movement in the painting (fig. 65). The stretched musculature of the leap, the supine plummet, the headlong dive, or the wrenched turn of each horse is "seconded" by a Hora in its immediate vicinity.

The fully extended body of Phaeton is a jarring rupture in the otherwise contorted rhythm of the scene: by reason of his swoon, his anatomy seems to have escaped the chaos of the foreshortened bodies. His pose is heroic, a stop in the midst of great turbulence. He recalls the central corpse, arm arched over its head, that Menelaus carries in Giulio Romano's *Battle around the Body of Patroclus* (and this pair, in turn, is strongly influenced by the famous antique group in the Loggia dei Lanzi in Florence) (fig. 66). During his long residence in Mantua, the young Rubens could have studied Giulio's enormous fresco in the Palazzo Ducale's Sala di Troia. Phaeton also bears a strong resemblance to the dead soldier dramatically draped across the back of his horse in Giuseppe Cesari's famous battle painting—the legs, one outstretched, the other bent, have had their positions exchanged (fig. 67). Regardless of which is in fact Rubens's model here, each of these renderings shares the generalized image of a body whose affective significance derives from the pathos figure visualizing complete surrender.

Phaeton's fall is set off by the rebellious dappled gray, whose abrupt reversal of momentum has caused the chariot to tip over. Its broken shaft, prominent against the backdrop of the radiant white horse, underscores in its phallic form the physical potency of the powerfully rearing equine. Its placement above the groin of Phaeton is significant and confirms the impression so aptly formulated by the art historian Frances Huemer: his Michelangelesque body is stretched out "as if lost in a sexual dream." The helpless, limp, "impotent" body that seems to be "wounded by the scarlet red drapery" discloses Phaeton's fatal destiny: he is to become an emblem of youthful presumption.[83] Phaeton succumbs to a "sexual dream," a fantasy of virility and omnipotence. He demands the sun chariot of his father in order to assuage his doubts about his paternity and to confirm the identity of his true *genitor* (in Ovid's Latin, literally meaning "generator").[84] The "organ of generation" that is

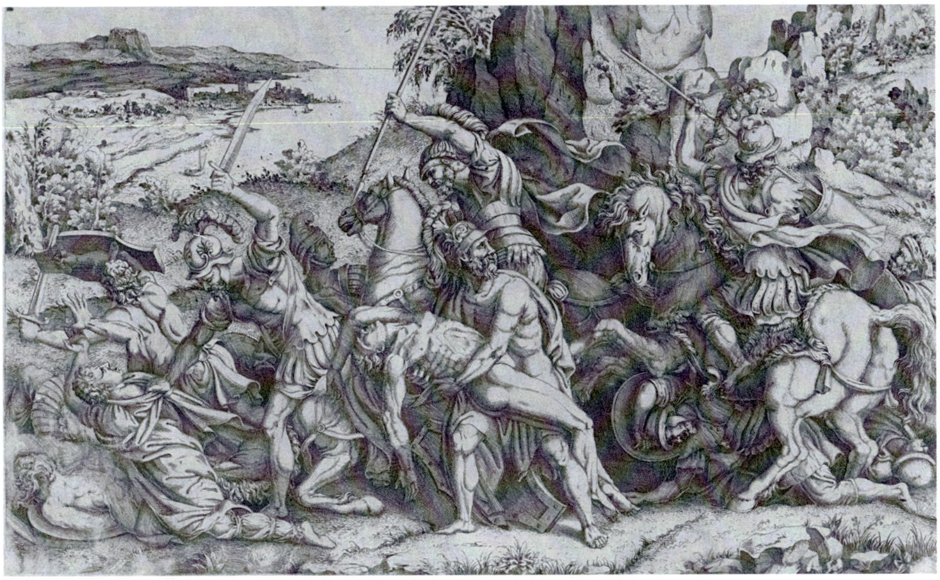

66
Anonymous, after Giulio Romano, *Battle around the Body of Patroclus*, ca. 1543–1547. Etching, 38 × 60.5 cm. Metropolitan Museum of Art, New York.

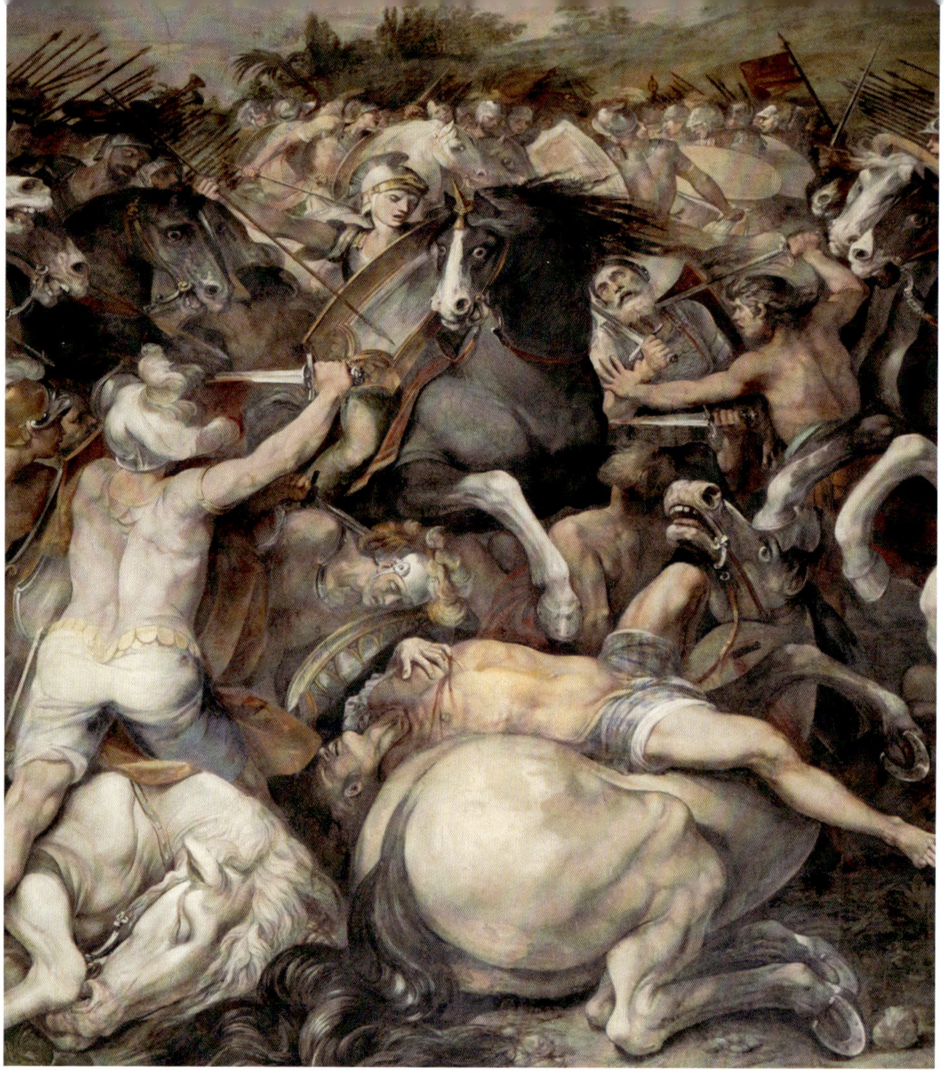

67
Detail of fig. 28
[*Battle of Tullus Hostilius: dead soldier*].

68 (FACING, LEFT)
Detail of fig. 61
[*The Fall of Phaeton*].

69 (FACING, RIGHT)
Detail of fig. 57
[Nicolas Beatrizet, after Michelangelo, *The Last Judgment*].

veiled as Phaeton's body falls is elicited—for the art connoisseur unmistakably—a second time in his close proximity by a Hora tumbling headfirst, her legs splayed in the air.

Phaeton's desire is foolhardy; when he endeavors to take on his father's role he renounces his own, despite his father's warning: "Thou askest too great a boon, Phaeton, and one which does not befit thy strength and those so boyish years. Thy lot is mortal; not for mortals is that thou askest here."[85] He comes to realize his own hubris and the knowledge leads to impuissance and ultimately destroys his desire: "Over his eyes came darkness through excess of light. And now he would prefer never to have touched his father's horses, and repents that he has discovered his true origin and prevailed."[86]

The cultural historian Hartmut Böhme, who described Phaeton as the "first hero of the ongoing immortality project," and also identified him as the "first case of the god complex," underscores the significance of speed in the myth.[87] We see that temporality was also of central importance to Rubens through his elaborate use of the Horae, contrary to pictorial tradition; we notice also that one of the twelve hours is missing, as if the crash has triggered an acceleration of time.[88]

A desire for immortality[89] that takes the form of a headlong rush of youthful

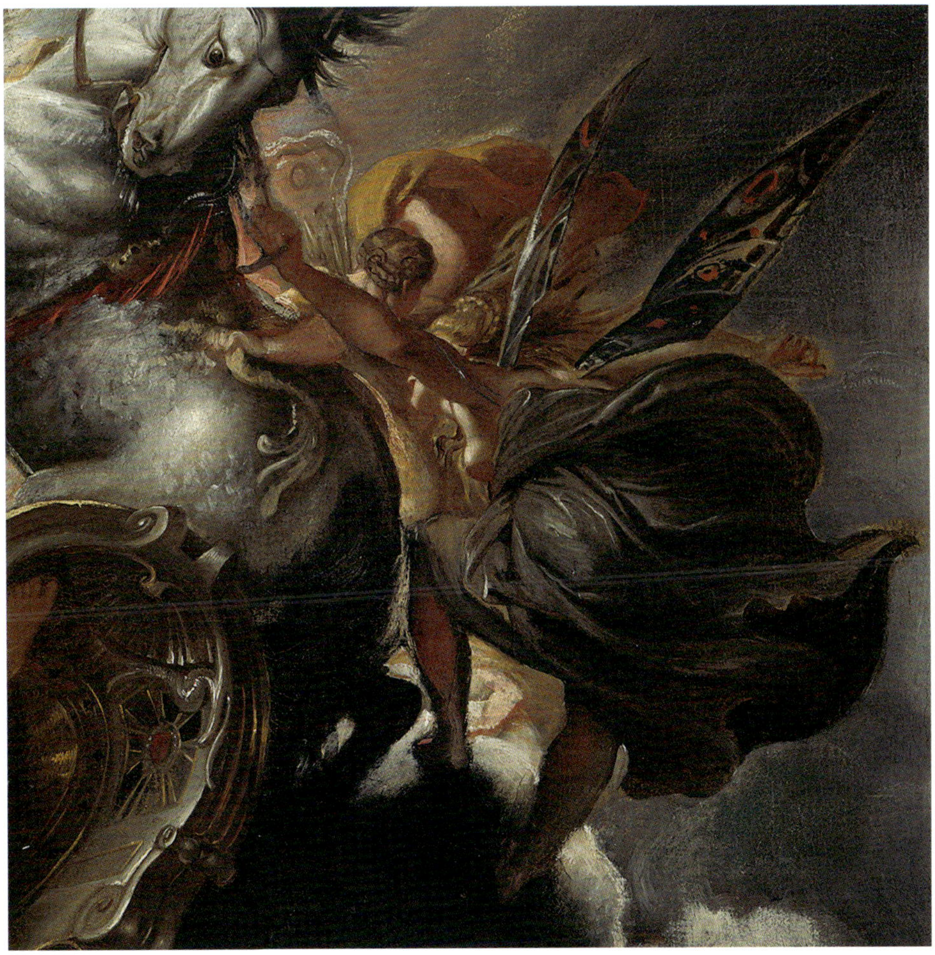

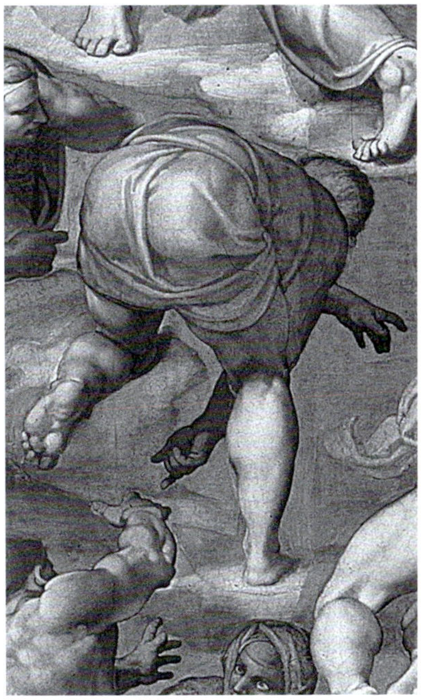

daring would not have been completely foreign to Rubens. His own haste, however, was more likely fired by impatience for the immortality granted by earthly recognition than by any yearning for eternal life. His younger colleague Joachim von Sandrart (1606–1688), whom Rubens personally met in Utrecht in the atelier of Gerrit van Honthorst and accompanied on his two-week tour of Holland, wrote about Rubens's artistic development in his *Teutsche Academie*: "According to the first *manier* he brought back from Italy, he industriously endeavored to imitate the strength of Caravaggio's coloring, whose hand he closely copied [*als dessen Hand er sehr beobachtet nachzuahmen*], but because the same proceeded too heavily and slowly, he adopted a quicker and lighter manner."[90] This change in practice encouraged his ability "to operate with the hand most masterfully and quick, and to finish his works when anyone else would just be starting." Sandrart's accolade indirectly points out that Rubens's new orientation gave him the opportunity "due to his skill to splendidly raise himself up on high."[91]

The kinetic potential of Rubens's falling bodies is achieved by a drastic chiaroscuro that sets up a vivid contrast between areas of light and darkness. Sandrart's colleague Giovan Pietro Bellori, who attributed to Rubens great speed and a fiery spirit (*la gran prontezza, e' l fuoco del suo spirito*),[92] as well as a fury of the brush (*la*

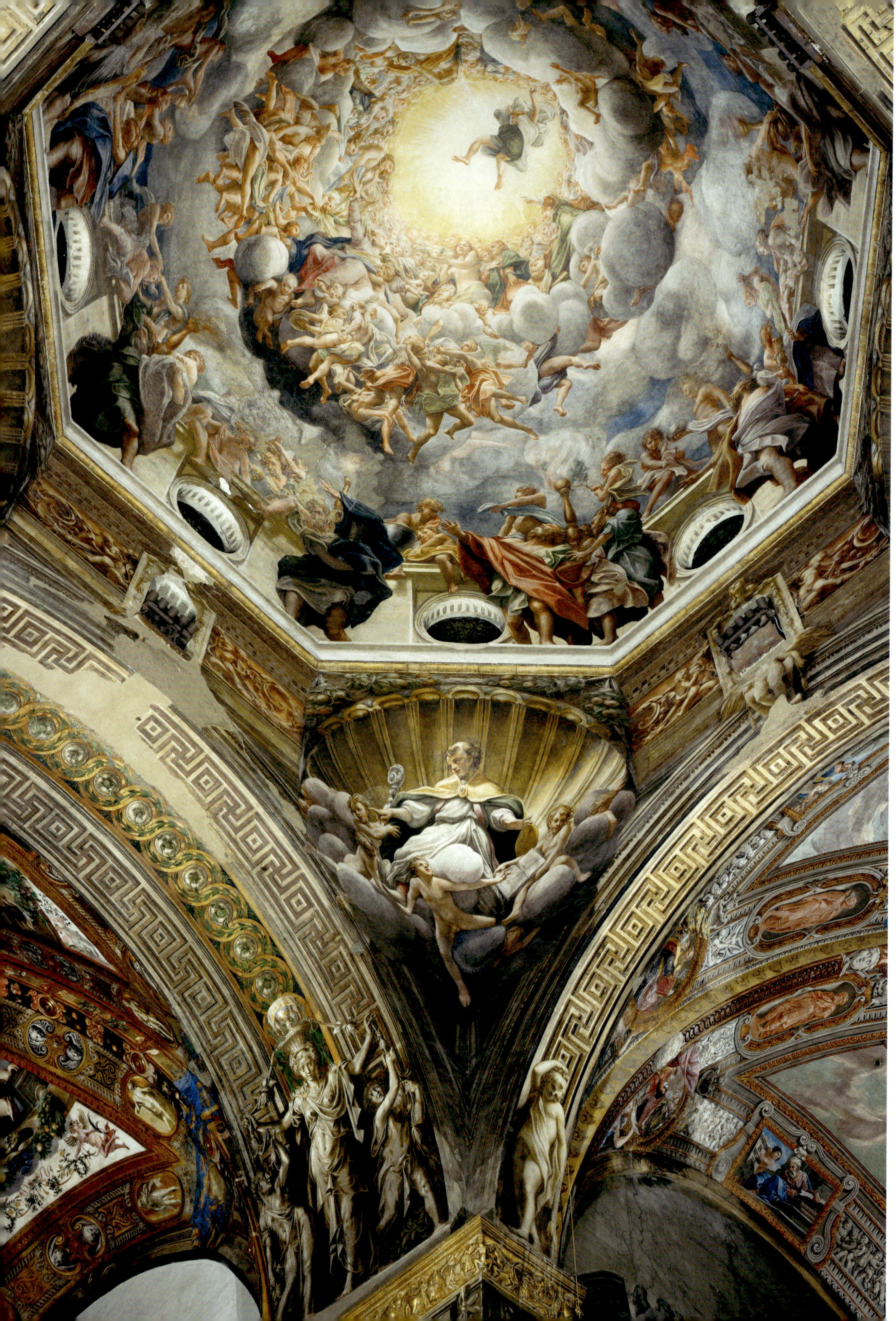

furia del pennello),[93] grounded these qualities in the artist's intensive study of Venetian painting, which taught him the proper distribution of color and chiaroscuro.[94] According to the painter and art critic Roger de Piles (1635–1709), Rubens went "further than any other painter" in this science.[95]

Rubens seems to have studied not only Michelangelo's *Fall of Phaeton*, but also his magnum opus *The Last Judgment*. The energetic pose of the Hora at the right margin, who leans deeply forward as she grabs the bridle of the rearing gray with her left hand, echoes a similar figure in *The Last Judgment*, but the Hora's elongated arms extended to the side as she turns her back to us bestow on her a grace that Michelangelo's struggling figure lacks (figs. 68, 69). In addition, Rubens casts an all-encompassing chiaroscuro over his figures that obscures their contours and draws them into the picture's overall gyre of action. The effect is very different from that of Michelangelo's precisely defined figures, each positioned on its own cloud. Rubens's terrain, a heavy billowing mass, seems to lose its solidity from right to left in harmony with the descending diagonal movement of the whole.

The most daring figure in the work, however, plunges headfirst as she tries to grab the neck of a horse that threatens to trample on Phaeton. Both she and the horse are viewed from below, her legs widely spread as if she were striding in midair. Nevertheless, their gazes strike us from underneath their inverted bodies, catching our eyes with their spectacularly precarious position that so loudly proclaims painterly bravura. This minor figure may be a reference to Antonio Allegri da Correggio's nude angel in the cupola fresco of the Parma Cathedral (fig. 70). However, Correggio's extreme foreshortening, which shifted his figure's genitals to the center of his anatomy, is in Rubens modestly consigned to the beholder's imagination by the Hora's garment. It might be that Rubens's depiction of the fall of Phaeton, a theme that would have ideally suited ceiling painting because it features a cascade of figures who all appear to be overhead, was meant as a showpiece to inspire such a commission. In addition to Correggio, Rubens also cited another famous artistic model who excelled in ceiling painting.

The impressive equine hindquarters so liberally dispersed throughout the painting are inspired by Giulio Romano's ceiling painting in the Palazzo del Te, representing Apollo and Diana on their chariots in *di sotto in sù* perspective (fig. 71). As De Piles noted, Rubens diligently studied the works of Giulio Romano while in Mantua.[96] But he deliberately stopped short of Giulio's most daring foreshortening, seen in the bodies of the two gods. Rubens's reasons for this might be simply that the *Fall of Phaeton* is not a ceiling painting and therefore does not open up an *al di sotto in sù* view; on the other hand, Rubens may also be bowing to an opinion widely held in his day that urged moderation in the use of foreshortening.

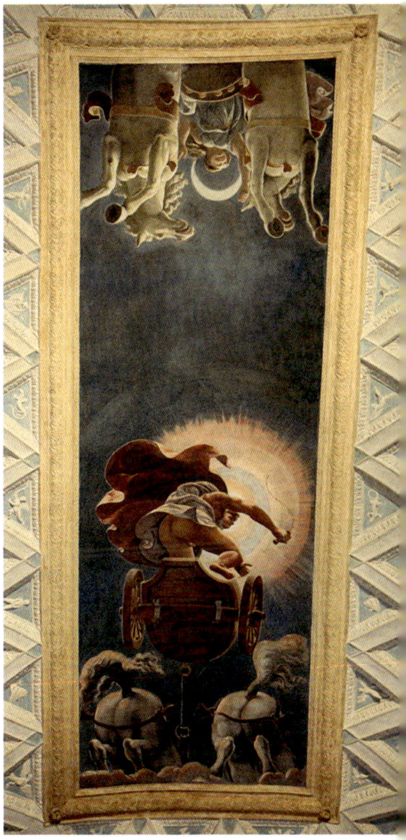

70 (FACING)
Correggio, *Assumption of the Virgin*, 1526–1530. Dome fresco, 1,093 × 1,195 cm. Cathedral of Parma.

71
Giulio Romano, *Chariot of the Sun*, 1526. Ceiling fresco. Stanza del Sole, Palazzo del Te, Mantua.

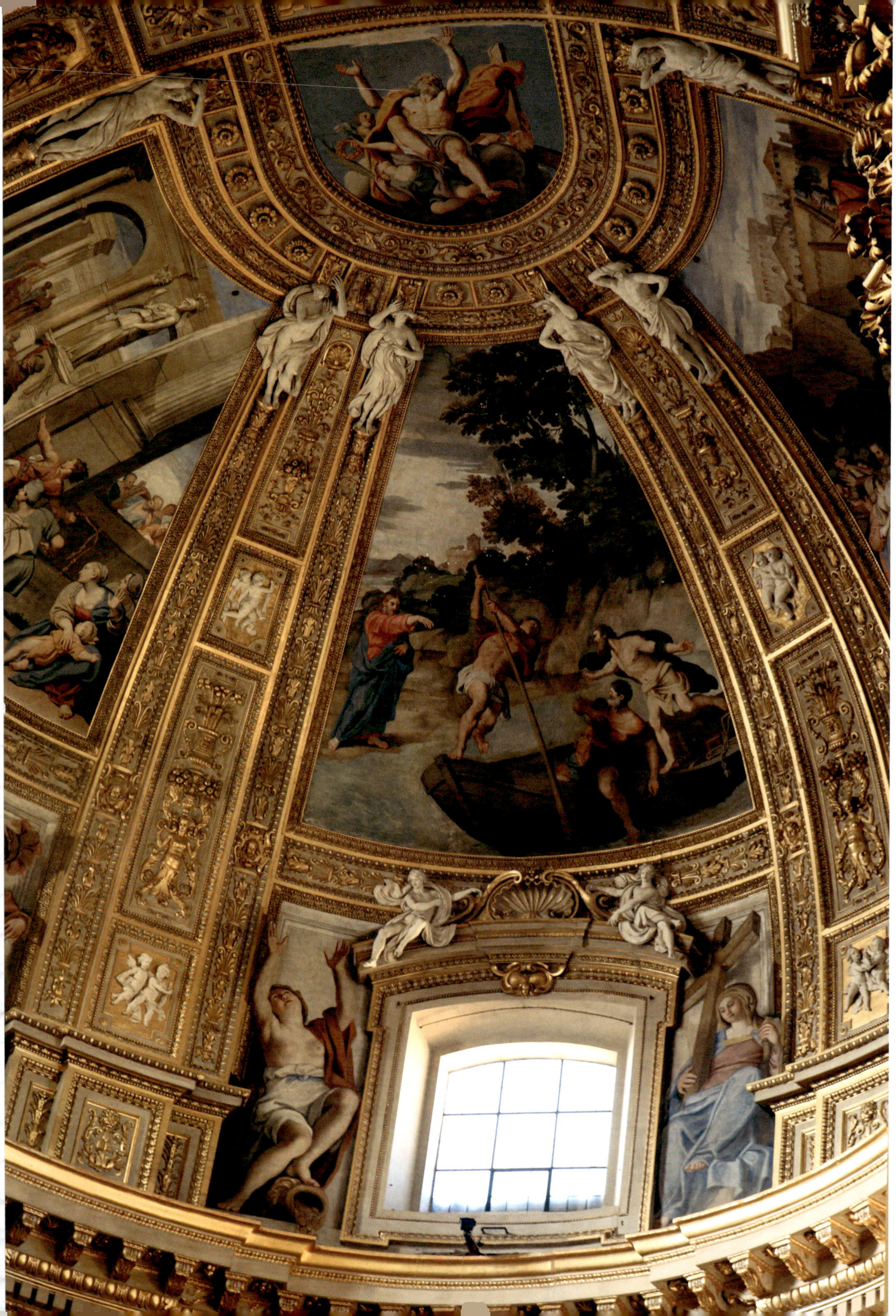

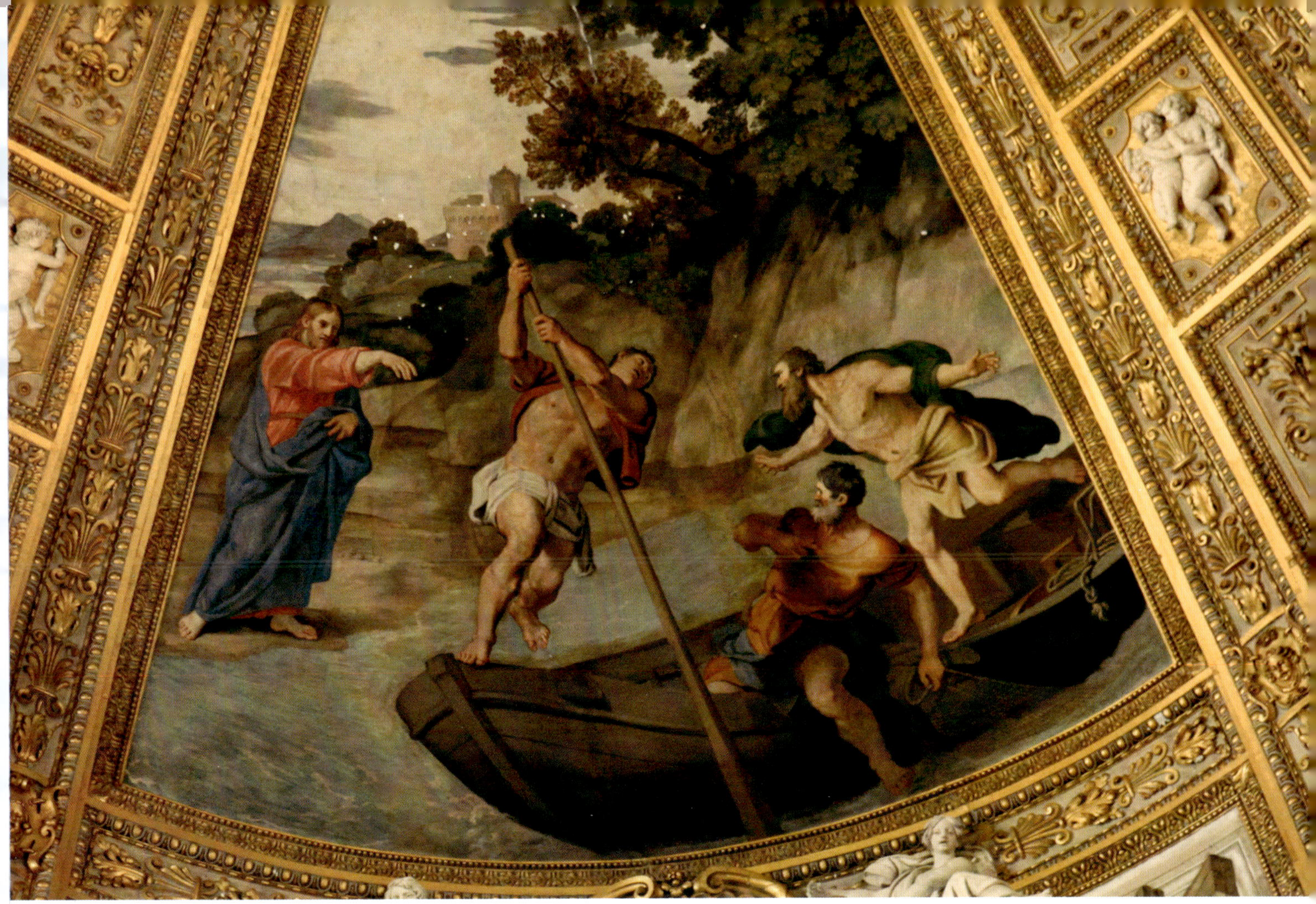

in the direction of Jesus waiting on the lakeshore, while the other steps out of the boat seemingly to flee in the opposite direction; he turns his head toward Jesus and points to himself with his right hand as if questioning whether he too has been called. Their actions are counterbalanced by the figure of the boatman, whose entire physical effort is engaged in propelling the vessel away from shore, thereby acting against the narrative arc of the story. He balances on the gunwale with one foot and pulls back with all of his weight to move the immensely long oar. And curiously, in carrying out his task, he turns his gaze to the two fishermen. Perhaps he is somehow mediating in their calling.

Bellori's observation that the oar not only appears to us as perfectly straight despite the steep curvature of the apsis, but even protrudes into space, points to an aspect of Domenichino's bravura feat that is not immediately apparent. By placing the oar's blade at the lower margin of the picture field, the boatman's corporeal effort expressed in his body's foreshortening transforms the concave form of the apsis into what looks like a convex form, an illusion strongly reinforced by the spatial setting of the figural composition. He seems to push the boat (Italian, *nave*) forward into the sacred space of the church's nave. Bellori emphasizes the virtuosity of this accomplishment when he adds: "Since the rules of perspective

73 (FACING)
Domenichino, *The Calling of St. Andrew*, 1625–1628. Apse decoration. Basilica of Sant'Andrea della Valle, Rome.

74
Detail of fig. 73 [*The Calling of St. Andrew*].

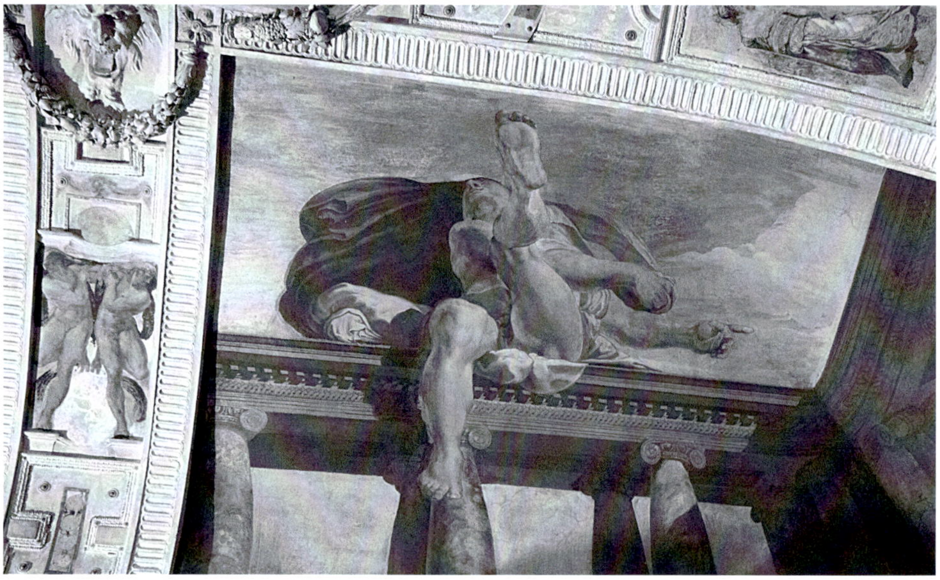

77
Pellegrino Tibaldi, *Ignudo*, ca. 1550. Fresco. Sala di Ulisse. Palazzo Poggi, Bologna.

78 (FACING)
Detail of Pietro da Cortona's *Allegory of Divine Providence and Barberini Power*, ca. 1633–1639. Fresco. Galleria Nazionale d'Arte Antica, Palazzo Barberini, Rome.

kneels awkwardly on a cloud. His position is precarious as he leans forward in order to create a link between the two realms in the scene (composed of the damned and the saved), holding one hand back between his legs and stretching the other forward. Caravaggio also configures Jupiter's arm between his legs, but he pulls it forward in such a way that it has almost the same size of the leg adjacent and parallel to it. The juxtaposition of the two extremities is intriguing but at the same time deviously undermined by the viewer's awareness of their differing orientations in space. Whereas Jupiter's right hand clearly touches the transparent sphere from above (and shines through—a significant gesture toward his model, Raphael's Urania in the Stanza della Segnatura who only touches the contour of the sphere), Caravaggio did not clearly define the spatial relationship of the god's foot to the sphere. The toe only touches its contour, leaving the question of distance open.

Cole Wallach references another plausible model based on the position of Jupiter's legs: Michelangelo's epigone Pellegrino Tibaldi and his fresco in the Palazzo Poggi in Bologna (ca. 1550–1551), likewise a ceiling painting, that shows a naked figure seated on a balustrade seen from below (fig. 77).[15] But unlike both models, Caravaggio severed his figure's extremities by completely covering the torso with the eagle's body. His tactic of avoiding the *difficoltà* of the extreme perspective by concealing the junction of limbs to torso creates a most convincing foreshortening because it engages the beholder's imagination. This "trick" had been earlier brought to perfection by Correggio, the first artist whose figures were allowed to fly with their feet dangling down in midair. Caravaggio thus took on a bravura exploit that had already been brilliantly solved more than half a century before.

CUTTING EDGE SOLUTIONS

The extreme *di sotto in sù* perspective was calculated to trigger amazement, and it did; but the wonder lessened over subsequent decades and the device became

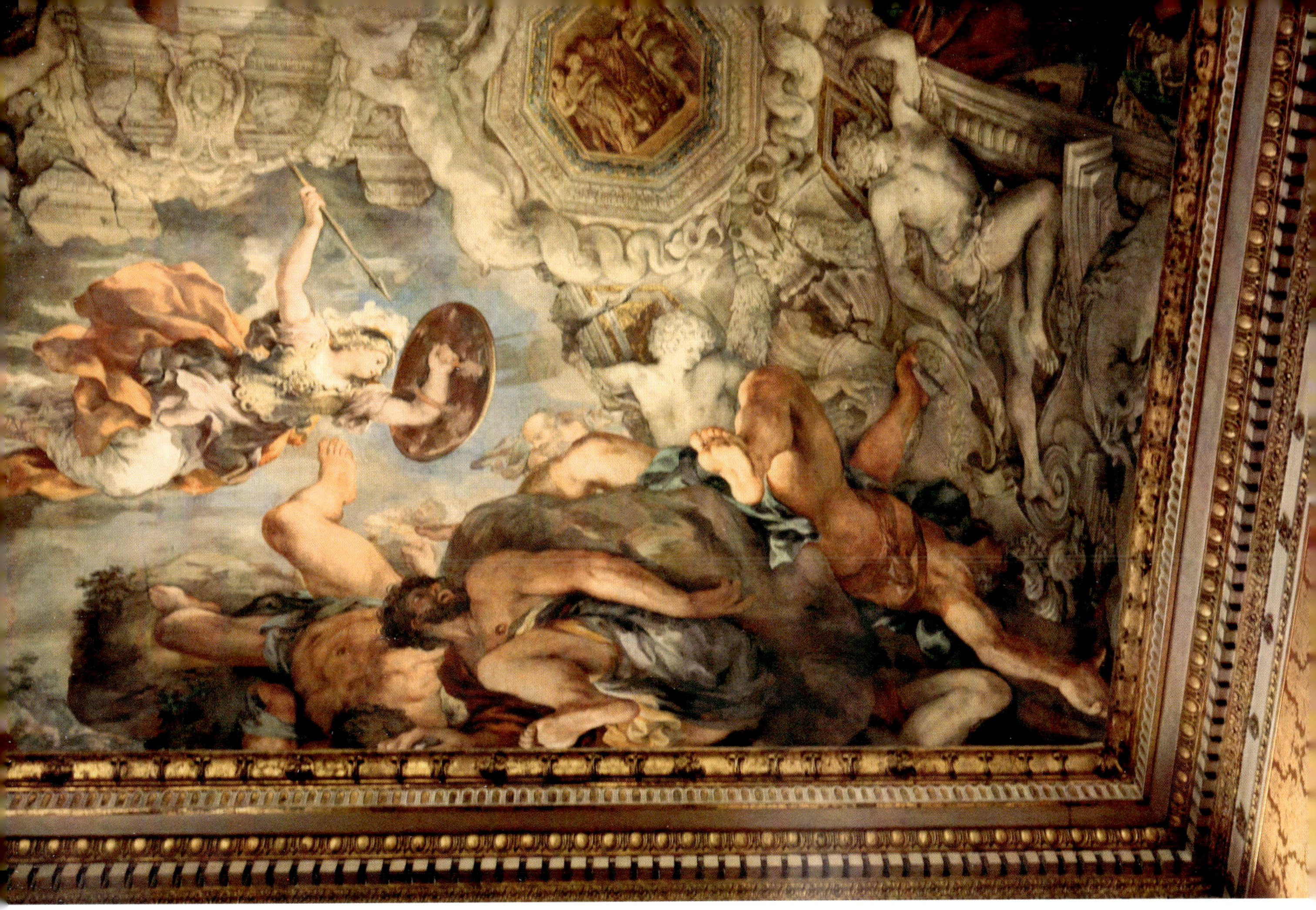

a bit passé. Intriguingly, remarkable displays of bravura like Caravaggio's are found in private houses, where they may be best understood as demonstrations of skill and expressions of a sophisticated humor enacted for knowledgeable art patrons. In the highly ambitious ceiling painting by Pietro Cortona (1596–1669) for the massive *sala* of the Palazzo Barberini (Cortona's construction of the vault's immense span is an architectural feat in itself), we find a group of three defeated giants with monstrously foreshortened bodies. The soles of their feet have left the ground, leaving them suspended in midair (fig. 78). While one figure positioned in the middle ground tumbles in what is bound to be a fatal fall, the other two are pushed so forcefully into the cornice that they have lost their balance and become a threat to the viewer below. We can see the soles of their unsupported left feet. One of these giants, stepping into the gaping void that opens below him, seems in special danger of being hurled down into the beholder's realm by the heavy rock-like weight on his shoulders, while his companion already falls headfirst through space.

This drama required very elaborate foreshortening to make such a striking impact on the beholder, and it happens in a zone of ceiling painting that poses the most formidable challenges: the corner areas of a barrel vault, where the different

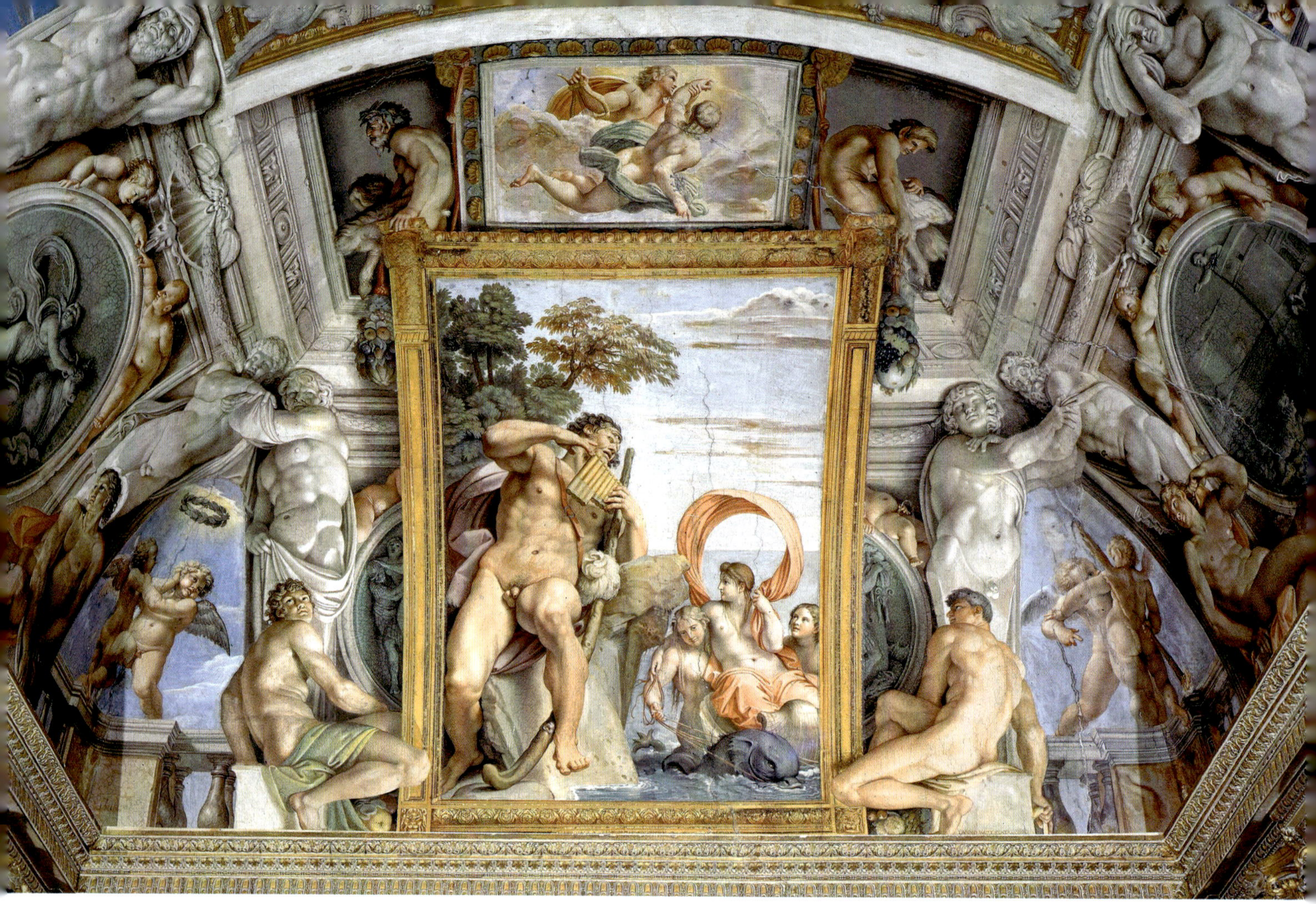

perspectival axes of the adjoining scenes come together. Cortona was not the first to wittily conquer this optically sensitive zone by covering it up with a narrative intermezzo. The most famous example may be Annibale Carracci's masterful handling of a similar challenge in the ceiling painting of the Palazzo Farnese in Rome, painted with the help of his workshop in the years 1597–1608 (fig. 79). In Bellori's extensive description of Carracci's masterpiece, he praises the illusionary space opened up where the end and side walls of the curved vault come together:

> Among other remarkable effects of perspective to be found in this artful work is the one in the four corners of the Gallery, where the figures of Terminus meet and embrace from one wall to the other with admirable visual sense; because without being cut off or breaking at the corners of the wall, they come together from one side and the other with their arms in relief and projecting outward as if painted on a flat surface; and a similar effect is also produced by the Loves painted in between and inserted in the spaces of the same corners.[16]

Cortona's eye-catching motif of the giant's foot suspended in air is also here in Carracci's ceiling: An amoretto, one member of a corner pair scuffling for a crown that hovers above them, steps over the architectural frame and into the spectator's

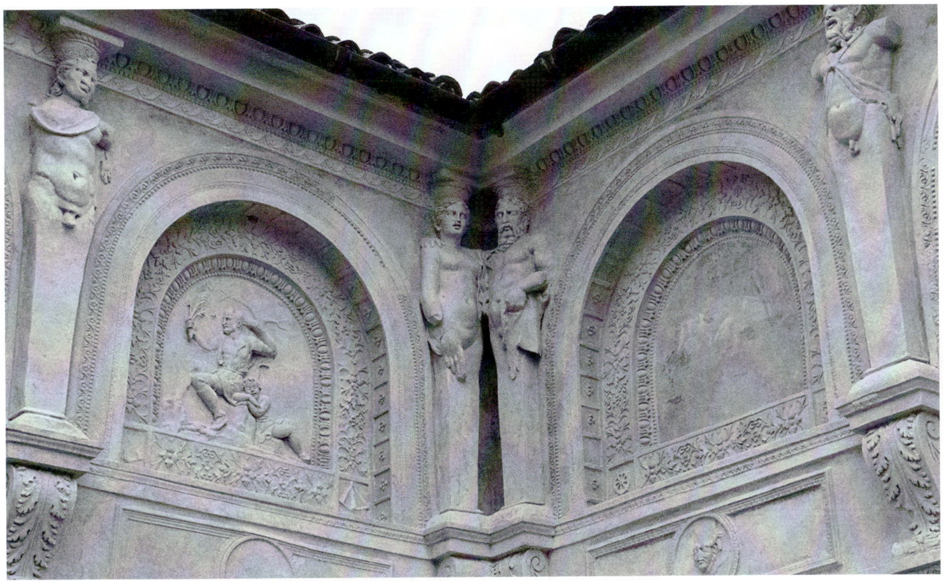

79 (FACING)
Annibale Carracci and workshop, *Love of the Gods*, 1597–1607. Ceiling painting. Fresco. Palazzo Farnese, Rome.

80
Giulio Romano, stucco decoration of the court of the Secret Garden, Palazzo del Te, Mantua.

space.[17] The ceiling's multiple stagings of conflict and resolution between pairs of amoretti—grabbing, embracing, bickering, or struggling—act to smooth over the clash of divergent illusionary spaces (which can only be appreciated by successively changing one's orientation in the room—observation from one single viewing point does not suffice). Terminus figures in more uniform embraces occupy the transitional zones between the ends and sides of the vault. Carracci must have seen Giulio Romano's paired corner Termini in the courtyard of the Palazzo del Te in Mantua, who in contrast to a series of solitary Termini along the walls, have arms with which to embrace each other (fig. 80).

Carracci mastered the complex configuration of a corner by foreshortening an amaretto's foot in midair, itself a breathtaking feat. In Cortona's ceiling painting this device is taken to an extreme (fig. 81). Cortona moreover pushes the carefully balanced arrangement of Carracci's work, its playing amoretti sheltered by hugging Termini who support a fictive entablature on their shoulders, into quite an opposite mood. One giant clings in vain to a similar architectural device that divides the ceiling into narrative sub-scenes. It looks as if this figure is the chosen victim of the goddess Minerva as she rushes to drive the giants away. But at this perilous moment, we become the targets of Cortona's ingenious and multivalent humor. The giant's desperate attempt to find a handhold in the carved decoration demonstrates his shocking ignorance of the structure's load capacity. He is going to bring it all crashing down on us: cracks and splits are spreading; pieces of the weakening architectural frame have already fallen out.[18]

There is an animated Atlas "sculpture" at the left of the pillar depicted in this scene, who has lost his right arm but reaches his left hand toward the giant's ill-fated grasp. His still unscathed counterpart on the right seems to leap away from the accident. As the attacking figure of Minerva approaches, the palpable threat posed by the giants to the surrounding protagonists (and to us) becomes a source of ridicule: how could this giant have hoped to take a firm hold on a flimsy piece

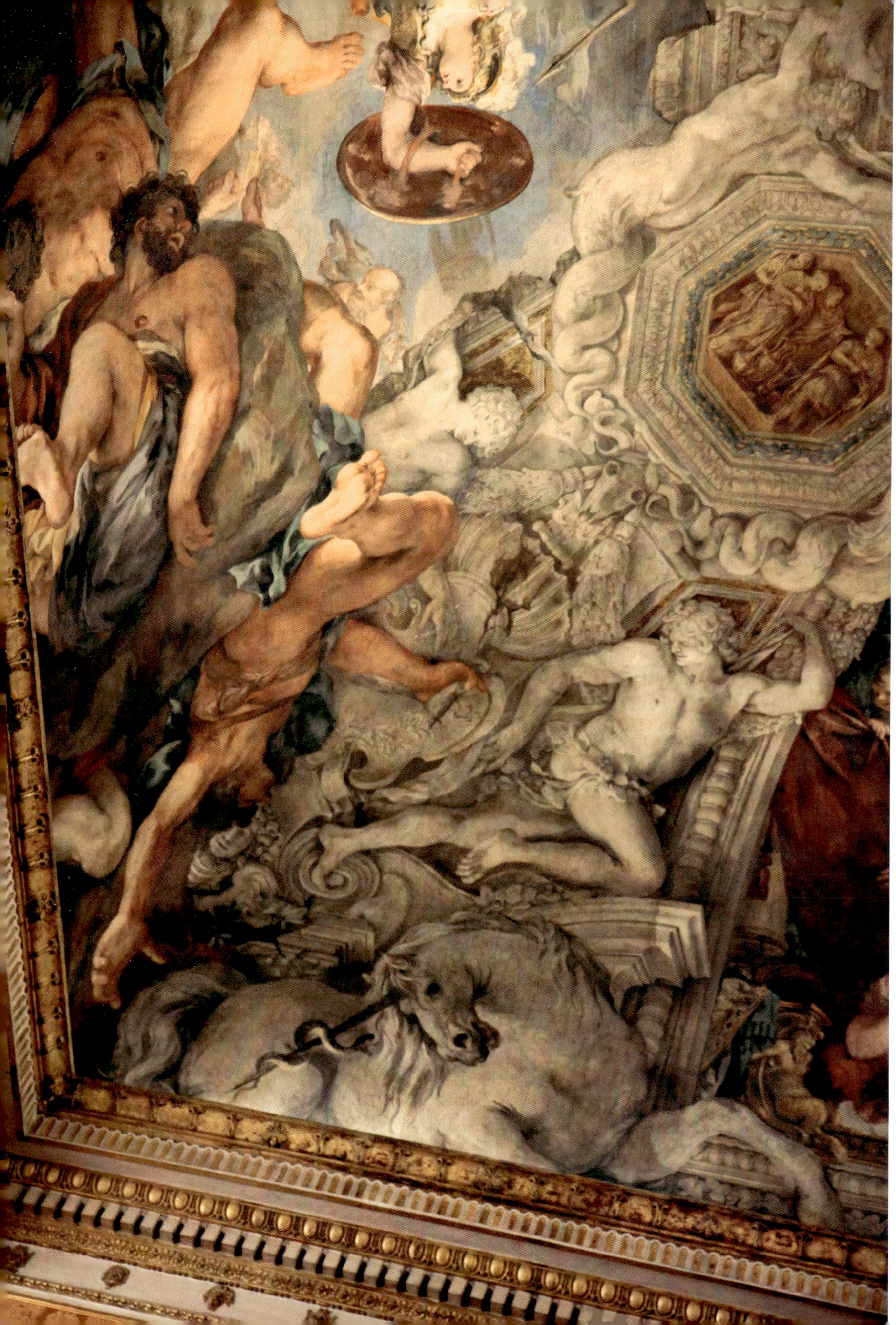

of decoration, and how could we, on a second level of deception, think that the fiction above our heads would come tumbling down? The remarkable effect of these foreshortened figures on the astonished viewer testifies tremendously to the artist's skill, and when the whole amusing causality behind this small scene with its false bottom is realized, the knowledgeable beholder responds with relieved laughter and applause.

THE GLORY OF THE DOME

Giorgio Vasari, who called Correggio a most extraordinary painter (*pittore singularissimo*) and a rare and wonderful artist (*raro e maraviglioso artifice*) because he excelled in both *disegno* and coloring, praised as a most incredible miracle (*stupendissima maraviglia*) his dome fresco in the cathedral of Parma with its *di sotto in sù* perspective (fig. 82). A spiral of bodies fills the dome; at its forefront we see the ascending Mary flanked by Adam and Eve and other saintly figures. They float in the heavens supported by thick swirling cumuli in whose lower registers putti playfully romp about. A dazzling bright yellow suffuses the center of the cupola, where the extreme reduction of the figures situated behind and above the lower rows of witnesses creates the impression that a vertiginous cone of light is drawing them into heaven. A figure suspended in midair seems to be caught in the luminous whirlpool. Christ, offset from the center, is not the hub of this vortex but rather a mediator, whose highly animated pose and billowing garments appear to draw Mary upward, although her ascent is also displaced to one side, seemingly in order to provide space for the upward movement of her gaze. Christ's flying movement connects him more closely to the romping putti of the lower cloud register than with the seated and expectant witnesses above him. This figural resonance gives the putti the corresponding function of generating uplift for the spectators below.

Painted balustrades encircling the dome's oculi enable a transition between the cathedral's architecture and the fictional celestial sphere (fig. 83). The cornice above is populated by *ignudi* (naked young men) occupied with lighting altar candles and burning incense. The most stunning feature of the tambour decoration, however, is the figures of the apostles placed before the angled sides of the octagon, all highly excited to witness the assumption of the virgin depicted in the dome above them. Their presence transforms the angles of the building's structure into an encompassing fictitious scene that causes us to overlook the odd connection of the octagonal tambour to the round dome. In a stunning effect, bent knees, billowing garments, and gesticulating arms seem to project forward to initiate the maelstrom above.

It comes as no surprise that Correggio's dome fresco had a lasting impact on the next generations of painters. In his vita of Giovanni Lanfranco (1582–1647), Bellori reports that Lanfranco

> took such a fancy to the cupola of Parma Cathedral that he made a little sketch of it in watercolors, practicing the unity and style of the figures seen in *di sotto in sù*. For, as we have heard from Giovanni himself, it is not enough to understand perspective and to know how to measure figures high up according to rule if

81 (FACING)
Detail of Pietro da Cortona's *Allegory of Divine Providence and Barberini Power*, ca. 1633–1639. Fresco. Galleria Nazionale d'Arte Antica, Palazzo Barberini, Rome.

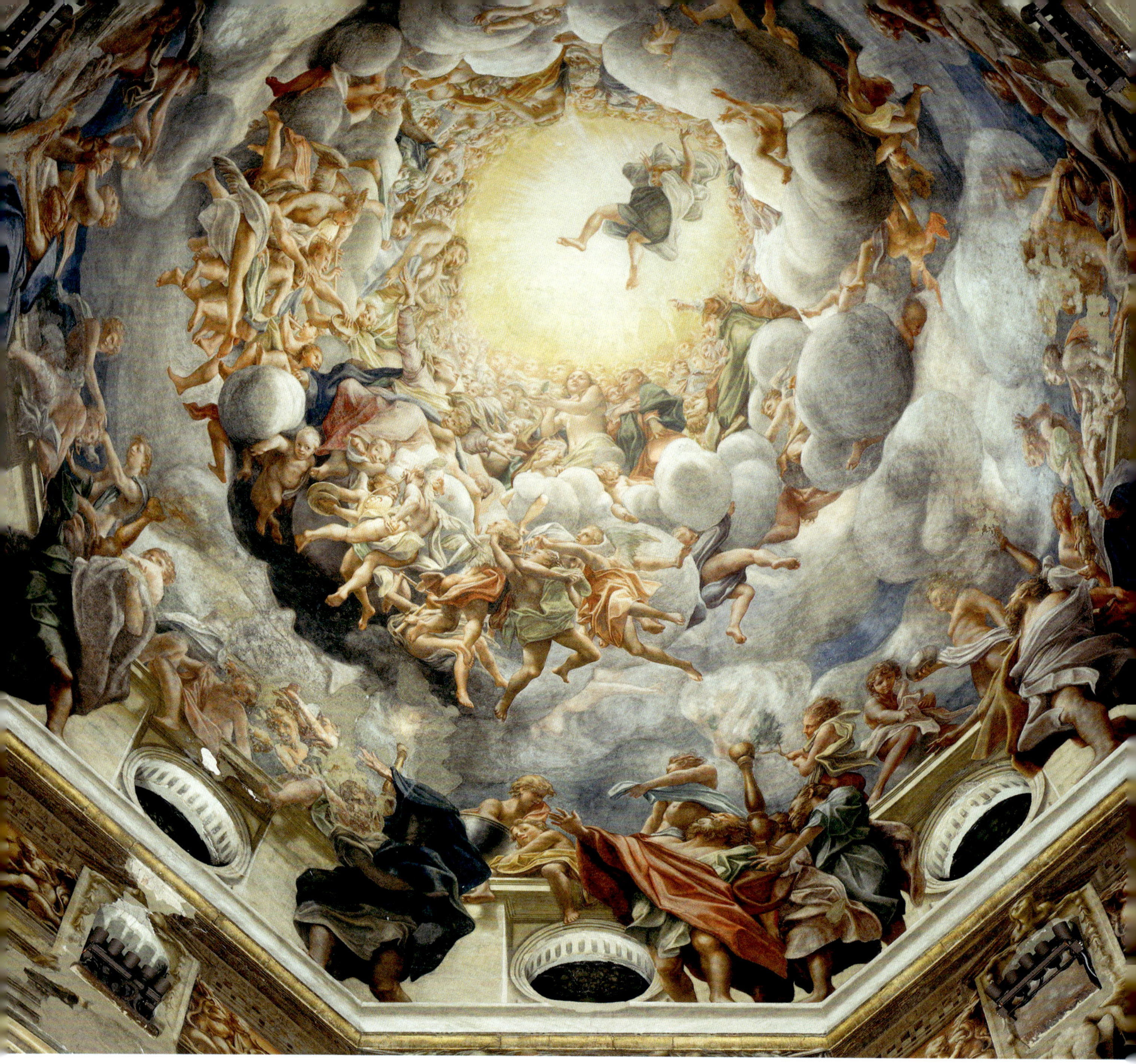

82
Correggio, *Assumption of the Virgin*, 1526–1530.
Dome fresco, 1,093 × 1,195 cm.
Cathedral of Parma.

83 (FACING)
Detail of fig. 82
[*Assumption of the Virgin*].

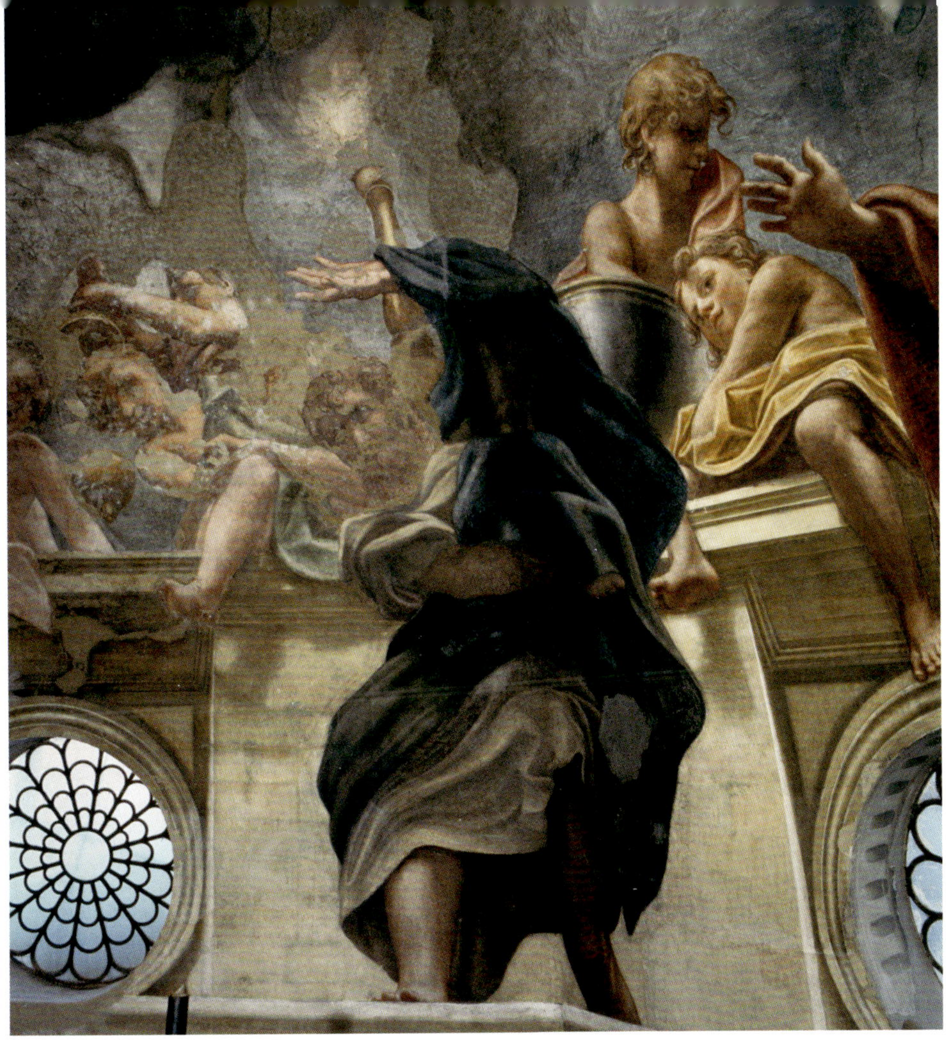

these are not accompanied by a certain grace in their movement to render them attractive.[19]

Watercolor was also the medium Lanfranco used for developing his own ideas; input and output were seemingly enmeshed in his creative process. Bellori writes: "In drawing he captured life with few marks of charcoal or chalk; he conceived his ideas easily, and he would immediately give form to his thought in a sketch, mostly in watercolor."[20]

Bellori, who puns with Lanfranco's name—"it was luck and heaven that put 'franco' in his surname and frankness in his spirit"[21]—and praises the "beautiful and harmonious facility without a trace of difficulty of invention or hesitation of the brush"[22] that characterized even his large works, also discusses an ingenious trick of artifice that Lanfranco employed in his own cupola painting in the Basilica of Sant'Andrea della Valle: he depicted in dark green colors a festoon encircling the aperture of the roof lantern that creates a strong chiaroscuro effect and opens up an astounding spatial illusion (fig. 84). Because of the festoon's darkness and precise rendering, it appears to hang suspended in midair, over the beholder and yet under the encircling congregation of saints. The art historian Alba Costamagna interprets the asymmetry of this arrangement of fruits and flowers as a "device of

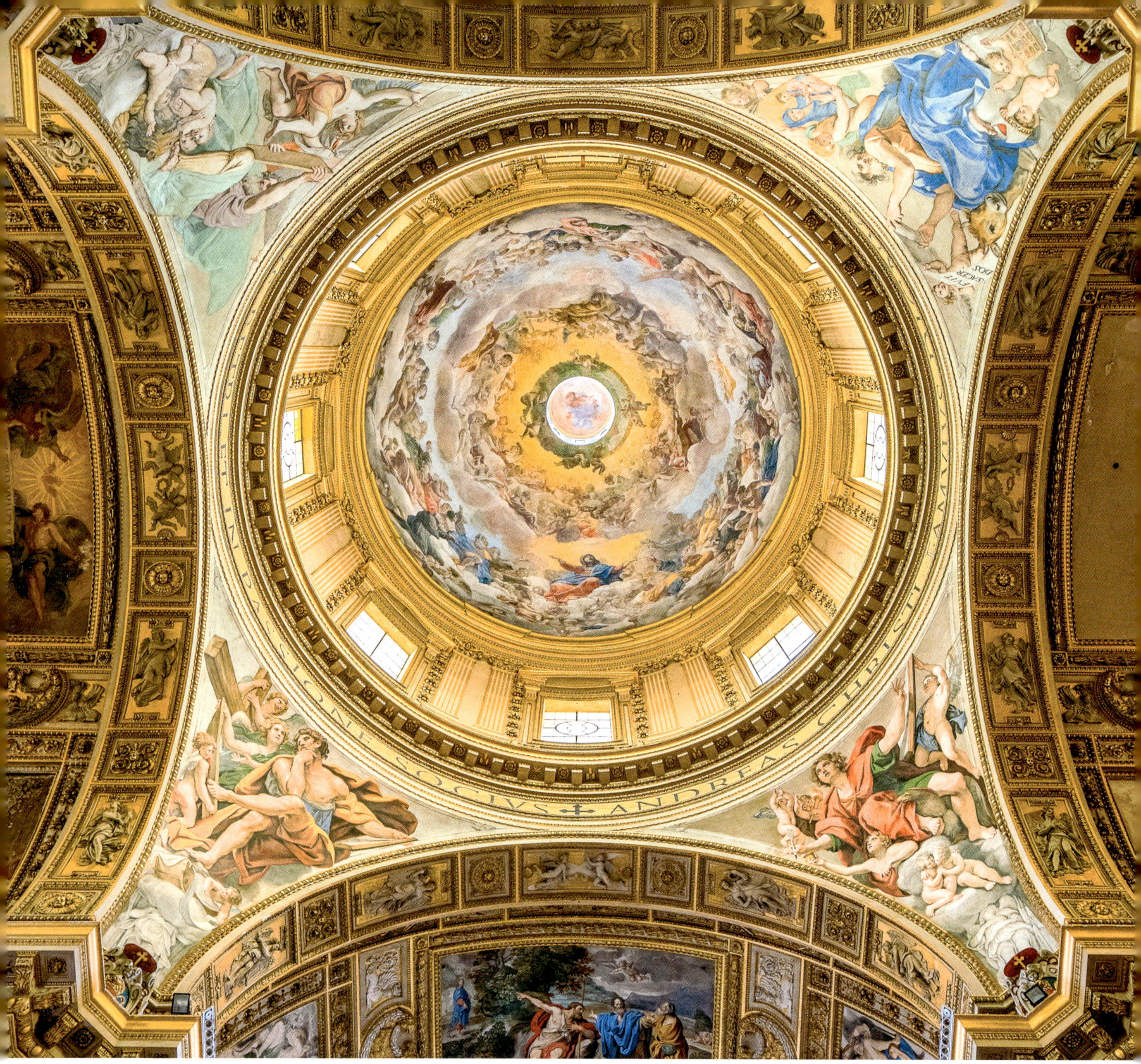

84
Giovanni Lanfranco, *Assumption of the Virgin*, 1622–1628. Dome fresco. Basilica of Sant'Andrea della Valle, Rome.

perspectival illusionism" that creates a swirling movement. On one side the green wreath thins out and we see an outer ring of gold, a fictional decorative stucco festoon resembling those that traditionally frame the oculi of roof lanterns (as, for example, in the same basilica's small Cappella Rucellai). Here, between the gold molding and green garland, Lanfranco has inserted a small strip of blue sky, creating an illusion of open space and suggesting continuity with the natural light that comes through the windows of the lantern.

The saints are seated on several rings of clouds, their orderly arrangement moderating the, in Lanfranco's opinion, annoying difficulty of foreshortening (*la difficoltà noiose di scorci*).[23] Their reduction in size stretches the perceived height of the dome's curvature to an extreme. Bellori noticed this effect: "When seen from below it expands into a very ample space before the eyes, and then when one mounts to see the painting up above at close range, the cupola diminishes and its circumference narrows to half what it appears from below, as everyone can grasp."[24]

In an extensive description of the dome, written around 1627, the writer and art collector Ferrante Carlo (1578–1641) explains how Lanfranco created illusionary depth by foregoing precision: The higher the figures' position toward the central oculus, the more their heads are immersed in what he terms a "superior light" that eventually renders them imperceptible. Underscoring the divine origin of this light, Carlo paradoxically describes the effect as "great light casting a shadow" (*adombrare dal gran lume*).[25]

Christ, at the center of the congregation, flies head lowermost through the air and gestures downward with his left hand. He shares this peculiar positioning with the spectacular figure of Christ in Taddeo Zuccari's *Conversion of St. Paul* for the Frangipani Chapel in San Marcello al Corso (1557–1564) in Rome (figs. 85, 86). This clear pictorial reference endows Lanfranco's figure with the power to convert the "unbelieving" beholders looking up at the dome from below. The extreme foreshortening of Christ's body, with its planimetrically joined left hand and foot, is concealed by a fluttering bright blue cape whose color evokes the open sky, and, in fact, Christ is spatially separated from the dome by the tambour of the roof lantern on whose apex his figure is portrayed. The natural illumination flooding in through the windows of the lantern not only bathes Christ's figure in light, but also creates an aura miscible with the depiction of golden heavenly light that envelops the seated figures of the saints below and progressively gains in substance near the center—an apparent continuum that relies on the interruption of the dark festoon, whose suspension in an illusionary space disguises the real disconnectedness of the two realms of light. Spatial continuation is conveyed and natural light is given a supernatural quality within the illusion of the image. Bellori states that Lanfranco's style, although "resolute from practice" rather than from the "sfumato" of Correggio's paintings, was in its essence "imbued with the idea and composition of Correggio."[26]

Bellori's contemporary, the writer Francesco Scannelli (1616–1663), affirms the enormous influence of the Parma dome on subsequent artists; the best masters studied it as a demonstration of Correggio's command of the "greatest challenges of the profession."[27] At first sight, the dome's "great composition articulates all the most disastrous difficulties that were in the past considered insurmountable and

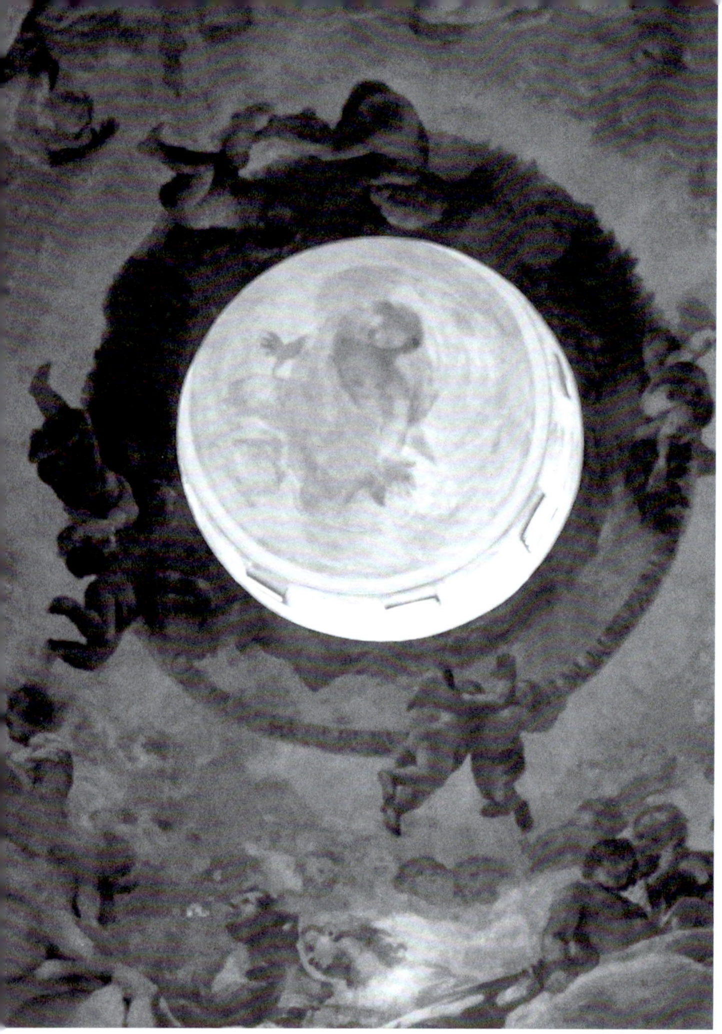

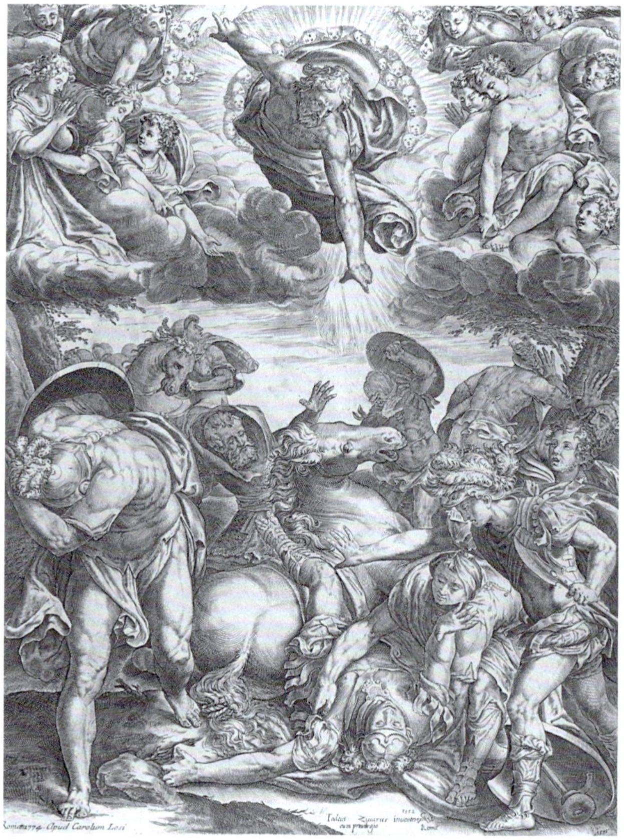

contemptible" and thus visually displays Correggio's "supreme understanding."[28] Scannelli especially praises the delicacy of the *scorzi*. They manifest finesse and decorum and are expressions of the device at its most true and proper.[29]

A sinopia made for the dome's Ascension of the Madonna illustrates why Correggio was such an important model for bravura renditions of foreshortened figures in cupola decoration (fig. 87). The beauty of Correggio's graceful conception of the figure lies in the clear definition not only of her body seen from an extreme low angle—we can see the tip of Mary's nose from below—but also in her ascending movement that seems to be mediated by resonating linear waves. A curving line, articulating the right side of her face by defining her forehead, and a similarly long and slightly undulant line marking her cheek on the left side, open up her features and contribute to an overall sense of rising motion. Another sequence of lines—the sweeping stroke that describes a fold of skin at the boundary between her throat and chin and links with two others that evoke her bosom—loosen the body's silhouette and at the same time make it receptive to a spatial treatment that deforms and reconfigures her to meet the optical requirements of *di sotto in sù* perspective.

This fine-tuning of line, which causes the beholder to overlook the body's loss of anatomical coherence was what made Correggio's name famous in art history.

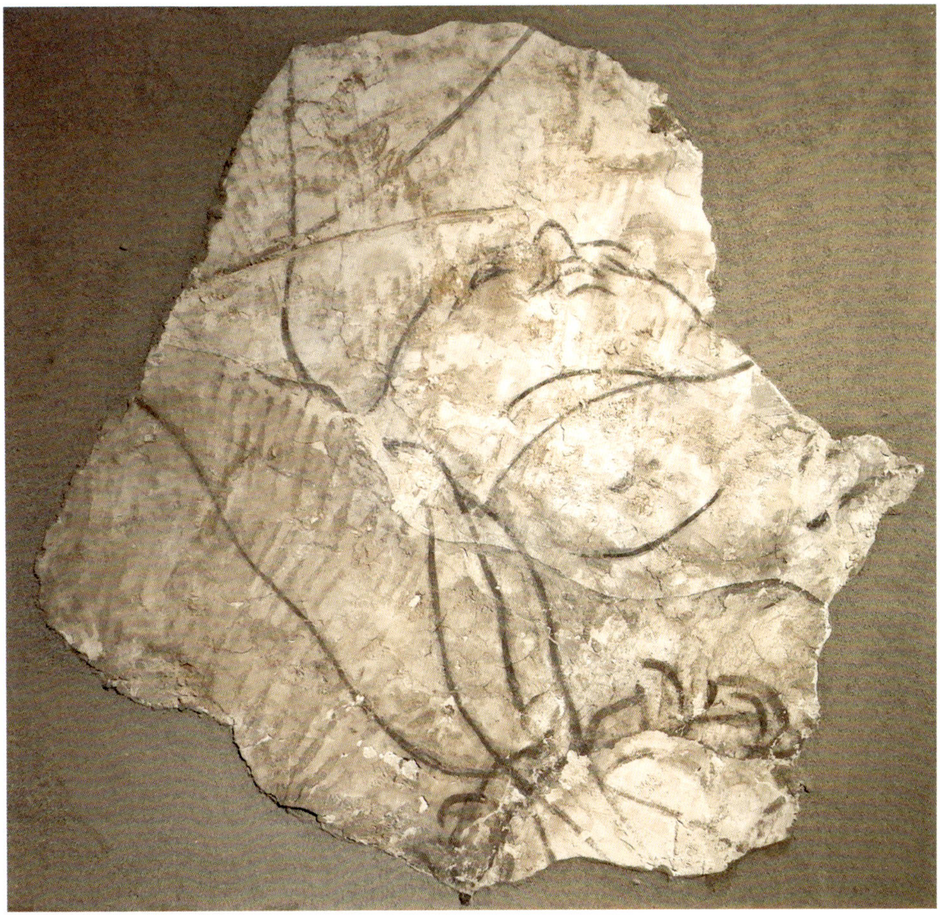

85 (FACING, LEFT)
Detail of fig. 84 [*Assumption of the Virgin*].

86 (FACING, RIGHT)
Cherubino Alberti, after Taddeo Zuccari, *The Conversion of Saint Paul*. Etching, 47.1 × 34.5 cm. Metropolitan Museum of Art, New York.

87
Correggio, *Ascension of the Madonna*. Sinopia. Galleria Nazionale, Parma.

On July 8, 1713, in a letter to his son titled "Le goût du dessin" (the taste of design), the "premier peintre du Roi" Antoine Coypel wrote that "one can also draw with great taste without being completely correct, as one sees in most of Correggio's works." The grand character of drawing, he says, consists in the mastery of enormous masses of light and dark and in the avoidance of all that is "dry, hard, and cut." Correggio's wavy lines admirably serve this end, enlivening bodily form and endowing it with grandeur and elegance, a quality that Coypel defines as the very "spirit of contour."[30]

CHAPTER FOUR

Bravura as Painterly Style

SPREZZATURA ARTIFICIOSA

According to Francesco Scannelli's treatise *Il microcosmo della pittura* (1657), what Correggio expressed in the Parma dome had never been thought of before in the human mind.[1] Later on in the book, Scannelli tells us Correggio once boasted "that he had his drawing at the tip of his brush," a remark preceded by another insight into the artist: the man who possessed "the most exquisite excellence in painting" detested the practice of drawing. Scannelli sharply distinguishes Correggio's attitude in this regard from Raphael and Parmigianino (ten times the number of their drawings are extant today). The latter, he says, carefully finished their pictures *con longhe fatiche di studiosi esercitij*, on the basis of detailed preliminary studies executed "with extreme perfection." Correggio, on the other hand, captured "his inspired ideas" (*pensieri accenati*) in sketches drawn so quickly they seemed to appear miraculously, as if of their own accord.[2]

The interesting idea that not only is painting a physical act, but that creativity can be generated in a quasi-corporeal fashion, is reflected in the rhetorical conceit that undergirds Scannelli's treatise. He imagines the artistic world as a single organism in which different artists and their styles of painting play the parts of various bones and organs of the human body. In this "microcosm of painting," the "three most noble parts" are Raphael as the liver, Titian as the heart, and Correggio as the brain. Veronese is identified with the genitals due to his "learned, easy, and fecund execution."[3] Michelangelo, the spine, supports the inner organs and guarantees the vitality of the whole being.[4] As the liver, Raphael draws the substance of knowledge from "Mother Antiquity" and extracts what is fine and tender in painting from the hard stone and bronze of art's classical legacy.[5] The heart, personified by Titian, is the origin of life, invigorating the spirit through the circulation of blood; Scannelli links this physiological trait to a stylistic one when he categorizes Titian's manner as "bold and true" (*gagliarda, e vera maniera*).[6] Correggio's ability "to temper excess in each part because of his unusual and subtle procedure" (*con modo d'insolita, è più fina operatione ha saputo temperare per ogni parte i vitiosi eccessi*) is equated with the body's highest functioning organ, the brain. Scannelli's metaphor of art as a well-functioning human body reflects the long-held notion that creative productivity arises from a process of "embodied" imitation.

Seneca's famous 84th letter to Lucilius, "On Gathering Ideas," may explain the metaphor's deeper meaning:

> The food we have eaten, as long as it retains its original quality, and floats in our stomachs as an undiluted mass, is a burden; but it passes into tissue and blood only when it has been changed from its original form. So it is with the food which nourishes our higher nature—we should see to it that whatever we have absorbed should not be allowed to remain unchanged, or it will be no part of us. We must digest it; otherwise it will merely enter the memory and not the reasoning power.[7]

To have creativity "at the tip of one's brush" does not entail preserving artistic conceptions in a fixed state, rigid in the mind and bound to tradition, but instead requires keeping them liquid (or, indeed, "liquidated them"), flowing, as they are seamlessly incorporated into practice. The process of obliterating the original form of what enters through the senses "naturalizes" its content and enables virtuosity.

In his *Recueil des essaies des merveilles de la peinture* written in 1635, the painter Pierre Lebrun made a similar argument: "Poets have their inspiration in their heads, which is where their poetic nerves are located, and painters at the end of their fingers and on their brush-tips."[8] The basic difference between the creative processes at work in poetry and painting is that in the former the imaginative faculty is the seat of invention, whereas the *poiesis* of painting is released in execution. While the writer's hand is not granted a role in the creative process, the painter's fingers—and the paintbrush as their extension—are understood to stimulate the development of pictorial ideas. Lebrun's remark stands opposed to the predominant view articulated in Early Modern art theory that the creation of art is above all a product of contemplation, and thus spiritual in its essence.

The latter attitude is programmatically displayed in Marcantonio Raimondi's engraving of *Raphael in His Studio* (1520). It depicts the hero of academic art theory absorbed in thought: The painter sits on a step in a contorted and crouched position (fig. 88). His knees are turned to the right, his slightly shaded gaze in the other direction. A second step serves as a shelf where, behind Raphael's back and to his left, a blank panel rests. To his right we see the artist's instruments, palette, and paint cups. The most stunning feature of the engraving is the wide cape that completely covers Raphael's hands and arms (so that he can't use them), thereby isolating him from his external surroundings. The cape accentuates the artist's concentration on "a certain idea that comes to the mind," as he worded it in a letter to Baldassare Castiglione,[9] and at the same time gives the strange impression that he is literally cold. The fire of enthusiasm with which he will take up his work does not yet burn. A later description by Bellori of the young Domenichino attests that this image of Raphael's artistic attitude had been handed down to the succeeding generation: "He had a habit of hiding under his cloak to draw, and while studying in his youth he persisted in going about swathed like a philosopher in his pallium."[10]

Against this foil, Correggio's assertion that he had his drawing "at the tip of his brush" is striking. Here the tip of the tool is the contact point where the pictorial idea

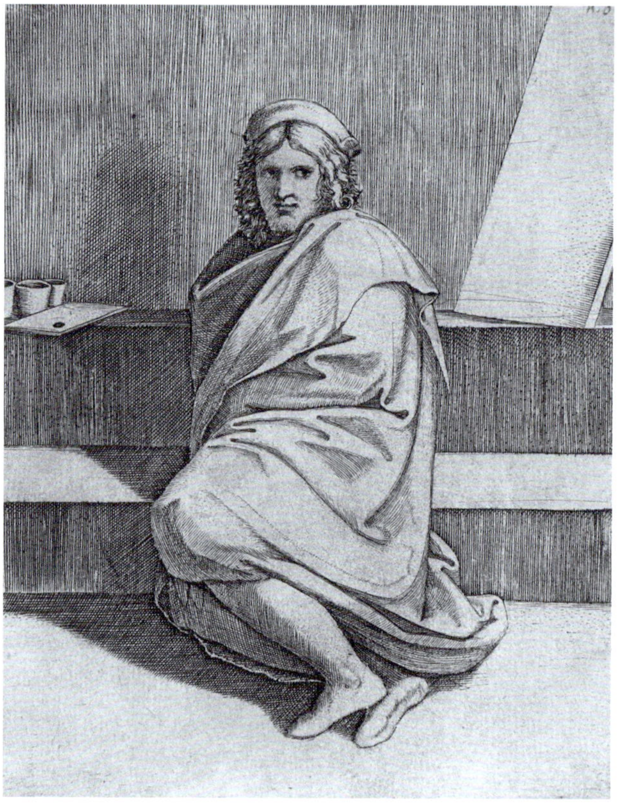

88
Marcantonio Raimondi,
Raphael in His Studio, 1520.
Engraving, 13.7 × 10.6 cm.
Yale University Art Gallery,
New Haven.

takes material form. The traditional hierarchy of invention that sees drawing as the paramount activity and coloring as a second subordinate step is reversed, and with this turnabout a highly controversial experimental field opens to experiment. In fact, Correggio's figure of speech had embedded within it an underlying element of criticism: His remark, as recorded by Scannelli, is actually a direct citation of another artist. In Vasari's vita of Perino del Vaga, Girolamo da Treviso congratulates himself in precisely the same manner, exclaiming: "What cartoons, they are nothing but cartoons! I, I have art at the tip of my brush!" (*Che cartoni e non cartoni! Io, io ho l'arte su la punta del pennello*).[11] Here the artist elevates his own talent above the practice of intensive preliminary study employed by Perino and other competitors with whom he worked from 1527 to 1528 on frescoes at Casa Doria in Genoa. As Vasari records, Perino eventually heard of these boasts and responded by publicly exhibiting his cartoons at the spot where the final work would be located. Girolamo "took fright at the beauty of the cartoons," left his frescoes unfinished, and immediately fled Genoa.

There were thus two different implications contained in the same idiom, and together they illustrate the ambivalence of an underlying concept known as *sprezzatura* (*s-prezzare* literally means "dis-prize," but in this context it should be understood as deliberate and artful negligence), a cultural aesthetic and behavioral ethos that greatly influenced and defined the Early Modern artistic attitude. Scannelli explicitly echoes Baldassare Castiglione's *Book of the Courtier*, the literary source of sprezzatura's conceptual framework, when he defines "true art" as that which contains "everything to an eminent degree but without showing it."[12]

Castiglione (1478–1529), who was a close friend of Giulio Romano and sat for a portrait by Raphael, identified a second attitude intricately tied to sprezzatura. He precedes the description of his model courtier with a counterexample of one who continually sings his own praises while disdaining and reproaching the people around him, a figure reminiscent of our *exemplum in malum*, Girolamo da Treviso. Such conduct, Castiglione explains, is nothing other than "the affectation of wanting to appear bold" (*affettazione di voler parer gagliardo*).[13] The person who forces things (*il sforzare*) or "drags [them] by the hair" contradicts the maxim "true art is that which does not appear to be art" (*quella esser vera arte, che non pare esser arte*)[14] and brings about his own disgrace because such affectation is "a very steep and dangerous cliff" (*come un asperissimo e pericoloso scoglio*) that must be avoided as much as possible.[15] The prospect of losing one's credibility (*leva in tutto il credito*) is caused in this case by "showing art" (*mostrar l'arte*) in an overt striving for sprezzatura, and thus contradicting its ethical-aesthetic stance.

The counterconcept of *affettazione* designates an attitude against which the ideal of sprezzatura not only distinguishes itself, but also a state into which sprezzatura always threatens to degenerate. Castiglione describes a dancer who, in a calculated move while performing, lets his frock slip from his shoulder and his slippers glide off his feet in order to demonstrate that he is not thinking (*mostrar ben di non pensarvi*) but just moving spontaneously. Here the affectation of being unhindered by thought ironically arises from "thinking too much" (*questo è il pensarvi troppo*).[16]

Castiglione's enumeration of the dangers inherent in sprezzatura underscores a fundamental vulnerability inherent in all artistic performance: namely, that sprezzatura has the potential suddenly to capsize into its opposite. When dissimulation fails to convince the audience then artistic pretension is all the more revealed. Even though Castiglione places a negative stigma on this type of defective sprezzatura, which is unsuccessful in its purpose and is equated with the counterexample of *affettazione*, he still employs the same term "sprezzatura" for both the laudable and defective varieties. Sprezzatura is thus inherently contradictory: *virtù* and *vizio* lie at either end of its conceptual spectrum, and the few pages of *Il Cortegiano* where this aesthetic is outlined caution that the ideal of sprezzatura will inevitably lead to instances of pretense.

Scannelli's treatise in the first instance associates sprezzatura with *moderanza, facilità, e gratia*. In line with Castiglione's ideal, he holds that a work of art should appear to be created "without thinking," arising as if "from itself" (*senza pensarvi, e da se stesse*). He further relates the degree of a work's "naturalness" to its visual proportionality (*soggetti talmente alla natura, e all'occhio proportionate*)[17] and sees in Correggio one of those most excellent artists who accurately "hit the target of beautiful naturalness."[18]

And yet the word "sprezzatura" appears a second time and in a different context in Scannelli's writings, in his formulation *la Veneta sprezzatura de'colori*.[19] Scannelli explains that this type of media-bound sprezzatura results from the artist's taking into consideration the distance between a painting and its viewer; if the viewer is far away, a more open facture is necessary to create, with a *forza di straordinaria Maestria*, the impression of beautiful and natural effects. That the second type is associated with Venice may echo one of Castiglione's examples of defective sprezzatura, namely, the "cavaliere alla veneziana," who haughtily rides tall in the saddle. Castiglione contrasts such a horseman with the true sprezzatura of a rider who, without thinking, sits naturally in his saddle as if he were walking. He is a "modest gentleman who speaks and boasts little," in contrast to the former who "always praises himself and swaggers about threatening the world just to appear brave [*gagliardo*]."[20]

The martial undertones of Castiglione's concept of sprezzatura become evident when he instead pictures the positive example of a man well versed in handling weapons assuming a battle-ready stance (*in una attitudine pronta*) and, once again without thinking (*senza pensar*), holding his sword in such a relaxed manner (*scioltamente in una attitudine pronta*) that he gives the impression his body and limbs naturally and automatically (*senza fatica alcuna*) assume such a contrived pose.[21]

In this regard, Scannelli's category of "Venetian carelessness" is only indirectly related to forceful brushwork; its primary concern is with illusionistic impact. *Sprezzatura veneziana* is the consequence of an economy of labor calculated on the visual effect of distance, which acts to simplify finishing the artwork. The recognition of this attribute as something positive, however, requires connoisseurship.

Much later, Antonio Maria Zanetti's commentary on Jacopo Bassano in his *Della pittura veneziana* (1771) also notes this requirement and, more implicitly, that the beholder's aesthetic perception needs time to grow accustomed to novel painting practices. The connoisseur will always lag behind the artist in recognizing art. Zanetti's analysis of the quality of apparent carelessness in Bassano's painterly execution, by which he demonstrates his "art," provides us with a concise articulation of the concept of bravura:

> JACOPO da PONTE, called Il Bassano, made for himself a way of painting [*una strada di dipingere*] with so much wisdom and boldness [*con sapere, e fierezza*] that he stunned even those most knowledgeable. His manner consists in carefully executed strong and scornful strokes [*colpi massicci, e sprezzanti*] of the brush mainly characterized by spontaneity and intention, which produce such power and plasticity in his figures that they stand out from their canvases. He put aside the great *diligenza* and *finitezza* and replaced them with bravura. Nevertheless, one cannot say his things were not complete, for each part was sought out and highly intentional; but he omitted the gradual shading [*la sfumatezza*] and smoothing over [*i lisciamenti*] that were hitherto common practice in order that his speed and mastery could better come to the fore; truly a way of painting that shocks because for those who do not know much and view his paintings from up close, they appear like a randomly produced indistinct confusion of colors. If one moves back somewhat, they wondrously have their effect; and in this way the rationality is addressed of those who understand that all of this is derived from the finest art and intelligence, only accessible for those who know how to conceive it.[22]

Zanetti's astute assessment includes some of bravura's essential components, such as brushwork that does not comfort but rather affronts the eye, and the ostensible removal of an all-encompassing illusion, which reappears from a more distant viewing point with the help of the beholder's imagination. These characteristics marked a transformation in painting that paved the way for a new perception of pictorial phenomenality. But change is not always welcomed, and this change raised

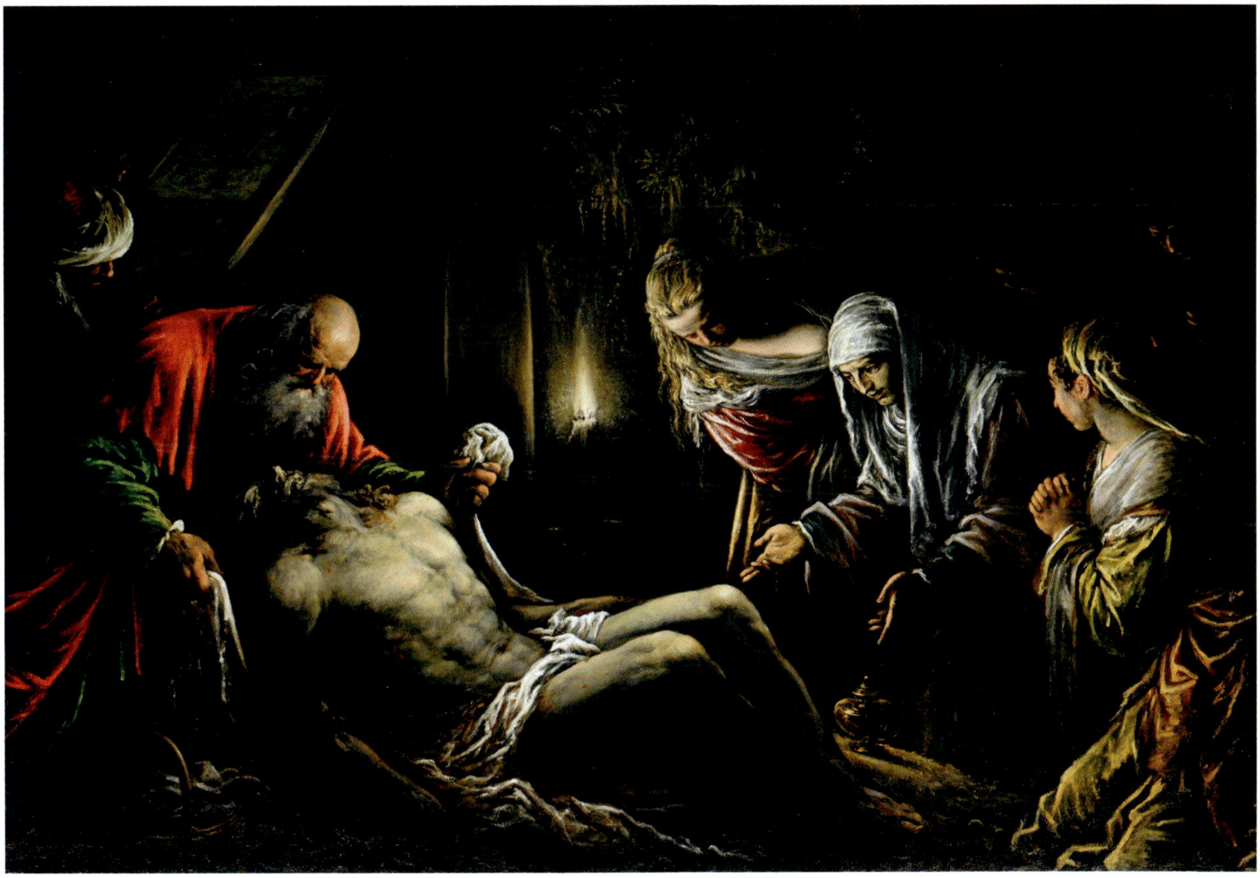

89
Jacopo Bassano, *Descent from the Cross*, 1580.
Oil on canvas, 154 × 225 cm.
Musée du Louvre, Paris.

an intense wave of criticism preoccupied with bravura's destructive potential rather than its innovative force. Zanetti seems to have taken such concerns into account in the eulogy cited above when he characterizes the first impression of Bassano's paintings as a "randomly produced indistinct confusion of colors." But he explains his rejection of the accusation of incompleteness in Bassano by pointing to the wisdom and intelligence explicit in the visible stroke of his brush. As we shall see, the recognition of these attributes requires erudition and in the end enables the beholder to experience a marvelous effect—the dispersal of coloristic confusion that follows from "moving back" from the work.

The painter and writer Giovanni Pietro Zanotti (1674–1765) highlights the aesthetic benefits of bravura's "manipulations" and "blows" of the brush by noting that although these stratagems are specifically calculated to work at a distance, connoisseurs privy to this new knowledge are able to detect the "bravura" and "felicità" of the artist who made them even when viewing up close.[23] Zanetti's observation of a *confusione indistinta di colori formata accaso* is superbly corroborated in Jacopo Bassano's *Descent from the Cross* (fig. 89). Because Bassano shrouds the scene in the darkness of night—an isolated candle standing in the center is the only source of illumination—the contours of the individual figures are lost in the gloom. When viewed nearby, the linen cloth grasped in the hand of Joseph of Arimathea completely dissolves. Its substance drains away into rivulets of shadow, revealing the rough painterly sketching of the cloth as well as the body of Christ. Jesus's reclining form observed at close range seems to lose its material stability. His right foot and right hand are completely imperceptible. The linen cloth is only white at the crests of its folds, and the color of the weeping Mary's undercoat is likewise determined solely by blue flickering ridges limned on the furrowed fabric. However, from a distance the extreme contrast created by these broad streaks of canted light abruptly dispels any impression of confusion and melding. This liquidity becomes mimetically "composed" in the motifs of the woodland grove's hanging branches behind the cross, in Mary Magdalene's flowing hair, and in the tears dropping into the air from the cheeks of both Marys.

The artists' conscious adaptation of their painting method to best serve a work's appearance in the specific place where it would eventually be mounted—Tintoretto was an absolute trendsetter in this regard[24]—often led to the viewer's misunderstanding of the artwork. Carlo Ridolfi reports that there were those who disparaged Tintoretto's work because it lacked *sfumato*, a quality that pleases the eye of the "less knowledgeable" because it creates smooth transitions between color tones. He responds to such uninformed disregard for the art involved in painting:

> It is not always praiseworthy when the painter uses refinement and finish [*le delicatezze e'l finimento*], which are undoubtedly superfluous when those works are located far away. For the air in between contains a rare spice [*raro condimento*] that, by virtue of our vision, unifies the vigorous brushstrokes [*pennellate gagliarde*], rendering them soft and pleasant [*soavi e grate*].[25]

Ridolfi's comparison of a viewer's standpoint to an optical "condiment" is stunning. The metaphor is primarily employed to address the sensory impact of an individual style, but the "condiment" as a visual surplus that can change the perception and therefore reception of an artwork addresses a *way* of seeing rather than *what* is seen. It takes in aspects of both location *and* style.

Castiglione's concept of defective sprezzatura, the demonstrative rather than courteously inconspicuous expression of one's art, faults not so much an artist's technical immodesty as their attitude of indifference or outright disdain of "sprezzare," a concept interchangeable with bravura. We find this word often in descriptions of bravura's painterly appearance: Ridolfi speaks of *un certo sprezzo di maniera*, Zanetti notes *colpi massici, e sprezzanti*, and Boschini praises strokes that evince *un sprezzo di pennello*.[26] Baldinucci's *Vocabolario* (1681) addresses *bravura pittoresca* as a countermodel to *sfumato* painting under the dictionary entry "Di colpi." According to Baldinucci, the term refers to a painting

> that is comprised of brushstrokes by which the artist places pigments with great spontaneity [*franchezza*], whether by means of light and dark or medium tones... in order to give the painting a strong relief and allow the great bravura and mastery of the brush and colors to become apparent—in contrast to those paintings we call '*sfumate*' or fatigued [*affaticate*].[27]

Baldinucci concludes by equating the concept of bravura with *franchezza* and daring (*ardimento*).

The frescoes by Lodovico Carracci (1555–1619) in the Cappella Lambertini in San Domenico (Bologna), extant only in poorly preserved fragments, evidence in a single work Carracci's remarkable skill in both of these diametrically opposed modes of painting. For his biographer Carlo Cesare Malvasia, this artistic tour de force consists in the union of two extremes with contrasting affective impact: the rendering of Francis of Assisi is *terribile, facile, resoluto*, conveying virtuosity with only a few strokes and colors in a way pleasing to the connoisseur, while the figure of Caritas is *gentile, finito, amoroso* and captivates those less knowledgeable. The former is connected with daring, the latter with the concept of *grazia*.[28]

Sprezzatura's relationship to technique, already evident in Scannelli's addition of the words "de'colori" to the term,[29] is reflected in the conceptual shift from *nascondere* (to conceal) to *mostrare l'arte* (to demonstrate art). Ridolfi accordingly lauded Titian's St. Nicholas altarpiece in San Sebastiano: "The beauty of the painting does not consist in its finesse or purity of colors [*nella finezza o nella pulizia de'colori*], but in its mastery of execution [*nella maestria del fare*] shown in the figure made from solitary brushstrokes and with marvelous spontaneity [*sprezzo*]."[30]

The rhetorical power of sprezzatura, according to Castiglione, consists in the suggestion that one knows more than one lets on, and in the implication that the act one performs could be done even better, that is, with greater emphasis on accurate draftsmanship, had the artist so desired. The air of effortlessness appears spontaneous and uncalculated, even though it proceeds from the highest degree of calculation. Castiglione gives the following illustration of his point: "An unforced line, a single stroke of the brush drawn with such ease that it seems like the hand, without being guided by study or any skill whatsoever, proceeds by itself to the line's terminus according to the painter's intention."[31]

According to an anecdote Ridolfi relates, Tintoretto ridiculed the conventional charge that Venetian painting after Giorgione possessed no *disegno*. As the story goes, several young Flemish painters living in Rome sought out Tintoretto and presented him with meticulously drawn head studies in red chalk. When Tintoretto asked how much time they had spent on these drawings, they answered ten to fifteen days. Tintoretto's sympathetic response that one indeed could not have done them any faster was countered in the same breath by a brush drawing he executed as he spoke. In vigorous brief strokes (*brevi colpi*) he sketched out a complex figure with black ink and lead white, which he then held up to his visitors and said: "We poor Venetians only know how to draw like this." The young Flemish artists were equally astonished at the prontezza of his genius and by how much time they regularly squandered with their fastidiousness.[32]

Ridolfi also reports that the Bolognese painter Odoardo Fialetti[33] visited the elderly Tintoretto to ask him what he could do to improve his practice. Tintoretto answered him: "You must draw," and when asked for further advice, the old man added: "You must draw, and draw some more [*disegnare, e ancora disegnare*]."[34] His insistence on drafting as an exercise was not meant to raise the value of drawing per se, but instead to raise the value of proficiency in this specific skill—the ability to mentally conceive a figure and execute it in the shortest time with the least amount of effort.[35]

In 1756, Dandré Bardon would explain the confidence demonstrated by the virtuoso placement of a figure on paper in "four elegant strokes" as reward for many years of drawing: "The masters of a *style prompt et hardi* have been familiar with Nature for a long time, they know it, so to say, by heart."[36] The fluency evident in a bold and vigorous painterly style depends on a "perfect knowledge of forms, of tones, and of effects."[37] Without this knowledge flowing as if in the artist's veins, there could be no *disegno* at the tip of one's brush.

THE APPEAL OF SKETCHINESS

Leaving a sketch-like passage in a work is perhaps the most easily discerned expression of sprezzatura in the bravura artist's toolkit. The deceptive nonchalance of this device deliberately disappoints the naive spectator who wants to be deceived by an uninterrupted illusion, even as it opens their eyes to the "reality" behind the picture (and thus to the artistic maneuvers that create the picture's fiction). The visibility of the sketch or of some early stage of work in the finished painting fuses both phases of pictorial development into a single operation. The conventional distinction between drawing and painting thus becomes blurred, because the former no longer exists on a separate sheet of paper. Tintoretto's name became associated with "sketchiness" during his own lifetime, and over the intervening centuries art literature has continued to reaffirm his works as the apotheosis of this phenomenon.[38] Carlo Cesare Malvasia's assessment of *The Assumption of the Virgin* by Annibale Carracci, whose art he termed *coraggioso, sprezzante, e impaziente,* runs as follows: "It [Carracci's work] seems to be more like a sketch than a finished painting [*più tosto una bozza che un quadro compito*].... Annibale cast his eye toward Tintoretto."[39] Malvasia makes a similar reference to Tintoretto in his vita of Guido Reni when he writes about a Madonna with child made "from strokes, from manipulations of the brush with the sure sprezzatura of a great master... uncommon in Roman and Lombard painting, although sometimes practiced by Tintoretto."[40]

Tintoretto's reputation as a paragon of sprezzatura was founded not only on his manner of painting, but also on the legendary daring of his professional persona. One of his particularly spectacular coups marks a historic milestone in artistic self-conception. To briefly outline the story: The Confraternity of San Rocco had asked Salviati, Zuccari, Veronese, and Tintoretto to submit proposals for a commission. While the other candidates were laboring over their presentation drawings, Tintoretto took measurements of the location where the finished work would be positioned to decide how exactly he would proceed. He then painted a canvas of what he had determined to be an appropriate size "with his own unique swiftness" and installed it at the premises. The confraternity was not pleased: drawings were requested, not completed works. Tintoretto replied with contrition that this was his way of drawing, he did not know any better. His self-criticism disabled their ire, but Tintoretto then went on to qualify his apology by adding that such drawings and proposals should, in fact, always be done in this way to avoid misleading commissioners, thereby turning his self-incrimination into self-praise. He concluded by offering to give the confraternity the work as a gift if they did not want to pay for it or for the effort of its creation. His overture paid off: The Scuola Grande di San Rocco is the most impressive monument of Tintoretto's art, dominating both floors and every surface of the building's interior (fig. 90).

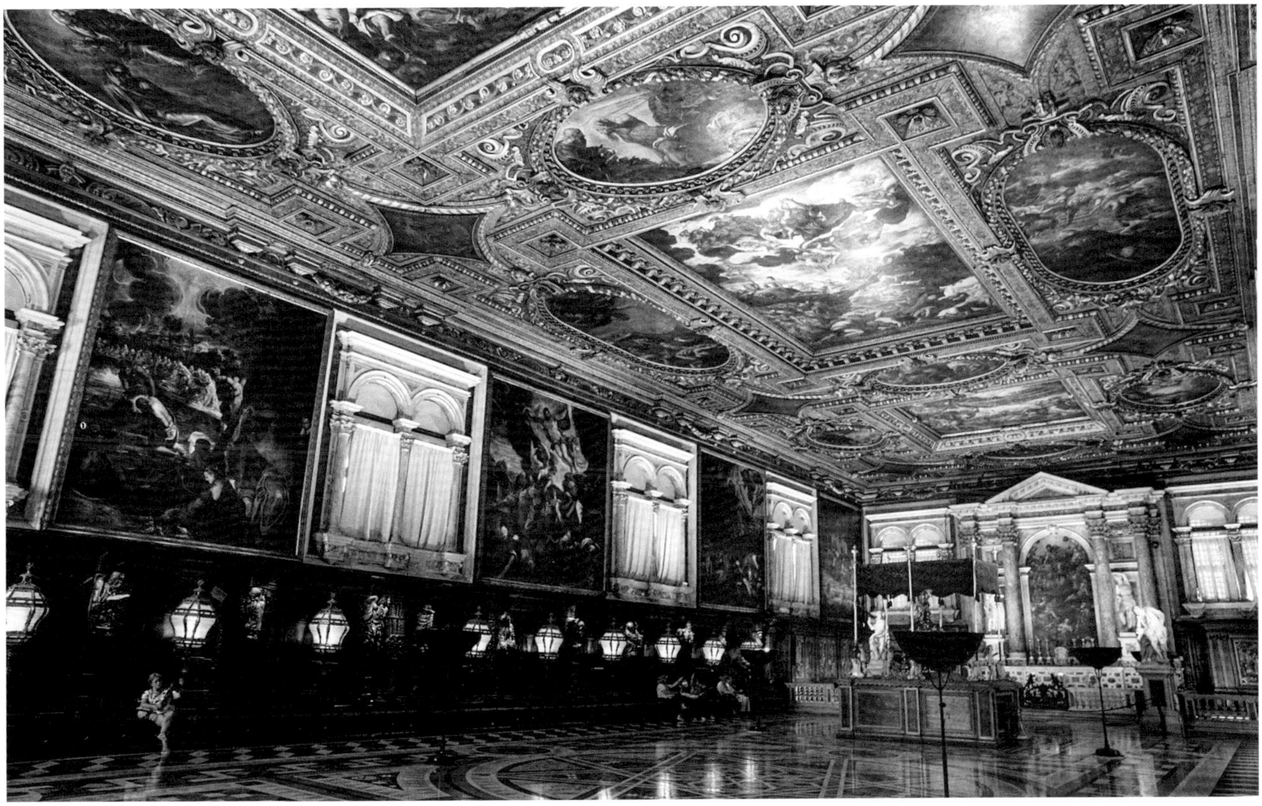

Joachim von Sandrart adopted this anecdote from Vasari's *Lives* in his *Teutsche Academie der edlen Bau-, Bild- und Mahlerey-Künste*, and praised Tintoretto's astonishing inventiveness and his quickness of execution: "Tintoretto finished still many other paintings because he was so quick and prepared that when others meant he had not yet properly studied the matter [*noch nicht recht nachgesonnen*], he had already brought his work to an end."[41] He describes Tintoretto's technique, however, with a critical undertone, describing his sprezzatura as presumptuous negligence:

> He also works according to his own pleasure without any previously made drawing, as if he thereby wanted to show that painting was not an onerous tedium but only a leisurely pastime [*Kurzweil*]; many times he merely underpainted and left his paintings in oil so raw that one found on them the brushstrokes and gobbets of paint, and regarded such a piece as an abandoned work of desperation without any design.[42]

90
Sala Superiore of the Scuola Grande di San Rocco, Venice.

Similar criticism of Tintoretto persisted over the centuries. In the *Dictionnaire des arts de peinture, sculpture et gravure* (1792), Lévesque called the painter a "deplorable draftsman" in his entry on *Prestezze*, but then qualified his remark: "He owes his reputation more to his quickness than to the perfection of his work. One can criticize his mistakes, one can complain about what is lacking in his works, which appear to be not so much made as thrown down, but he amazes and is applauded."[43]

Aretino expressed, though with some forbearance, his disapproval of

Tintoretto's haste in a letter to the artist. In a tone of paternal counsel, he excused Tintoretto's negligence-inducing speed as a sign of youthful overconfidence, which time would eventually teach him to rein in.[44] His praise of *The Miracle of St. Mark* was nothing short of euphoric, but he objected to the painting's sketchiness. This failure to reach the highest degree of perfection was, in his view, deliberate: "Your name will be blessed," he wrote," if you are able to turn the speed of getting it done into the patience of doing. Nevertheless, little by little the years will take care of this, for they and nothing else will suffice to slow down the rush of carelessness, to which youth willingly and quickly submits."[45] Aretino thereby addresses the conflict that so often arises between the impulsiveness of youthful creativity and the aspiration to finished perfection. Aretino's choice of the word *trascurezza* for "carelessness" instead of the rhetorically weightier *sprezzatura* is noteworthy.

We also find rueful understanding for Tintoretto's *non finito* in Francesco Sansovino's guide to Venice, *Delle cose notabili che sono in Venezia* (1561). After characterizing Jacopo Tintoretto as *tutto spirito, tutto prontezza* and highlighting the overwhelming power of his imagination, the author voices a reservation: "But he doesn't have much patience.... This is perhaps due to eagerness or to the great love he has for art, or to caprice; for the men of this profession are very unusual."[46]

Significantly, this passage in Sansovino presages a repudiation of contemporary Cinquecento criticism of Tintoretto and the beginning of a paradigm change in the understanding of his art. The censorious judgments of Cinquecento art literature will in the seventeenth century undergo a curious metamorphosis. When Boschini acclaims Tintoretto as having "the most terrible mind painting has ever seen [*Un cervel più terribile de quelo No fu mai visto certo in Pitura*]...as may be recognized in each of his works [*come se vede in ogni so fatura*],"[47] he takes up Giorgio Vasari's not necessarily complimentary designation of Tintoretto as "*il più terribile cervello che abbia avuto mai la pittura*,"[48] thereby turning critique into panegyric. His use of *terribile* clearly suggests "fearsome" in the sense of awe-inspiring by its daring brilliance. The phrase will become a stock epithet, employed, for example, by Antonio Maria Zanetti in his *Istoria di pittura veneziana*: "JACOPO ROBUSTI, called TINTORETTO...was the most fearsome [*terribile*] painter who came from this school; he is truly the Master and we can rightly call him the Disposer [*disponitore*; in the sense of 'marshal'] of Painting."[49]

Boschini's contemporary Carlo Ridolfi praises Tintoretto's creation of a woman's portrait as done with "masterly sprezzatura."[50] The positive reevaluation of this painterly style will remain standard scholarly opinion for more than a century, as for example when Zanetti speaks of Giorgione's *pittoresca sprezzatura*, by which "the possession of art is manifested" and through whose "action much spirit and vitality will be instilled in works of art."[51] Zanetti once again gives voice to the shift mentioned above: his sprezzatura is a *demonstration* of art and not, as Baldassare Castiglione's *Cortegiano* defined it, artful concealment.[52]

TINTORETTO AS *PRIMUS INTER PARES*

In his comprehensive paean to Venetian painting, the well-known *Carta del navegar pitoresco* (1660), the Venetian artist and art dealer Marco Boschini equates what he deems a superior, "valiant" style of painting with bravura, and so expands the theoretical scope of the term. He associates "bravura" with martial skill, singling out Salvator Rosa's battles for example, as "histories of bravura" that exalt painting, but then he goes further.[53] He not only cites the bravado articulated by artists working in other genres, but also specifically relates bravura to a certain style of painting that originated in Venice, describing its Venetian proponents as "gran Guerieri" and "valorosi Capitani" committing "ferocious deeds" (*ati sì fieri*) in their paintings.[54]

Boschini then further refines his concept of bravura by means of a series of rhetorical associations. He asks what makes a soldier valiant (*bravo*) and answers his own question: "To be full of courage for improvisation, for in the end the man who has no blood on his face is just a poorly groomed slave."[55] To the question, "What does painting consist of?" he answers, "of bravura."[56] As for Tintoretto, he has "never been seen a greater bravura which terrorizes every *bravazzo*."[57] With these associations he establishes an aesthetic model that will be perpetually linked with Tintoretto's name. Zanetti's *Istoria della pittura italiana* further elaborates on the passages of Boschini that we have previously cited, in which he lauds Tintoretto as the most terrible (*più terribile*) painter and "the master and munificent lord of painting," who unleashes terror and handles chiaroscuro with daring (*fierezza*) and extraordinary intelligence.[58] Tintoretto becomes not only the epitome of a specific manner of painting, but also a stylistic reference point: Vincenzo da Canal, for example, commenting on Gasparo Diziani, characterizes his *maniera* "as resolute and swift in the gusto of Tintoretto."[59]

Boschini decisively shaped the concept of bravura with his military imagery,[60] and in this regard he ranked Tintoretto as *primus inter pares*. Regarding Tintoretto's *Conquest of Zara* in the Palazzo Ducale's Sala dello Scrutinio, he warns, "Whoever does not award first place to Tintoretto in war, and does not make him the master and general of the field, knows nothing about the steel of his resilient and strong armor. As for bravura, every soldier is depicted; and in his sword is life and death; and he spreads out a vast array of warriors in the painting."[61] Even when praising Tintoretto's biblical histories, Boschini employs a martial vocabulary to convey the violence of his bold figural compositions. Reminiscent of Esteban March and his use of military music to fuel his creativity, Boschini's panegyric—beginning with the words: "This is the doctrine and noble artifice!"—celebrates the overwhelming impact of the Scuola Grande di San Rocco's Sala Superiore by conjuring the "fired salvo of muskets, trumpets, tambourines, and similar dignified things" that greet the beholder who enters the *sala*. This rhetorically motivated, synesthetic depiction of the hall's decorative program also has a deeper significance that goes to the issue of painting as art. According to Boschini, "[It is] a signal of victory, signal of imperial rule, signal of absolute power, signal that the painting dominates and is enthroned with the battle ensign." Boschini concludes with the exaltation, "This is the arsenal that provisions painting with muskets and cannon; here breastplates and helmets are dispensed to those who eagerly give themselves over to bravura!" It is clear that the theater of war he visualizes is nothing other than a stage for art.[62]

The modern weaponry named in Boschini's extended metaphor—a separate ekphrasis mentions "flintlocks and bombards, along with swords and arrows for the naval wars"[63]—underscores the novelty of bravuroso painting, which entailed constructing *per forza*, by means of foreshortenings and dramatic chiaroscuro, a canvas-shattering, spatially projecting fiction of strongly animated bodies: "[Tintoretto] put great effort—as do today's soldiers in their drills with buried mines, incendiary devices, bombs, grenades, and similar things—into making his figures leap from the canvas [*far balzare le figure fuori delle tele*]."[64]

In his poetic guide to Venetian painting, Boschini makes two observations about Tintoretto's chiaroscuro that elucidate specific technical aspects of bravura. Tintoretto's powerful and daring distribution of *tutta la massa*, he writes, is most notably evinced in reflected light and cast shadows (*apparir sempre fierezze de lumi, ombre, riflessi e battimenti*). The artist further employs stark contrast to construct the spatial distance between near and far; figures near the beholder are formed from darkness, while light is projected (*gettar*) into the distance. Boschini's choice of the pair "*formar*"/"*gettar*" to distinguish these reciprocal treatments is quite appropriate. They describe the impactful distinction between detailed modeling in the foreground and rough sketching in the background. The backlighting intentionally shatters the pictorial space, recalling Boschini's association of Tintoretto with new, explosive war technologies. Boschini goes on to associate Tintoretto's application of chiaroscuro with "painterly freedom and artful stratagems, new statutes and reforms for new laws of painting" (*licenze pittoresche ed artificij industriosi, nuovi statuti e riforme di nuove leggi alla Pittura*), an opinion echoed by another author of the period.

91 (FACING)
Tintoretto, *The Baptism of Christ*, 1579–1581. Oil on canvas, 538 × 465 cm. Scuola Grande di San Rocco, Sala Superiore, Venice.

In much the same way, but in a less martial tone, Carlo Ridolfi not only asserts the didactic value of the Scuola Grande di San Rocco, which he describes as "always an academy and refuge for every scholar of painting," but also lauds Tintoretto's works as lessons in how to compose *invenzione*, harness *disegno*, and exhibit the boldness and force of coloring (*la franchezza e la forza del colorire*). In addition, he commends the disposition of the artist's chiaroscuro, which serves to distinguish one figural group from another (*staccare con lumi e ombre i gruppi delle figure ne'componimenti*).[65]

With his light placements that were able to cleave and define areas in his representations Tintoretto had invented nothing less than a new painting technique, one that facilitated his rapid completion of more than thirty paintings in only a few years. His compositions were worked from a foundation of brownish-black-toned ground, which made it much easier to model bodies, because he often shows them emerging from shadow. As soon as he sketches them onto the ground's surface they are already embedded in a desired ambient that does not have to be created in a separate step. This extreme economy of execution (in brushwork) also extended to an economy of materials (in the usage of paint). We know from scientific analyses of the paintings in the Sala Superiore that his dark-toned primer consists partially of paint residues Tintoretto must have scraped from his palette.[66]

The Baptism of Christ impressively showcases Tintoretto's extreme chiaroscuro (fig. 91). The sacrament seems to take place at night, as do many of the scenes depicted in the Scuola Grande di San Rocco. Their nocturnal aura is certainly not just a consequence of low levels of light inside the building.[67] Boschini glorifies Tintoretto's orchestration of extreme lighting effects on a dark ground when he celebrates the artist as a "divine spirit who came into this world with a torch in his hand."[68] The dim setting of the *Baptism* is pierced by rays of sacred light that guide the radiant dove of the Holy Spirit. Brilliance spilling from an opening in the heavens designates

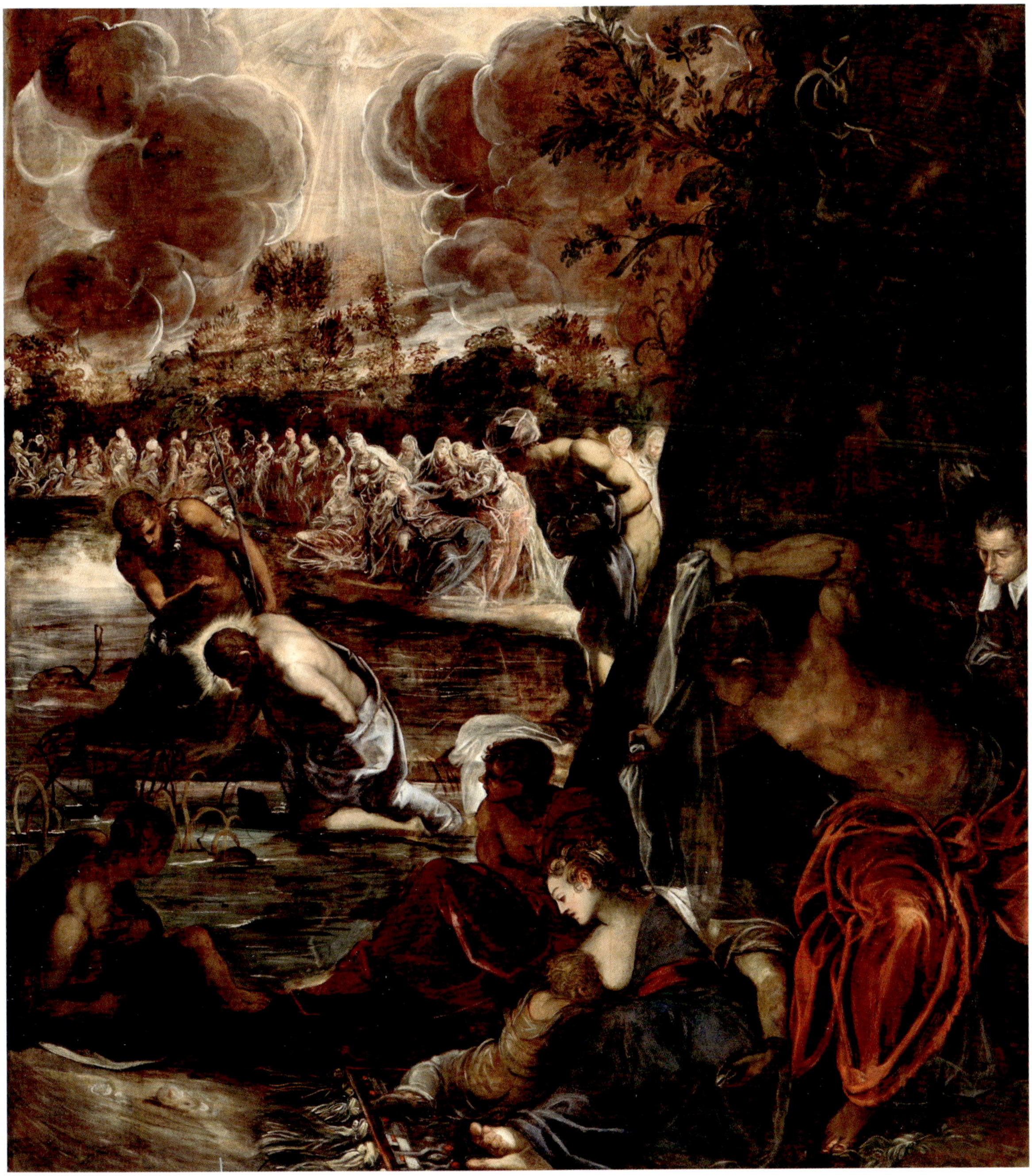

Christ as the Son of God. It pours over the group of figures in the background and illumines the baptismal ceremony in the middle ground. The exaggerated contrast is highly dramatic in its effect on Christ and the disrobed baptizand behind him; both bodies have strongly lit backsides and are deeply shaded in front.

This differential in the painting's formal arrangement, so accurately described by Boschini ("nearby figures are formed from darkness, and light is projected into the distance"), dictates the composition of the densely populated scene, which reoccurring serially on the same compositional plane and accentuating the two-dimensionality of the picture surface, but also interwoven across various planes and maneuvering in the fiction of depth by virtue of foreshortening. The many paintings mounted on the ceiling and walls are configured along diagonal axes that create correspondences across all the works in the vast architectural space, as noted by the art historian Astrid Zenkert in her iconographical analysis.[77] These relational axes reinforce the decorative program's narrative structure and unity as it spreads over walls and ceiling. Each composition's dual spheres of resonance (as a single work and as a part of the whole) explosively animate the individual motifs' potential to "shatter" the confines of their individual spaces and seize the beholder.

93 (FACING)
Tintoretto, *Moses Strikes Water from the Rock*, 1577. Oil on canvas, 550 × 520 cm. Scuola Grande di San Rocco, Sala Superiore, Venice.

Tintoretto's intense engagement with extreme perspective in the paintings on the lateral walls of the choir (the so-called *quadri laterali*) and on the ceiling was undoubtedly a catalyst driving his search for innovative technique. His sketchy execution allows insight into his creative process and gives clues to the compositional methods that Boschini saw as revealing the "scienza" of his painting. After he praised the figure of the Eternal Father as *maestoso* in his panegyric on *Moses Strikes Water from the Rock*, declaring it "made with a compass" and therefore perfect as *disegno*, he extolled the brushwork: "Oh, how they are keen and daring [*Oh come le xe pronte, oh come brave*]! Look how well he keeps these figures together in the act of painting, this bright one with this dark one that dips water."[78]

Here Boschini apparently refers to the two figures standing next to each other directly above the nursing mother in the left corner. One with dark skin establishes a connection to the shaded area of the cliff, while the other is almost completely immersed in the gleaming light of the background where a battle rages (fig. 94).[79] Boschini concludes by lauding this work as "monstrous art" (*l'arte mostruose*) and quotes Pietro da Cortona who reportedly said of the ceiling painting: "This makes me believe I am standing at a place where [water] is actually cascading down, such that I would like to distance myself because otherwise I would surely get wet at once, at once."[80]

Long brushstrokes in lead white create this illusion that at any moment one might be splashed by the miraculous effluence gushing in great arcs from the rocks. Vessels held up high to catch the water are filled to the brim. A white contour line skirts the rims of some of the bowls, and white sloshes running down their sides engendering a mirage of water spilling over. Here we see Tintoretto's "white sword" (*spada bianca*)—the free-fall and rotation of the firm brushstroke that Boschini sees as central to the master's "great bravura."[81]

The Venetian critic explicitly alludes to fencing to describe Tintoretto's developmental progress between his work at the Chiesa and the program at the Scuola Grande: "Let us proceed from the Chiesa to the Scuola of the Saint to observe the swordplay and bravura in the painting of our Tintoretto!"[82] The metaphorical references to sword fighting frequently found in the *Carta del navegar pitoresco*[83] are not, however, empty rhetoric, for they vividly call to mind the image of Tintoretto at work. Drawing swiftly with the medium of paint the white lines used to contour, mark, and sketch out his images, he seems possessed of a bravura very like that of a swordsman.[84]

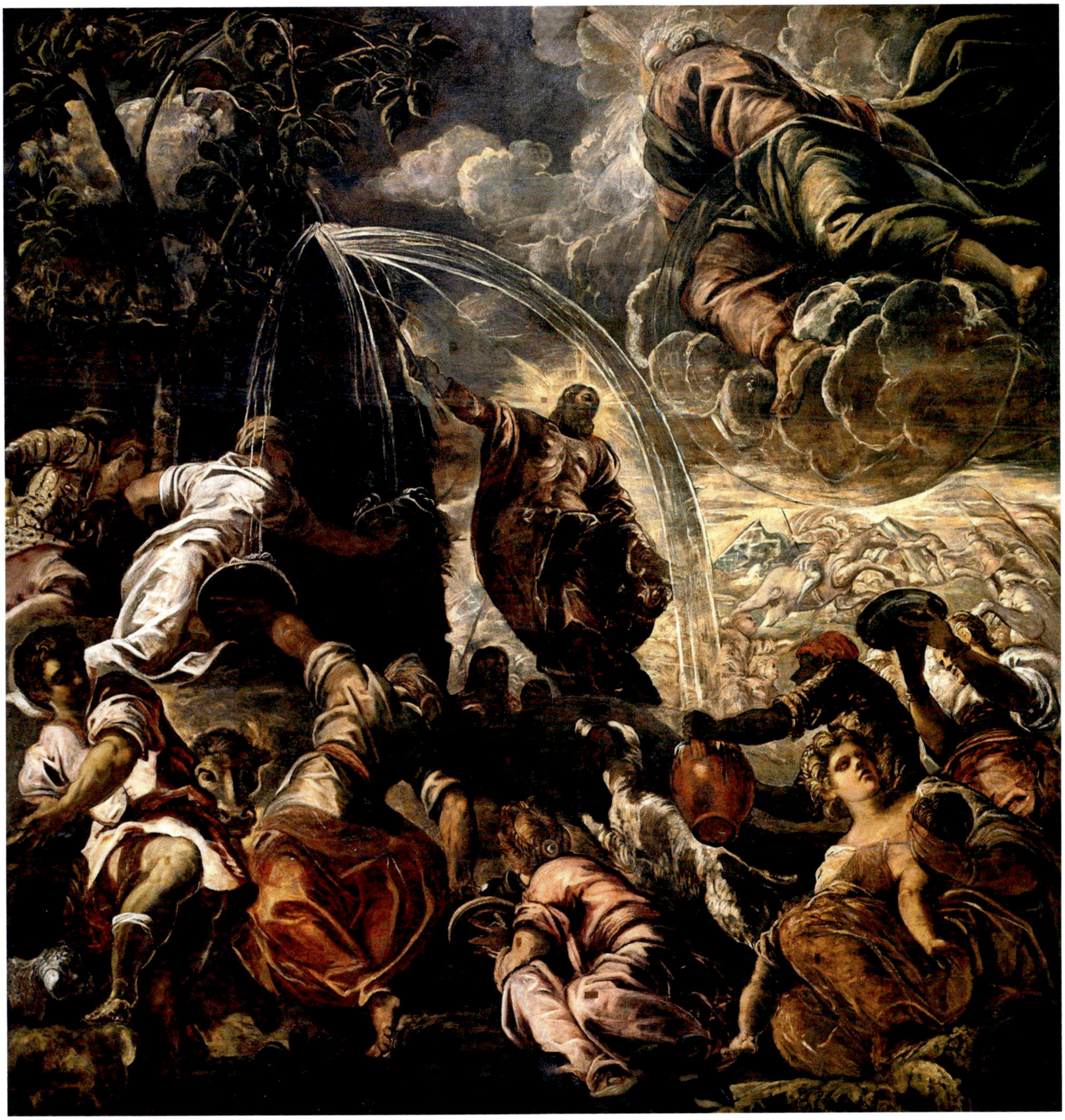

Boschini's image of Tintoretto as a swashbuckling painter fighting his way to a new art of painting, a "true paladin" who struggles against all warriors present and past and exacts more injury on his opponents the harder he is attacked,[85] is not the author's invention. Fifty years earlier, in *Il franetico savio ovvero il Tasso*, Alessandro Guarini had compared Torquato Tasso with Tintoretto (and Tintoretto in turn with Dante).[86] He characterized the artistic temperament of the latter as follows: "As quick with his hand as with his ingenuity, but quick like a good fencer with art, who

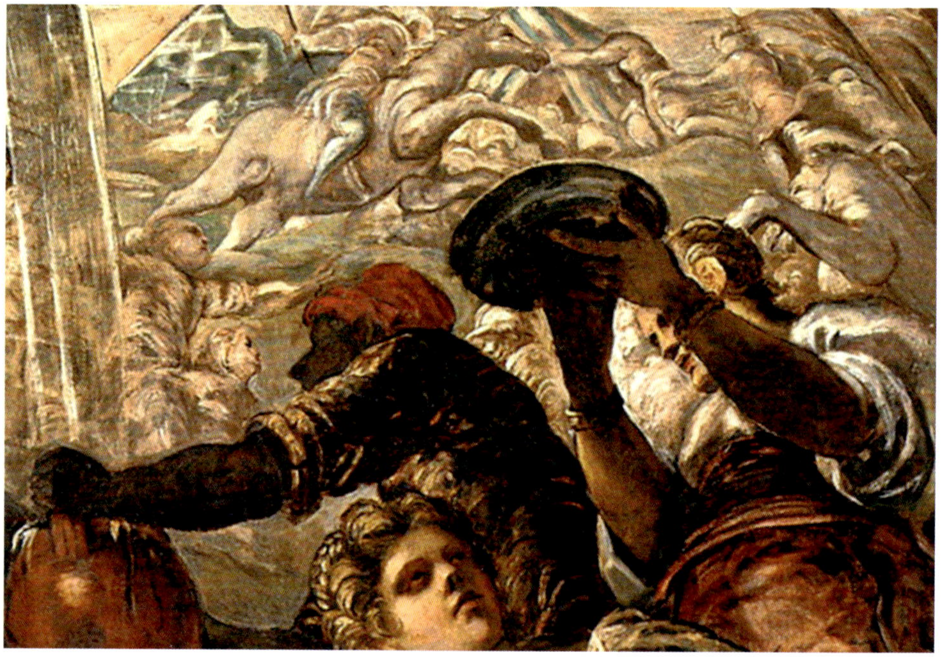

94
Detail of fig. 93 [*Moses Strikes Water from the Rock*].

with only two brushstrokes makes all appear full of life, whereas others touch and retouch a thousand times, hardly managing to make an outline."[87]

Nor was Guarini the first to link Tintoretto's swift and efficient "fencing with brushstrokes,"[88] a practice that required an equal contribution from hand and mind, with the idea of prontezza. During Tintoretto's lifetime, Francesco Sansovino in his 1561 guide to Venice affixed to the artist's name the words *tutto spirito, tutto prontezza*, thereby at one stroke invoking both his intellectual and practical abilities.[89] When Sansovino attests that Tintoretto's hand is accompanied by a quick intellect,[90] he refers to a concept of mastery previously formulated in the earliest art-theoretical treatise, *De pictura* (1435/6), written by the architect and art theorist Leon Battista Alberti (1404–1472): "Talent [*ingenium*] roused and stimulated by practice turns easily and readily to work, and the hand swiftly follows when guided by a sure and ordered judgment."[91] Alberti defines *ingenium* as being *accinctum expeditumque* (armed and ready for battle) and makes an unmistakable connection between creativity and warfare.[92]

THE ART OF FENCING

In aesthetic discourse, martial tropes have a long history stretching back to antiquity. Quintilian's widely read treatise on the education of the orator compares different oratory styles to the various ways men handle their weapons (one always fights with the tip of his sword, the other puts his full weight into the blow),[93] and advises keeping one's "weapons" polished and clean from dust and rust, so that their brilliance will threaten the enemy's eyes and mind. But this shininess, he explains, is not like that of gold and silver (in other words, not of material worth), which is powerless and more dangerous for the owner than for any foe;[94] "brilliance" here is not a superficial quality but an indication of preparedness (and thus of spiritual worth). Quintilian compares the power of speech to muscular strength, but warns against modeling oneself after the "athlete's bulging muscles" and recommends instead emulating the "soldier's strong arms."[95] A trained body is not in itself the goal of exercise, but rather improved physical stamina that will enable one to take action at a moment's notice. Judgment is needed; no matter how rapid the response is required, a combatant does not strike without a plan. In his *Metaphysics,* Aristotle tellingly illustrates his critique of praxis without principles with a comparison to "untrained soldiers in a battle, who rush and often strike good blows, but without science."[96]

Interestingly, the training necessary to prevent warfare from becoming mere savagery, a blind acting out of aggression, is the same as the training that turns craft into art. The first influential treatise on single combat, Camillo Agrippa's *Trattato di scienza d'arme* (1553), was motivated by the desire to condense the "science of arms" to a manageable "language" in the form of an alphabet of moves or "guards"[97] so that opponents could communicate. Just as Alberti proposed learning the alphabet as a primary exercise[98] and determined geometry to be the foundation of painting,[99] Agrippa likewise attempted to base sword fighting on geometric principles.[100] He recommended tracing "all sorts of geometrical figures—circles, squares, triangles, octagons, and so on" in the air with a wooden stave (fig. 95).[101] Several illustrations in the first book depict abstract geometric figures that hover in front of a single fencer and seem to stand in for a potential exchange of blows with an adversary, but the text provides no further instructions that would explain their abstract design, its different lines and their order. This shortcoming is discussed in the appendix of the treatise in a dialogue, where the playwright Annibale Caro cautions Agrippa against publishing these illustrations because they could confuse the reader. Agrippa responds that the geometric figures could be easily produced with the aid of a forked stick, but he still refrains from relating them to the four specific guards that he sees as basic principles of the art of fencing. In the main text of the treatise, Agrippa only states that lowering the point of the sword to the

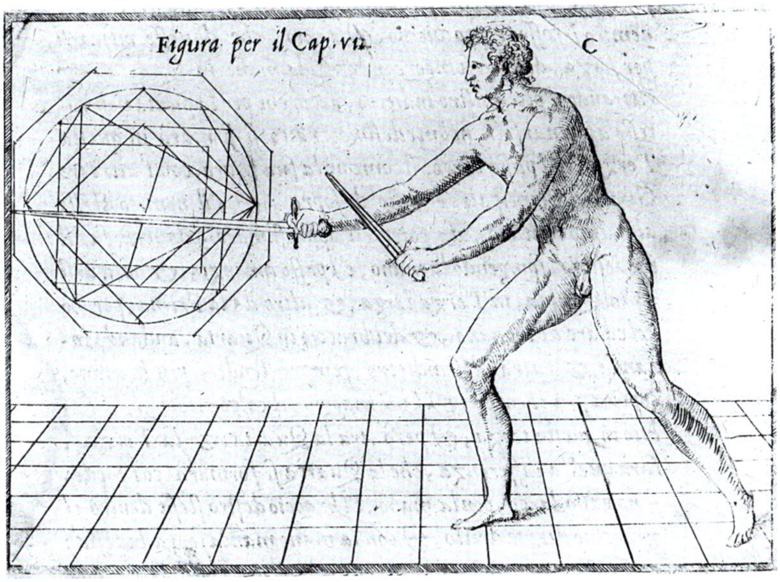

95
Camillo Agrippa, *Trattato di scienza d'arme. Et un dialogo in detta materia,* 1568, page 20. National Central Library of Rome.

The "one-day-painting" as an artistic feat became the preeminent topos for mastery in seventeenth-century vitae, as numerous anecdotes in the writings of the period attest.[20] Passeri's praise of Cortona's ceiling painting in the Barberini palace as "a wonderful work of great study and effort, worthy of highest praise for being so creative in invention, copious in composition, diligent; and truly marvelous, lavish, and beautiful in ornamentation" culminates in the paradoxical assertion that "it is carried out with such mastery of the brush that it seems as if it were all painted in one day" (see fig. 81).[21]

Giambattista Langetti, described by Zanetti as possessing *brio di pennello, buon maneggio di colore, forza e vivacità*,[22] is said to have easily completed a bravura piece—a beautiful half-length figure of a philosopher—with great *prontezza* in a single morning, for which he exacted a goodly sum from his admirers (*dilettanti innamorati*).[23] A *speditezza del suo pennello* allowed Guercino, who "worked in a manner only slightly more than *alla prima*, meaning sketching and immediately finishing,"[24] to conclude a figure of God the Father in one night by torchlight.[25] His colleague Alessandro Tiarini commented on this feat: "Signor Gio. Francesco, other painters make what they can, but you make what you want."[26] Salvator Rosa painted so fast that he often finished a medium-sized painting in one day.[27] It was said of Matteo Verona that "[i]n the morning he sketched the figures, then dried them in the sun, and before evening completed them."[28]

On December 2, 1690, at a memorial held in honor of Claude Vignon at the Académie royale de peinture et de sculpture, one of the speakers recounted the legendary story of how Vignon once "invented and produced a painting in twenty-four hours" after allowing the agreed-upon time for the commission (six months) to lapse without working on it at all. In order to calm the upset client, Vignon made a bet with him that he would have it finished in a day. The painter even allowed his client to change the commission at the last minute; he now wanted a multifigured painting instead of the three-figure composition initially agreed upon. When the man then saw the completed work, instead of finding just a first draft as he expected, he had to "admit that this was one of the best paintings ever done by Vignon. All Paris went to see and admire the painting that gave Vignon the nickname of 'the painter of the wager.'"[29]

It was said that Anthony van Dyck always produced his portraits "in one go." The son of a cloth merchant who was "eager to become famous," Van Dyck went to great lengths to present himself to his clients as their social equal: "In addition to his fine clothing, he adorned his head with plumes and hatbands, wore golden chains crossed on his chest, and kept a retinue of servants, and so, by imitating the pomp of Zeuxis, he drew all eyes to himself." The outcome of his profligate spending, as Bellori reports, was that "for all the riches he had acquired, Anthony van Dyck left little wealth, as he spent everything on the sumptuousness of his way of life, more that of a prince than a painter."[30]

In his *Self-Portrait* as a young man of about twenty-two years, Van Dyck's pretentious posture attests to his aristocratic aspirations (fig. 97).[31] And although his demeanor seems somewhat inconsistent with his astonishingly timid facial expression, shy smile, and the uncertain, wary look in his eyes, the artificiality of his pose and his silky, sumptuous black mantle and soft, velvety, burgundy-red jacket rein-

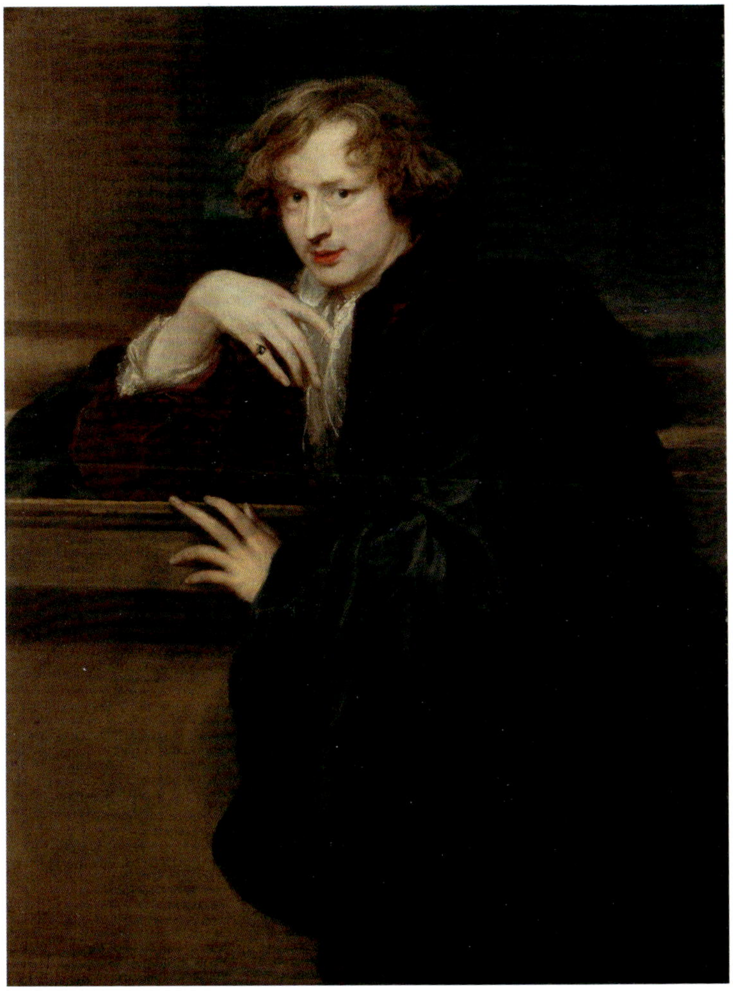

97
Anthony van Dyck, *Self-Portrait*, ca. 1620–1621. Oil on canvas, 119.7 × 87.9 cm. Metropolitan Museum of Art, New York.

force the impression of hauteur. Van Dyck displays courtly sprezzatura not only by means of his pose, which mimics the nonchalant air of his aristocratic clients (and by the prop of a formulaic column as a backdrop), but also in the mannered gesture of his hands with their remarkably long fingers. The index finger of his right hand, rests against his extremely thin, nearly transparent white chemise, its index finger pointing to streaks of white paint laid down on gray imprimatura. The delicate way he touches this diaphanous garment mirrors the fragility of its depiction, which nonetheless gives the stunning impression of costly fabric.

Van Dyck's exorbitant lifestyle included bountiful generosity toward his clients, for whom he provided lavish entertainment: "They went there gladly, as if for recreation, attracted by the variety of the entertainments. . . . When they stayed on, he would provide the most sumptuous repasts for them at his table."[32] Given these no doubt time-consuming dalliances, his quick practice seems more than sensible. He began in the morning, then invited those sitting for him to lunch, and afterward took up his work again, bringing everything to completion "with promptness and great intelligence," as Félibien noted in his résumé. With expert bravura he was usually able to paint two portraits a day, to which he then only added a few finishing touches.[33] His speed, facilitated by a painterly style grounded in practical expertise, enabled Van Dyck to complete even history paintings in a day, as Bellori recounts: "He would calculate how much work he could complete in one day and no more. He employed reflections and cast shadows, and since he would determine the lights in advance, he produced his work on time, with grace and power; in this he was like his master, Rubens, following the same rules and principles of coloring."[34]

As speed of execution became compulsory and artists came to a new understanding of art, the question arises as whether or to what degree this behavior was encouraged by impatient patrons. There are many recorded anecdotes of artists being summoned to contests of speed. Guido Reni, who in contrast to some of his contemporaries did not paint quickly à la Tintoretto and didn't produce *una abbreviatura, e un certo facile Tintoresco*, but according to Malvasia found pleasure in a more meticulous painting style,[35] expressed his outrage over a timed competition announced by the pope (the prize being a golden necklace for the painter who finished his commission first): "How preposterous! Are we Barbary horses, whose greatest and best is deemed the one who first reaches the finish line?"[36]

Arnold Houbraken records the story of an artistic race against time held for the amusement of aristocratic patrons. It came about when the German animal and landscape painter Philipp Peter Roos (1657–1706), who had moved from Frankfurt to Rome in 1677 and was elected a Virtuoso del Pantheon in 1683,[37] was summarily challenged to take on a timed bravura piece:

> The imperial emissary Duke Martinitz and General Roos, a Swede and famous duelist, were talking to each other in Rome about the great speed [*vaardigheit*] of our painter [Philipp Peter Roos]. This seemed impossible to General Roos and consequently, they decided to wager a number of golden pistols, whereby Martinitz was obliged to prove to the General that the painter Roos could complete a painting before they concluded a certain card game, which usually took half an hour. Our painter, who was not far away, was summoned and asked if he would be willing to undertake the challenge, and when he answered yes, they told him he could begin. Palette, paints, easel, and a small board called a *tela di testa* by the Romans, large enough to paint a human head on, were brought into the room and Roos began to work, the others to play; but the game was not yet over when our quick Mercurius stood up and presented his picture as proof that he had won. He had painted two or three goats or sheep, and a half-figure with the usual requisites of a landscape [*met hun voeglyk bywerk of lantschap*], this to the wonderment [*verwondering*] of the Swedish general who acknowledged the loss of his bet.[38]

The alacrity with which Roos complied with their request to produce what was surely an artistically dubious specimen of his talent is startling. Orlandi, in his *Abecedario pittorico* (1753), also mentions this contest and states that Roos, also known as Rosa di Tivoli, was able to please everyone with his great quickness.[39] His speed, which inspired his nickname "Markurius" (Mercury) in the Schildersbent [40]—the band of Dutch artists in Rome to which Roos belonged—is also emphasized by Nicola Pio, who praises the painter as "a man of great spirit, nice appearance, good behavior, and great bravura in his paintbrush"; because of the rapid execution of his subjects with "such boldness and resolution," he was also nicknamed "Il Fulmine" (lightning).[41] His willingness to measure his pace against the duration of a card game was not due, however, to a zeal for work. Ticozzi relates that Roos was more interested in hunting than painting, even though "the extraordinary effortlessness of his brush fills the art dealers' shops with his landscapes."[42]

LUCA GIORDANO AND *IL FAR PRESTO*

The Neapolitan painter Luca Giordano (1634–1705) likewise rejected a detail-oriented and time-consuming painting practice in order to cultivate prestezza. His capacity to complete an enormous number of works and accept every commission he received was due to "the speed of his brush; for a thousand times he was observed painting a half-figure in less than an hour, beautiful and finished, or sometimes a Madonna with Child."[43] Due to his storied speed, his name is linked in the literature to Tintoretto and other Venetian painters.[44] According to Bellori, his colleagues Carlo Cignani, Carl Loth, and Carlo Maratta called him "the Veronese and Tintoretto of modern times."[45] Later art historiography also links the practice of this Neapolitan directly to Venetian painting culture. Luigi Lanzi, in his *Storia pittorica della Italia*, writes that over time it has become a customary expression of "modern style" to paint "with a certain carelessness [*con certo sprezzatura*] as some call it and [which they] attribute to Giordano and several Venetians."[46] Antonio Maria Zanetti even categorizes Luca Giordano as a "Venetian" in his *Istoria della pittura veneziana* (1797). Zanetti, who praises in equal measure Giordano's quickness and erudition, explains that he is numbered with the Venetians due to his ability to use the brush in such a candid and intentional manner as to shock his artist colleagues (*i professori*),[47] here repeating a formula previously applied to Tintoretto. According to legend, Giordano's father, a painter as well as his son's first teacher, spurred him on to do his best with the words "Luca, make haste" (*Luca, fa presto*).[48] This eventually became his nickname,[49] personalizing by conjugation the infinitive phrase *far presto*, a term used disapprovingly in Armenini's *De' veri precetti della pittura* (1586) to refer to hurried painting deemed suitable only for ephemeral festival decorations.[50] The negative significance of *far presto* is also evident in Filippo Baldinucci's *Vocabolario toscano dell'arte del disegno*, where he defines the verb *acciabbattare* as "to do anything in a coarse manner, to botch; derived from slippers, worn-out shoes; and our artists do this in coarse works, [those made] without consideration and, as we would say, with a mind to work hastily and badly [*con animo di far presto e male*]."[51] The "Fa presto" directly associated with Giordano's name became an established cognomen in art literature and we can also find it used for painters who came after him.[52]

De' Dominici's story of an altarpiece made by Giordano for the Jesuit Order gives us a detailed description of one dramatic incident featuring fast work. Giordano had repeatedly delayed starting the commission, until his patrons finally threatened to penalize him. Under enormous pressure he then completed the painting extremely quickly: "This sensational news spread throughout all of Naples, and suddenly the church was full of artists and aficionados who came to view the masterpiece that was a hastily but excellently executed work of art, completed in one and a half days and one night."[53] This legendary act of bravura not only pacified his angry patron, but also swayed other viewers, and the church where it was displayed became a prime locus of art. Giordano's painting depicted Francis Xavier, but homage was paid instead to the "depicter."

Speed became a quality that allowed artistic achievement to be quantitatively measured. This led to the theatrical demonstrations of rapid execution we have described and also to numerous publically staged competitions in which two painters strove against each other to prove their superior skill. Palomino records another legend concerning Luca Giordano and a competitive outperformance between him and the Spanish painter Claudio Coello (1624–1693). The goal of their contest was to complete in twenty-four hours *The Battle of the Archangel St. Michael against Lucifer,* a work commissioned by the Spanish royal court. When Coello realized he would not finish in the allotted time, he was allegedly so stricken with grief that he died of a broken heart. Palomino voices great skepticism about this legend, but he does credit Luca Giordano's with the ability to paint incredibly fast and accepts a causal connection between the arrival of the acclaimed high-speed painter at the Spanish court and the demise of Coello. He attributes Coello's downfall and death more to the emotional pressure that Giordano's presence placed on him as a threat to his position at court than to any legendary contest. In fact, Palomino introduces himself as an eyewitness in order to discount the story's veracity: "In truth, it is all rumor, for I witnessed everything and there was neither such a contest nor the twenty-four hours. The king even ordered that no one should disturb the painter." According to Palomino, Giordano did not even produce an oil sketch in twenty-four hours, much less the painting, which took more than twenty-four days. He could, however, verify "that Giordano painted the head of St. Michael in one morning, but it was not finished."[54]

De' Dominici gives an account of this same painting, but with some variations: Coello, motivated by jealousy to discredit his Italian colleague, convinced Charles II to put the new painter to the test. This entailed painting *all'improvviso* a composition containing nudes. Doubts about Giordano's *alla prima* competence had stoked rumors that he relied on sketches after classical masters, which provided him with a ready-made image bank.[55] To see if these accusations were true, the king had a canvas set up measuring 15 hands in height, where in his presence the artist was asked to portray the Archangel Michael driving Lucifer and his followers from paradise. Giordano immediately set to work. He made a few marks on the canvas, whose purpose was unintelligible to the observers and even to his rival Coello. In the upper pictorial field he placed St. Michael, who would bring about the devil's fall by the mere act of displaying a banner with the words "Quis ut Deus;" and on the right, a "gloria of the most beautiful angels." Then he set about painting. He began with St. Michael and some of the more central demons, setting out only the light and dark tints of their flesh and establishing the surrounding color field, while leaving their faces as blotches without distinguishing the eyes, noses, mouths, or other parts. "Then the painter began to sulk and intended that the king would grow weary of observing." And the king did become bored, after three hours. He withdrew from the room with his courtiers and a triumphant Coello to discuss what they had witnessed. The king complained that his expectations had been high, but he had seen nothing. While they were gone, Giordano harmonized his colors, which were already set in their proper places, and brought all the parts of the painting together with dazzling speed and care in the short time allotted. When the king returned and saw how beautifully St. Michael was executed and how ugly and fearsome the devils, he was amazed and turned to the shocked and shortly thereafter deceased Coello with the words: "This is the best painter in Naples, Spain, and the entire world."[56]

TO WITNESS PAINTING

The king's desire to witness the painting process reflects an established custom at the Spanish court. According to Palomino, Philip IV had decreed that a studio be set up for Velázquez in the northern wing of the royal palace. Here the king had a seat placed for himself so that in his leisure time he could observe Velázquez at work,[57] just as his great-grandfather, Emperor Charles V, had watched Titian paint whenever he could spare the time from the numerous wars that monopolized his attention.[58] Charles II of Spain, accustomed to observing Coello at work,[59] offered Giordano a high sum and prestigious position at court not only because he wanted his paintings, of which he already possessed several before Giordano's arrival in Spain, but because he expressly wished to watch Giordano paint.[60]

This habit of sovereigns vis-à-vis their artists was widespread by the sixteenth century,[61] but its roots reach far into the past. Alexander the Great is the ultimate point of reference.[62] In his popular *Dialogo della pittura,* Lodovico Dolce tells of the military commander and almighty ruler Alexander receiving great pleasure from art, and of how he would often visit the studio of Apelles to spend many hours with the painter, discussing and watching him paint (*ragionar seco domesticamente et in vederlo dipingere*).[63] By Giordano's time, royal interaction with painters—visitation as leisurely pastime—was already commonplace. Roger de Piles reports that Maria de' Medici "who loved painting and also liked to practice her own drawing skills, desired that Rubens would create two works for the Medici Cycle in her presence so she could have the pleasure of seeing him paint."[64] The custom ultimately became almost routine. It was said of Salvator Rosa that he painted at the bedside of an indisposed prince to provide him with a source of diversion.[65]

If demonstrations of skill were to double as entertainment, then it was critical that the artist amaze. As a general rule, it would not do for royal spectators to become bored. Giordano's near defeat at the Spanish court, which according to De' Dominici was only averted in miraculous fashion, conveys also how strongly public interest in an artist's work depended on an understanding of painterly praxis. For Giordano's triumph was not effected by his execution, which actually bored the king (whose eye had been schooled in the praxis of Coello), but instead by its unexpected result. It was not what the king saw, but what he did *not* see that secured success.

It is questionable whether Giordano's initially disappointing performance was a ruse to intentionally bore Charles II, even though De' Dominici construes it as such in order to heighten the drama and make Giordano the man of the moment. It seems more likely a misunderstanding; the king simply had no prior knowledge of Giordano's method of painting and did not know what to expect. His style was familiar, however, to another of his princely patrons, Cosimo III de' Medici. De' Dominici reports that the Grand Duke of Tuscany visited Giordano at the house of marchese Andrea de Rossi to commission a ceiling fresco from him. He found the artist standing in front of a canvas 4 hands high with nothing on it except the imprimatura. When Giordano asked what he should paint, the Grand Duke permitted him to choose any subject whatever. He then requested a chair, because his main reason for visiting was to watch Giordano paint. Giordano then set to work on the *macchia*. "With a few marks of white chalk [he developed] an idea, began to paint it, driving the figures back with light and shadow, and then perfected the different parts"—all of this to the great delight of Cosimo, who was transfixed at Giordano's performance for four hours without pause and in the end awarded him with high praise: "Marvelous painter, created by God for the satisfaction of princes."[66] The grand duke ultimately requested to keep in his possession this *bozzetto* for the *Allegoria della pacificazione tra fiorentini e fiesolani*, in remembrance of the astonishing speed with which it was made (*in memoria della stupenda velocità con cui era stata fatta*).[67]

Giordano's *bravuroso* tempo is the subject of yet another anecdote by De' Dominici. It tells of a meeting between Giordano and the virtuoso French draftsman Raymond Lafage (1656–1684), who had commissioned Giordano to transform one of his *all'antica* drawings using "his dazzling and modern paints" (*con suoi vaghi, e moderni colori*). Giordano declined the request, but proposed instead to teach Lafage how to paint so that he could do it himself.[68] Giordano's rejection of Lafage's initial offer is interesting. It likely arose in reaction to the common understanding of the period that painting was subordinate in status to drawing. Consider, for example, Michelangelo's disparaging comment about Sebastiano del Piombo, the artist who often translated Michelangelo's preliminary drawings into paintings: "Painting with oils [is] an art for women, and for well-off and lazy people like fra' Bastiano." Vasari, who recorded this statement, also tells us that Sebastiano's colleagues had reproached him for giving up painting after he joined a religious brotherhood, to which he replied: "Now that I have the means to live, I no longer wish to do anything more, for there are men of genius in the world today who do in two months what I used to do in two years."[69] Vasari himself shared this view: "Whereas earlier masters needed six years for one picture, today they make six works in one year."[70]

Giordano placed a canvas 4 hands high on an easel, upon which Lafage drew a design for the worship of the brazen serpent "with such goodness and perfection as one can only imagine by such an expert draftsman."[71] Giordano then tried to teach him about color tones and how to mix them, without success. Realizing the futility of his efforts, he finally turned to Lafage and said: "My monsù, do you see what a difference there is between a painter and a draftsman? For anyone who applies himself can draw well, but not everyone can paint equally well. I am indeed quite pleased to be Luca Giordano, and not Monsù Lafage or any other draftsman in the world. So therefore look what a painter does that a draftsman cannot, as you now realize!" He then took up his palette and brush and painted, *pieno di bizzarria*, the worship of the brazen serpent "with a wonderful harmony of color and exceptional bliss." He joked that he would add to the antique scene something unique and modern, and in the center produced a group of figures being bitten by snakes and caught in their coils. (With this addition he seems to have challenged Lafage's artistic model Michelangelo and his spectacular depiction of *The Brazen Serpent* on the Sistine Ceiling.) Lafage was duly impressed and acknowledged Giordano as the world's best painter "because of his quick intellect and his rapid hand in execution" (*a cagione della menta pronta, e della mano veloce nell'esguire*); he also offered his apologies and tried—without success—to keep the painting for himself. Giordano's display of skill was not a rebuke of a minor painter, but rather a lesson to a renowned virtuoso of the limits of his discipline.

Further to Raymond Lafage, Arnold Houbraken shares the following story about another bravura piece. Lafage, who lived in Paris, was invited to Brabant by the art dealer Jan van der Bruggen to meet a local group of painters.[72] When van der Bruggen introduced him to his artist colleagues with the words "Lafage is in our company," one of them pointed at the artist and asked, "Is this *la Fagie*? It sure looks like him." Their disrespect galvanized Lafage. He answered: "It is indeed I, and if you want me to prove it to you, bring me paper and ink."[73] Houbraken continues:

> Lafage asked what they would like him to draw. One of the group called out he should depict the demise of Pharaoh in the Red Sea. The others objected to this request; they felt it impolite to require from their guest a work that would take the entire evening. But no sooner was it said than Lafage had already begun, to the astonishment of all. He sketched here an arm, there a leg, here a head, there a foot, then several groups in the background and others in the foreground, such that in a short time the entire sheet was littered all about with limbs of humans and horses. Finally, the chaos of entangled corpses had grown into an artistic, well-ordered drawing and was finished in two hours to the astonishment of all; in it he portrayed the downfall of Pharaoh in the Red Sea and the armies, horses, and chariots with which he had pursued Moses.[74]

Lafage's desire to live up to both the *fama* that preceded him as well as the *invidia* that followed on its heels (and the two factors met in this particular challenge) seems to have been the engine behind his art. His extempore bravura piece served as an effective way to introduce himself to the unknown painters. Pierre-Jean Mariette (1694–1774) in his *Abecedario* remarks that Lafage was so dependent for his livelihood and self-esteem on impressing witnesses with stupendous drawing performances that he eagerly accepted challenges on any proposed theme "with great promptness and minimal preparation."[75] Mariette also reports another event that accords with Houbraken's anecdote: "Lafage was so proficient [*si practique*] in drawing that it was all the same to him where on a figure he began drawing; sometimes he started with the big toe, at other times with the navel, or at any other place one pointed out to him. Sometimes he would be seen drawing a figure in this manner in one stroke without raising his pen."[76]

No such drawings are extant from Lafage, but several studies attributed to Agostino Carracci (1557–1602), depicting body parts such as a foot, heads, or ears, drawn in a calligraphic manner, illustrate that bravura drawing techniques of this sort were indeed practiced.[77] The simple virtuoso exercise of drawing a figure with a single line in fact may have had important art-theoretical implications in Agostino's and Lafage's time. A written account of a similar performance, this one by Salvator art a noble occupation linked the recognition of art to the exhibition of the creative act, which always risked disappointing the art devotee, and perhaps also devastating the artist.

Agostino Carracci is reported to have taken a bolder line with an annoying client who "would come up very close to Agostino while he was working, hovering over him and fussing around in such a way that in the end it was impossible for Agostino to work his brush properly." Instead of panicking like Garofalo, he went on the offensive:

> Agostino eventually grabbed a large hard brush, which he thrust at the canvas with such force it pierced through to the other side, and then, pulling it downward, made such a large gash that the whole picture was virtually cut in two, so that he could pass through the center and emerge from the other side. Agostino's excuse, when the patron flew into a rage over this piece of foolishness, was that there was no room left for him to paint unless he made some for himself behind the canvas.[92]

Agostino here ironically evokes Apelles, who hid behind a canvas so he could overhear what his studio visitors were saying about his work. He may also have had in mind the legend of the ignorant shoemaker rebuked by an annoyed Apelles, who sprang from his hiding place after the shoemaker overstepped the bounds of his expertise by commenting on some aspect of the artist's work that had nothing to do with his depiction of sandals.

A self-portrait attributed to Nicolas Régnier (1588–1667) comes with a story that suggests how strongly painting under the gaze of a patron could affect the finished product. The work in question again manifests the painter's social ambitions (fig. 98). Elegantly dressed in a coat and wide-brimmed hat, Régnier depicts himself in the act of painting his patron's portrait; the portrait, supported on the easel, is so lifelike it seems to emerge from the tondo. The inevitable foreshortening of the portrait due to the easel's position is cancelled out, so to speak, by the turned face of the portrayed. Painter and model look at us with an attentive gaze. The painter's black clothing makes him recede into the background and his corporality is flattened into the darkness of his surroundings, only a single bright area of light brings forth the contour of his shoulder area. In contrast, his model, Marchese Vincenzo Giustiniani, is more gently embedded in his surroundings. His saturated red mantle and beige fur collar communicate his physical presence. His clothing, as yet unfinished, is set out in bravuroso strokes of the brush generating shadows and ridges of light, placements that prefigure the velvet cloth's materiality. The emergence of mimetic materialization increases in an upward progression: facial features gain in detail and intricacy; the shininess of the man's hair, in contrast to the fur, evidence artistic maturity, an impression deepened by the image's phase-like development.

The lowest region of the portrait is cut off by the artist's palette, which is tilted toward the beholder and testifies to an economic use of materials. There is only a modest assortment of paints, and these in small quantities. The painter's hand, which seems to come forward toward the viewer more than either of the faces, and in this respect compensates for the painter's turned-away body, slips in between painter and model and in this central position captures the attention of the beholder. The little finger is elegantly raised; the index finger and thumb loosely grasp the shaft of the brush under whose bristles an ocher dab of pigment resonates with the color of the fur collar.

With a look of concentration, the painter scrutinizes his model. He compares the "original" to his depiction on the easel, the same depiction the patron must also be intently observing. Giustiniani is the model shown in the portrait and at the same time, as the intended recipient of the commissioned painting, he is the sovereign observer of the scene. Two gazes, that of the artist studying his sitter and that of the sitter, who verifies the resemblance of his image and attentively watches the artist at work, meet in the gaze of the beholder (now not only Giustiniani's, but also ours).

Régnier's self-portrayal acknowledges and responds to the scrutiny of the marchese. It functions in this sense like a mirror, not for the artist himself (who indeed must have used a mirror in the execution of this painting) but for his patron. The scene-dominating gaze of the connoisseur unites with that of the artist, who throughout the production of the painting likewise occupies Giustiniani's

98
Nicolas Régnier, *Self-Portrait*, 1623–1624. Oil on canvas, 110.5 × 137.5 cm. Harvard University, Fogg Art Museum, Cambridge.

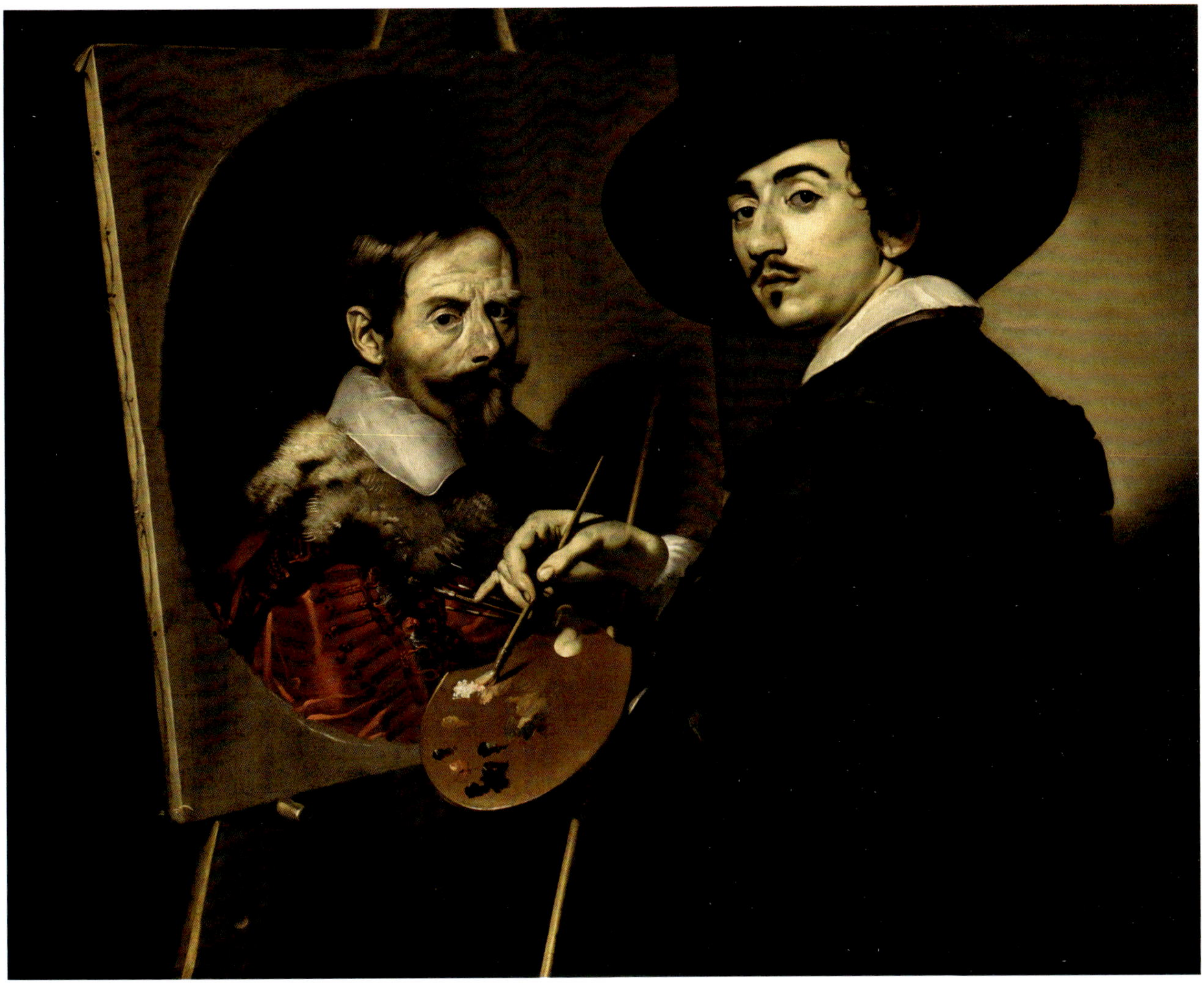

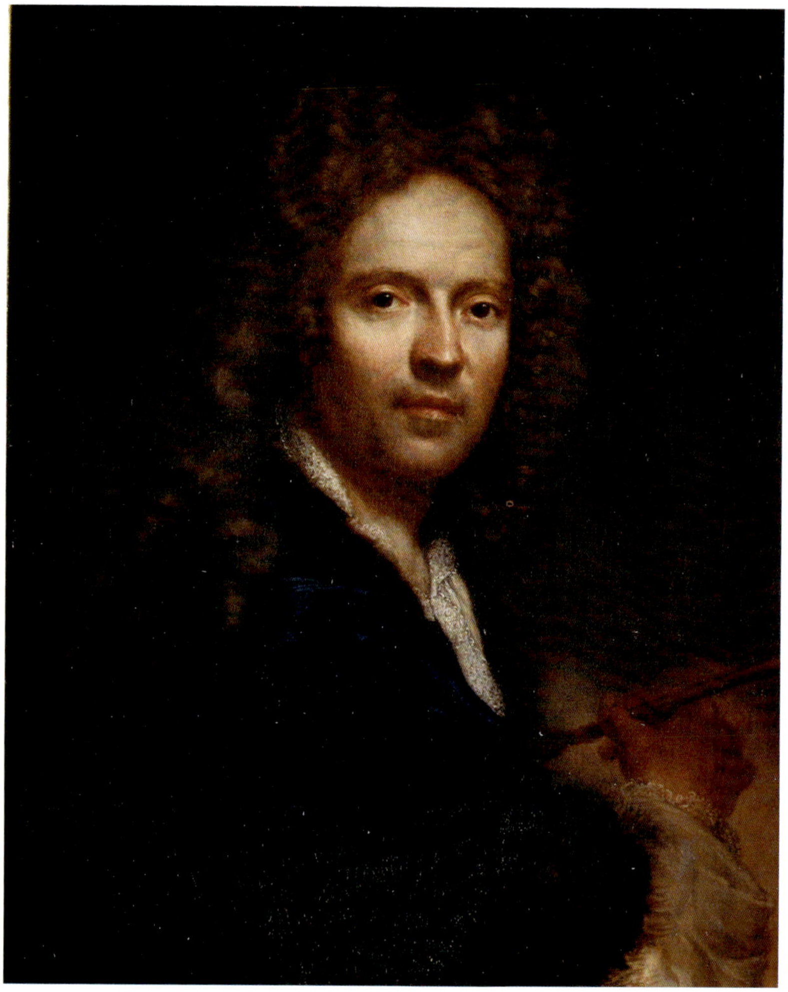

99
Niccolò Cassana, *Self-Portrait*, ca. 1695. Oil on canvas, 72.5 × 58.5 cm. Galleria degli Uffizi, Collezione degli Autoritratti, Florence.

standpoint as observer. Ingeniously reflected in this complex double-portrait is the functional dependence of the portrayed on the portrayer, doubtless the reason why the patron keeps a watchful eye on the artist, as well as the existential dependence of the portrayer on the portrayed, who determines whether the artist is successful or not. In the work, the two heads are the same size, but their eyes are not placed at the same height. The superiority of the painter as he works is perceptible in his slightly elevated position, which in turn compels the beholder to assume the portrait-sitter's perspective.

An anecdote about Tintoretto illustrates how the social intricacies of sitting for a portrait can be mastered with bravura while the painter remains in command of his own autonomy.[93] According to the story, a foreign prince wished "to have his portrait painted by the rapid brush [of Tintoretto]." Tintoretto was alerted beforehand that the prince traveled in the company of an artist in disguise who wished to surreptitiously study the painterly technique of the Venetians without being recognized. As the sitting began, and before the prince had even made himself comfortable, Tintoretto finished the portrait swiftly, and quite slyly, in one go. The incognito painter, to whom this artful stunt or "capriccio" was addressed, considered Tintoretto's manner of painting miraculous (*una magia*) because its execution was invisible, "and Tintoretto was pleased to the depths of his heart by his skillful demonstration of his own artistic ingenuity." More than anything else, the words used by the patron in recognition of Tintoretto's talent—"You are in painting a terrifying commander-in-chief.... This is truly a stroke of bravura. Such are the [brush]strokes of the Venetians!"[94]—communicated to the artist that he had delivered precisely what the prince had desired to see.

In the course of the seventeenth century, the pictorial trope of painting practice—that is, of painting a picture of an unfinished picture still in progress, as in the fiction of Giustiniani's portrayal, became increasingly en vogue. A curious example is a self-portrait from the Galleria degli Autoritratti by Niccolò Cassana (1659–1714),[95] an artist whose turbulent character was introduced in the first chapter of this book (fig. 99). Cassana was subject to bouts of rage while painting and, as previously described, he would follow these fits by making appropriate corrections to his canvas: "He realized what was missing, took up his brush once again, corrected and renewed and incorporated that which was lacking. And thus it continued. He was either pleased or gave himself over to great rampages." His biographer Carlo Giuseppe Ratti explained this unusual, if not outright unhinged, behavior as incited by the artist's ambition: "So great was his zeal to be better than good."[96]

Artistic ambition was also clearly a factor behind Cassana's persistent pressuring of the art dealer Del Teglia to arrange for the inclusion of his work in Cosimo III de' Medici's (1642–1723) Collezione degli Autoritratti. This collection of famous self-portraits initiated by Cardinal Leopoldo de' Medici (1617–1675) and continued by his nephew Cosimo III, was considered one of the most illustrious showcases for artistic self-representation. With a self-portrait in the Galleria, usually given to the collector as a gift, a painter could number himself among the greats, those whose names and faces were deemed worthy of remembrance by future generations, and thus secure in his own lifetime a place in the Olympus of immortal artists. The gallery made a significant contribution to the artistic development of the self-portrait genre, for each of the works had to prove itself against the others if it was to stand out in these ranks of supreme achievement. In his correspondence with the Grand Duke Cosimo III, Del Teglia reported annoyance with Cassana, with whom he associated "more smoke than fame" (*più fumo che fama*).[97]

Cassana's self-portrait contains a clever iconographic joke: the artist is depicted setting his hand and paintbrush to his own image. Whereas all the details of his appearance are rendered with mimetic precision, the dark background in the right lower corner of the painting dissipates to expose an ocher-colored field. This apparently still unfinished area, tonally distinguished from his hand and arm, is in the process of being filled by Cassana's broad brush. Significantly, he starts to paint at his own outline, which diffuses into the dark background. In this self-referential gesture, the brush points in a peculiar fashion to the body of the painter. Cassana provides a new vehicle whereby the pictured subject can reference his or her own person without losing the meaning a pointing finger would provide. However, now that the painter's instrument has taken the place of the index finger, the symbolic gesture is converted into a practical act: the identity of the painter, which the gesture affirms, produces itself in the moment of painting.

CHAPTER SIX

Economies of Practice

CARLO DOLCI'S EXCESSIVE DILIGENCE

In contrast to Régnier's and Cassana's celebration of painterly potential, a self-portrait by the Florentine artist Carlo Dolci (1616–1686) displays an ambivalent approach to practice, one that underscores the tedium of the work. The painter depicted himself twice in a piece commissioned for Leopoldo de' Medici's portrait collection (fig. 100). We see him life-size and *en miniature*. The latter takes the form of a simulated "drawing" (a painting of a drawing) held in the right hand of the former and presented by him to the beholder. Dolci's picture within a picture takes on the difficult challenge of constructing an identity across two markedly dissimilar yet corresponding self-portraits.

The dominant, format-filling portrait shows Dolci elegantly dressed with a plain collar of fine white fabric over his black coat, while in the smaller, minutely detailed "drawing" executed in oil paint, he cuts a rather humble figure. The wart awkwardly prominent on his cheek is hidden by the shadow of a lock of hair in the larger, representative image of his doppelgänger. Calligraphed inscriptions frame the drawing's octagonal format, including the work's year of creation (1674), the artist's age (*Di anni 58*), and a dedication to its intended recipient, Cardinal Leopoldo de' Medici, addressed as "the Most Reverend Highness" (*per la Alteza R[everendissi] ma*); the signature, *Io Carlo Dolcj*, is in the shaded right corner. Here, Dolci does not wear the outfit of a burgher, but the modest garments of a working artist. The elaboration of the simulated drawing is so extraordinarily fine that delicately drafted lines are visible as individual strands of the artist's hair, while the "paper's" surface appears to have a powdery quality that imitates the materiality of red chalk and charcoal. This composition held out for our inspection represents, in fact, a meticulously finished cartoon. In it we also see a bundle of artist's implements, composed of four different types of fine hair brushes, fanning out at the left margin. In his right hand, the painter uses a brush truncated by the picture edge, and judging from the visible quill, it must also be a brush made of fine hair. The missing head of his instrument wittily evokes the invisible brushstroke so characteristic of Dolci's *maniera*. He works with an open mouth, a token of his intense concentration. This

100 (FACING)
Carlo Dolci, *Self-Portrait*, 1675. Oil on canvas, 74.5 × 60.5 cm. Galleria degli Uffizi, Collezione degli Autoritratti, Florence.

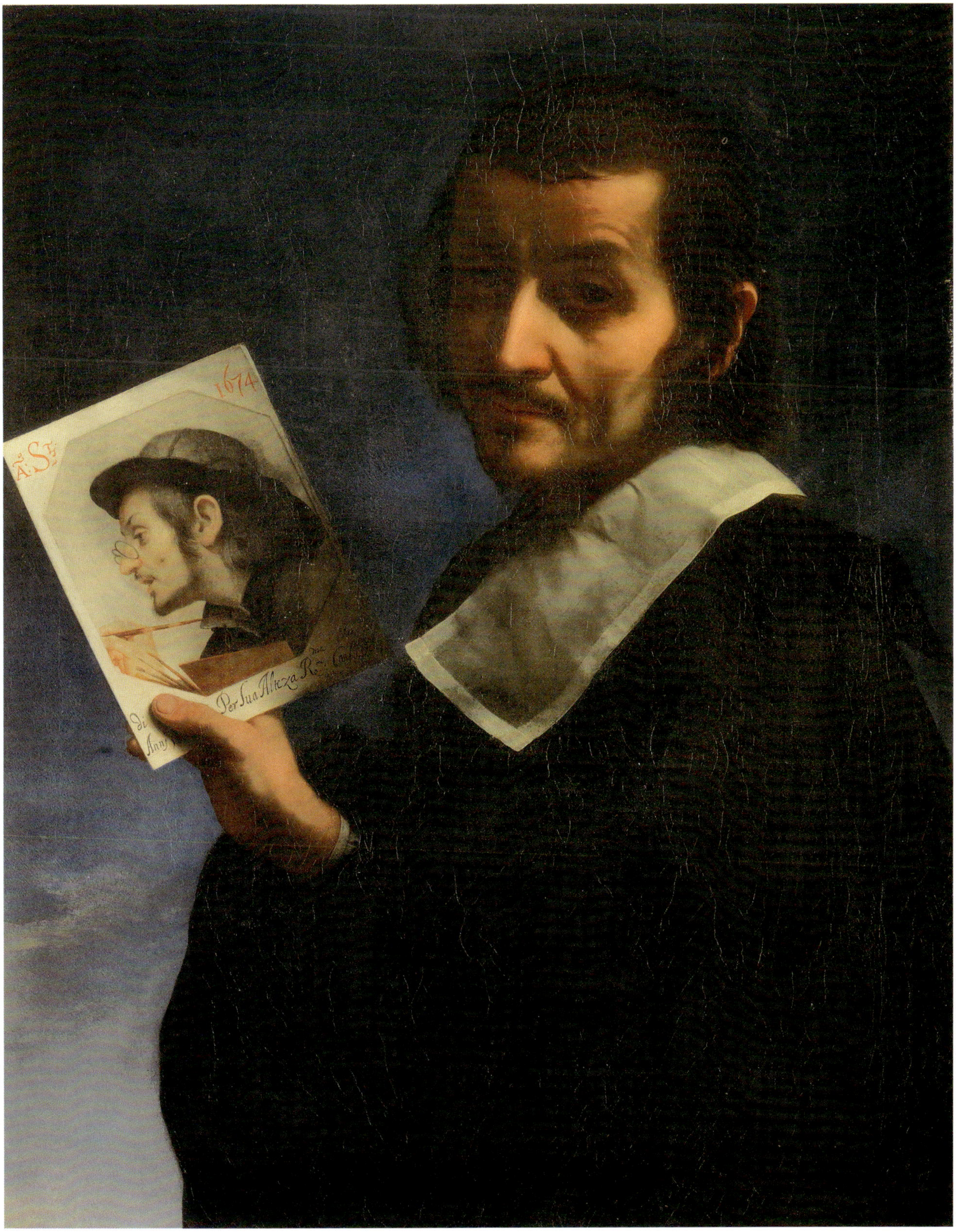
1674

and indeed every element of the drawing speaks of an unpretentious and austere artistic existence of complete sacrifice to one's work, while the larger representational self-portrait mirrors pensive restraint.

There is a correspondence between the way Dolci holds his brush in the simulated cartoon and his cartoon in the larger image. In the latter, Dolci substitutes for his painting instrument a portrait of himself as an artist so involved in his craft that he loses his noblesse. In comparison to Régnier's self-staging, in which painterly activity projects an image of the highest refinement, Dolci's self-portrait in the painted drawing bears no trace of gentility, and the dedication to work that it depicts undermines the model image of a "well-mannered" painter conceived a short time later by Roger de Piles:

> In order to paint gracefully, one should hold the brush as far back [on the shaft] as possible and sit upright in one's chair, with no sense of constraint, at a proper distance to the work. Thus one can work much more freely. In contrast, there is nothing more ungraceful than holding the brush short and pressing one's nose right next to the painting. . . . Those who are just beginning to paint usually fall prey to three mistakes: the first of these consists in using a brush much too small.[1]

The nobility of the artful attitude is created by maintaining the proper distance between body and canvas. Only this stance allows ample space for the artist to operate masterfully.

The nesting of one self-portrait in another deepens the introspective aura of the commissioned work, and Dolci's split self-perception unmistakably adds an element of ironic distance to his own practice. The tired smile that plays around the corners of his mouth, as well as the melancholy displayed in his shaded eyes, are expressions of a contemplative detachment from one's own activity. However, the counterimage of a laboring craftsman presented *en miniature* within the distinguished self-portrait strikes the spectator as a self-reproach which the artist communicates to the beholder. Dolci's "humbling" drawing, as an auxiliary to his dominant self, brings before our eyes the reason for the somber mood resonating in the *colorito* of the artist's face—the extremely tedious work of painting is wearing Dolci down.

Filippo Baldinucci, a childhood friend of the artist who tenderly called him "Carlino" in his *Notizie di Carlo Dolci*, had little sympathy for the unrelenting diligence of Dolci's execution.[2] His brush brought forth *opera rarissime*, but his "extremely patient practice of painting" ultimately prevented him from finishing his works. Baldinucci introduced this grave consequence by way of the eminent antique artist Protogenes, a painter who never knew when to take his hands away from his work, thus employing an *exemplum in malum* (although not for Dolci's highly praised paintings) that had become a topos in Early Modern art theory because it so aptly illustrated a key principle: that economy of artistic labor was a basic constituent of *ars*.[3] Baldinucci distinguished between two kinds of diligence, "experienced" (*diligenza pratica*) and "inexperienced" (*diligenza inesperta*), describing the latter as useless because it comes from an ignorance of painting practice.

At the conclusion of Dolci's biography, Baldinucci relates an incident that provoked a mental breakdown in the artist and led to his death. The Grand Duchesse

Vittoria summoned the painter for an audience to praise him after she received his *Adoration of the Kings*, Dolci's last work. During their conversation, she asked for a painting by Giordano to be brought in, another commission that had also just been completed for her, and asked, "What do you think about this painting, Carlo? Can you believe that it was in reality only made in a few days?" Her question should be understood as a well-intended criticism intended to spur a productive rivalry between the two artists. But Dolci instead fell into a deep depression, tormented by the idea he was "good for nothing in his art,"[4] allegedly refused to eat, and died a short time later. It would seem that Giordano's work, which locates art in prestezza, was dangerous, fatal not only for his Spanish rival Coello, but also for his friend Carlo Dolci.[5] Bellori also recorded Dolci's encounter with the art of Giordano and his tragic end, but in his version the crisis was sparked by the rapidly executed Galleria in the Palazzo Medici Riccardi, which Dolci studied at Giordano's invitation.[6]

Baldinucci's blamed Dolci's melancholy on his timid, fastidious, and anxious nature,[7] taking up a topos formulated earlier in several of Vasari's biographies. Lorenzo di Credi, whose style was so finished and "clean" that all other painting seemed in comparison sketch-like and "impure," was not very productive, as Vasari avers, due to his *fattica incredibile*: he spent too much time on each work, much of it spent mixing his paints in countless gradations of color. It was said that he arranged as many as twenty-five colors on his palette in order from the lightest to darkest tones and used a separate brush for each. This overzealousness was no more praiseworthy, according to Vasari, than an abundance of negligence, because extremes are generally immoral and one should not succumb to them, but observe moderation in all things.[8] The vice of such exaggerated *diligenza* lies in its excessive attention to methods, which take on a life of their own until the artist finally loses control over them. When that happens, the intellectual power of discernment that steers the painting process "from outside" becomes fatigued over time.

There is one object in Dolci's self-portrait that has still gone unmentioned—the artist's eyeglasses, which in the painted drawing are perched on his nose. This optical aid calls attention to the sharp eyesight demanded by his detailed practice, closely linking vision and pictorial execution. By overexerting his eyes Dolci was able to produce a virtually invisible brushstroke, but only with the further aid of a technical instrument superimposed onto and therefore subordinating his own vision.

Interestingly, a self-portrait by Dolci's *advocatus diaboli* Luca Giordano likewise focuses on this prosthesis (fig. 101). Here, however, the evaluating gaze is directed not at the canvas but at the beholder. We take part in the painter's confrontation with his own gaze as somewhat secondary observers. Giordano does not identify himself as an artist in his portrait by displaying this tool of his trade, but instead stages himself, with a penetrating stare passing through his eyeglasses, as the personification of *visus*.[9] Interestingly, the thicknesses of the two lenses differ. The painter's right eye is larger and somewhat more distorted than his left eye. This imbalance is exaggerated by an accented light-to-shadow ratio that divides the face into two halves much more markedly than in Dolci's self-portrait.

The light reflected from the upper area of the black frames and from the edge of the lens at the side of Giordano's nose, builds a coloristic relationship to the

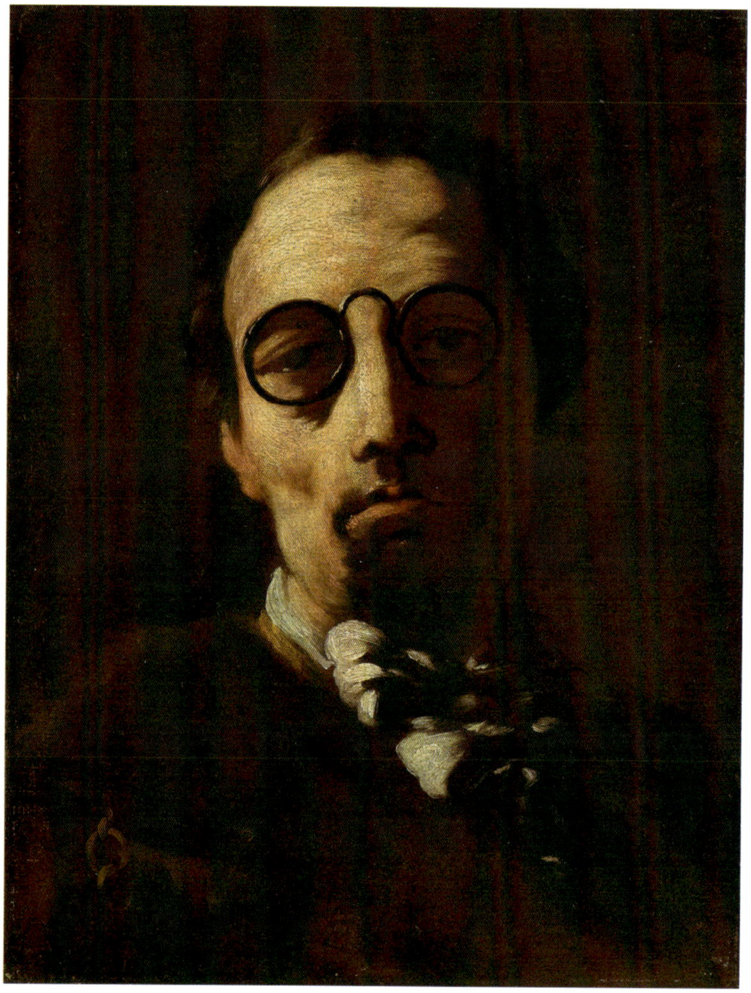

101
Luca Giordano, *Self-Portrait*, ca. 1688. Oil on canvas, 46.8 × 35.3 cm. Staatsgalerie, Stuttgart.

white cravat whose shaded areas are tinted black. The curvilinear knottiness of Giordano's neck band is in eye-catching contrast to Dolci's stiff collar. Whereas a pointed brush was employed for the highlights on the glasses, the soft flowing loops of fabric were painted with a thicker brush. The energetic movements composing the knotwork are clearly visible in the ridges left by the bristles on the picture's surface. Also, none of the flesh areas are fully saturated; rather, the brushstrokes trace and create facial wrinkles, expression, and volume.

How much the paint substance informs these mimetic features is best seen in the traces visible in the neck area, where the materiality of skin, cravat, and outer garment coincide. Giordano's evocation of different materials here avoids diligenza, for operating in that mode would obscure the paint as medium. Instead he boldly showcases the virtuoso speed of his brush before the eye of the beholder. In another self-portrait, created shortly after this one and belonging like Dolci's to the Medici portrait gallery, Giordano demonstrates the accuracy of his prontezza when he places a single black flourish on a reddish ground and thereby captures his expansive shoulder, turned to us along with his contemptuous gaze.

Giordano's depiction of himself wearing glasses surely stems not only from a wish to create a realistic portrait; with the optical aid signifying his far-sightedness, he also underscores the foresight with which he planned his often immense works of art. His glasses designate him as a scholar, a *pictor doctus* in the newest sense—not an erudite artist but an expert who understands the science of painting and articulates his knowledge by calculating the effects of his brushwork from a distant viewing point. In Giovan Pietro Bellori's vita of Giordano, he praises the supreme mastery of the artist's contours, made with rough lashes of the brush (*con grossi trattizzi ne'contorni*) that then converge and harmonize when the eye is at a certain distance—a phenomenon that can only be exploited by a *practico professore*.[10] Giordano's learnedness, which his glasses thematize, likely relate to the concept of *acutezza dell'ingegno* as developed by Vasari in his reflections on sculpture. According to him, sculptures or frescoes designed to be viewed from a distance must be executed more with the mind than with the hand, "for the diligence of the *ultimo finimento* cannot be seen from far away."[11]

In the same vein, the British portraitist Jonathan Richardson (1667–1745) would discover that the time-consuming, careful elaboration of objects depicted in the far distance was effort wasted: "The more remote any thing is supposed to be, the less finishing it ought to have. I have seen a fringe to a curtain in the background of a picture, which perhaps was half a day in painting, but might have been better done in a minute."[12]

THE INCALCULABLE ARTIST

The economy of visual representation appropriate to a particular work was based on the relationship between its destined location (taking into account not only the viewing distance, but also the buyer's monetary means) and the amount of artistic labor required. These issues also impacted, for Giordano, the pricing of his paintings. Bellori reports that he "never refused any commission," even those from humble clients, in keeping with the popular saying "everything left is lost"—a principle shared, as is well known, by other artists.[13] However, Giordano's lightning-fast execution came at a price, *especially* if the pay was low. De' Dominici faulted the artist for the sometimes meager quality of his work and disallowed modest recompense as an acceptable excuse:[14] If Giordano had agreed on a price, he was obligated to paint in a manner commensurate with his own self-respect, the decorum of art, and the honor of his fatherland (*al decoro dell'arte, ed all'onor della Patria*).[15] He goes on to lament Giordano's excessive greed as "the only reason why he occasionally painted pictures that were much more inferior than his knowledge."

Giordano's approach to time and money is also reflected in his advice to Carlo Dolci. Baldinucci reports that Giordano, after having praised Dolci's work, jokingly said to him: "I like it all, Carlo; but I must tell you, if you continue working this way and take up so much time executing your works, I think it will take a long while until you have collected the hundred and fifty thousand *scudi* my brush has already brought me. I have to believe perhaps you will die of hunger."[16]

Accusations of greed against artists were nothing new; they were commonly leveled at prestezza painters.[17] According to Tintoretto's contemporary Carlo Ridolfi, Paolo Veronese greatly appreciated Tintoretto's lively genius, but allegedly regretted the damaging precedent Tintoretto set by choosing to paint in any *maniera* whatsoever (including, by implication, rapidly), for this damages the profession's status.[18] De' Dominici gives, as an example of shoddy procedure resulting from speedy execution, the use of too much oil to thin down the texture of the paint and accelerate the painting process. This practice began in the seventeenth century and became widespread within a short period of time. It had the side effect of exposing the imprimatura, which was at first unintended and lamented, but later, as described chapter 2, was deliberately incorporated into the bold painterly style as a display of prestezza.

De' Dominici describes works by Giordano showing this kind of "damage"; in his opinion caused by avarice, *troppa avidità del danaro.*[19] After criticizing the results of what he called "sovereign prestezza," he adds that Giordano used to say "he had three brushes, one of gold, one of silver, and one of copper, with which he pleased the nobility, burghers, and common folk, respectively." For all three classes, the merit of the work was proportionate to the price.[20] The three-brushes trope, also associated with Tintoretto, generally appears in art literature as a criticism of irregularity in painting style,[21] but how should we interpret its tripartite gradation of artistic production? It certainly alludes to quantitative measurements of time invested by the artist. But the time dimension seems hardly a valid gauge of the true value of a painting, for that depends more on ideal qualities than on pragmatic quantities. How applicable is the imagery of the three brushes to the phenomenon of speed painting as practiced by Giordano and others? The whole point of sprezzatura lies in its "de-valuation" (in the sense of s-prezzare, "to dis-prize") of a pragmatic appraisal that overprizes labor and underestimates art. So does the trope express the fact that only someone, more than likely a wealthy patron, who knows how to estimate value added (a surplus of demonstrated expertise causing the price to rise) can accurately appreciate the worth of an artwork? Or does it reflect an alternative economy that views art as a commodity that can be produced at different levels for different customers?

The three brushes also appear in the Dutch painter and author Samuel van Hoogstraten's *Inleyding tot de hooge schoole der schilderkonst* (1678).[22] He cites Pieter Cornelisz Hooft, who used the trope to explain the stylistic diversity of Dirck Barentsz, a student of Titian: "He had three kinds of brushes, gold, silver, and copper, and he gauged the use of each according to the payment."[23] He then adds as a general comment: "Although not all works are finished with the same carefulness [*zorgvuldelijk*], those artists who have more lively control [*wackere toezicht*] and rush ahead probably have more gold in their brush than those who are slowed down by the last touches."[24] It would be too facile to "cast" the metallurgic element of this metaphor, which symbolizes nothing more than stylistic pluralism in Giordano's work, as a literal three-tiered price policy.

But the imagery of the three brushes has further potential for explaining the value increase with the transmutative process of alchemy. The following anecdote from Joachim von Sandrart's *Teutsche Academie* provides some insight into how the mysteries of this science might resonate with the pursuit of art. A London alchemist by the name of Brendel tried to convince Rubens to build him a laboratory, promising Rubens in return a share of the profits. The artist declined his offer with the explanation: "M. Brendlin, you've come about twenty years too late, for it was then that I found the right true LAPIDEM PHILOSOPHICUM by way of brush and pigments."[25]

De' Dominici records a comparable story regarding the teacher of Giordano's father, one Jusepe de Ribera.[26] He was once visited by two Spanish officers, who mused about the famed stone that could change any metal into gold. Ribera was more bored than entertained by their many "ridiculous arguments," so he decided to have some fun while also imparting an important lesson. Putting on a serious face, he told them he knew the secret of making gold and actually possessed the *lapis philosophorum*. If they wished to see him conduct the procedure, they should come the following morning, while he would spend the evening getting everything ready. The officers arrived early the next day and found Ribera painting a half-figure of John the Baptist. It soon became apparent that he would not to stop painting, no matter how many times they asked when the alchemy demonstration would begin. Each time Ribera answered, "very soon, very soon." He continued to work until he finished the figure *alla prima*. He then gave the picture over to one of his assistants with the instruction he should deliver it to a certain *cavaliere* who was waiting for it, and should receive from the gentleman that which they had previously discussed. When the helper left, Ribera told the officers they would see how gold was created just as soon as his assistant came back from the *cavaliere*, who would contribute the most important and essential element of the mystery. The messenger finally arrived with a folded piece of paper. The officers were beside themselves with anticipation. Ribera led them into another room, opened the envelope, and tossed on the table ten gold ducats with the words: "Here you see how I make gold—alchemy, gold, lapis, these are all decoys that mislead the mind and drive you crazy. Learn from me how to make perfect gold. I, with my painting, and you with your service to His Majesty, here we have found the true secret."[27]

The art-theoretical punch line of Ribera's practical joke is the astonishing fee he had charged for a half-figure in *alla prima* that he had produced in half a day! And interestingly, we should note that a *lapis* actually *did* effect the miracle. The preparations made by the artist the evening before the demonstration, whose importance he had underscored in his parting words to the Spanish officers, give us a decisive clue. As we learn in a passage preceding the anecdote, it was Ribera's custom in the evenings to entertain visitors while sketching out what he planned to paint the next day. After he had determined the object to be represented, he elaborated it after a life model in either pen or *lapis* (lead pencil) and watercolor, often also with red chalk (*lapis rosso*), and sometimes also with charcoal. According to De' Dominici, the large number of Ribera's extant drawings bear witness to his constant study.[28] The practice of drawing in the evening in preparation for the next day's work was not unusual, in fact quite a common procedure in many workshops.[29] Luigi Scaramuccia's maxims explicitly recommend that painters spend the hours of night or daybreak in drawing, sketching, and translating thoughts onto paper in order to fix in the imagination that which they intended to make during the day.[30] In De' Dominici's anecdote, however, the Spaniards did not witness Ribera's development of the pictorial idea in the medium of drawing; they came in the morning to study an alchemical miracle but instead were confronted with the sight of the painter at work. The hidden preparations kept the spectators in the dark, so to speak. They were permitted to witness the "wonder" of an *alla prima* work swiftly blazed onto the canvas in a few hours, but were granted no insight into the development of the image, and so missed the transformational process that was art. In an exhibition of painterly bravura, hiding one's skills behind one's back is acted out as a triumph.

De' Dominici explores the subject of price negotiations in an anecdote in the vita of Ribera's student Salvator Rosa. A *cavaliere* who fell in love with a large landscape painting in the artist's workshop found Rosa's price tag of 200 *scudi* too high. They dithered over the amount, with the *cavaliere* entreating Rosa to reconsider and lower the price. On his next visit, he again inquired about the price and thought surely the artist was joking when Rosa answered "300 *scudi*." After he spent some time discussing the work with a courtier who had accompanied him and gave it much praise, the *cavaliere* decided he was at last ready to pay the 300 *scudi*. He asked a third time for the price, and received a caustic reply: "The price is 400 *scudi*, and each time you ask it will go up 100 *scudi* more." Finally, unable to contain his rage, Rosa stormed over to the painting in question, ripped it to pieces with great ferocity, and declared: "Your stinginess has destroyed a painting that would have been one of the most beautiful of its kind when finished; the negotiation is hereby ended."[31] The theatricality of the artist's outburst, as described by De' Dominici, was more a grand gesture than an act of blind temper. It was a proclamation on the independence of the artist and the uncontestable value of art.[32] In a letter of April 1, 1666, Rosa explained to his patron Antonio Ruffo that he did not paint to make money, "but solely for my own satisfaction; therefore I must let myself be carried by surges of enthusiasm, and pick up my brush only at those times when I feel violently assailed by them."[33]

The sovereign act of wrecking one's own artwork was the stuff of legend long before this incident was recorded. When Rosa blamed the destruction of the painting on the *cavaliere*'s greed, he was voicing the moral of the story, a moral also found in a number of *vite*. Vasari offers in his biographies (which were well known and critically read by many artists) several tales of artists' destructive fury when faced with the ignorance of their clients. In one of these anecdotes, the artist's anger backfired with lethal impact.

The arrogance and irascibility of the "soldier sculptor" Pietro Torrigiano (1472–1528) was evident already during his artistic apprenticeship as a youth in the garden atelier of Lorenzo de' Medici. Because he could not endure having any of his colleagues surpass him, he regularly destroyed any works "from the hands of others" that he felt threatened his status. But these notorious attacks (allegedly culminating in his punching Michelangelo in the nose in the Brancacci chapel, which led to Torrigiano's falling out with Lorenzo and being compelled to enter the military) were not the only reason he was publicly condemned. His own works also fell victim to his tantrums. When he felt cheated of a princely sum promised by a certain Duca d'Arcus in Spain, he destroyed a painting of the Madonna and Child that had already passed into Arcus's possession. As this was a sacred image, Torrigiano was accused and arrested for committing heresy. While under interrogation by the Inquisition, he undertook a hunger strike and died, which, as the legend goes, saved him from decapitation.[34]

Vasari recounts another furious incident of destruction in his vita of Donatello. The target of wrath in this case was an art dealer who was acting as an intermediary between Cosimo de' Medici and Donatello and trying to get the purchase price of a bronze bust lowered. His argument tellingly rested on calculations based on a daily rate of pay: the work had been finished in just over a month, meaning that Donatello was charging more than one *fiorino* per day, which the dealer deemed excessive. Donatello was so offended that he struck the bust hard enough that it fell from the window and smashed into pieces on the street below, and then he proceeded to accuse the dealer of destroying a year's worth of effort and merit in the space of a hundredth of an hour. The dealer, he said, would be better off buying and selling beans rather than statues. Accepting his responsibility in the matter, the ridiculed man offered double the price if the artist would remake the work. Donatello adamantly refused, even when the duke personally interceded and pleaded with him to change his mind.[35]

This anecdote is also cited in Carlo Cesare Malvasia's notes on Giovanni Andrea Donducci, called Il Mastelletta (1575–1655). According to Malvasia, Donducci had a similar confrontation with an art dealer, which ended with his cutting a painting of a Madonna into pieces before the man's eyes—an act of defiance[36] that Salvator Rosa would repeat years later. It should come as no great surprise then that when Caravaggio's painting of the *Resurrection of Lazarus* commissioned for the high altar of a church in Messina was criticized by the local literati, he unsheathed his dagger and cut it into shreds. Eventually, however, Caravaggio offered to paint a second version, which is still in Messina today.[37]

Public executions of innocent artworks are of course tragic and disturbing events, but the legendary killings described above functioned also as sacrifices whereby art successfully defended itself against its own marketing apparatus. De' Dominici's anecdote, for example, is about more than cunning tactics for raising prices or turning the tables on an adversary in negotiations; it also addresses the issue of an artist's ownership of their own work. The ultimate message is that bargaining should play no role in the acquisition of art; an artwork's value is determined by the artist alone, not by the rules of the marketplace. Filippo Baldinucci remarks several times in his *Notizie* how anxious Salvator Rosa was to get a high price for his works, insisting always that the interested party pay the amount he asked.[38] The reason, Baldinucci says, was Rosa's experience of having sold pictures for a few doubloons that were then quickly resold by the buyer for ten times that price.

The refusal to relinquish a work if its artistic worth was not adequately appreciated, even if that meant its destruction, was a gesture of sovereignty proclaiming that the price of art was basically incalculable. There was no standard unit of value by which its worth could be established. It was thus literally without price. Pricelessness was at the heart of selling and also, interestingly, at the heart of giving. With the generous gift of an artwork, an artist surrendered evaluation of its artistic worth to the recipient; it became dependent on their connoisseurship. However, this also could engender resentment in the artist.[39]

Artists worked at different speeds. This variability, an inherent aspect of the creative act, according to De' Dominici and Baldinucci pardoned the annihilation of one's own work, because the value of that work was not reckoned in labor and materials, but rather reflected the artist's disposition toward their art. Rosa's self-righteousness typifies an attitude, already perceptible in the art theory of the sixteenth century, toward an economy of artistic practice encapsulated in the notion of prestezza, which would be increasingly thematized in the painting of the seventeenth century. Rosa's aggressive pricing strategy, as well as the fact that he never agreed on a fixed fee before finishing a commission because he wanted to be paid for the result and not the work,[40] reflects a similar position taken earlier by Michelangelo toward one of his clients. Vasari relates that Michelangelo doubled his rate for the Tondo Doni because Agnolo Doni balked at his initial asking price.[41] The exemplary *terribilità* of Michelangelo enabled the generations after him to more self-confidently establish the worth of their work in the mind of the art collector.

Purchase price as a symbolic value, one that does not reckon on the amount of time and effort expended by the artist, but depends instead on the recognition of art as such, was a continual source of tension between artist and patron. Rapidly executed works were especially prone to having their expense challenged, for in such cases artists had to bring to the negotiating table the rather esoteric claim of an *ars* unique to the fine arts. Michelangelo is alleged to have said on the subject, as reported by Francisco de Hollanda in his *Dialogos em Roma* (1538):

> The work of art that I consider worth a high price is one done by the hand of an exceedingly able man, even if it was done in a short time, for if it took a long time who would be able to calculate its worth? And one that I consider to be of very little value is one painted over many years by someone who does not know how to paint, even if he is called a painter; for works are not to be evaluated according to the length spent on them uselessly, but according to the merits of the knowledge and the hand that executes them; for if this were not so, they would not pay a learned man more for an hour of study spent examining an important case, than a weaver for all the cloth he weaves in a lifetime, or a ditch digger who spends the whole day sweating at his labor.[42]

The calculation of price according to a daily rate, seen by artists as an affront to their art, met its match in the justly celebrated work of one day. Here, unmistakably, it is the art that is paid for, not the expenditure of labor. What should be placed on the weighing scales and therefore evaluated in price negotiations, the artist argued, was creative ability as revealed in the skill that makes rapid execution possible. When Salvator Rosa imperiously tore up his painting before the eyes of a potential buyer and blamed the man's miserliness for causing the destruction, he was justified in doing so, according to Michelangelo: the interested party had neither respected nor perhaps even recognized the art of the work when he decided to haggle over its price. In such cases, buyers in their ignorance miss the point that a rapidly executed bravura work is, more or less (as each case may be), an effortless articulation of the highest art and, as such, an object of value worth collecting; instead, its art is nullified on invalid grounds. Rosa forestalled this symbolic loss of value by obliterating his creation. De' Dominici concludes his account of Rosa's deed by recording a rumor he had overheard: "Some say that Salvatore did not make too much out of the destruction of his work, for he is very quick in execution and usually when he begins a painting in the morning, it is already finished in the evening." De' Dominici, however, expresses skepticism at the possibility of such an extreme tempo—Rosa's landscapes consisted of numerous single motifs, and even Luca Giordano, "the fastest painter," needed at least one day and one night for a history painting, and on others he actually worked eight days.[43]

VANAGLORIA

In art theory of the sixteenth and seventeenth centuries, as well as in modern scholarly literature, greed is named again and again as the impetus behind rapid painting, especially when Tintoretto and Giordano were discussed.[44] Yet it was not only a desire for money, but also the pursuit of a glorious reputation that spurred these artists to compete for the title of leading painter in their city and, with that goal in mind, to accept as many public commissions as possible. Of Giordano, Bellori says there were few churches in Rome where one could not see his works,[45] an observation also applicable to Tintoretto in Venice. His striving after omnipresence was allegedly stronger than his avarice, and in truth, both artists took on just about every commission, however humble and, as we saw earlier, executed these with a diligence commensurate to the payment. Tintoretto sometimes even painted for free or solely for the cost of materials.[46]

The different motivations posited for a so-called "cheap" painterly style—the artist's greed on the one hand, or what could be seen as a deliberate debasement of their own market value on the other—are at first glance contradictory, but they actually demonstrate internal consistency. Benedetto Varchi in his first *Disputa della maggioranza delle arti* (1547) identified the driving forces behind art as a scramble after fame on the one hand, and on the other the desire—and need—to be well paid.[47] However, Varchi's formulation cannot definitively explain why the bravura artist's desire to reap the rewards of ambition, namely money and success, through art was interpreted as an expression of personal greediness. Don't these incentives motivate most human endeavors? Isn't what bravura exposes, and what perhaps bothered its detractors, the very nature of human ambition? This novel concept of an art that lives in legendary and brilliant performances of prestezza was conceived, at least in part, as a means to an economy of execution; that is, with the goal of creating the greatest possible impact for the lowest possible investment (of work, material, and time). And it is this motive that opens up a conceptual space for the understanding of art as an asset, one that is carefully controlled by sprezzatura, and hinted at in showpieces dashed down with a few strokes of the brush. The staging of promise in that which is unfinished, as a preferred method of design, broadly aligns with the idea of ambition as an expression of potential.

The lofty goal of prestezza—to be able "at one stroke to give birth and to paint,"[48] or in other words, to simultaneously conceive of and execute a pictorial idea—is well represented by Paolo de Matteis's (1650–1710) audacious bid to outdo his teacher Luca Giordano.[49] His parade piece was the cupola fresco of Il Gesù Nuovo, executed in "sixty-six days and a few hours" (later destroyed and no longer extant). Another artist also submitted a proposal for this commission: Francesco Solimena (1657–1747), likewise a student of Giordano, who according to Palomino "imitated Giordano in everything his master did well, and [in] what his master did not do well, he superseded him through study, so that he is today the best known [artist] in Europe."[50] Solimena, who had demanded a proud price of 16,000 *scudi* for his proposal (a bid De Matteis significantly undercut to get the commission), later allegedly remarked in reference to De Matteis's work: "Paolo de Matteis does not need to go on about how little time he spent on the cupola, it speaks for itself."[51] His words not only echo Apelles's response to the unknown fast painter, but also resonate with an accusation of pretentiousness advanced by De' Dominici, who reported that De Matteis liked painting "bizzare fantasies" *all'improvviso* in front of an audience, accompanied by "elegant discourses" intended to augment the adulation of his works.

In these speeches he allegedly compared his art to the works of great masters, the likes of "Titian, Correggio, Veronese, the Carraccis, Guido Reni, Domenichino, and all the most singular painters," and he finished off by crowning himself with the (self-bestowed) title of *Il Creatore*.[52] (Other sources report that these ostentatious displays made him a laughingstock at the French court.)[53] Solimena goes on to say: "It would have been much better had he taken sixty-six months and made [the cupola fresco] properly with a corresponding amount of study, instead of executing it hastily only for the vainglory of being considered fast, to no avail."[54] De' Dominici shared Solimena's distaste for an artistic practice reliant on speed: "Paolo's sole purpose for working quickly was to make himself be seen as miraculous." He also notes that this demonstration of painterly recklessness, which exhibited no trace of study or diligence, was the fault of his *vanagloria*.[55]

De Matteis's improvisational showpieces, which he so eloquently accompanied with spoken commentary, were described by De' Dominici as follows: "And many times he commenced the work without even making a sketch on paper beforehand; actually without having given the slightest thought . . . he dropped certain figures randomly, as if they were generated from the hand and not from contemplation! All the effect of a reckless opinion of himself."[56] Orlandi in his *Abecedario* (1753), on the other hand, would pay homage to De Matteis's self-staging and define him as an extremely quick (*velocissimo*) painter with the natural ability to "invent, paint and finish at once [*in un subito*] large works in fresco or oil."[57]

The sprezzatura that doubtlessly constitutes the backdrop for this artist's behavior, with its "as-if" spontaneity, is unmasked by De' Dominici as affected and therefore contrary to art. The forced character of De Matteis's technical performance, especially in *all'improvviso* demonstrations, which rank as the highest of artistic challenges, annoyed De' Dominici to the point of unleashing on him a barrage of devastating critique.

Pierre-Jean Mariette, who concurred with Orlandi's judgment of De Matteis and praised his extremely lively and effortless genius, would later add: "He was a practitioner and that is all. In the celebrity of his operations he outdid Giordano; but he did not in any way possess the brilliant seduction in his brush that made the works of his master successful. On the contrary, he had an insipid and languishing *coloris*."[58] Mariette's criticism echoes that of his contemporary, Le Comte de Caylus (1672–1765), who in his lecture "De la légéreté de l'outil" distanced himself from Paolo de Matteis as a role model. One should certainly not join the chorus that sings the praises of his painting style, he said, for it results in a hardly finished work whose appearance of impatience and promptness give only a bogus sense of what is meant by *légéreté* (ease), which Caylus understands in a positive sense; De Matteis's pictures are instead "faux-semblants."[59] Caylus's critique took in the majority of Tintoretto's works, because he as the "first of the moderns" provided models of ease "that encouraged and at the same time set adrift such a great number of artists because they were unable to successfully imitate him in the interrupted works he produced."[60] And keeping Paolo de Matteis in mind, one can only concur with the judgment of the first president of the Royal Academy of Arts, Sir Joshua Reynolds (1723–1792), who in his speech before the academy on December 10, 1784, disparaged the rhetoric artists use to promote themselves with their actual painterly practice. Here Reynolds painted with a rather broad brush: "However extraordinary it may appear, it is certainly true that the inventions of the *pittori improvvisatori*, as they may be called, have—notwithstanding the common boast of their authors that all is spun from their own brain—very rarely any thing that has in the least the air of originality: their compositions are generally commonplaces; uninteresting, without character or expression; like those flowery speeches that we sometimes hear, which impress no new ideas in the mind."[61]

Paolo de Matteis's attempt to outdo his teacher's genuine achievement of *far presto* seems to have been in vain. There is so far no catalog raisonnée or monographic study dedicated to him, notwithstanding that he was considered one of the best painters of his time.[62] In Paris, he was entertained by none other than the Earl of Shaftesbury, who commissioned from him a *Hercules at the Crossroads*.[63] It may be that his own pompousness sabotaged his fame (in any case, Matteis is only noteworthy in art history for the place he occupies in his teacher's shadow). But it is also possible that his failure to achieve enduring success despite obvious talent has its roots in Giordano's attitude toward teaching, as Palomino suggests: "Luca Giordano had innumerable students, but only a few proved themselves, for he was more practical than theoretical and his students were attracted by the ease with which they saw their teacher paint; and because they wanted to follow him in this, they lost their way for they lacked the fundamental teaching Giordano was taught at the beginning by his teachers José de Ribera and Pietro da Cortona."[64] And regarding Claudio Coello, whose rivalry with Giordano at the Spanish court came to such a lethal conclusion, Palomino records a verbal exchange with Don Cristóbal Ontanón. In response to the remark, "Now Giordano will come and teach you all how to make a lot of money," Coello allegedly replied: "Yes milord, and absolve us of many sins and take away many of our scruples."[65] De' Dominici tells a similar story about Giordano's students: they were satisfied with copying his inventions and figures and transmitted these as stock motifs in their own works. They tried to imitate the "magic of his colors without plumbing the profound depths of their master's knowledge."[66]

THE FRAGILITY OF FAME

Critics of a highly economic painting style also targeted the work of Andrea Schiavone (1522–1563), another today-forgotten artist who was nevertheless cherished by his contemporaries. According to Baldinucci and Ridolfi, Schiavone was ranked by connoisseurs as one of the best colorists of the Venetian school,[67] outdoing "those before and after him in felicity, facility, and the bravura with which he handled his brush."[68] And if we believe Baldinucci, Titian likewise "cast his eye" on this less well-known figure, or more precisely on his coloring, which Baldinucci defined as a "bravura of the brush that put fear into everyone who worked with paints."[69] Tintoretto kept one of Schiavone's works next to him while painting as an aid to replicating the great daring of Schiavone's coloring; Federico Barocci (1535–1612) was known to do the same.[70] It was mentioned earlier in this book that Vasari commissioned a battle painting from Schiavone. Boschini linked him with bravura when he exhorted the artist with the words: "Andrea Schiavone, come here with your power, come here with your infinite bravura, with this impasto that contains fire and life."[71] His "painterly stroke made with a scornful blow of the brush" (*il tratto Pittoresco, con il colpo sprezzante di pennello*),[72] according to Boschini, surprises even the "Marvelous itself"—probably in the sense that such a manner first neglects and suppresses the (quasi divine) marvel of complete illusion in order to have it appear unexpectedly from pastose brushstrokes. In his ode to Schiavone, Boschini enumerates all the various aesthetic tropes expressed by his bravura: boldness, forcefulness, resolute technique, and frenzied artistic potential that inspires dread and causes fear, panegyric ciphers that also align Schiavone with Tintoretto.[73]

It is remarkable that such effusive praise and recognition were accorded to a painter whose financial circumstances at the beginning of his career forced him to paint furniture (the so-called *cassone*) and hire himself out as a day laborer. After his death his paintings experienced an enormous increase in value and were sought out as objets d'art,[74] but during his lifetime Schiavone was a marginal figure, and indeed he remains of limited interest in art history to the present day. Ridolfi traces his lack of popularity with his contemporaries to the prevailing taste for a *delicatezze* of style such as exemplified by Giorgione, Palma il Vecchio, and Titian. Despite his *buona maniera* and *toche con molt'arte*, Schiavone was more appreciated among painters than by the general public[75] because, as Ridolfi notes, "the recognition of this art is not possible for everyone, rather it is reserved only for those who are able to comprehend the concept [*i termini*] due to a long study of such difficult and laborious material"[76] (an argument we also encountered in the previous chapter à propos Martin Fréminet). Pietro Aretino, who chided Tintoretto for his prestezza, also asked Andrea Schiavone in a letter "to transform the haste of execution into the carefulness of perfection." Aretino prefaced this quite conventional opinion with a nod to the intelligence and erudition manifested in Schiavone's style: "I have always praised the learned prestezza of your intelligent execution."[77] That his insight was keen is certainly borne out by Aretino's earlier exchanges with another "worthy painter" deeply impressed by Schiavone's methods, namely, his friend Titian.[78]

Ridolfi mentions a technique Schiavone originated that produced a remarkable stylistic effect: he used the paint left over on his palette from the previous day to mix lifelike flesh tones.[79] Such intentionally messy, or in Joachim von Sandrart's words "dirty" practices, were also reported in connection with Tintoretto and Titian—the former used old, dried up paint in his imprimatura, the latter loaded his brush with more than one color at a time. The resulting qualities derive from the material itself, that is to say, they are inherent in the process of painting. Boschini found in this pioneering colorism of Schiavone's yet another opportunity to make use of the central metaphor in his ode to the Venetian school, tellingly titled *La Carta del navegar pitoresco* (A Chart for Painterly Navigation). "Through his command of coloring," he wrote, "[Schiavone] executed nudes so plastic and daring with their forceful forms and bulging muscles that these angular figures in their greatly varying skin tones seemed to be born from the ocean like Tritons, Glaucons, and Neptunes."[80]

Boschini may be referring in this passage to two of Schiavone's works "in the houses of the noble Zanni family," which Ridolfi describes as a nude Galatea sitting on a dolphin and a Triton blowing on a horn.[81] But Boschini goes beyond identifying the subject to seemingly visualizing in literary form one possible rationale behind the artist's choice of such painterly effects. According to him, Schiavone's figures were born in the oceanic depths of painting, and as gods of the sea they must remain optically detained there. One might read this as yet another allusion to a lack of *disegno*, a charge continually leveled against Venetian painters. But Boschini once used the same metaphor to characterize Titian's works, which he said gave the beholder a good pathway for "entering into the ocean of painting" (more on this below), a capacity that could have been inspired by Schiavone's technique.[82]

When Ridolfi writes that the "professori" are able to make splendid observations from Schiavone's "random mixtures of paints," and that "this accidental color mixture is wonderfully suited when it is well-employed by an intelligent painter," he is suggesting that methodical analysis by scholars might explain a practice that seems instead to arise from an artist's supreme self-confidence, the "disdain and daring of [his] brush."[83] Vasari in his vita of Tintoretto had ascribed what he viewed as unpredictable color effects to accident; they were determined "by chance" (*a caso*)—a negatively charged quality that would remain attached to this painterly style for centuries and a commonplace in the literature of art criticism. Ridolfi relates that Tintoretto, despite his own advice to artists that they keep Schiavone's example before them, objected to his lack of design, which he ascribed to the artist's shoddy artistic education. He admitted, however, that Schiavone did know how to cover this deficiency with a charming veil of nebulous colors.[84] Here Ridolfi repeats a criticism he once levied against Giorgione, the founding father of the Venetian school, and an artist whose name we continually come across linked to the names of other artists. Several times Ridolfi pointed out how little Schiavone's art was based on learning. For him it was clear that although nature makes prontezza available to the intellect, education is necessary to steer quickness in the direction of a well-grounded practice. He excused Schiavone's deficit in this regard as being due to his social circumstances.[85]

Boschini, by contrast, stood firmly with Schiavone and accused Vasari not only of treating the artist as if he were "scum" (*fezza*) and a "good-for-nothing" (*scoazza*), but also of oppressing Venetian style with his judgments.[86] Elsewhere in the *Carta*, Boschini upheld Schiavone's brush, a mate to his "Dalmatian fury" and thus a legacy from his birthplace of Zara, as "truly more quick than the filth drawn by a Saracen hand."[87] Vasari's characterization of Venetian practice as "confused, consisting of sketches [*abozzi*] and stains without finish" he countered with the following words: "Oh stains without fault, indeed brilliant, more flattering than any light."[88]

Schiavone did not cultivate carefulness, a trait which he "disdained, even trampled under foot,"[89] but rather an unusually bold painting technique;[90] in other words, he developed an experimental, innovative practice that sought to compensate for his lack of knowledge.

In Schiavone's own lifetime, the Venetian painter Paolo Pino linked rapid execution to his name—though in a thoroughly critical tone. In his *Dialogo di pittura* of 1548, Pino stated that painting rapidly was not in itself praiseworthy because, in Schiavone's case, it stemmed from a natural disposition rather than from a habit of tempered art. Accordingly, Pino dismissed Schiavone's style as "smearing manifested by a mere fabricator [of pictures]" and a "disgrace" demonstrating ignorance.[91]

102 (FACING)
Giovanni Andrea Donducci, called Il Mastelletta, *Genre Scene* (*Festa campestre*), ca. 1602–1604. Oil on canvas. Galleria Spada, Rome.

In his treatise, Pino developed a sophisticated concept of painting that differentiated the true artist from the one who draws attention to his works by merely exploiting the properties inherent in paint as substance. True art, he says, unfolds its potentiality only when materiality is turned into medium. Pino gives an example of this essential transformation by explaining that "green" may color many different things, but it does not possess the material qualities that distinguish velvet from wool. Thus the different tactile effects of green fabrics in a picture do not come only from the color, but from the painter's skill. For Pino, Schiavone's art lacked the subtle refinements of technique that can turn the matter of paint into the substance of the thing portrayed, and it was this shortcoming that made him such a bad example.[92]

There are in fact numerous instances in art literature of artists who had unmistakably high aspirations but failed in their quest for excellence because they lacked technical knowledge. One example, Giovanni Andrea Donducci, called Il Mastelletta (1575–1655), was admired by Guido Reni, according to Malvasia. Reni commented that he knew of no one more clearly born to become a painter, for he could launch himself with great determination into an oversized painting and finish it in a few days.[93] (Mastelletta was also one of those temperamental "incalculable artists" we mentioned earlier who slashed a work into pieces in front of an art dealer.) By Malvasia's reports, the work in question was a hurried production, rendered *alla prima*, not with thick [*di corpo*] but very fluid paint [*colore liquido*].[94] His *facile abbreviatura di macchia* (easy, abbreviated, and blotchy execution)[95] had the undesirable side effect of allowing the imprimatura to shine through the overlying layers of paint.[96]

In childhood, Malvasia tells us, Il Mastelletta displayed early signs of artistic creativity by using his fork to make all kinds of unusual figures on his plate.[97] His disinterest in eating, while it did nourish the power of his imagination, ultimately manifested in his work as a dislike of "digestion" in the mimetic process. He eagerly threw himself into the ideas that came to his mind, but was less eager when it came to the hard work of refining and metabolizing the fruits of his cognitive process.[98] Mastelletta, like Schiavone, had no formal art education, though in his case poverty was not to blame; according to Malvasia, he simply had no patience with the classroom. Instead of approaching his art studies in an organized fashion, he gave himself over to flights of fancy (*capricci*). Malvasia's lack of discipline made him a more or less self-taught painter. He refused to take part in drawing lessons, for example, and instead devoted himself to coloring, and he made his choice of whom he would

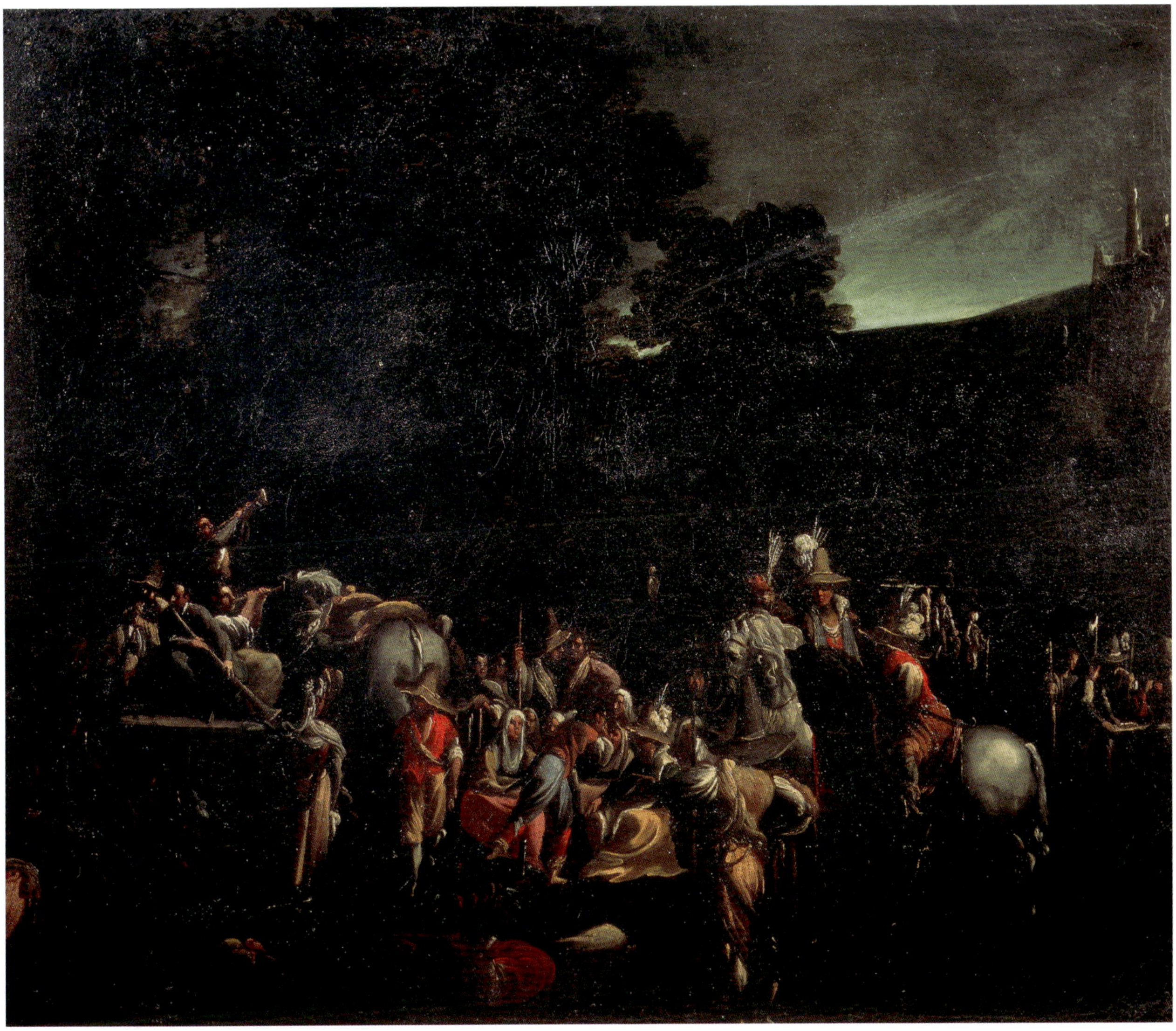

emulate on rather shaky grounds. Like Schiavone, he decided upon Parmigianino, because he found his "leggiadria" captivating. (Parmigianino, we might note, was already praised in his time for the *vaghezza* that made every beholder fall in love with his depicted subjects.[99]) Not only did Mastelletta refuse to participate in life drawing classes that took place in the evenings, he even made fun of such work (*fattica*) and deemed it a hindrance for young artists who wished to advance quickly. Undeterred self-confidence is no guarantee of success, however.

A genre painting from the Galleria Spada with a *soldatesca* in the background showcases Mastella's much praised *galanti e spirituosi figurine*[100] and also both the vices and virtues of his bravura (fig. 102). Anna Coliva, in her monograph on the artist, dates the work to around 1602–1604 and highlights the fixed repertoire of his figures and motifs that stylistically connects his works during this period with landscapes produced more than a half century earlier. Mastelletta diverges

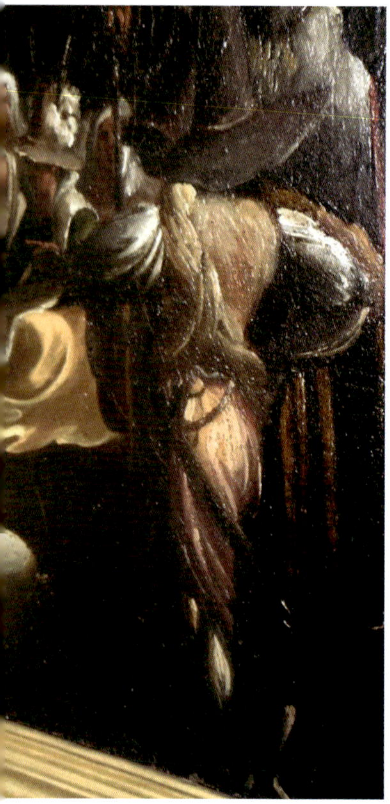

103
Detail of fig. 102
[*Genre Scene*].

significantly from this stylistic template, however, when he expresses his visionary disquietude (*ansia visionaria*) through the forced deformation and elongation of figures, and by using the painterly techniques of *pennellate veloci e sommarie* (quick and abbreviated brushstrokes) and intense and *dissonante* colors.[101]

The image shows a wooded valley—in the background we see a mountaintop settlement—and it seems to portray a number of separate events that lack any clear narrative connection. A pervasive darkness envelops the various groups of figures and gives a sinister feel to the whole that adds to the mysteriousness of what is being represented. The composition unfolds from the left foreground, where a band of musicians, three seated and one standing on a cart, plays wind instruments of different sizes. Almost like an overture to what follows, they set the genre scene's burlesque tone. Next to them is an encounter between a man and a woman who exchange glances as they walk past one another. Alongside this couple, a group of seated women, with men in peasant dress standing behind them, seem to watch a theatrical performance by a young man who gestures furiously toward a woman seated in front of him. Her strange headdress connects her to a group of riders to the right, comprising a woman and two men. As with the couple on foot, eye contact seems to be the central means of communication between one of the figures who is seen from the back and another who faces front, while a third rider leans forward on his horse in order to observe the central spectacle. This figure's stylish broad-brimmed hat resonates with one of the pedestrians, although there are clear class distinctions between the two. Farther to the right and toward the back, Mastelletta has placed a group of soldiers with halberds who seem to be bent over a plan of action. A split group standing even farther in the background is drawn only by means of bright lines in the highly economical bravura style of Tintoretto (see, for example, the group in the background of the *Baptism of Christ*; see fig. 92).

It remains unclear what brings all of these different episodes and people together, other than the general picturesque aspect they share. The tall, broad-brimmed hats are the work's most peculiar motif and they do create a certain sense of community. The tallest of these is worn by the figure standing nearest to the viewer with his back to us, moving toward and pointing at the central spectacle while turning to the rider who also observes the main event. (fig. 103) But this figure's quaint attire and energetic pose are less spectacular than the way his clothing is executed—with a few broad and confidently drawn strokes of a loaded brush whose flowing sprezzatura endows the figure with a particular elegance. The bright yellow skirt of the seated woman is likewise very fluidly rendered, catching the eye of the beholder as if spotlighted, but without making any particular compositional sense; her physiognomy, which might help us understand the scene, is lost in shadow.

Mastelletta's effort to flaunt his daring chiaroscuro is demonstrated, most awkwardly, in the shading of two white horses. The extreme juxtaposition of dark and light appears to depict a white horse adjacent to a black horse, but the whitish back of the latter clarifies that both are, in fact, of the same color. Anna Coliva speaks of "a lyrical rapport between the two horses," and defines the stark shadow as "unreal" and "without naturalistic justification," but "extremely delicate."[102] Their heads in profile seem to justify the common reproach that chiaroscuro hides in its shadows a lack of *disegno*, for they are certainly poorly drawn. This flaw is also evident in the figure lying on his back in the immediate foreground. Mastelletta's dilettantish foreshortening breaks this figure apart: his shoulder and arm become one mass that dissolves into darkness, as do the figures in the left foreground. According to Malvasia, their ghost-like existence is due to applying too quickly a paint that was excessively liquid, which caused it to be "drunk" or absorbed into a black imprimatura that had not been dried long enough.[103] This mistreatment of color lets the ground rise up and swallow not only details but whole figures. Nevertheless, the use of flashy highlights, which cleverly disperse the beholder's gaze, elicited great admiration. Mastelletta's biographer Malvasia calls such placements in dark areas a "sly style" (*maniera furbesca*); by "pushing everything into shadow, he avoided the difficulties [of art]." The surrounding darkness obscures contours and hides "disturbances and mistakes" (*scorrezioni e gli errori*). The "marvelous" lighting effects "at first wound the eyes" (*ferivano la vista*)—in a manner reminiscent of Boschini's *spada bianca*—but with an "extreme *vaghezza*, they satisfy the taste."[104]

Mastelletta's creative potential, somewhat misshaped by his resistance to education and discipline, is captured by Malvasia in formulaic praise that underlines the effect his unique practice caused his professional colleagues—namely "terror";[105] the word that had been used in association with Tintoretto and Schiavone as well, and of other bravura painters. Mastelletta's tendency to "flights of fancy" manifested in his childhood antics at the dinner table, his impatience for the rigors of training, and his undisciplined rush to begin learning coloring, which is traditionally taught at the end of a formal art education, sets before us a vulnerable young talent that ended up fooling itself. Mastelletta lacked a foundation and so was forced "to grope along blindly in the darkness."[106]

We may recall Sandrart's dismissal of the claims that artistic genius is apparent at a young age: "When youths in school, as commonly happens, sometimes doodle figures of little men, animals, cities, ships, and the like, and are even inclined to dabble with paints, their parents use this as grounds to proclaim: my child could, and for me he should, become a painter! But they ought to know better and consider that talent does not come from such hand-doodles, but must come from an extraordinary mind and spirit, and many years of work are required before one can be sure of such skill."[107]

CHAPTER SEVEN

Arte-Factum: The Feminizing Bravura

THE ARTIFICE OF PAINTERLY MIMESIS

Paolo Pino in his *Dialogo di pittura* explains the fundamental difficulty faced by all young artists inclined toward bravura painting: "Infinite are the things pertaining to coloring and impossible to explain with words, because every color can by itself or mixed produce many effects, but no color is able by its own property to make even a minimum of these effects because it needs the intelligence and practice of a good master."[1] The complexity of coloring arises from the intricacies of mixing and blending, an issue Plato addressed in his dialogue *Timaeus*: "The law of proportion, however, according to which the several colors are formed, even if a man knew he would be foolish in telling, for he could not give any necessary reason, nor indeed any tolerable or probable explanation of them."[2]

Early Modern art theory is replete with laments over the absence of precise rules on coloring (especially when compared with the plentitude of rules for *disegno*)—a deficiency that has significant repercussions for the quest for mastery. In Roger de Piles's view it was because of the extreme difficulty of painting (*une chose fort difficile*) that no more than six painters had achieved excellence "in the last three hundred years," in contrast to at least thirty draftsmen, and the source of the difficulty lay, he believed, in the absence of basic principles: ". . . drawing has regulations founded on proportion and anatomy, whereas *coloris* still has no well-known rules."[3] The futility of the painter's search for something so unfathomable as rules for coloring may be due to the much higher mimetic density involved in painting compared to drawing.

In his fifth *Entretiens*, the historiographer and art theorist André Félibien (1619–1695) distinguishes between the colors employed by painters (oil paint and distemper) and those naturally possessed by objects,[4] and further expands on the intricacy of *coloris* by differentiating so-called local colors from color effects produced by reflection. The former are "fixed and permanent;" the latter, purely "apparent and fugitive" (*passagère*),[5] are "foreign colors" (*couleurs étrangères*) that occur in conjunction with natural colors and are able to change them.[6] Félibien asserts: "It is very difficult to dictate firm rules that would allow us to penetrate this practice; one needs the understanding of a workman [*le jugement de celui qui travaille*], who orders all of his colors according to the subject, the distribution of the figures, and the light that illuminates them."[7] What makes a painting so captivating are the accidental properties that must be captured for a successful imitation of reality, which have nothing to do with the substance of what is represented, but solely with visual appearance. In other words, it is the rending and dispersal of the image into optical dazzlements that ensnares the eye of the beholder. The coherence of the composition amidst such distractions is achieved by chiaroscuro, an abstract principle and a "foreign" as well as fugitive element in nature that gains substance in painting.

In his own vita, Giorgio Vasari shares an important piece of advice he once received from a more experienced colleague when he was still a young artist.[8] While working on the portrait of Alessandro de' Medici, Vasari's efforts to meticulously reproduce the reflections of light on the duke's armor caused him such frustration he thought he was "losing his mind." In resignation he asked the older and more experienced Jacopo Pontormo to look at his painting and was given the following counsel: "My son, as long as real and shining weapons stand next to this painting, yours will always look painted; although lead white is the most intrepid color used in art, iron is nevertheless much more intrepid and shiny. Move the real weapons away and you will see that your make-believe ones are not as bad as you think."[9] The representational potential of color can develop fully only, it would seem, if its mimetic achievement is not relativized by direct comparison to the referent. Once the real is dissociated from the depiction, the viewer's eye opens to the power of artistic illusion.

In bravura, a "bold" application of color means successfully utilizing the materiality of paint, a medium whose substance, in the case of art, works against the artist's goal of deceptively faithful mimesis. Lomazzo describes piercing light as striking objects *gagliardamente* because it only reveals their illuminated parts, an effect especially evident in light reflected from metallic surfaces.[10] Baldinucci will later qualify the kind of intense chiaroscuro that gives objects a high relief and makes them stand out from the picture surface as an expression of a *maniera forte, o gagliarda*.[11] The power to generate plasticity or *rilievo* inherent in this style satisfies the central requirement by which the excellence of painting as an art is measured.[12]

In his lecture "On Disposition," held September 3, 1704, at the Académie royale in Paris, Roger de Piles explained the liaison created among pictorial objects as arising from the medium of chiaroscuro in concert with design (*dessein*). The commonly voiced reproach that "shadow" conceals a lack of competence in drawing misses the crucial point that, to a certain degree, chiaroscuro can be a substitute for design.[13] Later in the lecture, when discussing terminology used by Italian artists, De Piles added that contrast creates rapport not only between human figures, but even lifeless objects, "in order that they obtain soul and movement" (*pour leur tenir d'âme et de mouvement*). The opposition of light and dark validates the different parts in their visual relation to each other, gives them life and, last but not least, attracts attention.[14] In his *Dialogue sur le coloris* (1699), De Piles defines the "artifice" of chiaroscuro as the most powerful means of forcefully asserting (*faire valoir*) particular colors within a composition as well as the toute-ensemble of the entire composition.[15]

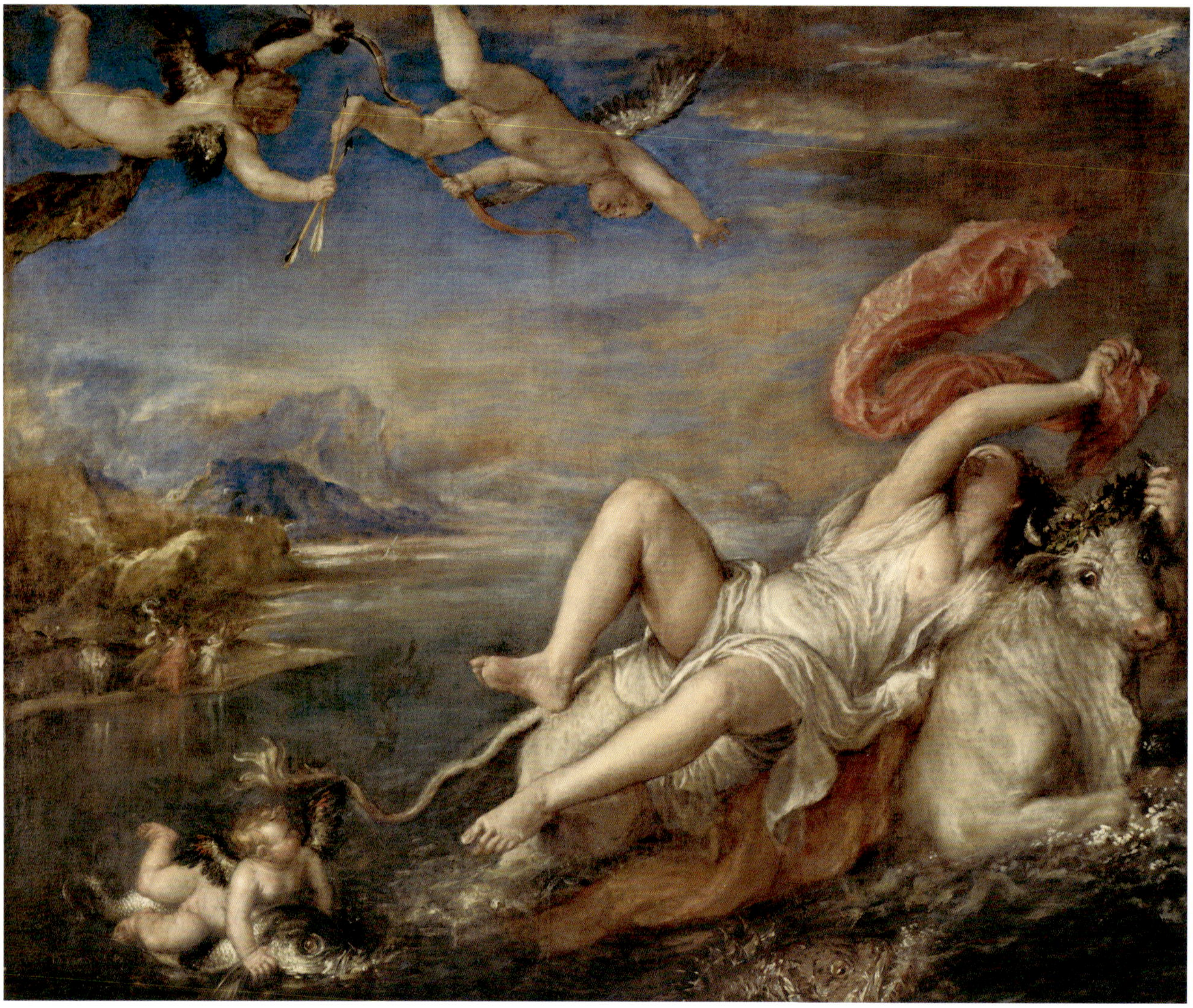

104
Titian, *The Rape of Europa*, ca. 1560–1562. Oil on canvas, 178 × 205 cm. Isabella Stewart Gardner Museum, Boston.

(*Un certo che inefabile e amirando, Che soto l'ochio ne va bulegando, Si che scovegno dir: questo e'l più belo*).[27] He here exaggerates an observation first made by Vasari, who described Titian's late style as making the painting, not its subject but the painting itself as an object, appear to be alive (*fa parere vive le pitture*).[28]

Boschini records an account of Titian's painting procedure as narrated by the Venetian painter and pupil of Titian, Palma il Giovane (1548–1628). He tells us that Titian's paintings were composed on top of a thick mass of paint that served as a "bed" or foundation for his subsequent *espressioni*. After first roughing out a figure with a few decisive brushstrokes on an amorphous, colored ground, Titian would turn the picture to face the wall and take it up again—but only after a certain amount of time had passed. This pause from the rough sketch opened up distance between the artist and his own placements, which he could then reclaim by reworking, and thus repossessing them. Palma compares Titian's correction of his first draft to operations performed by surgeons, who "excise" (*spolpargli*) swellings and tumors, and straighten broken arms. This "setting of bones," in order to bestow a perfect symmetry to the body in keeping with the beauty of nature and art, Boschini would characterize as a violent act: in his view, Titian did not ignore the pain he caused to his figures. This strange statement probably refers to the distorted anatomies in Titian's paintings, which take their logic from the composition as an organic whole. In a practice described by Palma, which Boschini terms as *riformare*, Titian progressively deconstructs the figure in order then to extract form from the substance of the paint (rather than from the outlines of a drawing). Boschini also observes that Titian used the same brush for applying different colors,[29] a habit that has left its traces on many of his later paintings. Following this *dottrina* (the rule), Titian was able to "promise a rare figure" with only four brushstrokes. His *abbozzi* (roughed out paintings) were devoured by the cognoscenti because they were aids to getting one's bearings and finding a good route for navigating "the ocean of painting."[30]

Titian's highly praised *Rape of Europa* may assist us in better understanding the challenges of sailing on these painterly high seas (fig. 104). In the right foreground, Europa is spectacularly staged recumbent on the back of a bull. We see the diagonal of her body stretched out before us, her bare legs sprawled. She finds momentary balance in a dangerously unstable supine position, somewhere between toppling backward and trying to sit up. A swathe of orange-colored cloth that has fallen into the water below lends a certain weight to the parallel form of her left leg suspended in the air and underscores our sense that she is in immediate danger of tumbling into the sea. Europa grasps the left horn of the bull with her left hand; her right hand raises aloft a rippling band of red cloth that communicates with the white cloth waved by a girl left behind on the shore, one of a group of three maidens occupying the picture's middle ground. While the repoussoir *amoretto* in the upper left corner grasps a prized trophy, a shawl of shimmering green and orange, another cupid in front of him dives toward Europa's fluttering band in order to capture it. The sash that would fasten her antique tunic has already been lost, and her loosely wrapped undergarment is about to fall open. This pictorial conspiracy threatening Europa's complete exposure animates the painting. Her navel, visible through her sheer chemise, informs the viewer that the entire garment is see-through; its woven

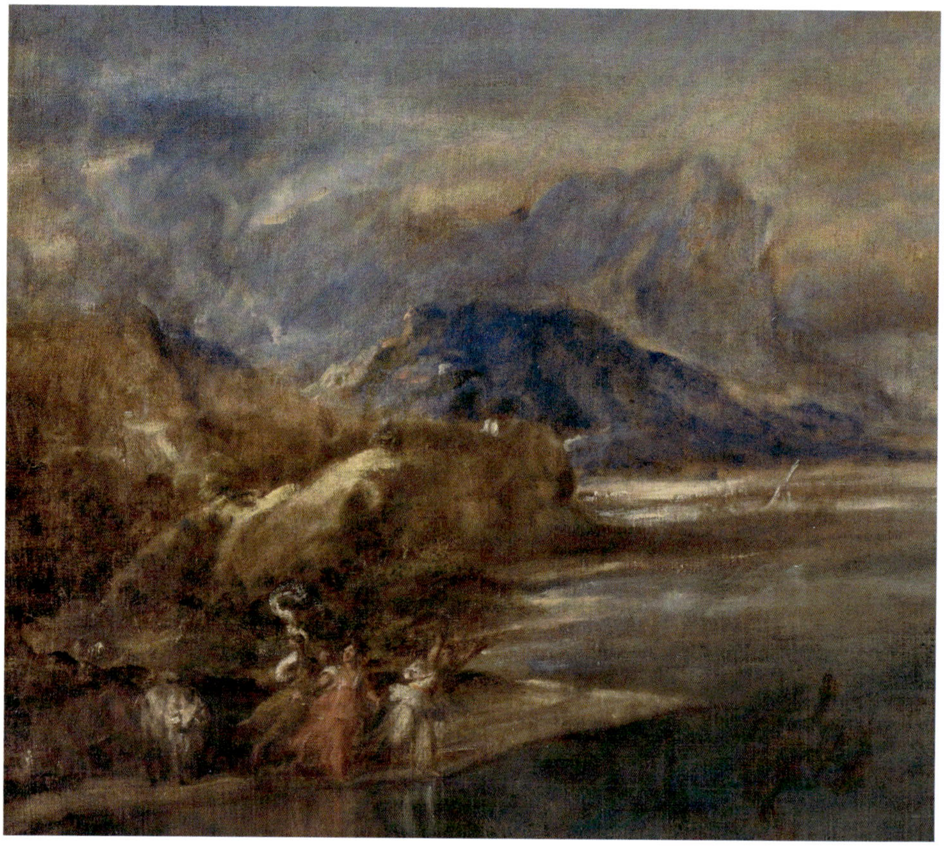

105
Detail of fig. 104
[*The Rape of Europa*].

texture, painted with fugitive brushstrokes, appears in some places even to merge with her body.

The bull's horn is Europa's sole anchor and lifeline, yet she looks back beseechingly, her gaze turned away from the animal. With panic-stricken eyes rolled upward, she searches for her companions, the vaguely sketched, indistinct group of maidens that the beholder's eye barely grasps. This countermotion jeopardizes her balance, while the disproportionally miniaturized scale of the maidens with their herd of cows opens up an indefinable distance between the far shore on which they stand and Europa. As she wrenches her head back, her raised arm casts a shadow across her face. The red cloth in her hand resonates with the redness of her countenance, and also with the hue radiating from the dark cloud formations overhead; her blush thus reverberates in the dramatic evening light that falls over the landscape. Europa's searching, over-the-shoulder gaze pierces the shadow covering it, an effect due to the luminosity of the whites of her eyes as they ecstatically roll back in her head.

The circumstances of Europa's abduction convey the significance of the picture's dense atmosphere (fig. 105). Her desperate situation—she has literally lost the ground under her feet and finds herself at the mercy of a foreign power to whom she has nevertheless turned her back—is palpable in the painting's disintegrating topography and melodramatic ambience. The foremost shore is clearly distinct from the dark green body of water, but in the distant depths of the landscape, solid ground, sea, and sky, clouds, and crags of rock, all become increasingly blurred as their zones of transition are softened by a reddish-orange mist. The haze behind the farthest ridge, of the same blue as the firmament above, contours the mountains and by setting them apart from the sky, gives them substance; it also, conversely, materializes as the mountains themselves and chromatically distinguishes them from the celestial blue. As the background grows increasingly nebulous, a space is created in which the signifying functions of the various colors oscillate and shift. As the concrete world recedes, the beholder's imagination takes flight and eventually is lost in the scene's unfathomable depths.

Two white pastose brushstrokes fixate the gaze, horizontal marks that replace the blurred horizon. The maidens lamenting Europa's abduction with emphatic gestures likewise consist of only a few strokes, and their reflections in the water of single vertical streaks. Because Titian used pictorial conventions to convey their emotions (both arms extended forward, or downward with palms upturned, etc.) the beholder is able to read their protestations. All of these techniques lead the viewer to perceive either more than what is actually represented, or less, depending upon whether they find something or nothing they can recognize. It is therefore in painterly indeterminacy alone, where the viewer's perception will unavoidably be under- or overinvested with meaning, that the potential of painting surfaces invigorates recognition as visual process, making the painting come alive.

MANU-FACTURE

Titian's *Rape of Europa*, one of a series of *poesies* inspired by Ovidian mythology, was made for Philip II of Spain.[31] It was one of the king's most prized paintings and was later copied by Rubens on commission from Philip IV.[32] Through these works and others in the royal collection, Titian decisively influenced the artistic taste of the Spanish court over a span of several generations.[33] The most telling testimony of the high esteem in which he was held by Spanish monarchs is found in the treatise *Arte de la pintura* by Francisco Pacheco, a painter from Seville who served at the royal court in Madrid for two years. According to his account, Philip III "followed the example of his father in his appreciation of Titian," and after hearing of the damage caused by the 1604 fire in the royal palace, inquired only after the condition of Titian's *Venus* (today in the Louvre). The other artworks in his collection were less important to him because, apparently, he believed they could be reproduced.[34]

Diego Velázquez (1599–1660), Pacheco's son-in-law, transformed Titian's *Rape of Europa* into a tapestry hanging in the background of his painting, *Las Hilanderas*. Along with *Las Meninas*, it is considered by art historians today to be among Velázquez's most enigmatic works (fig. 106).[35] Interestingly, the title *Las Hilanderas* (The Spinners) takes no account of the mythological content of Titian's painting and thus rather privileges a reading like that of the art historian Carl Justi, who praised this work as the oldest depiction of industrial production and saw it as representing a visit by noblewomen to the royal carpet manufactory.[36] The first breakthrough in deciphering the painting's iconography, published in 1940, seemed to turn its interpretation "upside down." The back chamber became the focal point, as it were, making the front room semantically accessible only via the back room.

The tapestry can be understood as Velázquez's cunning invention of an intermedium that "decomposes" its model, the *Rape of Europa*, in order to extract its painterly substance. The interpolation of Titian's painting into the context of the wool spinners is achieved on an iconographic level via the bridging device of the Arachne myth, which appears to be the subject of the performance by the two costumed actors in front of the tapestry. They have been identified as Arachne and Athena, the mortal and goddess who in Ovid's *Metamorphoses* participate in a weaving competition that ends in Arachne's death.[37]

In the myth, Athena wove an image of the assembled Olympian gods, ruled over by Zeus and framed by smaller depictions of various contests between gods and mortals, while Arachne chose the abduction of Europa as her central image and surrounded it with similar episodes from the *Metamorphoses*. In the end, Arachne's tapestry, with which neither Pallas Athena nor "Envy itself could find fault," was destroyed by Athena in a fit of rage at its offensive content: it portrayed "heavenly crimes."[38] It seems that Arachne, like Titian, was particularly successful in the erotic genre and, to assert herself as an artist, she chose her subjects accordingly.

106 (FACING)
Diego Velázquez, *Las Hilanderas*, 1655. Oil on canvas, 220 × 289 cm. Museo del Prado, Madrid.

However, the two protagonists in Velázquez's back chamber are unable to transform the room into a purely fictional space.[39] Three courtly ladies, standing before the tapestry and watching the actors' reenactment of the mythological contest, surround the costumed actors like spectators instead of entering the scene as participants. Even the tapestry's woven painting, which frames and dominates the conflict staged in front of it, has lost much of its mythological content and spatial depth. Most of Titian's abduction scene is obstructed from view; only the heads of the bull and Europa, very schematically represented, are visible to the right of the actor possibly playing the role of Arachne, who blocks Europa's spectacularly extended body from the beholder. This may be explained by constraints of decorum, for an erotic image would be inappropriate viewing for courtly ladies. Velázquez's abbreviation of the painting actually works to highlight the blotchy Titianesque style.

The actors' performance, accentuated with grand theatrical gestures, seems oddly stilted and fails to impart any flavor of ancient myth to this back chamber.[40] The genre aspect of the ladies' visit to the royal manufactory has the same effect: it is too prominent, and so is the conspicuous tapestry hung as the main attraction of the room. What is more, in Velázquez's depiction of Titian's *Rape of Europa*, he follows his model so loosely that it is hardly readable. Once the mythological "subtexture" is recognized, however, it appears to fully charge the activity spread across the foreground. Scholarship has almost exclusively taken the route of reading the ostensible genre scene alongside the myth staged in the back chamber, identifying the tale's two main protagonists as present simultaneously on both stages. Accordingly, the figure in the immediate foreground on the right side with her back to the viewer, winding a ball of wool from the spun yarn on her swift, is considered to be Arachne, while the markedly older woman sitting at her spinning wheel, who turns toward the viewer and is also distinguished from the other four spinners by her black clothing and white headscarf, is recognized as Athena. Yet as the art historian Friedrich Teja Bach has noted, the activity taking place in the foreground cannot be construed as a competition, if for no other reason than that it lacks the "fundamental structure of antagonism."[41] Instead of two protagonists facing off at

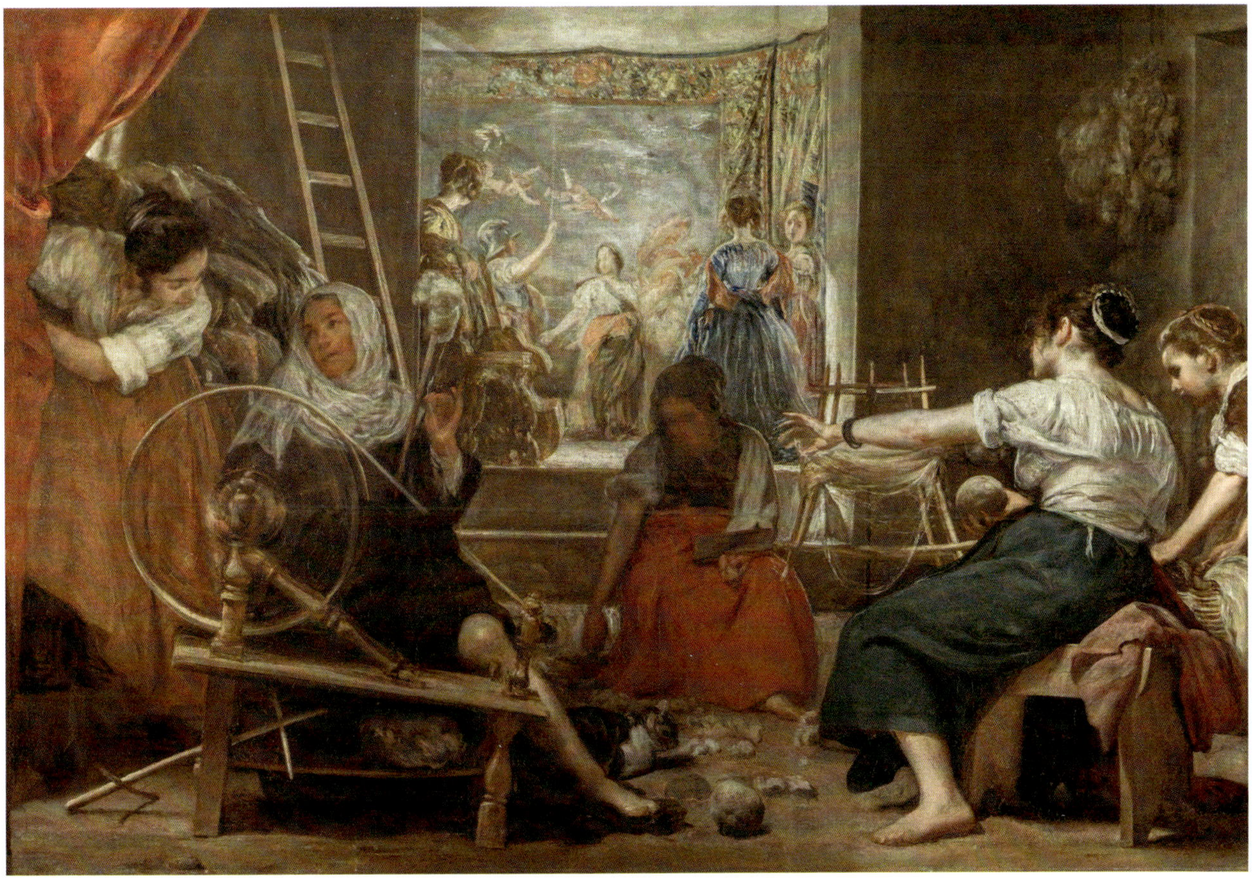

their looms, we see three craftswomen seated next to each other in harmony, occupied with various tasks in the preparation of woolen yarn, while two other helpers approach the group and close the scene at either side. The worker entering at the right margin is bent over a basket brimming with washed wool, while her counterpart, seemingly drawing a large curtain (we cannot see her hands because they are hidden behind it), turns her head toward the woman at the spinning wheel. A third woman, bent over her task in the shaded background, is occupied with carding fleece. None of them are weaving.

The hierarchy of the painting's dual tiers of meaning, the genre-based and the mythological, is reflected in the different floor levels of the two chambers. Reciprocal formal analogies between both groups of five figures serve to bind the spatially distinct events together, while the constellation of the figures as a whole manifests several parallels between the two scenes. These numerous correspondences between the visually detached scenes even out the constructed gradation (illustrated via the stairs and ladder) and thus "elevation" of meaning between the floors,[42] but the extreme steepness of the steps, as the art historian John F. Moffitt rightly emphasizes, makes the transition deliberately difficult and indicates an allegorical reading of the stairs as a *scala sapientis*.[43] Consequently, any effort to read both loci as belonging to one single narrative falls short. Only by unknotting their entanglements and discovering each room's conceptual principle does the nexus of their meanings become accessible to the viewer—with Titian's masterpiece apparently providing the story's plot.

We can reject the possibility that Velázquez's intention here was to make a subliminal moral critique of Titian—Athena punishes Arachne for her pride and arrogance by turning her into a spider. Not only Titian's standing at the Spanish court, but also Velázquez's high esteem for him, displayed in *Las Hilanderas*, rule this out. Arrogance, however, could be a motif that connects Titian to the mythical artist. Arachne's denial that she is in any way indebted to Athena, the patron deity of weaving and thus her artistic role model, which she justifies with the excuse: "I am quite able to advise myself,"[44] may reflect Titian's alleged claim of utterly peerless superiority, documented in Spanish art literature.

Antonio Perez, whose father commissioned Titian's *Adam and Eve* (ca.1550, today in the Prado collection), records a conversation with the artist: Asked why the Venetian painter associated himself with *borrones* (blotches) due to his carelessness (*al descuido*) and rough brushstrokes (*de golpes de pincel groseros*), and did not paint in the smooth manner (*dulzera*) of the virtuosos of his time, Titian answered that it was impossible for him to match the *delicadeza* of the brush of Michelangelo, Raphael, Correggio, or Parmigianino, and therefore he could not aspire to be an *imitador*, but rather he had to find a new way (*un camino nuevo*) to become famous (*celebre*).[45] Palomino, in his vita of Velázquez, interestingly has the artist echo this sentiment when he reports that in response to accusations of not painting objects earnestly with tenderness and beauty (*no pintar con suavidad y hermosura*) in emulation of Raphael, Velázquez countered: There is a greater force of will in being the leader of this rough style (*primero en aquella grosería*) than being a follower of *delicadeza*.[46] Here Velázquez paraphrases—whether in actual fact or as a figure of legend must remain uncertain—Titian's legendary formula. The affinity of their positions within art discourse is thus clear: Like Titian, Velázquez disavows the widely preferred stylistic quality of *delicadeza* in order to become successful in *grosería* (meaning "coarseness" or "rudeness"). In Palomino's opinion, Velázquez painted portraits in Rome *con la manera valiente del gran Ticiano*,[47] and in a description of the portrait of Don Adrián Pulido Pareja, he provides more details on Velázquez's *manera*: "He used brushes; sometimes those with long handles, to here and there paint with greater distance and boldness, such that nearby [the picture] is incomprehensible [*no se comprendía*] but seen from afar it is miraculous [*un milagro*]."[48]

This same dynamic between the experiences of near- and far-viewing is the *locus communis* for the reception of Titian's *maniera*, which Boschini mentions in regard to no other artwork so often as *The Rape of Europa* and *Venus and Adonis* (undoubtedly referencing Titian's later version).[49] Boschini's astonishment (*stupor*) over their *colorito* is such that he can hardly control himself (*no pode star vu medemo in stropa*). They are made from the brushstrokes of a style (*colpi de maniera*) he defines as *una machia de grosso*, and their impact comes from the fact that they cannot be viewed up close. He concludes by criticizing the idea that such a *maniera*, demonstrating skillful facility and quickness, could easily be imitated because concealed behind its *machia artificiosa* lies great artistic erudition. Immediately following this statement on the *imitatio* of Titian, Boschini segues to Velázquez: *L'ano mile sie cento e cinquantun Fu Don Diego Valasques, gran sugeto, Del Catolico Re Pitor perfecto, In sta Cità; no gh'e dubio nissun*.[50] He goes on to state that Velázquez painted Pope Innocent X in Rome using Venetian brushstrokes (*fato col vero colpo venezian*) and emphasizes how strongly the Spaniard "loved" the Venetian painters, *Tician massimamente*, with a true heart and purity of affection (*con vero cuor, con purita d'afeto*).[51] Boschini relates a discussion between Velázquez and Salvator Rosa, in which he repeats the rumor that the Spaniard did not care at all for Raphael's painting style (*E disse: Rafael... stago per dir che nol me piase niente*), and uses this to position Velázquez in opposition to Raphael, Titian's greatest rival. He affirms that for Velázquez, Titian was the standard-bearer (*Titian xe quei che porta la bandiera*).[52]

On what pictorial level does Velázquez reflect Titian's style in *Las Hilanderas*? Friedrich Teja Bach justifies the often-encountered interpretation of *Las Hilanderas* as "painted art theory" by demonstrating, via an etymological derivation of the art-theoretical term *borrones* from *borra* (wool),[53] that the depiction of a room where wool is being worked signals a certain manner of painting.[54] According to Bach, this goes back to Pacheco's equation of *borrones* with Titian's style. In his *Arte de la pintura* (more specifically, in the chapter "Que declara entre varias maneras de pintura cuál se haya de seguir"), Pacheco addresses the style of *pintura a borrones*, to which he attributes greater power and stronger relief (*mayor fuerza y relievo*) than more finished and smooth facture (*acabada y suave*) can muster. It is impossible to impugn this painting style, he insists, if one considers the mastery of Titian, one of Italy's best colorists. Pacheco records a common idiom, which, in his opinion reveals a fundamental ignorance about art: pictures with a lack of finish were supposedly called *borrones de Ticiano*.[55]

The art historian Gridley McKim-Smith points out that the art-historical term *borrones* underwent a change of connotation from explicitly negative to a positive via a subtle process of refinement in its usage, and he notes further that *borrones* would later again be used to discredit this style and consequently would regain its original negative significance.[56] The word's semantic flip-flopping is, however, precisely what gives it power, for it describes the material aspect of an image that viewed up close repels the viewer, yet has a surprising and even stronger effect seen from a distance. A negative experience when standing before the picture is an essential precondition for the realization that what causes the painting's illusion is the painting medium itself.

As McKim-Smith notes in her landmark study on Velázquez's painterly style, the poet and priest Hortensio Félix Paravicino (1580–1633) delivered a sermon on "the world as a painting" (2 Corinthians: 7) for Philip IV in the Royal Chapel in Madrid, where his treasured court painter might possibly also have been in attendance.[57] In his exegesis, he made an intriguing analogy between art and politics with respect to their appropriate appreciation. The light of the world (addressing the king as artifex of his empire) does not exist just for the purpose of seeing; light in and of itself must be contemplated and assessed. Paravicino went on to say that a painting by Titian not studied in the right light is hardly more than a battlefield of blotches (*una batalla de borrones*). Only when it is seen in the light for which it was made does a praiseworthy and heroic union of colors (*una admirable y valiente unión de colores*) take place; it becomes an animated painting (*una animosa pintura*) that on the "official orders" given by the eyes pleads its case before truth (*pone pleyto a la verdad*).[58] Because the painting itself demands from the eye of the beholder to be viewed in the right kind of light, the veracity of the picture can only be seen in a contemplative evaluation. Paravicino employs this original analogy to justify the political claim of absolute sovereignty, which tolerates no outside criticism; in like fashion, viewers must subordinate themselves to the specific rules and regulations of a painting if they are to see it properly.

McKim-Smith discovered yet another important contemporary source on the topic of pictorial truthfulness: the poet Francisco de Quevedo (1580–1645) in one of his poems singles out the naked materiality of Velázquez's painting style and relates it to the artist in a unique manner. Quevedo adjudged Velázquez's *manchas* (blotches)—which are not only to be viewed at a distance, but were also placed from a distance by the artist with his long-handled brush—as being "true" though they are "not verisimilar" (*que son verdad en el, no semejantes*).[59] The art-theoretical development of the idea of *borrones* as being the reverse of the illusion, so to speak, increasingly pits the substantiality of painting as an element of truth against its superficial illusoriness.

Returning to Bach's initial hypothesis concerning *Las Hilanderas* it is highly probable that the so-called *borrones di Ticiano* and the raw wool (*borra*) hanging at the right side of the picture, seemingly uncarded and unwashed, are conceptually connected. The processing of the *borra* as laid out step by step in the genre scene, is detailed in Ovid's Arachne myth. In order to explain the conflict with Athena and the reason for the goddess's resentment, Ovid premises the story with a description of Arachne's artistic talent, which does not so much feature her weaving as her spinning: "And 'twas a pleasure not alone to see her finished work, but also to watch her as she worked: so graceful and deft was she. Whether she was winding the rough yarn into a new ball, or shaping the stuff with her fingers, reaching back to the distaff for more wool, fleecy as a cloud, to draw into long soft threads, or giving a twist with practiced thumb to the graceful spindle, or embroidering with her needle."[60]

The art historian Jonathan Brown has underscored the great technical difficulty of depicting a spinning wheel in motion and suggests that it posed a challenge to Velázquez and was at the same time an opportunity to outdo Titian.[61] The woman sitting at the spinning wheel, distinguished from the surrounding young women by her clothing and age, operates the picture's machine, which requires the highest degree of skill because from it comes yarn so fine its materiality seems sometimes to completely dissolve before the viewer's eyes.

The transformation of the formless, dirty fleece into the ball of wool proffered to the beholder in the foreground can be metaphorically compared to the operations involved in painterly execution: the carding of the wool as the grinding and mixing of pigments, the spinning as a drawing out of nearly invisible contour lines from the paint's unrefined raw substance, and the rolling of yarn into a ball as the commingling of individual brush placements, via the arrangement and harmonization of color, into a *unión*. Velázquez directly relates the spun product to brush ductus when he paints reflected light as thin white lines, which, as the art historian Svetlana Alpers has observed,[62] were inspired by the exemplary bold brushwork of Tintoretto (Palomino notes that Velázquez studied Tintoretto while

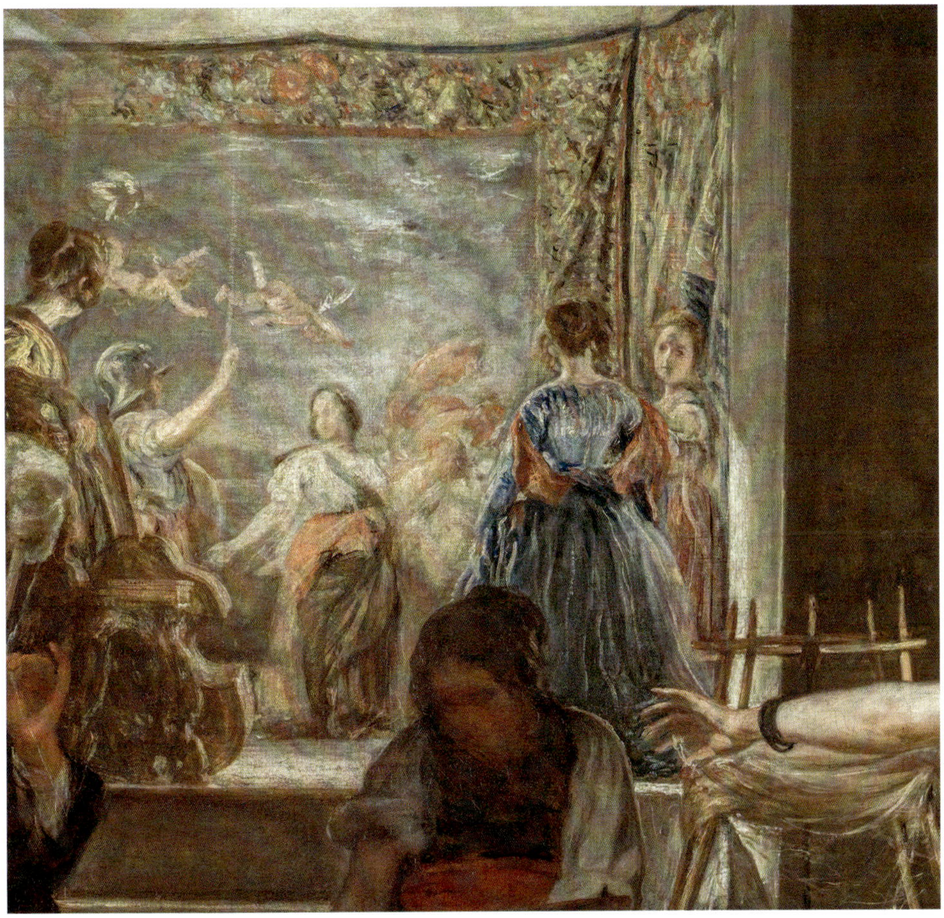

107
Detail of fig. 106
[*Las Hilanderas*].

he was in Italy).[63] Tintoretto's *spada bianca* (Boschini's term) seems to have maintained its "cutting edge" even a century later, although it is tempered here with a mimetic intricacy that points to Titian also as a model: the silhouette of the central shaded figure is outlined on her left side by a white line that visualizes the rays of sunlight striking her back. The splendid dress of the repoussoir figure in the back room is likewise accented by fine, vertical white strokes that enrich the blue cloth. These reflections interestingly interweave, via their planimetric proximity, with the woolen yarn being arranged by the woman whose back is also turned to the viewer and whose left hand reaches out to overlap the blue dress (fig. 107).

The rapid brushstrokes integral to bravura painting are cultivated through training in manual dexterity and, in *Las Hilanderas* the metamorphosis of material into medium—Ovid points out the wonder caused by Arachne's art as it was "*being* made"—is articulated via a bravura style primarily demonstrated in the back chamber and culminating there in the blotchy tapestry. This room is a light-flooded space drenched in fresh color tones, quite different from the dark and murky colors that dominate the foreground. The two zones, one of manual labor carried out by workers in the foreground, the other of aristocratic ladies examining tapestries in the background, are not only spatially separated from each other, but also divided by their distribution of light and shadow and the decorum of their painterly execution. There seems to be much more sophistication in the upper level, where nets of fine bright lines create a shimmer that reflects the costly textures of the ladies' clothing.

At the top of the steps we see a cello-like instrument that seems out of joint with its surroundings. So prominently positioned in the picture but left unused, it appears to function as an iconographic hinge. For John Moffitt, who identified the instrument as a bass lira, it signifies the faculty of reason, which distinguishes the liberal from the mechanical arts, and thus creates a conceptual threshold between the two floors.[64] In Francisco de Hollanda's widely read dialogues on painting, he often emphasized musicality as the measure of an art critic's discernment: Whoever is indifferent to the beauties of art and does not want to possess them is "unmusical" (*desmusicos*); he also reports that it caused Michelangelo "great pain" to receive payment from a *desmusico*.[65] Hollanda compares a good painting to a kind of music and melody (*finalement uma musica e uma melodia*) that only the cognoscenti can comprehend, and even then with great difficulty (*que sómente o inteleito póde sentir, a grande deficuldade*).[66] Velázquez's stringed instrument thus also occupies a threshold between manual production and mythologizing perception, separating the two related realms of art in the picture that are evidently not aware here of each other's presence. The instrument is not being played and therefore indicates only the potentiality of recognition between the two spheres.

Ariadne's centrally positioned expansive gesture, which blocks Titian's spectacular figure of Europa from full view may indicate that the ladies' conversation has shifted from mythology to painterly practice and style. Velázquez's decision to translate Titian's famous painting into a tapestry provides a decisive clue in this regard, and it could have been sparked by Vasari's introductory chapter to the *Vite* (Palomino claims that Velázquez studied the *Lives*).[67] In his *Proemio*, Vasari focuses on pictorial unification, which he tellingly describes as a harmonization of discordant colors (*L'unione nella pittura e une discordanza di colori diversi accordati insieme*). But if the colors are applied brightly and vividly (*accesament e vivi*) and with a heavy mass of paint, *disegno* is offended, for the figures in this case are drawn with the paint rather than the brush.[68] Vasari compares the resulting disorder (*disordine*) to a colorful carpet (*un tappeto colorito*).[69] Velázquez seems to have taken up Vasari's dismissive metaphor and turned it into praise. The courtly ladies in the upper chamber visiting the tapestry manufactory are presented with the myth of the weaver Ariadne as they appraise the carpet hanging on the wall. Velázquez here challenges the general accusation (associated with Venetian *maniera*) of rapid painting as purely superficial and ungrounded by inserting into the picture a workshop-like atmosphere that foregrounds an *industria* based on dexterity and skill (Pacheco says that Titian paints *con más destreza y facilidad*).[70]

The class distinctions between the two depicted realms of the art world could be interpreted as an expression of humility (the painter as craftsman), but could also be understood as a somewhat ironic commentary on the detachment of connoisseurs, who need a theatrical setting in order to mythologize the foundations of their own judgment. It is also worth noting that Velázquez designates the stages of both art production and reception as exclusively female domains.

ROLE REVERSAL

Velázquez's portrayal in *Las Hilanderas* of the courtly ladies' appreciation of bravura, which uncouples the concept of painterly boldness from the martial arts and reconnects it to female manual labor, was humorously and insightfully restaged by Francisco Goya (1746–1826) in a painting whose cutting irony manifests the spirit of the Enlightenment that would deflate bravura's overblown self-staging. Goya produced the small format cabinet piece, held in a private collection today, in 1774, the year before he assumed his teaching duties as deputy director of the Real Academia de San Fernando (fig. 108). His painting on the mythological subject of *Hercules and Omphale* shows the protagonists swapping gender roles. In its traditional rendering, the scene depicts a triumphant queen of the Lydians, more or less scantily clad in Hercules's lion skin and wielding the club he has given over to her, and a nude, seated Hercules who is spinning.[71] But here Goya has foregone the nakedness that would indicate they are lovers. The eroticism of their accustomed encounter has turned cryptic and mysterious.[72] Hercules's activity of threading a needle, in place of the usual motif of spinning, is vexing. The couple's actions and gazes seem to move past one another, even if their activities remain cross-referential: Hercules carries out his delicate manual task; Omphale watches him, visibly amused. They do not make eye contact, but their parted legs intersect.

Goya's rather casual and subdued handling of a quite provocative subject may be due to Omphale's resemblance to Maria Teresa, the young bride of the Spanish Infante Don Louis. The contemporary accoutrements of the scene—the club is replaced by a splendid sword, the lion skin by a luxurious golden yellow cloth draped over Omphale's throne—endows its mythological theme with new relevance. If Goya has indeed incorporated Maria Teresa as a possible addressee, his motivation is less to satirize one of her amorous escapades, as the art historian Manuela B. Mena Marqués has suggested,[73] than to wittily construct a personal relationship between himself and his patroness via the picture's playful hide-and-seek. Hercules seems to have Goya's profile. Disguised as the strongman performing women's work, he submits to his mistress in order to win her favor.

The third person in this enigmatic interaction is as opulently clothed as the others. Like Omphale she smiles, not so much from amusement as in thoughtful rumination, and like Hercules she keeps her gaze lowered and directed at the activity of his hands. She stands in the background but looms rather sublimely over the scene, triumphantly grasping an imposing sword. Isn't *she* Omphale, and the woman seated across from Hercules rather an illustrious witness?[74] While Hercules concentrates on his task, this second woman bears his sword, which has the artist's signature prominently inscribed in golden letters on its blade—"Francisco de Goya. Año 1784"—and recalls the pictorial tradition of comparing painterly practice with the handling of a weapon. Hercules, however, does not brandish his sword but rather a needle, through whose eye he draws a white thread. Its fine filament snakes across the red mantle of the "first" Omphale and disappears into a pink box that sits on her lap.

Hercules is part lost in shadow and part melded into the brown background, but like the task he performs, he "penetrates" into the room dominated by the presence

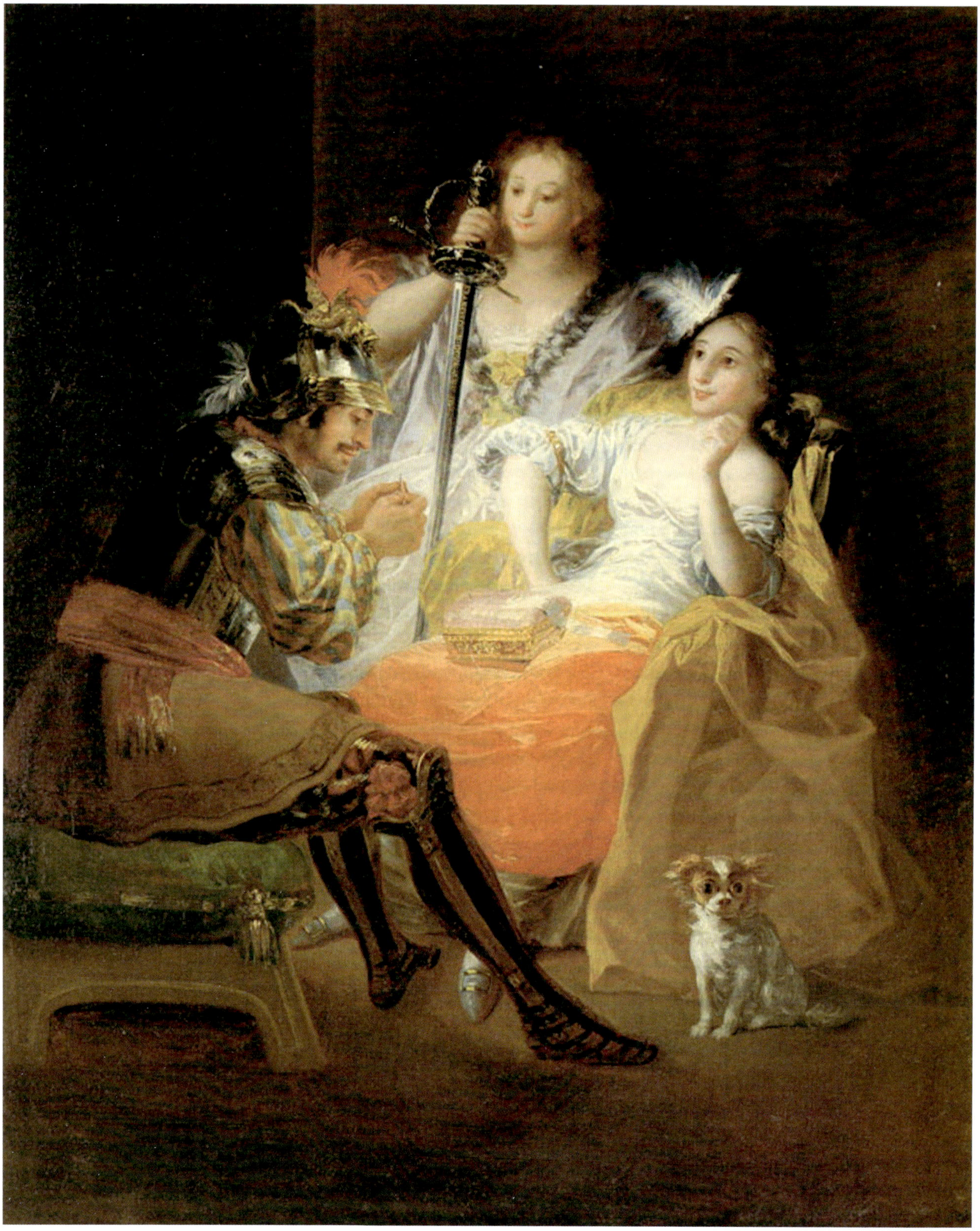

of the two women. His hands stand out to great effect in front of the white billowing cloth that forms a backdrop for the sword and at first glance appear to be folded, as if in prayer to the woman seated across from him. Although his body inclines slightly forward, she leans back in relaxed amusement, her eyes fixed on the bright red panache that tops his helmet; it sits just above a diminutive gilded dragon, and both objects appear to flicker vibrantly. The fiery bundle of feathers seems to inflame the queen's enthusiasm while distracting her from Hercules's occupation, which is anything but *bravuroso* and openly contradicts the signed sword and ostentatious armor that might otherwise visualize bravura. While the women's clothing is of the latest fashion, his extraordinary suit of armor is outmoded: cuirass, greaves, and helmet designate him as a figure from the Seicento.[75] The attention he receives from the seated woman is not prompted by his painstaking needlework, but solely by his outfit, which alludes to the mythological narrative's element of *furia*. His martial appearance may also encode the reason for his state of servitude: the insane rage that periodically turned Hercules into a murderer, even of his own children. This uncontrollable fury is here tamed. His hands are as if bound by his handwork so that his fury must retreat to the decorative ornamentation of his helmet. Hercules's ferocity seems to have leapt from his hand to his mind, or at least to the dragon that is its fantastical spawn; this to the delight of his observer, whose preoccupation with the ornament disrupts their visual communication.

108 (FACING)
Francisco Goya, *Hercules and Omphale*, 1784.
Oil on canvas, 81 × 64.1 cm.
Private collection.

The sword separates the two realms of the picture—*diletto* and *praxis*, and in the gap the artist's signature written on its blade has severed the zone of art from that of the audience. Hercules's amused observer, even as she hands over her sewing box, is not thinking about his skillful performance and therefore seems unwittingly to demand something from him that she cannot properly identify. Only the figure standing behind them is able to bridge the divide: the axis of her gaze connects sword grip to needle's eye. This synthesis, as well as her mirroring of the hero's facial expression, establishes her affective nearness to Hercules's ironic personification of the bravura painter and elevates her own figure as the mysterious personification of *Pictura*, so that she soars above the scene.

CHAPTER EIGHT

Endangering the Youth

CARAVAGGIO'S REALISM

In *Las Hilanderas*, Velázquez's investment of a quotidian scene with mythological significance shifted art-historical speculation about Titian's supremacy to a genre not associated with Titian, but rather with another artist. His works were not represented in the Spanish royal collection, but Michelangelo Merisi da Caravaggio was nonetheless highly important for Velázquez's understanding of art. During his sojourn in Rome, Velázquez had ample opportunity to study Caravaggio's works in situ; though Caravaggio had died years before, his impact on the following generation of painters would have been everywhere apparent to the Spanish visitor. In Rome, his artistic concept of *ritrarre al naturale* (in the sense of copying faithfully nature) was so impactful that it seems to have erased all memory of the pictorial tradition leading to it, which, as we have already seen, Velázquez brought so powerfully into play.

The painter Giovanni Baglione (1571–1643) was a vociferous opponent of Caravaggio's influence—even more of his influence than his art—though Baglione's own style also yielded to Caravaggio's dominance. He spread the rumor that "some believe [Caravaggio] ruined painting because many young painters following his example devote themselves to imitating a head from nature and do not study the fundamentals of design and the profundity of art; they are satisfied with mere *colorito*."[1] Baglione reports that Carlo Venetiano (Carlo Saraceni), whose name often appeared next to Caravaggio's in judicial court protocols, quit his formal schooling because of his determination to imitate his hero's *maniera* and thereby missed out on an education that would have helped him become an "excellent master."[2] The French art theorist Roger de Piles in his *L'Abrégé de la vie des peintres* (1699) comments on the bad taste of Caravaggio's design and then identifies the source of his painting's explosive force: "All of his effort was in coloring."[3]

Giulio Mancini (1558–1630), the papal physician, art collector, and critic, shared this conclusion, but in his *Alcune considerazioni appartenenti alla pittura* (ca. 1620), he remarked admiringly: "Our century owes much to Caravaggio for the coloring he introduced, which is nowadays commonly followed."[4] In the vita of

Salvator Rosa, his friend the painter Giovanni Battista Passeri (1610–1679) transfers to another venue an observation formerly applied to the Venetian school when he writes, "Neapolitan artists are not by nature much inclined to make a prolonged study of drawing, but they prefer from the outset to take up their brushes and oil paints and, as they say, 'to paint.'"[5] It may have been the immense sway Caravaggio held over Neapolitan artists of the generation before Salvator Rosa that gave rise to this new inclination.

According to Bellori, Caravaggio's coloring was limited to the manifestation of realistic flesh tones, facial complexion, and a "natural surface," because these mimetic intentions only depend on the eye and dexterity (*industria*); they disregard "the other concerns of art" (*gli altri pensieri dell'arte*).[6] Bellori ties this self-imposed limitation on *colorito* to a radical conceptual decision that became, even more than Caravaggio's coloring, *the* distinguishing feature of his art. As an addendum to the observation that Caravaggio quickly attained great recognition by means of bold, extremely blackened shadows (*oscuri gagliardi*), Bellori asserts that the method he used for lighting his figures, employing artificial light falling from above into darkened interior rooms to produce a vehement chiaroscuro, caused a sensation among his colleagues: "The painters in Rome were taken with this novelty, and the young ones in particular flocked to him and praised him alone as the unique imitator of nature; looking upon his works as miracles, they vied with each other in following him, unclothing their models and raising their sources of light; and in copying from life everyone readily found a master and examples in the piazza and on the street, without paying any further heed to studies and teaching."[7] Following Caravaggio's doctrine meant not only taking up coloring early, but also life drawing, both skills usually taught at the end of a traditional art education. The student would leapfrog over the first steps of a pedagogical program long based on an orderly succession of interdependent stages. The physician, author, and art connoisseur Giulio Mancini summarized two main features of the Caravaggist *scuola*: light projected from a single source to produce powerful chiaroscuro and relief, and a tenacious attachment to the live or "real" (*il vero*) model, which Caravaggio and his followers always kept in front of them. It amounted to a rejection of artistic tradition as the ideal course of training.[8]

Bellori intensified his already vehement criticism of Caravaggio when he described the artist's "disdain for the superb marbles of the ancients and the paintings of Raphael which are so celebrated"; as a substitute, "he took nature alone for the object of his brush."[9] On account of Caravaggio's negative example, "the antique and Raphael were deprived of all authority."[10] In an anecdote about Caravaggio's choice of the female model for his genre painting depicting a fortune teller, Bellori describes his reaction to the suggestion that he look to the ancients: "When he was shown the most famous statues of Phidias and of Glycon so that he might base his studies on them, his only response was to gesture toward a crowd of people, indicating that nature had provided him with masters enough."[11] Silence and a wave of the hand was for him an adequate response. By regarding the live model as his "maestro," without idealizing or improving its form (which would require an intellectual formula based on pictorial tradition), he was able "to surpass art without art" (*pare che senza arte emulasse l'arte*).[12] His concept of the model as the best teacher meant physical characteristics would specifically guide the conception of the image and guarantee the painting's semblance to life. Paradoxically, the viewer's perception of the live model in the fictive figure was criticized as "unnatural," because it was evidence of the scene's staging, and therefore highly artificial.

It is very unlikely that Caravaggio transmitted his doctrine personally; he was notoriously difficult and aggressive with other artists. A likely candidate for the driving force behind his school was Bartolomeo Manfredi (1582–1622), a mediocre artist who was highly receptive to Caravaggio's novelties and managed to derive from his engagement with Caravaggio's ownership of an eponymous technique, the *methodus Bartolomaei Manfredi*. Sandrart, who uses this term in his Latin version of the *Teutsche Academie*, does not suggest Manfredi's method was written down in treatise form. It seems more than probable, as the art historian Gianni Papi and others have suggested, that Manfredi's sociable personality and his workshop practice did the bulk of the work of conveying the new concept to the following generation of artists. Among them were foreign artists like Nicolas Régnier, Valentin de Boulogne, and Gerard Seghers. They helped popularize the subjects for genre painting made so fashionable by Caravaggio, such as card players and fortunetellers.[13] It was not only hitherto uncommon subjects that contributed to these artists' success, however, but also the daring way they were executed.

Caravaggio invented the single figure history painting, revitalizing and subverting the typical iconic images of saints with their attributes by exchanging their quality of eternal, ethereal presence for an introspective corporality, especially as embodied in a life-changing moment. Manfredi adopts these conceptual innovations in his depiction of King Midas bathing in the river Pactolus in hopes of washing away his fatal gift of turning everything he touched into gold—the divine fulfillment of his imprudent wish (fig. 109).

Midas sits on a river bank, leaning forward with one leg partially submerged and the other resting on a rocky mound in the water. Caravaggio's influence on the figure is most tangible in the posture of Midas's bent head, which bears a dazzling similarity to Caravaggio's Christ in *The Crowning with Thorns*.[14] The mixed message inherent in that subject, namely Christ's two natures and the crowning as humiliation, befits Midas.

Midas seems to squeeze his left foot, pushing down on it with his left hand. Drops of gold bubble up from the rock. Their color resonates not only with the crown that identifies him as a king, but also with the cape that seems to slip from his body. Whereas his right upper thigh is covered with the royal garment, the naked knee of his left leg is bare and projects into the viewer's space. That Manfredi looked also at Caravaggio's *Narcissus* for inspiration, with its compositional orientation around a central "phallic" knee, seems more than probable. Midas's eye-catching knee conceals his genitals. The sinful Adam-like state into which the royal figure has deteriorated is suggested by the brownish shading of his naked body and face, which vaguely suggests body hair and a downcast mood. The moral of the legendary story can be read in the earthy and naked appearance of the once insatiable king, who now sheds his wealth like an unwanted skin. And Manfredi is able to so clearly enunciate this message through heavy reliance on Caravaggio's most famous stylistic feature—the chiaroscuro on the live model's body that

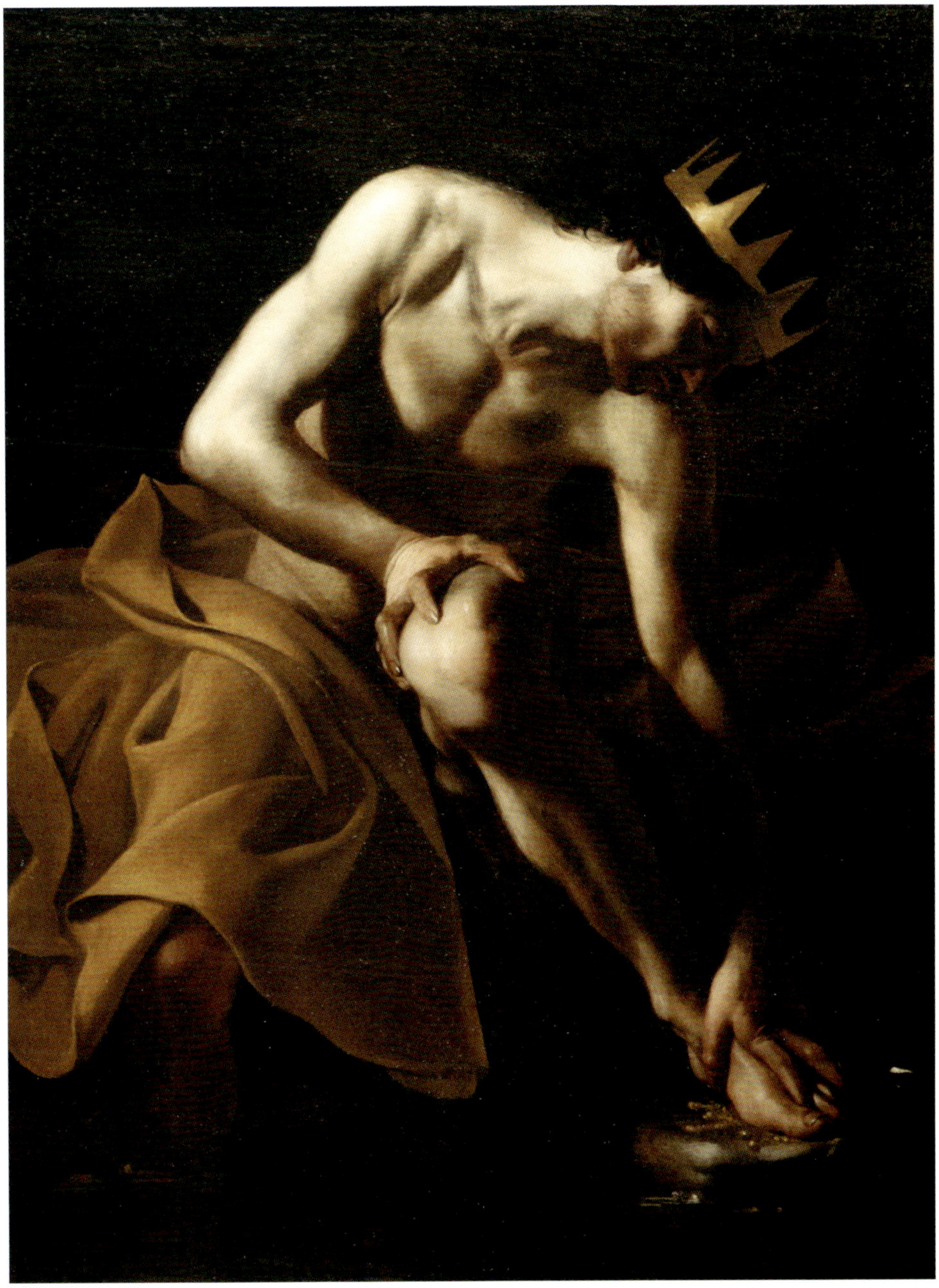

109
Bartolomeo Manfredi, *King Midas Bathing at the Source of the River Pactolus*, ca. 1617–1619. Oil on canvas. Private collection.

signals a dramatic turn of events and endows the mythological figure with natural emotional expression.

Caravaggio's forceful chiaroscuro is a common feature, adding drama to many of his paintings, but there is one work in particular where lighting intervenes in the narrative in a most astonishing way while at the same time trivializing its protagonists; here it is the medium alone that conveys the message. Bellori dedicates only a few words to this piece: "In the Church of the Madonna del Popolo, in the Chapel of the Assumption painted by Annibale Carracci, are two paintings from Caravaggio's hand on either side of the altar, the Crucifixion of St. Peter and the Conversion of

St. Paul; the latter history is completely without action [*questa storia e affatto senza attione*]."[15] The mention of Annibale's altarpiece underscores the contrast Caravaggio deliberately engineered between his work and his colleague's brightly colored, highly animated depiction of the Virgin Mary ascending to heaven. The latter unfolds in orderly fashion through various stages of emotional reaction as the Apostles witness the wonder.

In an open affront to any expectations that the chapel's central painting may have suggested, Caravaggio chose one of the most agitated of religious subjects, the conversion of Paul,[16] but represented it *senza attione*—in a state of stasis (fig. 110).[17] That Caravaggio was aware of the many earlier portrayals of this subject is evidenced by the clear references he wove into the figure of the stricken Paul. Caravaggio's figure seems to mimic the posture of the saint on Raphael's famous tapestry for Pope Leo X. And as in Zuccari's composition (see fig. 86), the saint's head is positioned near the lower border of the altar painting, its rotation to the right corresponding to the lateral viewing angle in the Cerasi Chapel. But in Caravaggio, the gesture of Paul's hands, articulating an openness and willingness to receive God's word, is answered with a blind silence: there is no wondrous arrival, no divine presence to communicate with the fallen soldier.

In *The Sacred Image in the Age of Art*, the art historian Marcia Hall explains how this painting expresses Caravaggio's typical attitude toward pictorial tradition and why it caused such offense among his contemporaries: "We see Saul experiencing his vision, but not the vision itself. It may be hoped that through contemplation of Saul's encounter, the worshiper may also communicate with God, but that can be only by grasping Saul's experience. There is nothing noble or distinguished, and certainly nothing saintly, about this soldier, seen from above, lying upside down on the ground."[18] Moreover, his figure is marginal in comparison to the dominant groom and horse, whose prominence and realistic rendition Friedlaender underscores: "The first thing to catch the eye would certainly be the enormous horse that fills more than three-quarters of the available space. It is a piebald, very bulky, and rather proletarian horse."[19]

110 (FACING)
Michelangelo Merisi da Caravaggio, *Conversion of Saint Paul*, 1600–1601. Oil on canvas, 230 × 175 cm. Cerasi Chapel, Santa Maria del Popolo, Rome.

In Lorenzo Pericolo's formative interpretation of the painting, he defines the animal, which in pictorial tradition rears up in panic at the presence of the divine, as a barrier blocking the beholder's view of the miracle taking place at the moment of Paul's collapse.[20] The substantial presence of Paul's "phlegmatic" horse therefore centers and anchors the picture conceptually.[21] "The immense beast," as the art historian Françoise Bardon has noted, occupies the "place of the hero in this history *à l'envers*."[22] Bardon understands its disproportionate and impressive presence relative to the narrative's main figure as communicating Paul's perspective to the viewer. She highlights how the mane mediates the connection between the horse's head and the arm of the fallen Paul, and rightly notes that the groom, who completes the scene as a witness, seems to be an extension of the horse's body, his legs continuing the horse's direction of movement to the right.

It appears that the two human protagonists are aware of each other, even though they move past one another. The old groom at first seems to be stooping down to address the fallen soldier, but if this was his intention it has miscarried for, on second glance, we see him taking a step to the right, away from the proceedings.

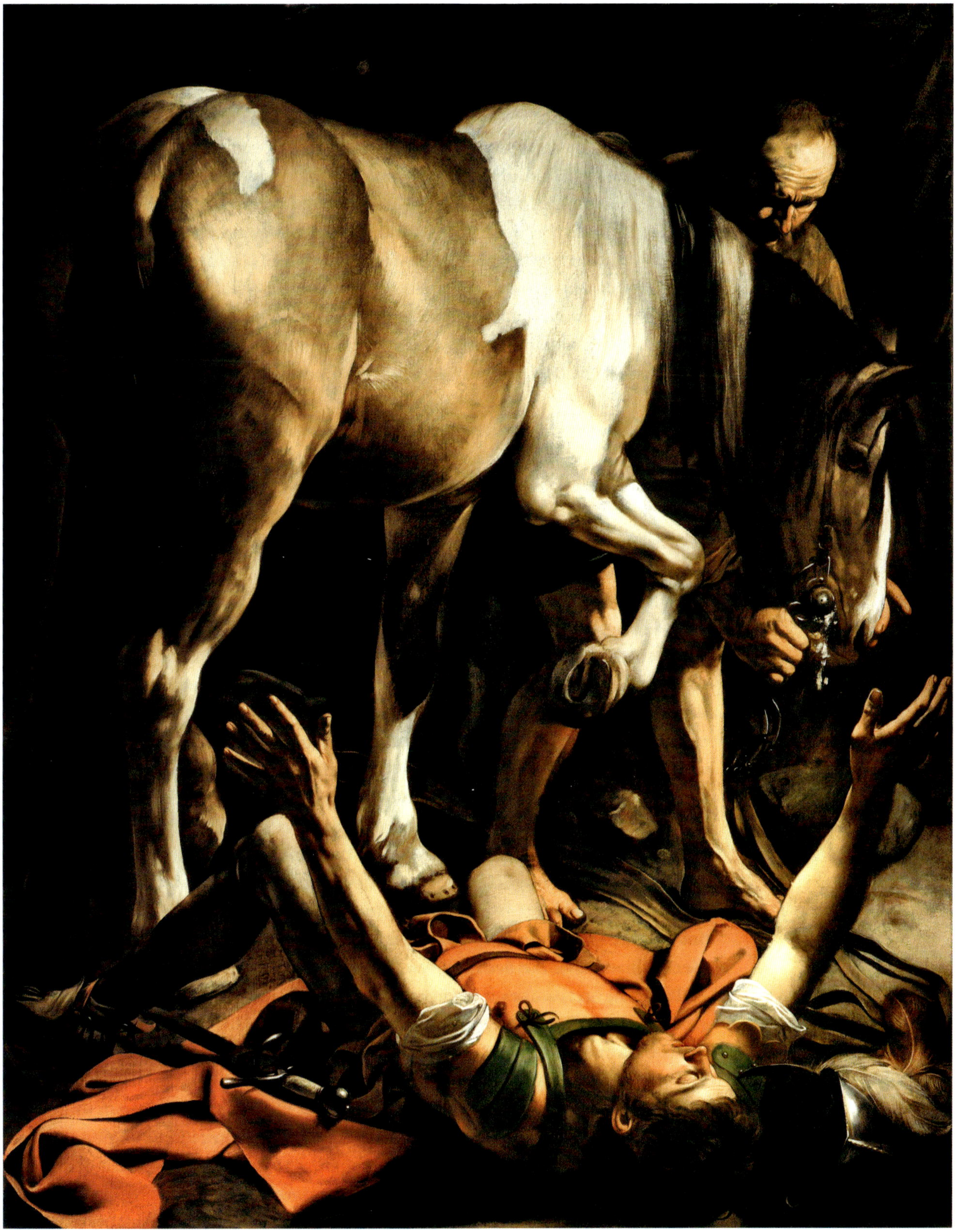

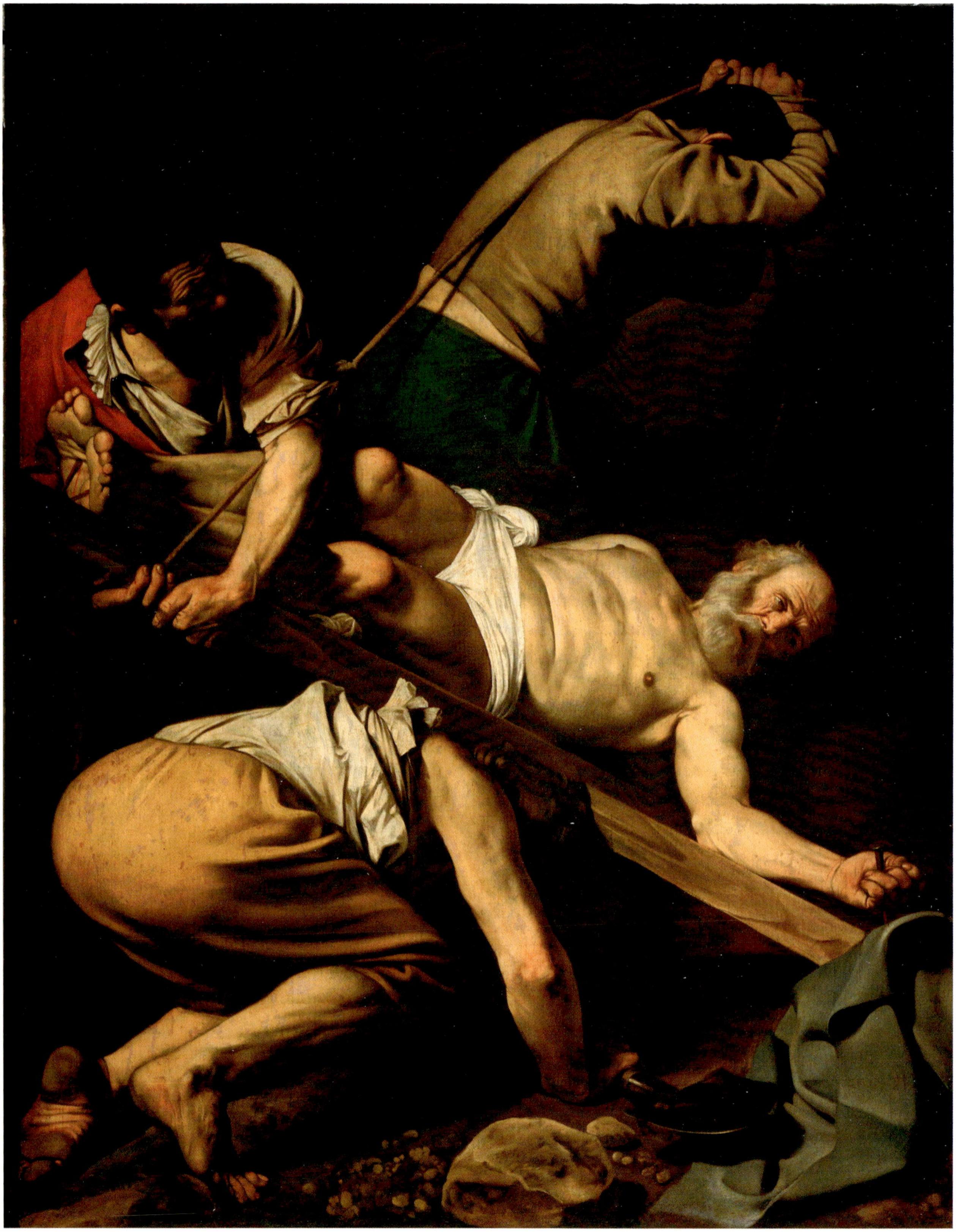

and shoulders. He is the closest figure to the beholder due to the painting's oblique viewing angle, necessitated by its position at the left side of the chapel altar; his illuminated buttocks seem to thrust outward into the darkness of the chapel's small space. The force of his toil is taken up by the standing figure who leans forward with his upper body as he strains against a rope that he holds taut across his back. A third man joins in, wrapping his arms around the upright beam of the cross where the rope is fastened to it. We see that the tensioned rope is the effective force raising the cross, because it is taut enough to catch onto and sharply tug the rolled-up sleeve of the third man. This moment also distances the latter's arm from St. Peter's legs. None of the three men touch the saint's body; their movements are all connected to the cross.

Remarkably, "a cross" as such is not visible: extreme foreshortening has reduced the two beams to one central diagonal,[28] and a blue cloth covering the end of the transverse beam adds to the spatial confusion. As a result, the lifting of St. Peter paradoxically gains visual clarity. Françoise Bardon has correctly pointed out that the cross's fugitive form is replaced by the figural composition of the scene's active participants.[29] The distribution of the primary colors marking the form's four components acts as a hint to the beholder's eye, which is then able to see "another thing" (in Paleotti's sense) through spiritual contemplation: the withheld image of a cross ghosted in the x-shaped figural composition. The decussate form of this imaginary cross strengthens the upright thrust of St. Peter's heavy cross, and it may also be read, simultaneously, as the Greek letter *chi* in the name of Christ. This thought may be too far removed from its visual basis, but theologically it is the cross of Christ, not St. Peter's, that is worthy of veneration according to the new Counter-Reformational understanding of the image.

We could even take Friedlaender's statement that Caravaggio's realism urges the beholder to "participate in the terrible work" a bit further. Does this participation also extend to imitation? The three actions depicted in this crucifixion appear in a different light if we compare them to Michelangelo's powerful image of several figures lifting the Cross of Salvation in the *Last Judgment* (fig. 112). Here we also see, at the lower end of the cross, a figure on hands and knees whose buttocks are thrust toward the beholder. Another angel carrying the heavy cross on his back resembles the workman leaning forward in Caravaggio's painting. The sight of the rope cutting deeply into this man's back, and the immediate bodily response may remind Christian viewers of the ritual reenactment of Christ's Passion by worshippers carrying a wooden cross in procession. The third man's gesture also is familiar, recalling the figure of Simon of Cyrene. From this perspective, St. Peter becomes an intermedium; his martyrdom both recalls and repeats the crucifixion of Christ although in reversed fashion. Caravaggio's blunt imitation of nature reminds the beholder in a most unsettling way of the need to imitate Christ, an imitation that begins as soon as they "fix their thoughts," as Paleotti would say, on the true cross "hidden" in the painting. The significant weight of the models' bodies, whose lifelikeness creates contemporaneity and thus urgency, breaks open the self-contained boundaries of the image, opening to the viewer an inner vision for which Caravaggio takes no credit. His representation is focused on, and excels in, the impact of the bodies' physical presence and the deep implications of their postures.

111 (FACING)
Michelangelo Merisi da Caravaggio, *Crucifixion of St. Peter*, 1601. Oil on canvas, 230 × 175 cm. Cerasi Chapel, Santa Maria del Popolo, Rome.

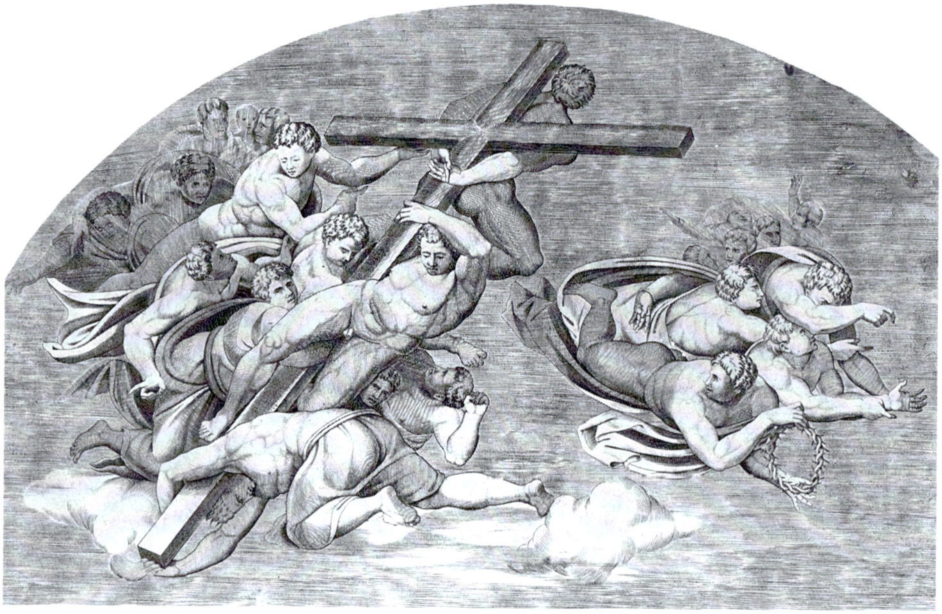

112
Niccolò della Casa, after Michelangelo, *Angels Carrying the Cross* (upper left section of the *Last Judgment*). Engraving, 83.6 × 67.5 cm. Metropolitan Museum of Art, New York.

Vicente Carducho (1576?–1638), a Florentine painter active at the Spanish court, anticipated De Piles's comparison of stylistic infection (specifically that of Caravaggio) to a strong aftertaste. He compares the artist's way of painting to a new dish "seasoned with a sauce so tasty, appetizing, and full of relish that all are swept up into overindulgence and licentiousness," which he fears is a sign of "some sort of apoplexy regarding the true doctrine." Carducho remarks worriedly that a large number of painters enthusiastically follow Caravaggio without considering whether they will be able to "digest" mentally this hard, unusual, and unbearable *maniera*. He asks: "Who could ever paint thusly and reach the level of this monster in talent and naturalness, who taught himself without recipe, without lessons, without study, alone by the power of his genius?"[30] It becomes apparent that the "contagion" of Caravaggio was symptomatic of a larger infection that was taken up and amplified by many of his contemporaries.

Alongside Caravaggio and Giordano, Simon Vouet was also the object of such acrimony. Roger de Piles praises Vouet's *facilité* and emphasizes Caravaggio's impact on the young artist during his stay in Rome, mediated by the French *Caravagiste* Valentin de Boulogne. Vouet's strong shadows and the "ease of his brush" reveal specific ways in which he absorbed the manner of his role model while at the same time developing his own variation on it that influenced a whole generation of French painters. De Piles adds that the French king liked to watch Vouet at work and even had the artist teach him how to draw in pastel, which of course elevated Vouet's reputation.[31] The author Charles Perrault (1628–1703) echoes both the praise and criticism of Vouet. He ranks the artist as one of the *hommes illustres*, not only due to his talent, but above all to the large number of his students. He calls Vouet the "Restorer of Painting" and cites as most commendable the "freedom and freshness of his brush," but then goes on to criticize his contrast of light and shadow as too strong and conspicuous.[32]

The *liberté* of his practice that enabled him to plant his own mark on Caravaggio's trendsetting doctrine would, in De Piles's view, become a trap for his successors. True, Vouet had destroyed a dull and barbaric style (Martin Fréminet is named as an explicit example), but the artist's *manière* was nevertheless "scarcely natural, untamed, and simple," and, alas, his technique was so enthusiastically adopted that it ultimately infected the imagination of all his students, causing them to form habits that could only be overcome with the greatest difficulty.[33]

In art literature, the classicists' disapproval persisted and was even incongruously espoused by one of Caravaggio's followers. According to De' Dominici, Ribera commented during his sojourn in Rome that he had great difficulty with the softness and correctness of Raphael's manner because it was so much the opposite of Caravaggio's, which he characterized as "fierce, coarse, and confused with shadow;" Caravaggio "proved to be disadvantageous, instead of providing useful lessons on truth, nobility, and corrections of contours, which were often lost in the overwhelming darkness of his fields."[34] Here Ribera complains about a compositional device he himself prominently employed: his insinuation of a *prejudicio* inherent in chiaroscuro, which causes a lack of clarity and is detrimental to contour, indirectly reiterates the principle charge against this practice, namely that it hid a lack of drawing ability under the cover of darkness. Bellori had earlier paired Raphael and Caravaggio as opposites and lamented the bad influence of the latter on the younger generation: "Once the majesty of art had been subjugated in this way by Caravaggio, everyone assumed license, and the result was contempt for beautiful things, and the antique and Raphael were deprived of all authority."[35]

Caravaggio's demonstrative *sprezzare* of classical models triggered the contempt of one of his French colleagues. Félibien relates: "Monsieur Poussin could not stand anything from Caravaggio and said he came into the world to destroy painting."[36] Poussin's condemnation is actually counterproductive, because his critique involuntarily helped to enhance Caravaggio's reputation as a rebellious innovator, an image that accorded with the artist's self-staging as an outlaw. Giovan Pietro Bellori, a friend of Poussin, would, as we have already shown, endorse Poussin's hostile image of Caravaggio in the portrait vignette that accompanied his vita, where the artist is shown holding the hilt of a dagger in his right hand (see fig. 26).

When the author Antoine-Joseph Dezallier d'Argenville (1680–1765) remarked in retrospect that "Caravaggio was lucky to exercise his talent at a time when they only painted from rote practice,"[37] it is not clear whether he too meant to classify Caravaggio's manner of painting as *de pratique*, or if he was singling him out as an exception and thereby explaining why the artist's novel way of painting caused such a furor. This second interpretation is supported by several examples of how the term "*pratique*" is used. Dezallier d'Argenville would reflect Bellori's judgment of the historical situation: "There is no doubt that Caravaggio benefited painting, coming at a time when working from nature was not much in fashion, and figures were represented according to artistic practice and style, and more was done to satisfy the sense of graceful beauty than that of truth."[38] Bellori's connection of both *pratica* and *maniera* with unnaturalness is common. Orlandi, for example, in his *Abecedario* characterizes the Venetian Antonio Cecchini as one of the painters, who "according to the taste of their times, around 1660, worked from practice or routine, without considering the effects of nature."[39] Dezallier d'Argenville also uses *de pratique* in this sense in a passage on the Genoese painter Bernardo Castello, an artist he initially called a good draftsman: "[Castello] had much genius and a good tone in coloring, but a painter who only works from practice reveals a savage disposition that is unlike anything else."[40]

GIUSEPPE CESARI LIFTING WEIGHTS

The rather unfavorable quality of *della pratica* is ascribed to the work of Giuseppe Cesari, also known as Cavaliere d'Arpino (1568–1640), whose daring self-inscription into his famous *The Battle of Tullus Hostilius against the Etruscan Cities of Veii and Fidenae* we encountered in the first chapter. Only nine years older than Caravaggio, he ran a thriving workshop at a young age and employed Caravaggio during his first years in Rome to paint images of fruit as decorative motifs. Shortly thereafter the two became fierce rivals, who regularly attacked and challenged each other verbally and artistically.

The famous accusation that Cesari's pictorial language lacked theoretical foundation (especially when compared to that of his role model Raphael), is echoed in a marginal gloss written in Bellori's hand in his copy of Baglione's vita of the artist: *Pittore di spirito (cioè di talento naturale) che non di scienza.* In an article on Cesari, tellingly titled, "A *bravissimo* painter, the most *bravo* of all, but not a great artist," Claudio Strinati explains that in Bellori's time it was no longer enough to be a skillful bravura painter; the new art was based on higher spiritual ideals that repudiated Cesari's style.[41]

The humanist and patron Vincenzo Giustiniani, in his *Discorso sopra la pittura,* filed Cesari alongside painters known for working *di maniera.*[42] He attributed to them the ability to form heads and figures without observation and solely by virtue of imagination, based on extensive practice in drawing and coloring.[43] Félibien felt obliged to repeat Giustiniani's authoritative judgment, likewise describing Cesari as the leader of a contingent of painters who "without adhering to nature are pleased to see great [visions from their] imaginations well represented," and admiring in him "this abundance, this facility, and that which the Italians call *furia.*"[44] It thus makes sense that according to Carel van Mander, Cesari was first noticed while still a boy as a "master" in dragons and grotesque masks, things that were in general regarded as products of pure fantasy.[45] This wunderkind discovered by the pope himself was the son of an "average painter" who preferred to "wield weapons in warfare against France instead of pigments and brush."[46] The youngster completed his first prominent piece, a grisaille representation of Samson carrying the gates of Gaza on his shoulders, in the Vatican's Sala Vecchia degli Svizzeri during the pontificate of Gregory XIII (fig. 113).[47]

In Cesari's representation, we see a brawny Samson striding forward like a young Hercules, shouldering the burden of the gate's wooden panels. Reminiscent of the demigod, Samson covers his nakedness with the skin of a lion he has dismembered with his own hands. The elongation of his body, an optical counter to its heavy weight, is violent in its impact. The planks he carries extend beyond the picture's edge and seemingly burst through the space between the framing columns

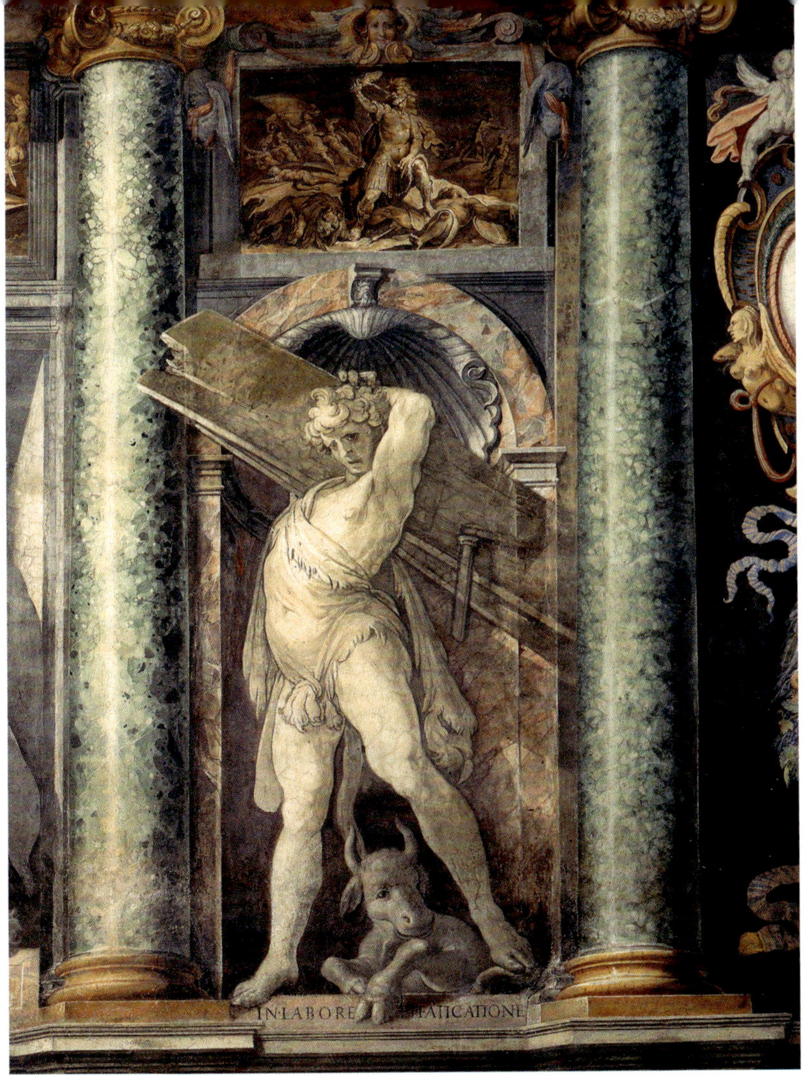

113
Giuseppe Cesari, *Samson Carrying the Gates of Gaza*, 1585. Fresco, height: 234 cm. Sala vecchia degli Svizzeri, Vatican City.

on either side.[48] The tense expression on his face darkened by shadow signals the terrifying temperament of this warrior known for attacking the Philistines. He is like a force of nature. The art historian Herwarth Röttgen, who pointed out the almost dance-like pivoting movement of the figure within its architectural niche, as well as the logic-defying motion that lifts his heavy, muscular physique up from the ground, understands the body's flexed-bow shape as rhetorical hyperbole directed against classical rules of proportion.[49]

Lying under Samson's striding legs, an ox points with its hoof to a motto inscribed along the picture's lower margin: *In labore et faticatione.* Samson effortlessly shouldering his burden is thereby assigned an allegorical significance that is reformulated on the architectonic base of the picture: *Per Labores Virtus Incedit.* In a drawing that parallels the fresco in many details—it is actually the earliest extant from Cesari's hand—the single word *laboris* is written under the crossed hooves of the ox (fig. 114). A second inscription adjacent to the ox, reading *io jos darpino,* is situated under the lion's tail hanging down between Samson's legs. Cesari's signature at this location creates an explicit correlation between the tremendous endeavors of the artist and the heroic figure. In contrast to the self-portrait of himself as a soldier that he inserted into a battle scene, the fifteen-year-old Cesari depicted

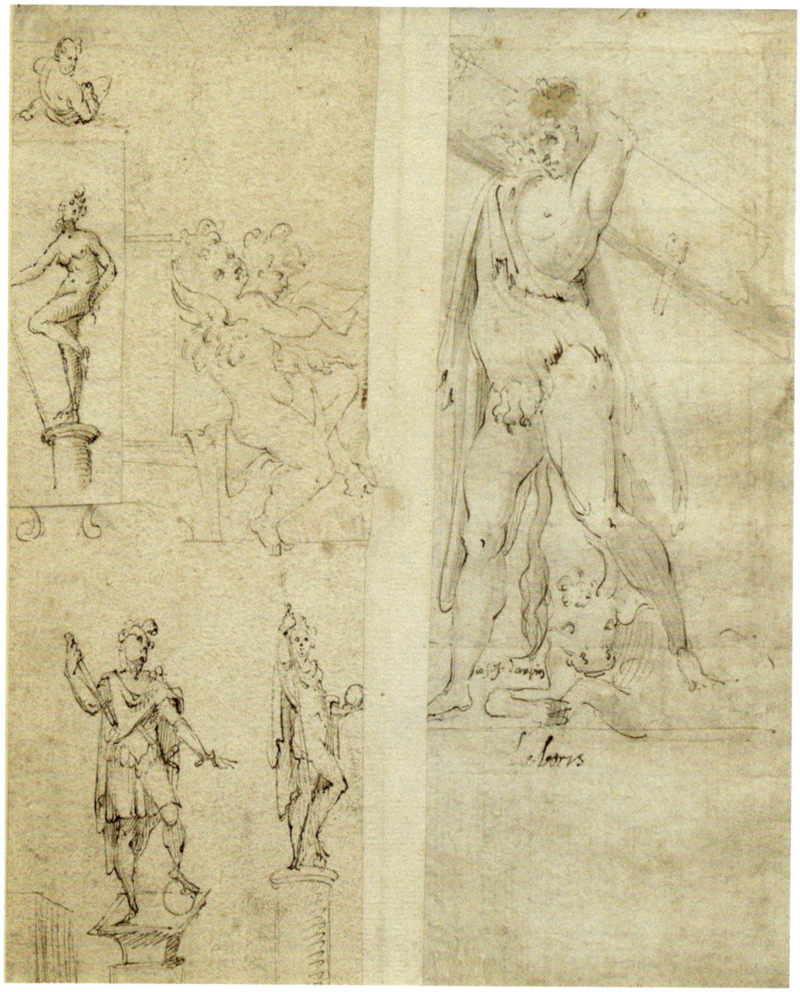

114
Giuseppe Cesari, sketch for *Samson Carrying the Gates of Gaza*, 1585. Pen drawing with wash, 19.3 × 15.6 cm. Kupferstichkabinett, Düsseldorf.

here seems to imagine himself as a monumental (eight-foot-tall!) grown-up. With a manly demeanor he bears his self-imposed burden as if destiny itself had laid it upon his shoulders. This painting, which indeed helped the young Cesari achieve a breakthrough in his career, unmistakably lays bare his ambition: every seeming difficulty is child's play for this boy, just another chance to exhibit his strength. Here he alludes to his own person as a personification of labor in a commission awarded as part of a larger decorative program. Cesari's mastery is such that he steps easily over the ox symbolizing work that lies at his feet.

The Latin *fatigatio* (fatigue) used in the inscription encapsulates the physical aspect of Cesari's artistic understanding. It further elaborates *labor* (work) and spells out what the grisaille piece portrays—the transformation of artistic effort into power (*virtus*). The terpsichorean torque of the stance he adopts while bearing his burden is doubtless in itself a physical performance that requires the exertion of the entire body. Caravaggio and Cesari thus share a certain corporeal view of art, but whereas the former uses the human body as a critical medium for contemplation of the *conditio humana*, the latter uses it to advertise his own muscular strength.

A polarization of opinion seemed always to surround these two artists, and it was categorically similar in the two cases in that it centered on practice. Bellori, in fact, mentions both Caravaggio and Giuseppe Cesari as negative examples in his vita of Annibale Carracci: "After a long, exciting phase, painting [was] pulled back and forth between two extremes, the one was in the thrall of the natural, the other fantasy; the instigators in Rome were Michelangelo da Caravaggio and Giuseppe d'Arpino; the first depicted mere bodies, as they appear to the eyes without any sort of selection, the second paid no heed at all to the natural and followed the liberty of his instinct." This appraisal Bellori preceded by a lament on the general decline in painting: "The Queen [i.e., Painting] became meek and ordinary... and artists no longer studied nature, making art invalid due to *maniera*, or more precisely, due to the fantastic idea that relies on practice alone, instead of on *imitatio*. This destructive abomination first germinated in masters having the best reputation and took root in the schools of their followers."[50] What unites both of these schools is a shared concept of art as based on practice rather than, as Bellori would prefer, an inner and higher "Idea" that foregrounds spiritual content over the forms of reality.[51]

The vice of *maniera* seems then to lie in the irresistible draw of certain artistic role models, whose exemplary works outshine the knowledge they embody, a knowledge necessary for, but absent from their execution. The prodigies Lafage and Fréminet, both imitators of Michelangelo, and Cesari who adopted Raphael, were accordingly founded on a shortcut that ultimately led to a developmental impasse (the fame of these men quickly passed and all three are of marginal importance in art history today), but during their heyday they were able to impress and win over the succeeding generation.

In a reformulation of Bellori, Félibien links the decline of painting even directly to the duo of Caravaggio and Cesari: "No one made detailed studies anymore of that which is necessary for the perfection of the artwork; everyone followed his own whim [*caprice*], and in Rome two different factions came into being that divided the entire youth... Caravaggio was the leader of the first group. Giuseppe d'Arpino was head of the second; and because of the daring of his undertakings and the brilliance revealed in his compositions, he acquired a great following."[52] In short, the ruinous consequences of working *alla pratica* strike at the very foundation of artistic invention. That, in its detractors' view, is the trouble with this kind of bravura. The first signs of "decline" manifest in painting practice as a "thickening" of the surface (most readily cognizable in the pastosity of the paint substance, as discussed in chapter 4), which blurs the knowledge that allegedly underlies it. This concealment induces a disregard of theoretical principles because raw materiality rendered with spectacular phenomenal effects captures the unschooled eye and promises the artist easier access to the elusive capital of art.

Public amazement at rapid execution encouraged some quite eccentric exploits. According to a report by Giovanni Battista Armenini, his friend Luca Cambiaso (1527–1585) was supposed to have used both hands while painting the frescoes in Genoa's Church of San Matteo, holding in each a brush fully loaded with paint and yet operating in a very expert and decisive manner. A drawing attributed to Cambiaso of a Madonna with St. Sebastian and St. Roch confirms this artist's curious ability with the inscription, *Luca Cambiaso dipingeva con due mani*.[53] It is thus not only paintings that open a space for experimentation, but also the drawings used as studies, where time- and labor-saving techniques can be tested in order to hone bravuroso artistic skills. The "incredible quickness" with which Cambiaso created his works brings him close to Tintoretto.[54] However, after seeing a drawing by Cambiaso, Tintoretto is alleged to have expressed both criticism and appreciation: "These are enough to ruin a young artist who does not yet have enough command of the fundamentals of art, but an honorable man who practices his craft may gain something from these because they are filled with expertise [*erudizioni*]."[55] This statement probably refers to Cambiaso's practice of rapidly putting form to his first pictorial thought: he drew the human body by breaking it down into cubes, diminishing the need for precise knowledge of the body's physical structure and thereby dismissing the need for a foundation in *disegno*. Such knowledge was, of course, already possessed by the *galantuomo*, but not the *giovine* (fig. 115). When young artists took to substituting such technical shortcuts for a proper artistic education, they committed themselves to a practice whose essential foundation—an understanding of the human anatomy—would remain always inaccessible to them.

The literature is full of descriptions of bad practices aimed at producing art in new and surprising ways. Carel van Mander, an important and often cited source, tells of Cornelis Ketel's (1548–1616) "inventive, productive spirit" (*vindinrijk en van een vruchtbaren Geest*) that appeared "to never rest." Ketel experienced, in Van Mander's words, "all sorts of impulses [*lusten*] and occupied himself with various efforts in the realm of painting." In the year 1599 he began to paint with his fingers, which "by many is held to be a ridiculous, abominable urge such as sometimes happens with pregnant women who crave to eat strange, raw, or uncooked foods [*die tot vreemde, raauwe of ongekookte soijzen trek krijgen*]."[56] The art historian Nicolas Galley interprets this passage as equating artistic invention with procreation and as an allusion to similar powers possessed by the divine,[57] but van Mander's comparison is undoubtedly meant ironically.

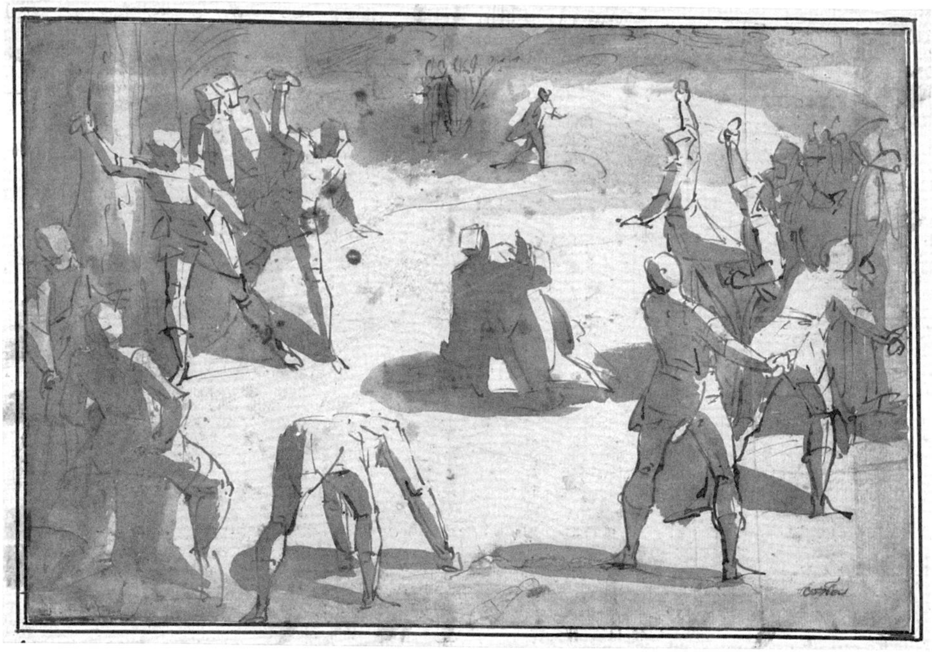

115
Luca Cambiaso (also attributed to his student Giovanni Battista Paggi), *Stoning of St. Stephen*, ca. 1554–1627. Ink drawing with pen and brush, 20.3 × 29.7 cm. Rijksmuseum, Amsterdam.

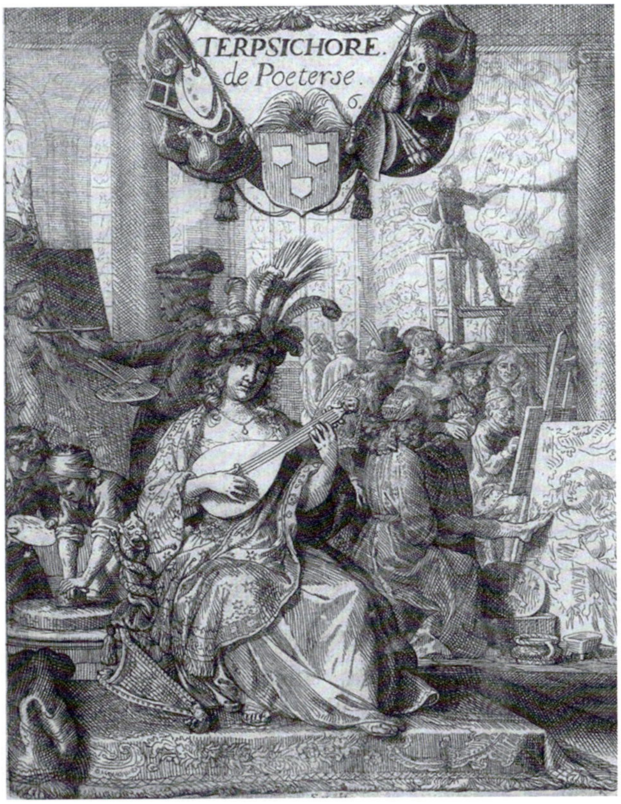

116
Samuel van Hoogstraten, *Inleyding tot de hooge schoole de schilderkonst*, 1678. Title vignette for *Terpsichore* [Cornelis Ketel painting with his feet].

Painting without the use of a brush as an act of bravura is mentioned in several artists' biographies. Even Giordano put on a demonstration of this kind for the Spanish king.[58] And earlier, Ugo da Carpi (1480–ca.1520–1532) had painted an altarpiece of the Volto Santo using just his empty hands, which Michelangelo did not much like: "It would have been preferable had he employed a brush and executed it in a better *maniera*."[59]

Ketel's later experiments prove that his interest in such techniques was about more than just about playing God in a creative sense, but also went to the issue of processual artistry. In the interests of experiment he did not hesitate to take his art down to even a quite literally pedestrian level—he painted with his feet! One of Samuel van Hoogstraten's titular vignettes in his *Inleyding* celebrates Ketel's feat (fig. 116). Ketel introduces his own corporeality as an obstacle to his art, then overcomes this self-imposed hindrance in a determined display of virtuosity, thereby circumventing conventional praxis and giving full sway to his idiosyncrasy. Van Mander underscores the gratuitous extravagance of such experimentation when he notes, more generally, that "there are also those who, in order to show their skill, do more such unusual things; some shoot with their guns on the back, or back to front, and hit what they aim at. Not to mention that some people walk on ropes when the ground, of course, is more suitable."[60] In ridiculing the figure of the tightrope walker, van Mander turns firmly against the notion of artistic genius proposed by Pliny the Younger in his illustrative use of the same metaphor. Pliny's famous letter to Lupercus the Rhetorician encourages him "to tread the edge of a precipice; for

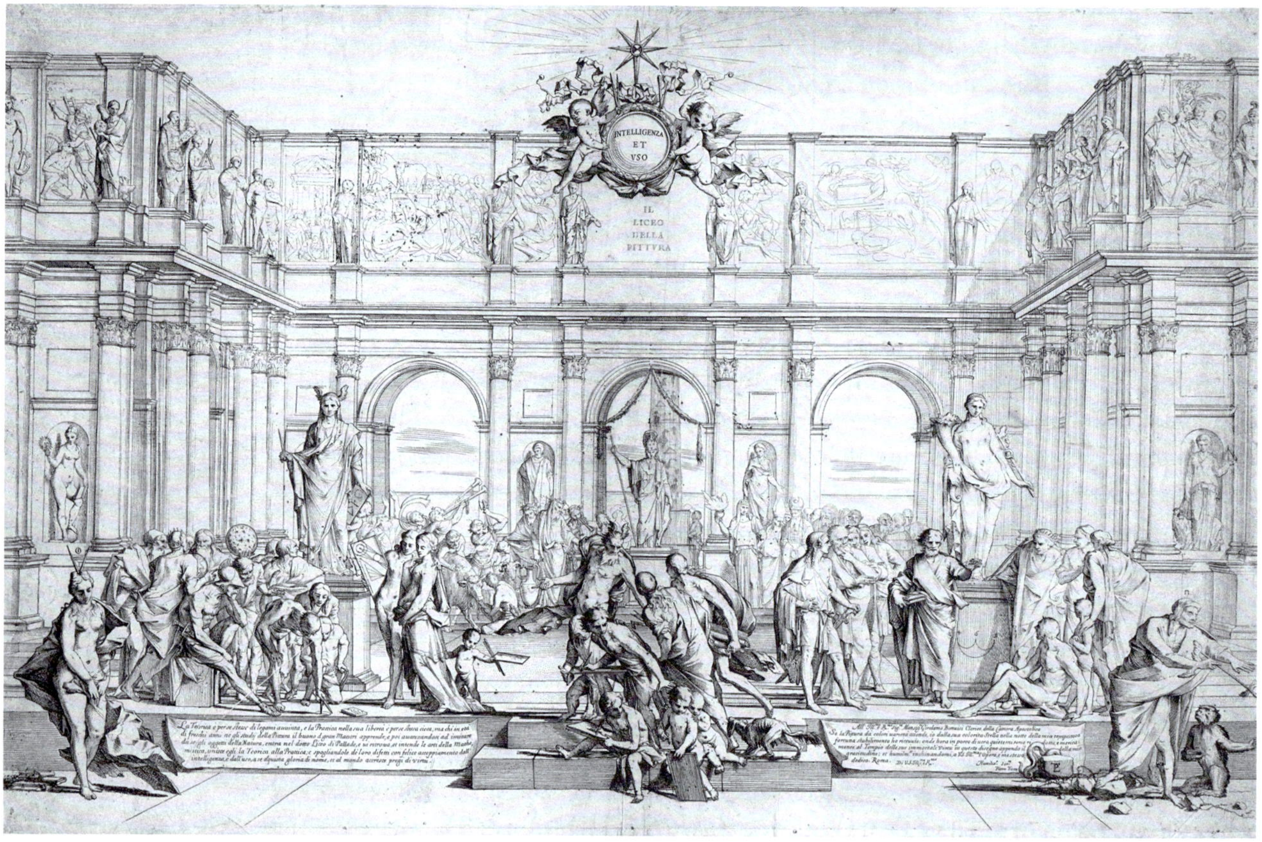
INTELLIGENZA
ET
VSO
IL
LICEO
DELLA
PITTVRA

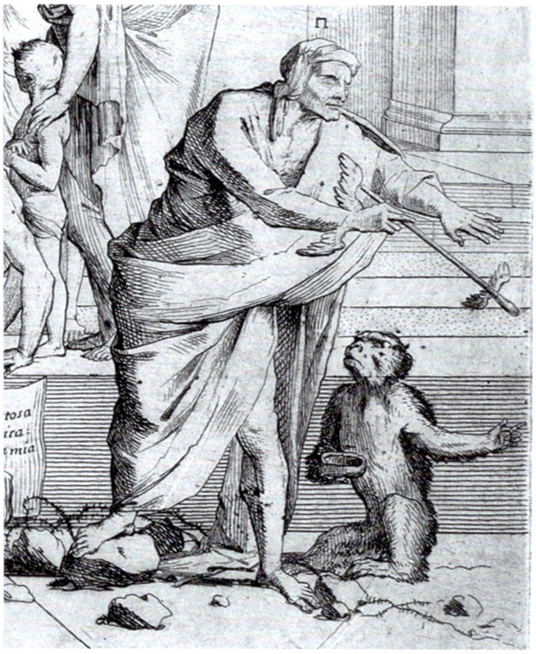

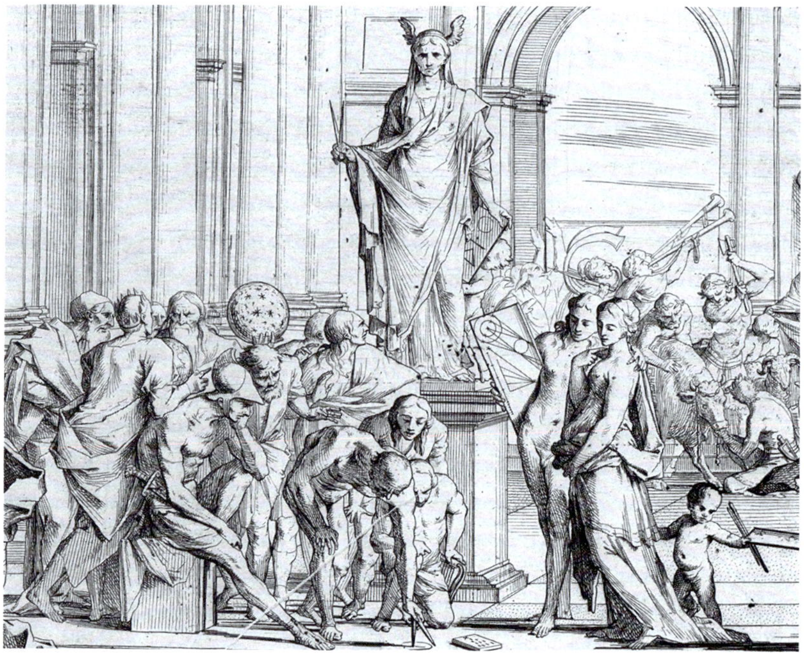

Testa can be considered a critic of Scannelli's *dissegni nella stremità de'Pennelli.* In his notes he frequently speaks out against an "ease of invention" (*facilità in far le cose*) that he excoriates as a "mad fury" (*furor matto*).[73] Here his depiction is unusual in the way he redefines praxis, most specifically in his use and amalgamation of different images found in Cesare Ripa's *Iconologia* (1603). His *Prattica* is derived from the same figure in Ripa, who likewise shows *Prattica* as an old woman (fig. 120). But Ripa's personification bends over a compass and a plumb line, rather like Testa's mathematicians. When Testa exchanges the compass for a blind man's staff and also removes the figure's fixation on the ground, he evokes, as the art historian Elizabeth Cropper has demonstrated, another of Ripa's personifications (fig. 121).[74]

Ripa's personification of Poverty—the poverty experienced by "one who [solely] possesses beautiful ingenuity" (*Povertà in uno c'habbia bello ingegno*)—is represented with wings on her left "inactive" hand, while her right hand is chained to a heavy stone pulling Poverty's right arm toward the ground. The "ingenious" painter's desire, which according to Ripa's explanatory text is a desire handicapped, indeed rendered impossible by *Povertà*, is visualized in the winged hand's extension. The blindness of Testa's *Prattica* links her to a third figure in the *Iconologia*, the personification of Will (*Volontà*): "She extends her hands forward, one more than the other, in order to hold fast to something. Blindness suits her, for in principle she sees nothing, but gropes along behind the sensual desires if she is weak and ignorant, or behind reason if she is bold and worthy" (fig. 122).[75] Ripa furnishes Will with wings (on her feet and shoulders) in reference to the Italian word for flight (*volo*) inscribed within her name (*Volontà*).

Whereas Ripa's *Povertà, in uno c'habbia bello ingegno,* is torn in two different directions and incapable of action, Testa's *Prattica* pursues her own will. In contrast to *Povertà* (fig. 121), her right hand is winged and gropes in a forward direction, while the assisting left hand reinforces the gesture and creates space. *Povertà*'s left hand, chained to a heavy stone, counteracts the winged flight of the right and brings about stasis, while Testa instead depicts the weight tossed aside, forming part of a path littered with stones and thorns that signifies setting out without the foundation of theory. An ape—symbol of the slavish imitation of nature—ushers her toward the exit off the stage of knowledge. The beggar's bowl in the ape's right paw may symbolize borrowing ideas from other painters, something spiritless, as reprehensible as slavish imitation.

The hands of Practice grope forward into the unknown, but those of Theory are bound; her gaze is lowered and the hinge of a compass rests on the part in her hair (fig. 123), the latter another motif from Ripa's *Iconologia.* Instead of stones, she has a pile of books behind her. On the base of the building's platform we can read the following explanation for both figure's circumstances: "Theory on its own is bound by attachments, practice on its own is blind in its freedom" (fig. 124). The distance between theoretical knowledge and practical ability is bridged by a group of eager students mounting the steps that lead into to the lyceum while shying away from the barking guide dog of practice (fig. 125).

Testa's inscription gives voice to a long-standing assumption that guided the understanding of art in the Early Modern period. "Freedom," illustrated by the winged hand of *Prattica,* was problematic because it runs contrary to the notion of art

117 (FACING)
Pietro Testa, *Il liceo della pittura*, ca. 1638. Etching on laid paper, 47.1 × 73.9 cm. The National Gallery, Washington, DC.

118–119 (FACING)
Details of fig. 117 [*Il liceo della pittura*].

as an activity steered by intellectual understanding, an idea eloquently formulated in a passage on aesthetics in Albrecht Dürer's treatise on human proportion (1528): "For understanding must begin to grow together with practice, so that the hand can do what the will would do within understanding. With time, the sureness of art and practice emerges from this. For these two things must exist together."[76] Dürer had only contempt for the blindness of praxis removed from theory: Works emerging "from a free hand's constant practice," he indicated, are "made forcefully but without reflection and according to pleasure alone." For artists, succumbing to the freedom achieved by "practice"—a freedom that releases them from the dominion of concepts—has fatal results: "But when you have no proper [theoretical] grounding, then it is not possible to make something proper and good, and this despite having access to the greatest practice in the world through your hand's freedom. For although it seduces you, it is more like a prison. Therefore, just as there should be no freedom without art, art remains hidden without practice. The two must exist together."[77]

The French painter Charles Alphonse Du Fresnoy (1611–1668), born the same year as Pietro Testa and an apprentice to Simon Vouet, would criticize artistic license—not of the hand but of the mind—by means of another carceral metaphor fully resonant with Testa's image of "chained theory." In his *De arte graphica*, translated by Roger de Piles and published in 1668 a few months after Du Fresnoy died, he strongly advises artists (as did Dürer, Testa, and many others before him) to coordinate hand and mind while being wary of blindness: "As solitary Practice discharged from the lights of Art is always close to falling into a precipice like a blind woman, without being able to produce anything that would contribute to a solid reputation, so will Theory without the aid of the hand never reach the perfection she proposes, but languish in idleness as if in prison."[78]

120
Cesare Ripa, *Iconologia*, 1618. Illustration of *Practica*.

121
Cesare Ripa, *Iconologia*, 1618. Illustration of *Povertà in uno c'habbia bello ingegno*.

122
Cesare Ripa, *Iconologia*, 1618. Illustration of *Volontà*.

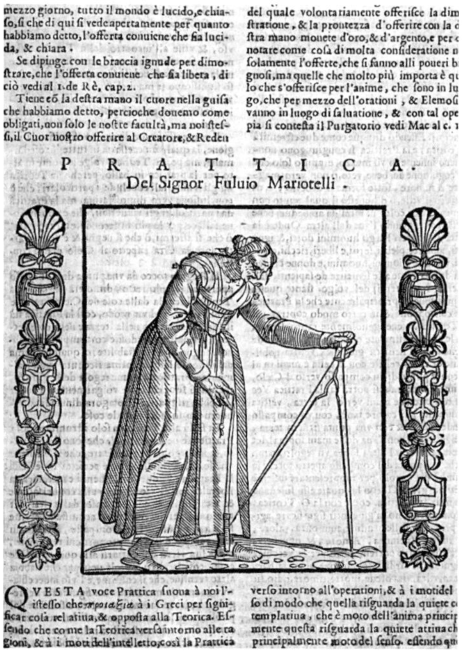

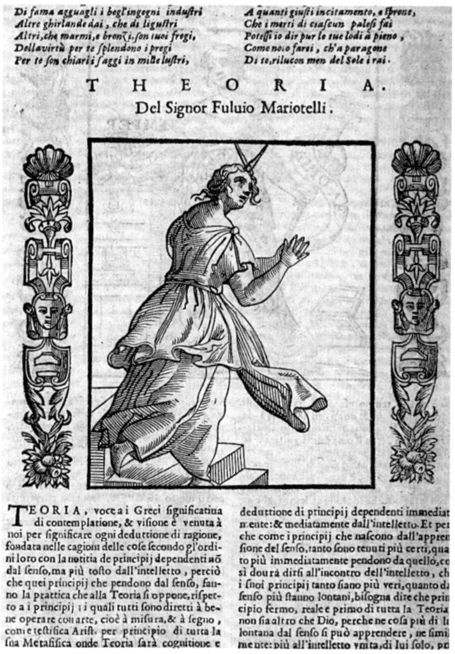

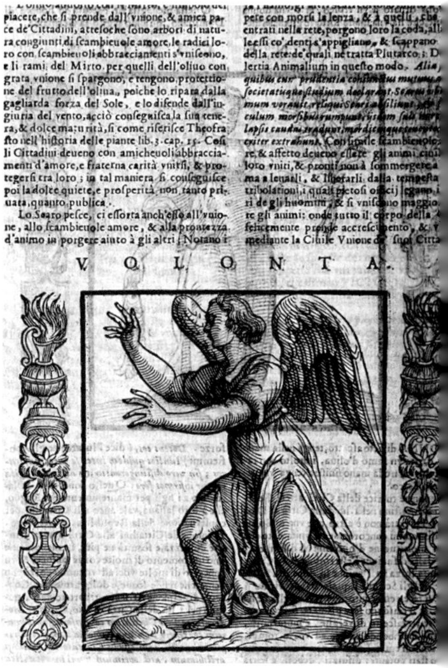

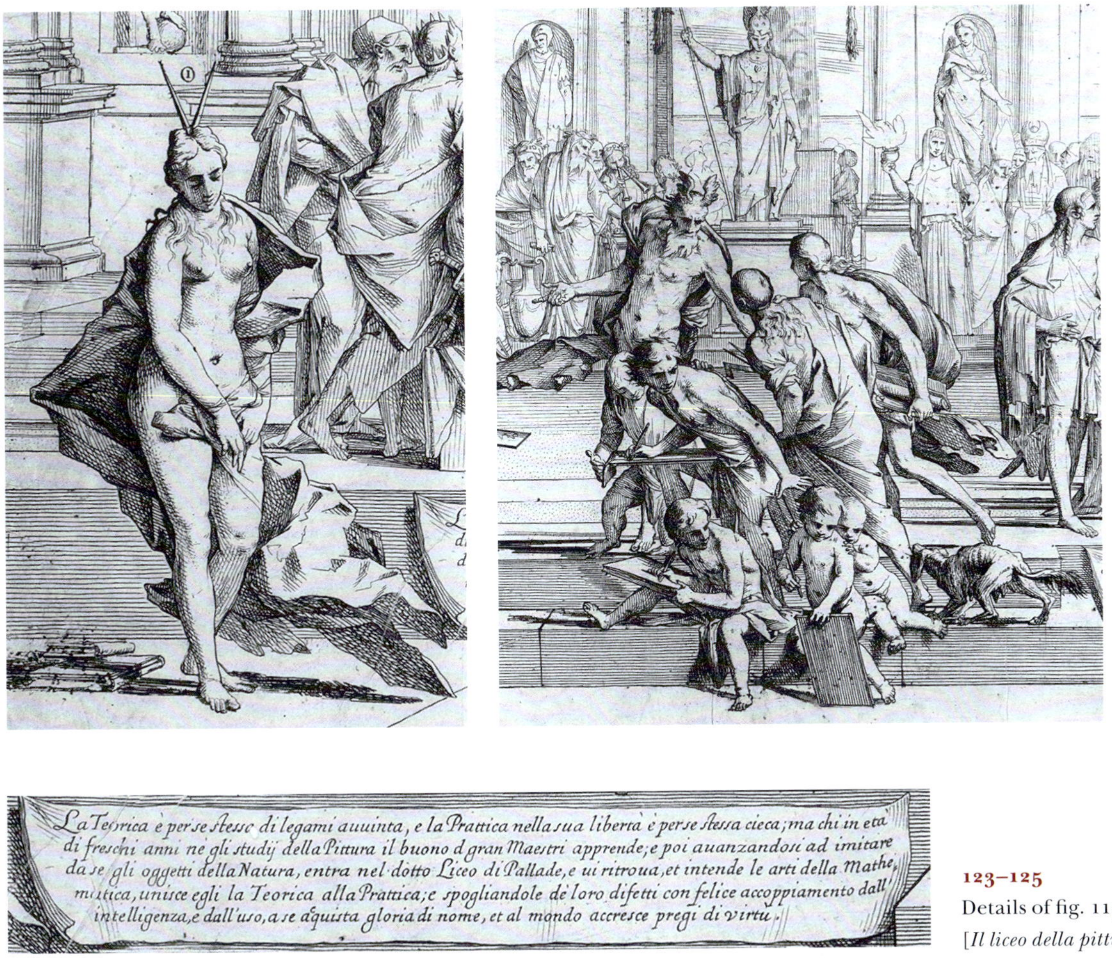

123–125
Details of fig. 117
[*Il liceo della pittura*].

However, at the beginning of his treatise, Du Fresnoy says that his prescriptions are not intended to imprison the hands of working artists (*les mains des Ouvriers*). He does not want either to choke "genius" with many rules nor to extinguish the "fire of a vein that is strong [vive] and abundant."[79] Du Fresnoy even questions whether the "hard science" of geometry may not be an impediment rather than an aid to art (in Testa's *Liceo* it guarantees certitude). To this end he uses the same argument we previously encountered against foreshortening constructed by purely perspectival means: it does not help one on the path to good painting (*acheminement de la Peinture*) because bodies are better represented according to how they are viewed than according to a geometric plan.[80] The successful interdependence of hand and mind produce an *ease* (*facilité*) by which things are made that were previously "pored over in the mind for a long time" (*après les avoir longtemps roulées dans votre Esprit*).[81] With this observation, Du Fresnoy brings into play a line of inquiry that will soon become central to deliberations on the subject of bravura at the French Académie royale de peinture et de sculpture, an institution founded, as it happens, during the same years when Du Fresnoy was composing his treatise.

CHAPTER NINE

The Academic Response

THE SOPHISTICATION OF *LÉGÈRETÉ*

On July 8, 1713, the painter and director of the royal painting collection, Antoine Coypel, expounded upon the problems inherent in rapidity and ease of execution.[1] He first distinguished between the instrumental component of painting and the inward learned component of painting, which might be termed the artist's acquired habitude, the former being "the brush," the latter an effortless, appealing, and light hand (*la main facile, agréable et légère*). He then goes on to describe a state of disorder that arises when the artist no longer respects the boundary between these two components, when instead: "The habitude of the hand is what painters call the brush."[2] Such a condition, he says, indicates the artist has taken a pernicious shortcut that too closely joins his habit to his hand and thereby suspends the intervention of the mind.[3] Coypel repeats many of the reproaches leveled against prestezza painting already noted in this book: its speed is motivated by avarice and its broad brushstrokes are undisguised ostentation. He particularly despises the arrogant attitude of the bravura artist: "The painters who affect these bold strokes and make them the basis of their beauty of execution resemble those insolent people who show up everywhere without respecting decorum. They are to painting what these tiresome bigmouths [*ces fatigants diseurs de grands mots*] are to conversation, who have nothing to say and in disputes use the power of their voice to oppose the power of reason."[4] He repeatedly counsels artists to periodically pause the flow of their execution, to slow down and avoid the "puerile vanity" of striving to be quicker than others because, citing Molière's *Le Misanthrope*: "Le temps ne fait rien à l'affaire."[5] Coypel understands work breaks as indicators of thought: "One retouches the same spot several times, for the mind [*l'esprit*] is not always content with a hand that executes with too much facility."[6]

Several years later in an address to the students of the Académie royale de peinture et de sculpture, Charles-Antoine Coypel (1694–1752), Antoine's son and like his father *Premier peintre du Roi* and director of the academy, blamed "self-love" for bravura's cult of *facilité*, a concept he considers to be a deception born of self-defense because "nothing is more devastating for a man born with feeling to then be forced to admit to himself that he is merely mediocre in an art that suffers no mediocrity." Before Coypel explains the self-deception at the root of *amour-propre*, he warned his pupils against the complacent use of their tools: "You mistake a love of handling the pencil or paintbrush for genius, and in this point your parents deceive themselves even more than you do. Without consulting your spirit or your strengths, and burning with a perilous ardor, you set out to pursue the thorniest of professions.... If [the misguided artist] is cold in the composition of his paintings and dry in their execution, self-love will persuade him that he has attained Raphael's sublime simplicity and perfection. If, on the contrary, he composes in an extravagant manner and draws incorrectly, self-love will bring him to compare himself with Correggio."[7] It should be noted that Charles-Antoine restored Correggio's heavily damaged *Leda and the Swan* and replaced its missing parts. Around 1731, Louis d'Orléans, the fanatically devout son of Duke Philippe II, had ordered Leda's head cut out of the highly sensuous painting and the rest ripped to pieces.[8]

Coypel's designation of Correggio as the antipode to Raphael comes from the former's having claimed to have *disegno* on the tip of his brush, but it also reflects his high esteem for the gentle and seductive qualities of Correggio's paintings. In the *Dictionnaire des arts de peinture, sculpture et gravure* (1792) under the entry "Pinceau," Lévesque locates Correggio's much-praised charm in his brushwork and describes his impact as follows: "He was eager to apply the paint thickly, to let it melt, and he enjoyed the pleasure of losing himself in the color and finding himself again, without enslaving himself to forms or caring about their selection. Such a bold brush, so in love, so tender, communicates to all those who see his works the delight and exhilaration [*le plaisir et l'ivresse*] which their author knew how to enjoy."[9]

In the eighteenth century serious misgivings about the value of bold facility paralleled a discourse on nuance in the sensory effects and components of coloring, topics touched on in the preceding chapter. The renowned antiquarian and "amateur" member of the Académie royale, Comte de Caylus (1692–1765), attempted to salvage the reputation of effortlessness, the quality so central to the concept of bravura. But his endeavor, in a lecture given at the Louvre in 1755, shows only too clearly how significant a loss of esteem painterly virtuosity had suffered during the eighteenth century. He began with a restrained praise of ease by justifying its importance for aesthetic judgment: "Even if a *légèreté* of the instrument is not the most essential thing for the painter, it is nevertheless one of the most pleasurable and enchants the process."[10] Caylus admiringly attributes the power of enchantment to an illusionary capacity that seduces rather than threatens the beholder. This foremost spokesman of French academic discourse thus demotes the martial masculine attitude of bravura and promotes in its place feminine charm and allure. Refinement trumps valor. In a similar vein, Roger de Piles also famously defined the art of painting as a cosmetic (*le beau fard*) whose essence is deception.[11]

The finesse of eighteenth-century art certainly speaks the language of gentle sprezzatura more eloquently than that of bold bravura, although bravura was nevertheless very present in discussions on the contested notion of *facilité*. As we have seen, Caylus vehemently criticized the lack of finish in works by the painters Paolo de Matteis, Pellegrini, and Tintoretto. The only counterexample he provided was Domenichino, but Caylus likewise pronounced him deficient in *légèreté d'outil*.[12]

His choice here of the Bolognese painter may reflect remarks made by the still-life painter Claude-François Desportes (1695–1774). In an address given to the Académie on May 4, 1748, Desportes singled out Domenichino as a foil to "precocious" painters: Whereas "insufficient nourishment" caused the vitality (*sève*) of works by the latter to dry up prematurely, Domenichino proceeded slowly so that his art was ultimately able to accumulate a "hidden treasury of solid merit" and thus prove worthy of posterity.[13]

Desportes, in turn, may have read Bellori's praise of Domenichino's diligent practice. The first sentence in his vita of Domenichino Bellori criticizes impatient youths who prematurely and single-mindedly set their sights on bravura: "We have seen some spring forth with such impetuosity that when they should have been pupils and remained in school, they have left in an instant with the ambition to be masters, carrying away nothing else with them but the audacity of their hands, while others, who appeared to proceed slowly but were confirmed in the end by their efforts, have their genius and the fame of their reputation ensured."[14] Domenichino's diligence was rewarded, Bellori explains, because while other painters boasted "of facility, grace, coloring, and other merits of painting," he focused his effort on interiority, on "limning souls and painting life." By striving for something beyond practical know-how in his art, Domenichino reached "greater glory."[15]

Back to Caylus's lecture at the Louvre. After praising the exemplary Titian for excelling in the "finesse of art," he came to the crux of his argument. *Légèreté* is expressed not in those first traces of the brush visible in the sketchiness of a seemingly unfinished painting, but in the final touches laid down on the canvas: *légèreté* is the "last stage of the essential parts of painting."[16] His Italian contemporary, the librarian of the Biblioteca Marciana in Venice Anton Maria Zanetti (1679–1767), in the preface of a treatise on Venetian painting published two decades later, would likewise describe how with a few brushstrokes Titian delivered his *finimenti*, which had the effect of making the *bravura* of the first phase of execution visible.[17] Baldinucci had earlier declared these ostentatious final gestures sprezzatura-like obfuscations. He mentioned an insight gained from Ludovico Cigoli's study of Titian's style: Titian executed his paintings with great care, and to make them seem more masterful, he hid this exertion behind a few brushstrokes executed at the end.[18] According to Caylus, it is through the recognition of *légèreté*, and not in *facilité*, that one can distinguish an original from its copy, because this quality encompasses a greater number of pictorial aspects and thus reflects the overall complexity of the art of painting.[19]

This raises the intriguing question of whether the imitated bravura brushstroke laid down by a copyist can convey art. A resolute brush movement embodies a certain disposition of the artist's; once the stroke is separated from the artist's work it may in a new environment become hollow. Or the opposite may happen: new insights developed in the rather mechanical practice of copying can retroactively bestow substance on the original and thereby unfold dimensions of systematic practice that the painter of the original work did not notice, as we saw in the case of Schiavone whose bold practice was meticulously studied by subsequent painters. The indeed fundamental difficulty of copying the appearance of *légèreté* by simply studying its surface attributes underlies Charles-Nicolas Cochin's remarks on

Sebastiano Ricci in his *Le voyage d'Italie* (1758): "The paintings of this master are worthy of admiration, but imitating them could be dangerous."[20] Luigi Lanzi in his *Storia pittorica della Italia* will term this danger a "degeneration" of style, for which he blames "Giordano and several Venetians," because when other painters tried and failed to imitate their methods, which abolish the old rules in order to make new ones (*far l'eggi nuove in pittura e abolir le antiche*), they ended up producing works that looked like preliminary sketches (*oprere che sentono dell'abbozzo*).[21]

The Venetian polymath and art dealer Francesco Algarotti (1712–1764), who wrote a widely read introduction to Newton's *Opticks* for ladies,[22] offered advice on how to protect oneself against the existential threat of an, as it were, ill-founded painterly manner. In the spirit of the Enlightenment, he recommended the science of optics as a helpful aid for the young artist because "it will teach how to read and translate such books where the rules of coloring are principally collected for him."[23] The works especially of Giorgione and Titian are, according to Algarotti, suitable models for the novice because they renounce "affectation" and exaggeration of style. Consonant with Castiglione's concept of sprezzatura, the student should seek out art in those who know how to hide art. Only when he has learned their fundamental lessons, Algarotti says, should he then study the bold strokes and effortless brushwork of Jacopo Bassano and Paolo Veronese.

This concern for young artists, who are more prone to fall under the spell of *facilité* or the bravura brushstroke, was a key theme of conferences held at the French academy during this time period. On November 8, 1749, in a lecture "On the knowledge of antiquity and anatomy," the miniature painter Jean-Baptiste Massé (1687–1767) condemned the "blind facility" that led those relying on painterly routine to "stray into dubiousness." He distinguished true fame from what he deemed "false and fugitive glory" (*la gloire fausse et passagère*), while admitting that the latter did attract a large audience, or what he preferred to call a *manège*, a circus. But he reluctantly conceded: "I know this unmerited glory is nevertheless brilliant enough to seduce the young artist."[24]

Charles-Antoine Coypel likewise diagnosed the premature sketchy execution of a pictorial idea as nothing more than a play for speed and a decidedly problematic phenomenon in the development of art. In 1750, Coypel remarked:

> In the art academy you can usually find a large group of young people who are capable of creating hasty compositions on paper or canvas, which promise to be exciting paintings. But when they then execute these paintings, you will immediately realize that their authors already placed the small amount of knowledge they possess in the preliminary drawings, where one is sufficiently pleased with the invention, and no detail is required. These young people will learn to their sorrow that the [preparatory] studies after nature they like to make [in order to elaborate the sketch] only serve to extinguish the sparks of the fire that appear in their sketches, for these studies are only gropings without discrimination, taste, or intelligence. That which usually enriches a carefully considered work by a person with principles, for them leads to impoverishment.[25]

Some of Coypel's imagery recalls Pietro Testa's figure of Blind Practice accompanied by a monkey holding a begging bowl.

In the *Dictionnaire des arts de peinture, sculpture et gravure* (1792) under the entry "Esquisse," the amateur painter and encyclopedist Claude-Henri Watelet (1718–1786) explains that young artists, with their easily inflamed imaginations, have a natural affinity for the sketch that puts them in danger of being led astray. For Watelet, this period in life is "the season of enthusiasm, the moment when one is impatient to produce; in other words, it is the age of the sketch." The sketch is inherently an immature thing, though one with some potential, a combination that has natural appeal to youth. It frees budding artists from the time-consuming and perhaps tedious task of perfecting their work, for the sketch permits "indecision in arrangement, inaccuracies in drawing, as well as an aversion to finishing."[26]

The presumption of youths, who pursue their bold creative ideas with passionate verve, but heedless of the dictates of art (whether due to indifference or ignorance), brings to mind a passage in Vasari where Michelangelo broods nostalgically over one of his early drawings. The picture, which Vasari owned and treated "like a relic," unified two separate sketches: one by a fellow student at Domenico Ghirlandaio's workshop and a bold correction by Michelangelo, drawn over the original with a broad pen. His adjustment of the outlines was an unmistakable critique not only of the student but of their teacher Ghirlandaio as well, whom the original drawing emulated and whose mastery Michelangelo impertinently challenged. When Vasari showed the drawing to an elderly Michelangelo in 1550, he relates that the artist was very moved and said *per modestia* that as a boy he knew more about art than now in his later years.[27]

What binds youthfulness and sketching together is the medium's inherent cache of promise, a promise that may not be fully realized at the end and therefore demonstrates pure potential. In another passage of the *Vite*, Vasari discusses the fact that the finishing process is not always of benefit but can in fact dissipate the energy of a sketch: "It can be said that Giulio [Romano] always expressed his ideas better in his drawings than in his paintings, since there is, in the former, more vitality, boldness, and emotion."[28] Here Vasari formulates an understanding of the sketch as a medium that not only makes the artistic effort of pictorial invention visible, but is also able to manifest art in a much more unfettered fashion than the finished work. Vasari relates his evaluation of Giulio Romano to the artist's working tempo. He tells us that while Giulio worked furiously on a drawing and finished it within an hour, he took many months and even years over his paintings. His works as a result lost "that fervent and burning love that an artist has when he begins something."[29] It became an axiom in art literature that the genuineness of the sketch disappears during the finishing of a painting due to the time-consuming process of elaboration, which quenches the fire of creative furor.[30] Cochin relies on this conception when he declares: "The great fire is the reason why Tintoretto is generally less admirable when he is more careful. His imagination cools during the period of cautious execution; he is left with little that is beautiful."[31]

But this oft-repeated argument could also be turned against a piece hastily and furiously dashed off because, as Félibien declares, the final result hardly withstands critical examination: their violent and forceful expression acts to negate "art."[32] Lévesque would later assemble a number of similar critical views in his entry on *Feu*: "That which is called *fire* in the arts should often be called quickness [*prestesse*] of composition, facility of execution, absence of reflection and of judgment."[33] In other words, an artistic concept that embodied inspiration can be flattened to mere phenomenality. Lévesque links this pseudo-fire to youth when he writes: "*Fire* is always vivacious, but vivacity is not always *fire*; [vivacity] can also be merely a puerile turbulence, a senseless petulance."[34]

"MECHANICK GENIUS"

A similar discourse preoccupied the members of the Royal Academy in London. The painter Sir Joshua Reynolds (1723–1792) addressed the most fervent arguments against bravura to art students at the academy, but long before he began counseling the young he had, surprisingly and cleverly, depicted himself in one of his works in a more uncertain pose often associated with the youthful artist searching for orientation.[35] Reynolds's self-reflection at an early point in his life, before he traveled to Italy, is reminiscent of Alberti's image of the forlorn seeker attempting to establish his bearings (fig. 126). Light streams onto Reynolds's face, whose soft features especially in the lower half indicate the painter's youth. His right hand (keeping in mind the mirror's inversion of the image) is raised over his eyes to shield them from the glare. An intense and concentrated gaze emerges from the resulting shadow, but do his eyes meet ours? The darkening of this area of the face makes the object of his stare elusive. He seems to be looking slightly askance, staring into nothingness as if momentarily blinded. What is he looking at? It seems that his mahlstick, an instrument whose usual function is to support the painter's hand, underpins the gaze seeking a firm footing. The mahlstick

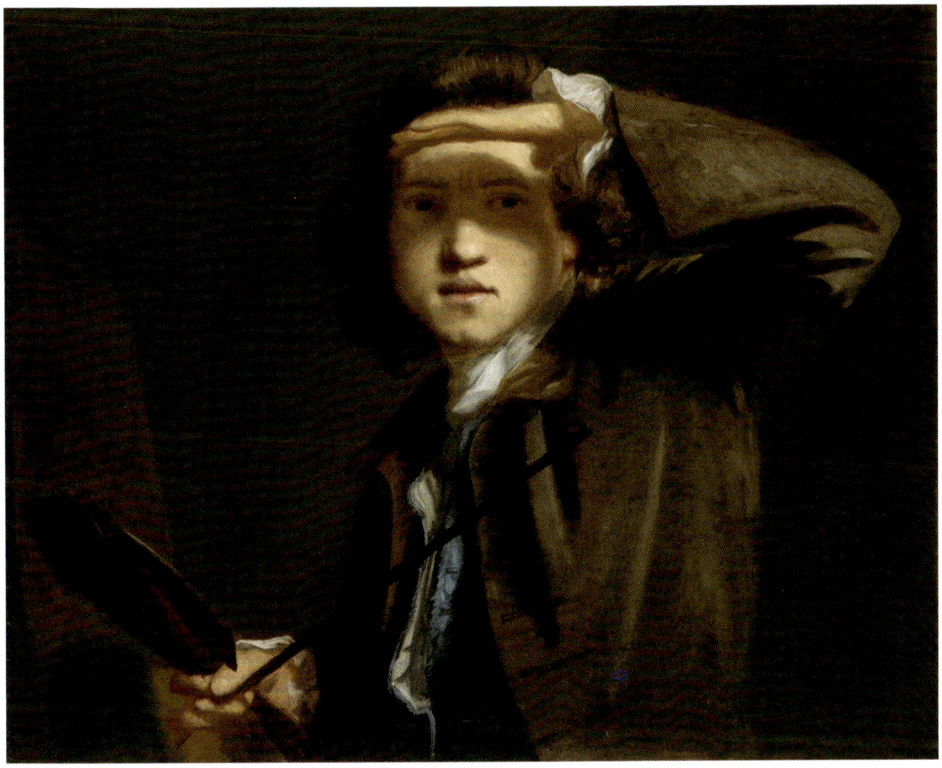

126
Joshua Reynolds, *Self-Portrait*, 1747–1749. Oil on canvas, 63.5 × 74.3 cm. National Portrait Gallery, London.

projects beyond the imaginary border of the picture, but is spatially retracted due to a lack of foreshortening. Planimetrically viewed, it cuts across several deeply shaded areas of the artist's coat that seem repeatedly to swallow the stick's contours. The tip of the instrument points in the direction of the shaded hollow under his arm, where the complex spatial relationship between shoulder and upper arm are cleverly obscured.

Whereas the left hand is exclusively engaged with mahlstick, palette, and brush (though these tools of the trade recede into shadow and therefore become intangible), his right hovers before his brow as if measuring its width. Overlapping the hairline, it screens the middle of his forehead. The back of the hand and upper forehead are illuminated to the same degree—*mens* and *manus* are merged together. While the left hand at the lower margin is preoccupied with the painter's instruments, the right is raised in a gesture that in pictorial rhetoric connotes wonderment (*thauma*). But what young Reynolds is experiencing here is not *ecstasis* in the face of a witnessed miracle. Rather, he marvels at his own mirror image, which channels the young painter's ambition. The shading of the eyes seems to be a precondition for visual acuity, sharpening the eyesight for something that is evidently difficult to apprehend. The constellation of hand, face, eyes, and forehead endows the artist's hand with a central, eloquent role in the painting's structure; it guides both vision and understanding, but the precise path, which praxis will open up for contemplation, is one yet to be determined. Alberti's metaphor of the blind man (borrowed from Platon's dialogue Phaedrus [270e]) who uses his brush like a staff to feel out "unknown paths," here adds an element of potential in the young painter's self-reflection. In Reynolds's self-portrait, the seemingly blind fumbling of praxis is caught, via the painter's astonished pose, yielding ground to an initiatory moment, to the *THAUMAZEIN*. The frustrating sensation of being blinded now paves the way toward deeper insight.

In a series of lectures delivered between 1767 and 1790 on the occasion of the academy's annual awards ceremony, Reynolds traced the historical development of painting, diagnosing along the way the causes of its decline, in what amounted to a vehement critique of contemporary style. A unifying trope in these speeches of this ilk is the danger youth faces from premature contact with a certain "infectious" kind of painting. This peril leads Reynolds to the term "affectation," in his words "that great enemy to truth and nature...which is ever clinging to the pencil and ready to drop in and poison every thing it touches."[36] Du Fresnoy—and De Piles shortly thereafter—had earlier stated his conviction that "bad" art taints the young painter. He compared the fatal situation of a boy entering the workshop of an ignorant master to poisoning. Such a teacher will "deprive the pupil of good taste through the many errors in his own painting, thus giving the pupil a poisonous drink that will infect him for the rest of his life."[37] But for Reynolds the metaphor of toxicity is less about the teacher depriving the student of art as a condemnation of his active efforts to prompt the student into creating bad art.

When Reynolds identifies the natural disposition of youth as being prone to such infection, because "at that age it is natural for them to be more captivated with what is brilliant than with what is solid, and to prefer splendid negligence to painful and humiliating exactness,"[38] he not only reformulates the well-known accusations we examined earlier in relation to the art-theoretical terms "sprezzatura" and "prestezza." Reynolds goes further to actually discourage pusuit of the visually attractive—the "brilliant" and "splendid"—for these qualities are not in his view the essence of art. Its essence derives instead from its foundation in a knowledge that can only be learned by means of hard work and cannot be directly communicated to youthful eagerness, for "enthusiastick admiration seldom promotes knowledge."[39] The youthful penchant for *bravissimo* role models and the ambition to emulate them seem to produce visibly seductive results remarkably early, because "boys" make "mechanical felicity the chief excellence of the art, which is only an ornament."[40]

Each year Reynolds would lament anew young painters' natural fascination for the painterly surface and reassert the academy's task: to counteract the damaging effect of such attractive painting practices by means of "enlightenment," that is, by unmask their seeming spellbinding magic as a false enchantment. According to Reynolds, "young minds" are primarily enthralled by "the splendor of style," which he locates in the optically alluring painting of Venice.[41] Tintoretto and Veronese are most often in the crossfire of his critique: "These are the persons who may be said to have exhausted all the powers of florid eloquence, to debauch the young and unexperienced, and have, without doubt, been the cause of turning off the attention of the connoisseur and of the patron of art, as well as that of the painter, from those higher excellencies of which the art is capable, and which ought to be required in every considerable production. By them, and their imitators, a style merely ornamental has been disseminated throughout all Europe. Rubens carried it to Flanders, Vo[u]et to France, and Luca Giordano to Spain, and Naples."[42] These painters' empty visual rhetoric follows on their desire for fame: "Tintoret, Paul Veronese, and others of the Venetian school, seem to have painted with no other purpose than to be admired for their skill and expertness in the mechanism of painting, and to make a parade of that art, which as I before observed, the higher style requires its followers to conceal."[43] The overwrought yet "impoverished eloquence," which according to Reynolds merely demonstrates its competence without aiming to express anything deeper, is denigrated as meaningless and summed up as being (and here he borrows damning words from Shakespeare) "a tale told by an idiot, full of sound and fury, signifying nothing."[44]

The impact of Reynolds's censure can be seen in the lectures of a later president of the Royal Academy, Henry Fuseli, whom Reynolds met in 1767 and encouraged to become a painter. Fuseli's disparagement of the artistic capital of Venice as a "splendid toy-shop," the contrast he draws between the "ornamental style" that originated there and the "grand style,"[45] his incrimination of Tintoretto and Veronese (they "spread the enchanting nosegay") while excusing Titian,[46] as well as his affirmation of a lack of substance in Venetian painting, all signal his allegiance to Reynolds. He outdoes his intellectual model however in the level of his verbal hyperbole, an excess that is ironically similar to the painting style he castigates. The crescendo reaches its climax whenever the word "bravura" is uttered: Giorgio Vasari is "the most superficial artist and abandoned mannerist of his time."[47] He is guilty of the same crimes as Tintoretto and Giordano: "He overwhelmed the palaces of the Medici and of the popes, the convents and churches of Italy, with a deluge of mediocrity, commended by rapidity and shameless 'bravura' of hand."[48] Fuseli ultimately turns his ultracritical eye to strong chiaroscuro: "It has often been employed by the machinists of different schools, for whom it became the refuge of ignorance, a palliative for an incurable disease, and the asylum of emptiness." And yet, Fuseli admits that there is in it sometimes "a certain vigor of mind" that provokes "unwilling admiration and forces applause."[49]

Along with Vasari and the Venetians, Luca Giordano, too, is an example of "fascinating but debauched and empty facility," another estimation he shared with Reynolds, who said that in painting Giordano exhibited a "mechanick genius" (Reynolds said the same thing of Lafage as a draftsman) "which operates without much assistance of the head."[50] Fuseli's "bravura of the hand" was doubtless not meant as praise; combined with the adjective "shameless" it describes a carelessness and liberality of practice that celebrate ability by means of ostentation and complacency, while disregarding concomitant losses in quality and content. It was in this context that the landscape painter John Constable (1776–1837) used the term when he said, "The greatest vice today is bravura, an attempt to create something beyond the truth."[51]

It is true of course that an image is upstaged when the artist egoistically promenades in the foreground instead of remaining discreetly behind the scene in order to serve the representation in complete self-abandonment. But how does Reynolds, according to his own logic, account for the attractiveness of the "ornamental style" for the young painter? One might well imagine that it would appear enticing to the novice as an illegitimate breath of fresh air, forbidden fruit not permitted by rigorous academic training, a loosening of the strictures of representation to allow a certain flexibility and enjoyment. Reynolds, however, took a dimmer view of young men's motives: "[They] have not only this frivolous ambition of being thought masters of execution, inciting them on one hand, but also their natural sloth tempting them on the other. They are terrified at the prospect before them, of the toil required to attain exactness. The impetuosity of youth is disgusted at the slow approaches of a regular siege, and desires, from mere impatience of labour, to take the citadel by storm. They wish to find some shorter path to excellence, and hope to obtain the reward of eminence by other means than those which the indispensible rules of art have prescribed."[52] For Reynolds then, the young painter who in his first steps tries to act like a master has only one goal—to display his own genius. Reynolds points out the enormous role this vanity plays in the development of artistic self-understanding when, in his eleventh lecture, he begins with the sentence: "The highest ambition of every Artist is to be thought a man of Genius." And then immediately he adds a more serious charge that goes to the impact of vanity on art itself: "As long as this flattering quality is joined to his name, he can bear with patience the imputation of carelessness, incorrectness, or defects of whatever kind."[53]

In his 1784 speech to the academy, Reynolds ascribes such tendings first and foremost to the artists of France, thereby taunting the leading center of art.[54] In France he detects among those old enough to know better what Coypel had believed to be an affliction specifically associated with youth: "Our neighbours, the French, are much in this practice of *extempore* invention, and their dexterity is such as even to excite admiration, if not envy; but how rarely can this praise be given to their finished pictures!"[55]

FOREVER YOUNG

The artistic fame of François Boucher (1703–1770)—teacher of Jean-Honoré Fragonard, court painter to Louis XV, and, like Coypel, Reynolds, and Fuseli, director of a royal academy—rested upon his predilection for arousing the excitement of the viewer. His oeuvre, which undoubtedly belongs in Reynolds's category of the "ornamental style," polarized critical opinion. We need only remember Diderot's rhetorical hypophora directed at Boucher's painting *Les Bergères*, exhibited at the Salon of 1765: "What does this say? Nothing."[56] Diderot here echoes Reynolds's assessment of Venetian painting as basically "signifying nothing." Boucher's art was, in his diagnosis, devoid of substance. It is hardly surprising then that Diderot also condemned its negative influence on academic teaching and feared the damage that its popularity might inflict on the young, an anxiety that Reynolds shared. In 1763 Diderot had been even more explicit: "This man is the ruin of all young students of painting... from him they only learn mistakes."[57]

In *The Young Landscape Painter*, Boucher paints an incognito self-portrait that celebrates the cult of the young artist (fig. 127). According to Melissa Hyde, the then thirty-year-old Boucher imagines himself as a boy seated at his easel in front of a medium-sized landscape painting.[58] Through the window behind him, light falls into the room and strikes the canvas that stands out in the dark and simply furnished room. The childlike facial expression of the young painter is in shadow; his head bends slightly forward as he directs his gaze at a sketchbook hanging suspended from the easel. This sketchbook, however, is not open to a preliminary sketch from nature that the young painter intends to translate into color, but rather a catalog of single motifs ready to be directly transferred ex tempore onto the canvas. The landscape panorama spreading across the work in progress is thus a freely invented composition but one made up of stock components: a watercourse, a mountain massif, a grove of trees, and an abbreviated grouping of ruins representing Tivoli.

Boucher, who received the Grand Prix de Rome at the age of twenty-three, here stages a painting that he had actually created earlier (though it has only come down to us via a print), in effect attributing an artistic accomplishment of his adulthood to his boyhood self (fig. 128). That the child is shown bent over a sketchbook testifies to the studious attitude with which he so masterfully executes this painting. Melissa Hyde associates Boucher's fictive return to youth with an anecdote told by one of his artist colleagues, Jean-Bernard Restout (1732–1796), concerning Boucher's first meeting with Louis XV.[59] At the installment of Boucher as the *Premier peintre du Roi*, the king was surprised at how old he was. Because of Boucher's painting style, radiating "warmth and vivacity," the king had expected a much younger man.

At issue here is the power of his works to deceive, specifically to disguise his true age, whether in the form of a pretended adolescence that is able to accomplish mature work, or a youthful-appearing work executed at an advanced age. The mannerism of his depictions here comes to his aid. According to Watelet, youth is "the age that most easily takes on mannerism," and he also notes: "Exercise in the arts of imagination prolong... in those that cultivate them, a youthful spirit. It is

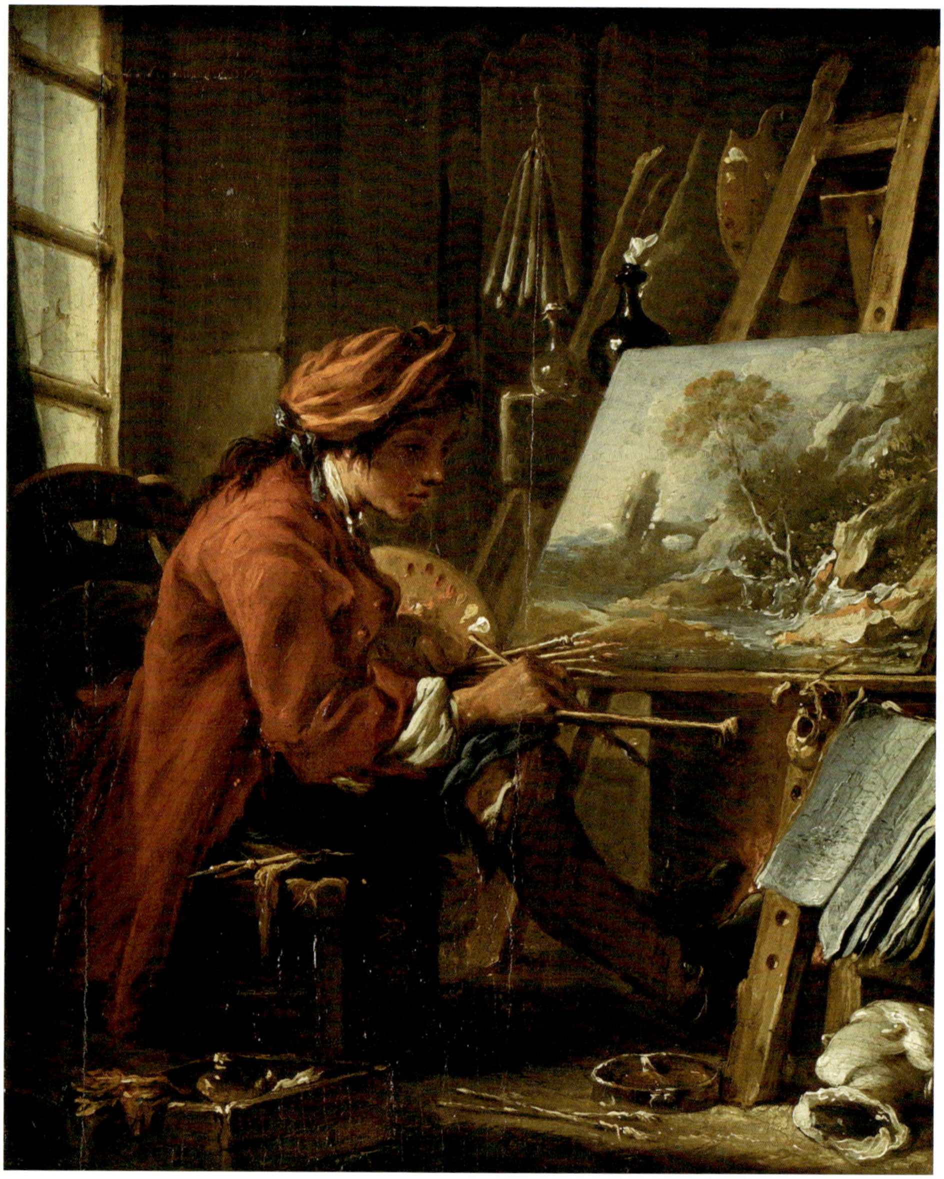

127
François Boucher, *The Young Landscape Painter*, ca. 1735. Oil on wood, 27 × 22 cm. Musée du Louvre, Paris.

also quite simple to recognize artists that remain forever young, whether it is by mistakes that are inherent to young age, or by their desire to please, which they naturally possess."[60] In Diderot's salon review of 1769, his mordant criticism would seem to suggest that Boucher's "forever young" self-stylization is in fact the product of senile dementia. He compares the painter to an old athlete who wants to appear one more time in the arena before his death and concludes: "One notices in these works the fertility, the facility, and the unbridledness; I myself was surprised that there was not more, for the old age of failed men disintegrates into blathering, triteness, and imbecility, while the old age of the foolhardy increasingly tends toward violence, exaggeration, and delirium.... Oh to still have the storminess of a young man after sixty-eight years!"[61]

Reynolds reports of his visit to Boucher:

> When I visited him some years since, in France, I found him at work on a very large Picture, without drawings or models of any kind. On my remarking this particular circumstance, he said, when he was young, studying his art, he found it necessary to use models; but he had let them off for many years. Such Pictures as this was, and such as I fear always will be produced by those who work solely from practice or memory, may be a convincing proof of the necessity of the conduct which I have recommended. However, in justice I cannot quit this Painter without adding, that in the former part of his life, when he was in the habit of having recourse to nature, he was not without a considerable degree of merit—enough to make half of the Painters of his country his imitators; he had often grace and beauty, and good skill in composition; but I think, all under the influence of a bad taste: his imitators are indeed abominable.[62]

However, Boucher's central place in artistic developments of the mid-eighteenth century was recognized even by Diderot, who, despite his sharp dismissal of the artist nevertheless saw some merit in him. He wrote: "The artists who saw to what degree this man had overcome the difficulties of painting—even if this is his only accomplishment, only they can recognize it—kneel down before him: He is their god. The people of great taste, of serious and classical taste, are in no way thus inclined."[63] Boucher is therefore not an artist of the educated bourgeoisie, but rather a painter's painter. He is similarly characterized by Edmond and Jules de Goncourt. In their seminal *L'Art du XVIIIe siècle* (1873), they label him a rogue (*canaille*) because he lacked refinement, but in the same breath commend the extreme enthusiasm of his powers of imagination and his joyful hand (*son imagination est la plus facile et sa main la plus heureuse*).[64]

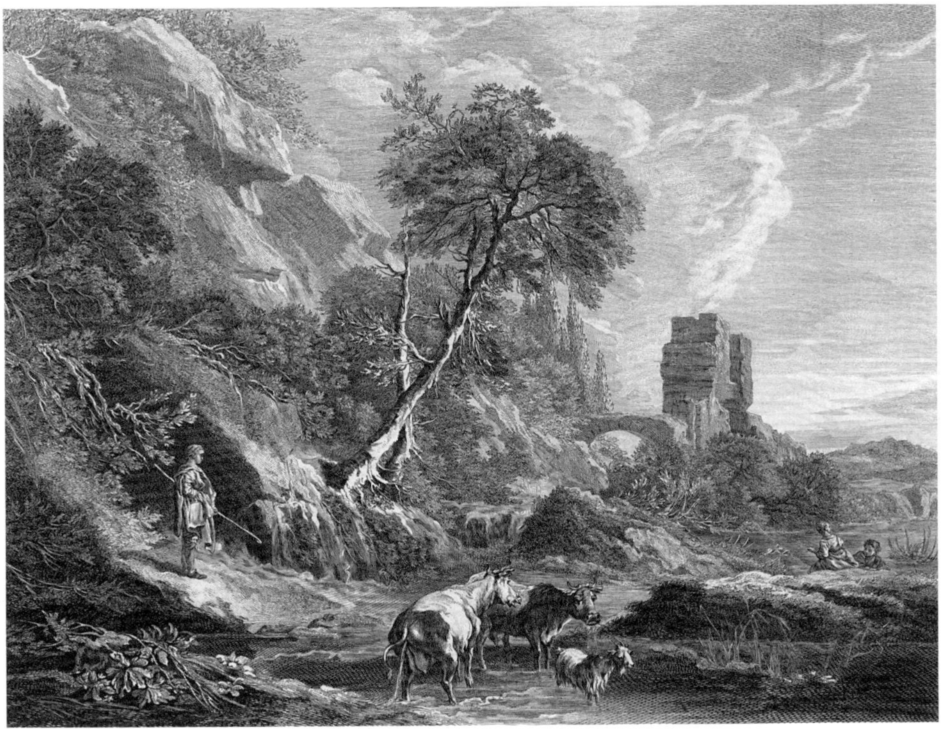

128
Jean Daullé, after François Boucher, *Neapolitan Shepherd*, 1758. Etching and engraving, 30.1 × 35.8 cm. Metropolitan Museum of Art, New York.

The charismatic influence of Boucher's style had on young painters is undoubtedly a product of his special teaching methods. The Goncourts report: "As a friend of the youths, he loved to surround himself with them, to dive into their midst. At this time he allowed them unrestricted entry to his studio. He had no hesitancy or unsureness of hand, the weaknesses that are the reason why artists hide away while at work. He taught with his door wide open and said he did not know how else to counsel than with brush in hand. And two or three strokes made on the canvas would give a young artist more than what he could tell him."[65] Staging live demonstrations in front of students is a style of teaching more appropriate to the master of a workshop than to the director of an academy, who might be expected instead to deliver theoretical principles from behind a lectern. But Boucher's motive was not to educate; he aimed instead for perfection in outward display, much like Tintoretto in his lesson to the young Dutch students. Boucher's pedagogy (to which Reynolds was, to say the least, not very receptive) consisted in self-aggrandizement, a personal display of his high art, whereby he modeled for the student on the one hand a total command of technique, on the other, the abandonment of models in order to find everything within oneself.

THE "INSPIRED WASTE" OF FRAGONARD

Joshua Reynolds declared the foreign academies nests of rottenness and "corruption."[66] The source of this "infection" lay in the poor taste of their directors and in the art politics of the previous decades: "The directors were probably pleased with this premature dexterity in their pupils, and praised their dispatch at the expense of their correctness."[67] We do, in fact, have evidence that the French directors were quite preoccupied with the proper institutional handling of early talent.

On October 11, 1759, the marquis de Marigny (1727–1781), director of the Bâtiments du roi, wrote a letter to the director of the French Academy in Rome, Charles-Joseph Natoire. In the missive, he voiced concern about academic training because, in his view, it dampened enthusiasm and caused the first fire of creativity to go cold. Marigny had in mind the troubling case of one of Natoire's students, Jean-Honoré Fragonard (1732–1806). He was pleased with the care and caution of execution shown by this artist in his academic drawing studies, but he feared that Fragonard's much-admired fire was in danger of being extinguished by excessive caution. The young man's diligence was still detectable, but no longer the joyful freedom and ease of brush (*point de ces heureuses laissés ni de cette facilité de pinceau*), that he had once possessed. In his earlier youth Fragonard had been "an artist who explored his talent and could abandon himself with full consciousness to the movements of his genius," but now in Marigny's opinion, his coloring had lost its freshness and daring: "*Tout est fondu, tout est fini.* It is time that *le sieur* Fragonard has confidence in his talents, and that working with more *hardiesse,* he rediscovers the first fire and happy facility he once had."[68]

Fragonard's *Portraits de Fantaisie,* probably painted between 1767 and 1772, spectacularly demonstrate how ten years after Marigny's letter, Fragonard's "fire" had been very much rekindled. This was due at least in part to a stay in Italy, where he nurtured a *facilité* that was calculated to overshadow, by virtue of his *genie presque italien*, the painting tradition in which he was trained.[69] Edmond and Jules de Goncourt aptly cited a "foreign touch" in these portraits in their *L'Art du XVIIIe siècle.* They recognized in Fragonard's speed of execution evidence of artistic skill, and somewhat comically termed him a "prodigieux *Fa presto,*" thus positioning Fragonard's virtuoso pieces against the foil of a bravura trope from the preceding century. Their discussion of one of the paintings in this series begins by noting the truly stunning inscription on its reverse: "... *peint par Fragonard en 1769, en une heure de temps*"; it was not a work of one day, but of one hour![70] To this day, these words with their emphasis of Fragonard's extreme prestezza are the standard introduction to any analysis of this work.

When the Goncourt brothers wanted to give full expression to their utter astonishment before the *Portrait of Monsieur de La Bretèche,* they brought the full force of their magniloquence to bear. The rhetoric and cadence of their description reflect the painting's display of virtuosity, which was intended to have precisely this kind of overwhelming effect on the viewer (though the Goncourts employ an irony that shows they see through its superficial bravura). After enumerating the picture's excellent qualities, their praise does an abrupt about-face—and they end by tossing the whole thing on the trash heap:

> "One hour! Not more than that. He only needed one hour to so boldly throw down, slap together, and quickly finish the large portrait, where the entire fantasy *à l'espagnole* unfolds and diffuses, and in which the painting of yesteryear clothes and ennobles our contemporaries. An hour to cover the entire canvas! Scarcely did he cast down his strokes and elaborate the faces with rough marks... as his brush then spread out the paints in stripes as if with a palette knife. Beneath the feverish back and forth of his brush, neck ruffs boil and twist, folds writhe, mantels wreathe, jackets billow, fabrics rustle and swell into great ostentatious drapery. Blue, cinnabar, orange stream into collars and hats... and the heads themselves leap from the canvas and fall forward out of this raging rubbish, this possessed and inspired waste."[71]

Such "rubbish" is also noticeable at the core of another of Fragonard's *Portraits de Fantaisie,* which allegedly bears the visage of the brother of La Bretèche, Abbé Claude Richard de Saint-Non (fig. 129). On the reverse of this painting there clings an old label with the inscription: "*portrait de Mr l'abbé de St. Non / peint par fragonard, / en 1769, en une heure de temps.*"[72] Here we see a thin film of dark brown paint applied unevenly over an ocher-colored imprimatura. Fragonard used the same dark brown on the imposing sleeve with marvelous results. In its shaded folds, the murky tone adds elevation by giving the impression that the imprimatura shines through from below (as in Vouet's self-portrait) although this effect was evidently painted in. The lambent red lappet of the cloak gliding over the Abbé's shoulder and the exposed upper area of his sleeve are thereby embedded in the background color in order to better reveal the traces of the few brushstrokes that render the luxuriousness of the fabric. The lappet's red paint is underlain with brown, while in the troughs of its deepest folds, brown paint mixed with black lies on top.[73]

The economy with which this figure was hastily and sketchily "slapped together" is indeed spectacular. The energy of Fragonard's bold painting style accords with

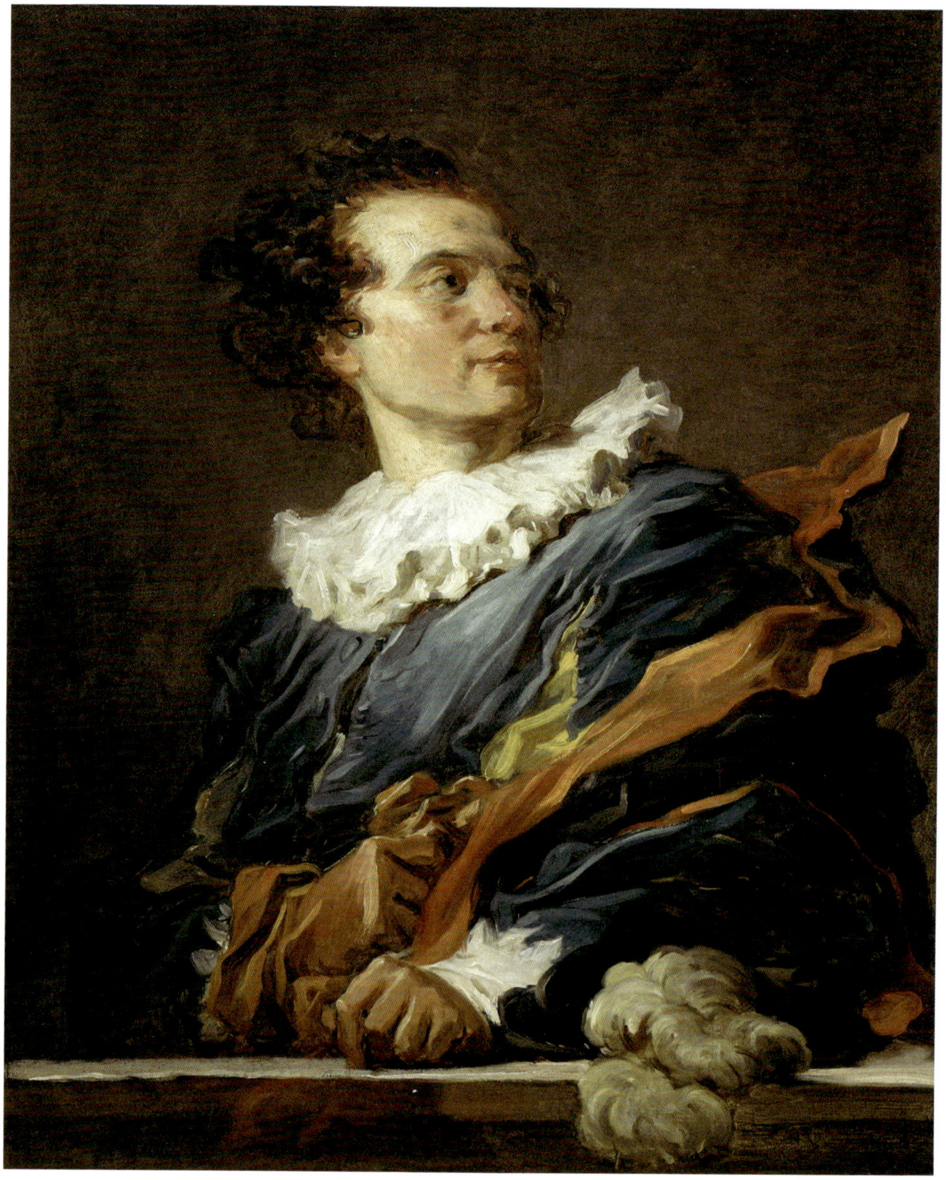

129
Jean-Honoré Fragonard, *Abbé Claude Richard de Saint-Non*, 1769. Oil on canvas, 80×65 cm. Musée du Louvre, Paris.

the portrait's intended impact. The proud, almost contemptuous gaze Saint-Non casts over his shoulder corresponds to the "disdain" that this type of execution communicates, its resoluteness concentrated in the gloved right hand, whose fingers are separated by broad, dark brown brushstrokes—each seemingly made in one single movement—while a single bright stripe configures the central row of knuckles. The marked contrast constructed between this gloved hand, holding a second glove, and the bared left hand is a traditional motif in works thematizing the art of painting, but here it is emphasized: the gloved hand is pressed close to the body and caught up in the surrounding zone of drapery folds, while the other hand, more clearly elaborated, rests on a parapet and appears to reach out into space. Its index finger marks the sharp edge that is only represented by a long white streak. This stroke is not actually continuous, but begins again on either side of the fingertip resting on top of it. A black hat lies next to the hand, and upon closer examination, surprisingly few brushstrokes articulate its exposed, showy bundle of feathers, whose airiness is due to the effect of the exposed ocher-colored imprimatura.

Fragonard's series of fantasy figures poses many questions. Were they commissioned by a patron? Did those portrayed actually sit for their portraits? Who is the ultimate referent here, the sitters, or perhaps more likely, the painter himself?[74] More than a dozen surprisingly homogenous pictures of the same size have been classified as belonging to the *Portraits de Fantaisie*, yet it is not facture and format alone that unify the group. All of them seem to depict either professional performers (singers, musicians, actors) or at least sitters who enjoyed the masquerade of pretending to be performers. The duc d'Harcourt, who Mary D. Sheriff posits as a possible patron of the series, owned a private theater where he wrote plays himself and even appeared on stage as an actor.[75] Whether it is La Bretèche in the role of musician, Saint-Non as a *bravo* in Spanish costume (Barcelona, Museu d'Art Contemporani), or the dancer Mlle. Guimard as an art connoisseur (Paris, Louvre), their dashing (or in female portraits, coquette) poses are all obviously disposed to garner applause. The art connoisseur to whom this spectacle is primarily addressed would recognize the dramatic posturing and gestures as components of a stock repertoire. Fragonard's assemblage of bravura painting devices gathered from the heroes of sixteenth- and seventeenth-century art are also on display, as if in a performance before this knowledgeable audience, and the theatricality of the entire affair is reinforced by the subjects' historical costumes. A familiar stereotype emerges when one views the series as a whole—for example, one identical head study served for the variously staged portraits of Saint-Non—which Jacques Thuillier critically, and fully in line with Diderot's and Reynolds's reproach of hollowness, points out: "Speed has become an end to itself. This art has its limits. However great the painter's virtuosity may be, there are times when speed leaves no more than a senseless trail."[76]

It is curious that while Fragonard was creating the *Portraits de Fantaisie*, which seem to deliberately parody and thus debunk outmoded bravura tropes rather than nostalgically revive them, he also conceived a remarkably fresh and stylistically forward-looking work literally on top of one of these portraits, overpainting it to give his idiosyncratic style a new look (fig. 130). In *La Liseuse* (*Young Girl Reading*) we see a delicate young woman immersed in a book, but a radiographic analysis has disclosed, underneath her and completely covered by this exemplary image of feminine refinement, a theatrical "figure de fantaisie" (to employ Michael Fried's polarizing category for eighteenth-century French art).[77]

Fragonard has not abandoned here the ostentatious demonstration of art, but his bold brushstrokes are more inclined to glide along folds of fabric, imbuing the painting with textural effects. One exception is the brilliantly placed long horizontal line that evokes, with astounding visual economy, the illuminated arris of the rail upon which the lady's arm rests (a line very similar to the one in the Saint-Non portrait in its gestural quality) (fig. 131). To create the undulations of her ruff, Fragonard scratched the wet paint with the tip of his brush handle to expose the light-colored ground underneath, a technique widely practiced since the seventeenth century. The overall impression of fluidity that embeds and cushions the reader

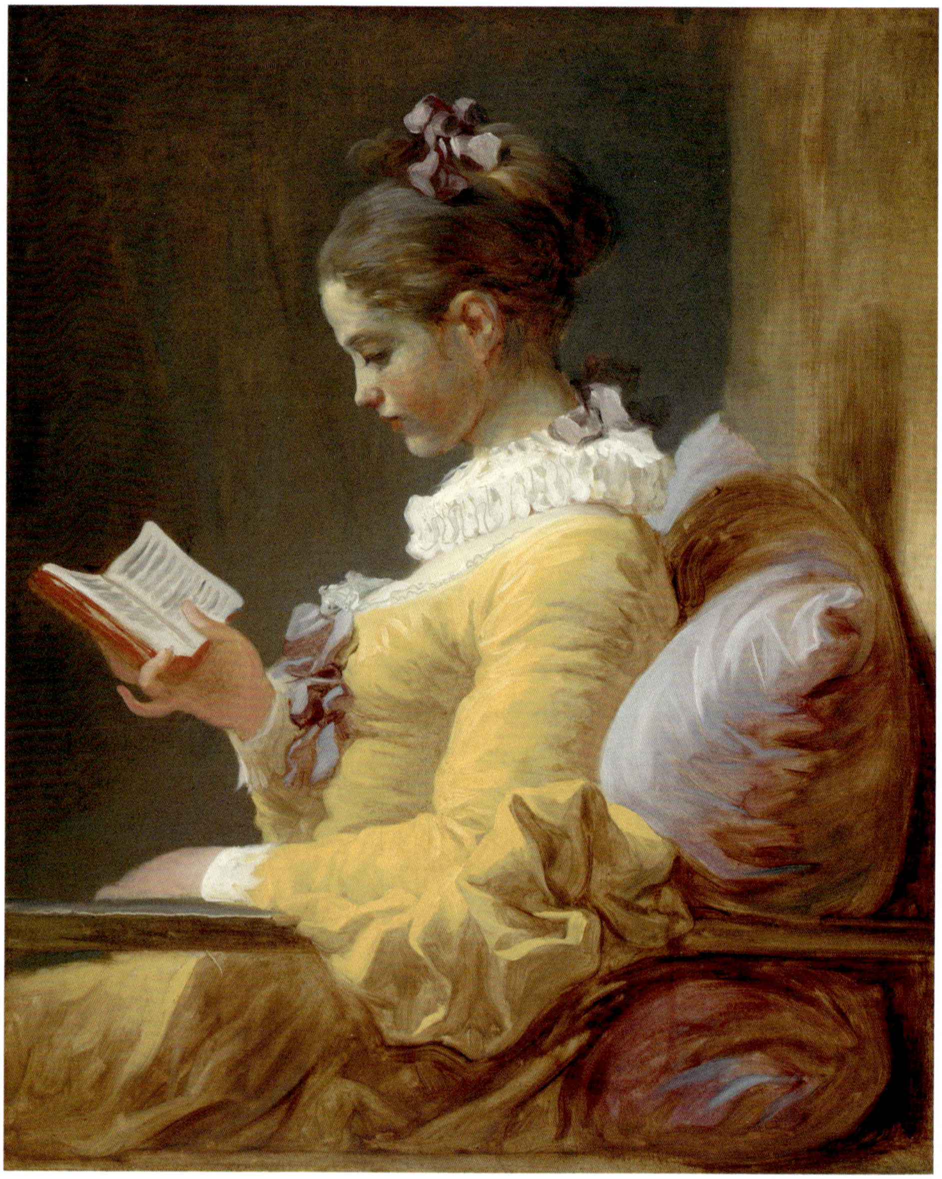

130
Jean-Honoré Fragonard, *Young Girl Reading* (*La Liseuse*), ca. 1769. Oil on canvas, 81.3 × 64.8 cm. National Gallery of Art, Washington, DC.

131–132 (FACING)
Details of fig. 130 [*Young Girl Reading*].

even infuses the elegantly raised little finger of her hand holding the book, a gesture emphasizing her refinement. The violet hue radiating from the ribbon of her bodice and the cushion supporting her back frame the yellow field of the dress in a cold bluish ambient, while the book's eye-catching vermillion edging resonates with the blush on her cheek and ears. Red lies uppermost on her lips, yet streaks of greenish-gray veil her forehead and temple. Their colder tone, traditionally used in lower paint strata and not on top, causes the underlying red to appear to flush to the surface (fig. 132). This depiction of a physiological response, which enlivens the image and spurs the imagination of the beholder, communicates an intimacy not shared with us: looking at the pages of her book, we encounter only horizontal bars of gray revealing nothing. The voyeuristic intrusiveness of our gaze is also drawn to the fervent execution of her skirt's churned up folds, whose magnificent swift

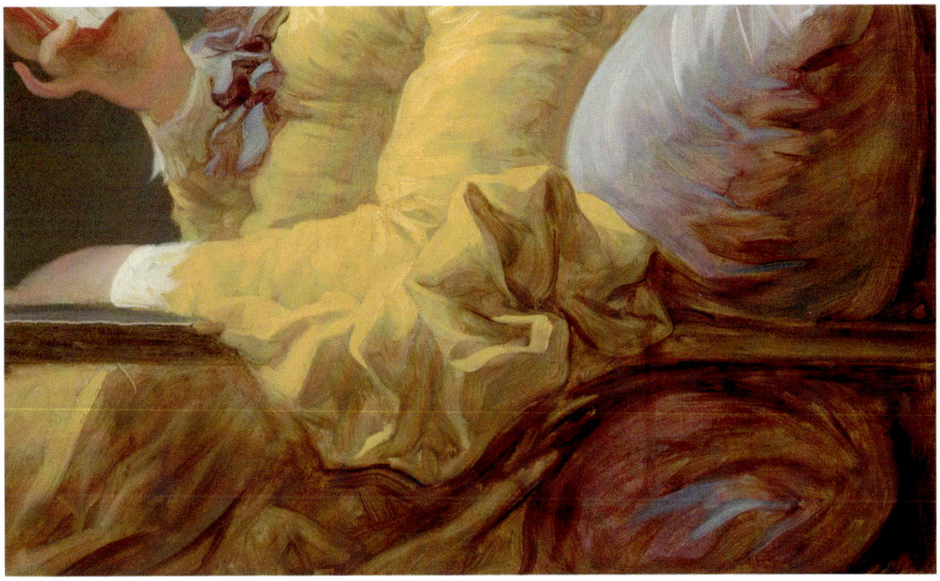

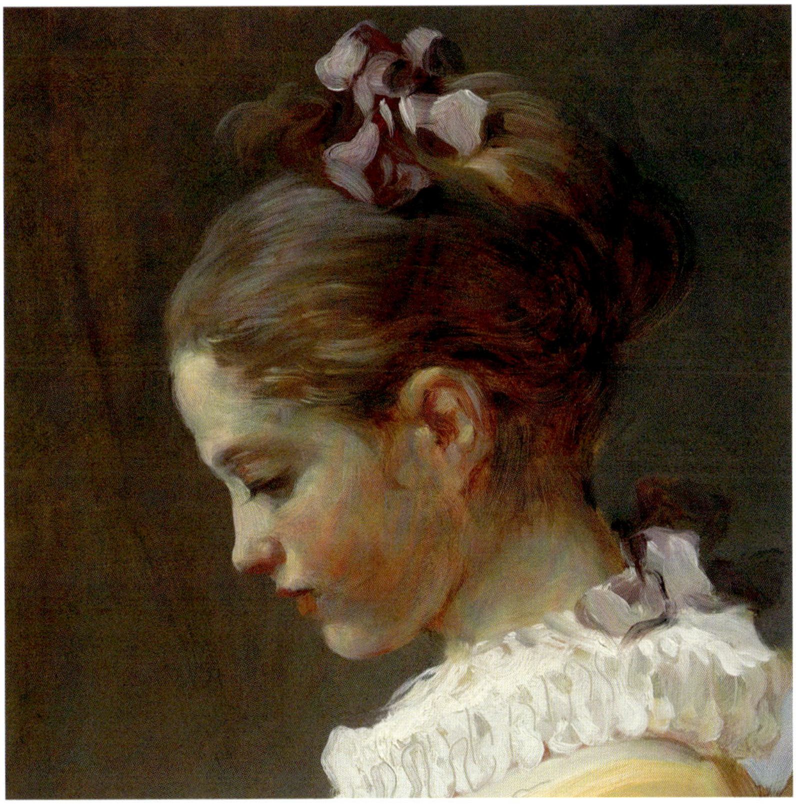

strokes reveal in their explicitness a desire to unfold the vortex they have so neatly embellished. Whereas in the areas bathed in light Fragonard's brushstrokes create plenitude and splendor, the girl's back and the shaded areas of her dress are mired in thin layers of brownish underpaint, a muddy ground she seems to slide into. Thus it seems the Goncourt brothers' metaphor of rubbish still holds true.

CHAPTER TEN

Reenactments and Echoes

FRANS HALS'S REALIST BRAVURA

During the nineteenth century's age of Impressionism, meaningful critique of "senseless" painterly affectation such as that voiced by Diderot seemed to evaporate. The Goncourts' takedown of Fragonard in the last chapter is an exception, and its literary qualities make it, ironically, a wry bravura piece in its own right. Their fickle celebration of the eighteenth century, written more than a hundred years after the creation of Fragonard's *Portraits de Fantaisie*, was doubtless a critical reaction to the dismantling of painting tradition that was underway in contemporary art discourse. Only a few years after the publication of *L'Art du XVIIIe siècle* in 1883, the engraver and author Baron Melchior-Roger Portalis (1841–1912) wrote the first monograph on Fragonard in similarly poetic prose: "And it was in the *belle pâte*, fluid and sparkling, that he drowned the features of his models with broad sweeps of his brush."[1] But for our purposes, his most important statement appears several lines earlier: "Portrait painting in his case almost touches on violence [*touche presque à la violence*]." This brings Portalis in the next sentence to humorously link Fragonard's art to the seventeenth century: "It's like an enraged Frans Hals!"[2]

The masterful "smearing" of paint, deployed to splendid effect by Fragonard in his *Portraits*, was indeed the subject of advice given by Frans Hals (1580?–1666) to his pupils: "You need only smear with daring; once you are steadfast in art, accuracy [*neitheit*] comes automatically."[3] However, the proposition that art will emerge almost spontaneously from "bold smearing"—from accidental painterly placements alone—is dubious. Techniques that have at least the appearance of accidents exhibit bravura—they are calculated for their impact. Whether such bravura is able to manifest art or not depends upon whether the result is successful or defective, although both outcomes may at first glance seem to be phenomenally equivalent. In other words, it depends upon the artist. Houbraken tells of the painter Abraham Diepraem (1622–1674):

> Just as the art of others grows and becomes greater with understanding [*verstant*] and the years, his art became worse as he got older, such that I have seen pictures of his where the colors are no longer blended together. But why

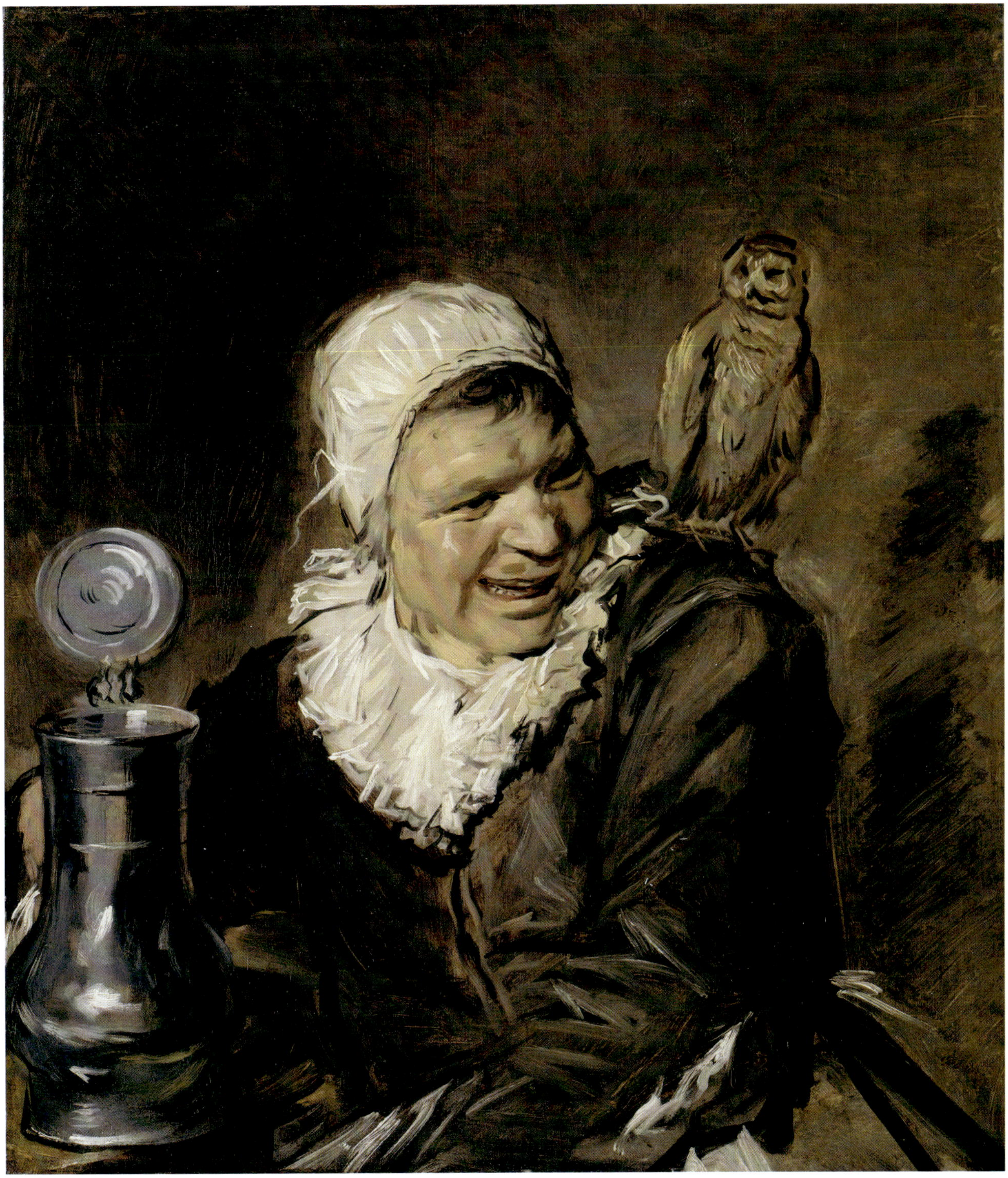

133
Frans Hals, *Malle Babbe*, 1633.
Oil on canvas, 75×64 cm.
Gemäldegalerie, Berlin.

talk about "blending"? The brushstrokes did not even touch each other [*de penceeltoetsen raakten elkander niet eens*]. Reader, you may counter that there are also such works by Frans Hals and that he is considered a good painter. To this I would answer that the execution [*handeling*] of Hals has not the slightest similarity to Diepraem. For the former showed therein his understanding [*verstant*], the latter his deterioration [*verval*]. The former operated purposefully to display his mastery of the brush, the latter could do no differently because his hands trembled from drinking too much brandy.[4]

The difference between *virtus* (understanding) and *vitium* (deterioration), between art and mere accident, is therefore linked to control (or lack of control) of the hand and thus to the motivation of the brushstroke. That Hals, according to Houbraken, was also inordinately fond of drink does not seem to interest him here, and he does not use it as an argument for or against his art.

One of Hals's most famous works is an intriguing case study in this regard, for it demonstrates artistic understanding by means of a brush ductus superficially reminiscent of that executed by a shaky alcoholic. *Malle Babbe* is the portrait of a laughing and apparently babbling drunken woman (fig. 133). Her uninhibited hearty guffaw, which Hals captures so masterfully, seems momentarily to galvanize Babbe's heavy, dull presence: jagged zigzags elaborate the left side of her body, while the right sinks into the imprimatura, steering the beholder's gaze toward something perhaps concealed behind her back. Her empty stare into space suggests a monologue, which the peculiar owl perched on her shoulder—symbolizing drunkenness—apparently visualizes.[5] Babbe's hand, grasping a pewter tankard, is an artistic feat of abbreviation, consisting only of an amorphous blotch of paint. Unremarkable on its own, it nonetheless serves Hals as the backdrop for a volume-creating play of reflected light across the vessel's metallic surface (fig. 134). It seems as if the tankard, from which crazy (*malle*) Babbe was apparently about to take a drink before she was distracted, projects from the surface of the picture—or more precisely, from the smudge of her hand—toward us.

The phenomenal aspects of this genre portrait do indeed recall Abraham Diepraem's style, as Houbraken noted. The materiality of the broad strokes that render the pleats of Babbe's cap are cast upon a canvas primed with a light-colored ground and belong to a similar compositional stratum as the markings of the collar below them; they do not dissolve when viewed from a greater distance. The collar, also rough in its outline, coalesces despite the rather chaotic arrangement of its brushstrokes, which increase in density and darkness where the low angle view of the collar switches to a high angle. The impression that Babbe has suddenly raised her left shoulder is achieved by the rendition of this collar, not that of the sleeve. Babbe's addled laughter resonates in the undulating black, white, and gray lines next to her mouth that can only with difficulty be identified as the ruffles of her collar. This reverberation of sound is also formally inscribed onto her face by a plump grayish-green dash of color—irritating, mimetically unmotivated, and disfiguring—above her mouth. The animated frills of her collar create a contrast to the taut pleats of the cap that securely and neatly frame the back of her head, and from which her face, distorted with laughter, seems to erupt.

One unbridled line, a zigzagging white brushstroke, bears sole responsibility for formal contouring in the right lower corner, where two long, thick black strokes (almost completely separated from the rest of the figure on the dark-colored, angular space of the background) configure Babbe's skirt. On its own, the white zigzag resists interpretation, but it stands in a convincing mimetic relationship with the rough white brushstrokes that mark the folds of the foremost part of the apron. The excellence of Frans Hals's *alla prima* technique is exhibited in his extraordinary ability to initially forego contouring in order to construct figures from placements of color and subsequent adjustments at their boundaries. These placements are differentiated as the painting progresses and gradually gain mimetic concretion. The openness of his style allows a reworking that is not a correction. The last step in this process—boldly executed lashes of the brush—brings the composition together. To quote Hals: "Now the only thing to add is that by which a master is recognized."[6]

The jurist and politician Théophile Thoré (1807–1869), who published art criticism under the pseudonym William Bürger, rediscovered Frans Hals after the painter had fallen into obscurity. He particularly commended *Malle Babbe* as the work where Hals "gave himself over most fully to the *furia* of his genius."[7] The "violence of his brushstroke" reaches a climax in this painting, Thoré says, and he links it to bravura through a fencing metaphor, in absolute accordance with seventeenth-century imagery: "All of his strokes are flourishes of adroitness and genius. One could say Frans Hals painted like a fencer and that he let his brush lash out like a

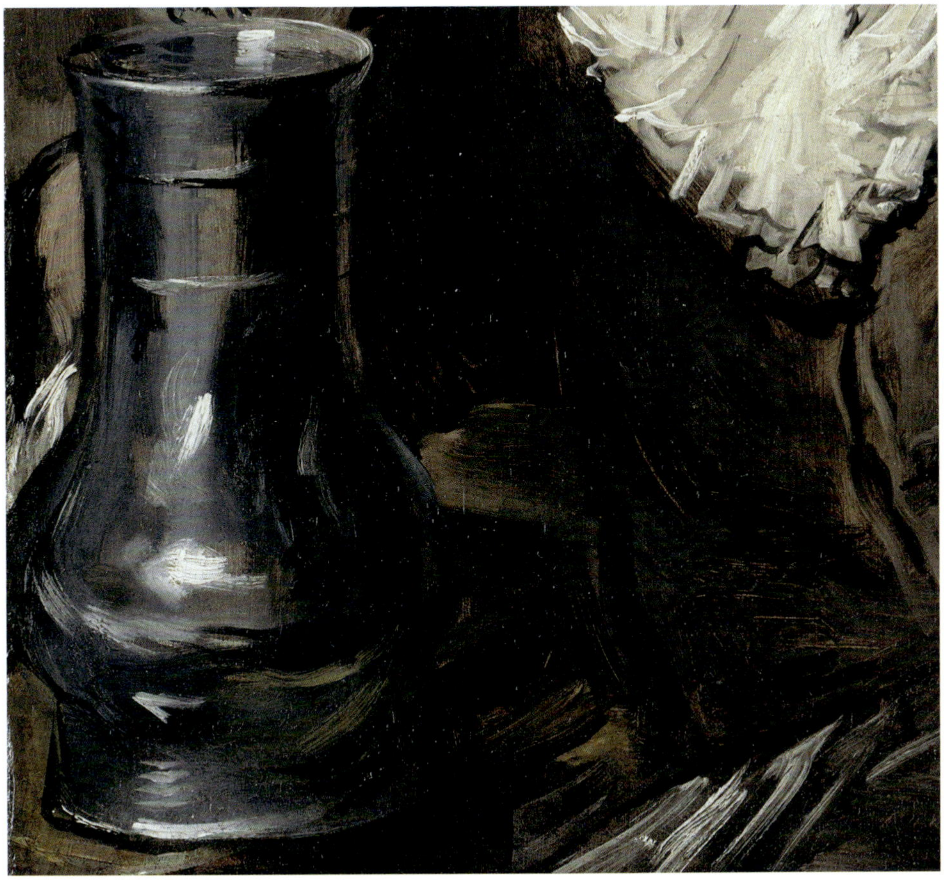

134
Detail of fig. 133 [*Malle Babbe*].

foil." Thoré's evocation of a beautiful exchange of blows that play out across the surface of the painting—"sometimes a bit reckless, without question, but equally experienced and unafraid"—befits Hals's bravuroso mastery of technique. Thoré also praises his construction of the picture from painterly placements that are "well-seated" from the very first stroke.[8]

The writer, art critic, and painter Eugène Fromentin would cast a critical as well as admiring eye on Frans Hals's virtuosity by reducing it to the concept of praxis: "Hals was nothing other than a practitioner; he is absolutely one of the most competent and skilled masters that ever existed, even in Flanders despite Rubens and Van Dyck, even in Spain despite Velázquez."[9] Fromentin sums up the abbreviated character of Hals's facture by comparing it to conciseness of speech, to "the art of being precise without explaining too much, of making everything understood intuitively... the right word and nothing but the right word, found at the very first stroke.... Never has anyone painted better, nor will they."[10]

Théophile Thoré's and Fromentin's eloquent rehabilitation of bravura by way of Frans Hals is remarkable insofar as Hals was unknown outside the Dutch Republic and until that time not a subject of academic discourse. But as he gained art-historical recognition, he came to be considered one of the most prominent forerunners of French modern art. In 1869 Gustave Courbet produced a copy after *Malle Babbe*, which however seems merely to congeal the sparkling vigor of the original and to be rather deaf to its bravura. The reason for Hals's belated fame has everything to do with institutional prejudices: As a "pure practitioner" he excelled in portrait painting, which in the academic hierarchy of genres placed "lower" than history painting because it was bound to the faithful representation of a particular reality (the sitter) and did not necessitate any further knowledge beyond that of painterly technique. Quite early on in the history of art theory, there was a prevailing view that not only portraiture, but Dutch art in general, lacked erudition. Francisco de Hollanda dismissed Netherlandish art as preoccupied with the purely mimetic and wanting in, among other things, "reason or art," "symmetry or proportion," "judiciousness of selection," and "substance or vigor."[11] This view was famously reframed by the art historian Svetlana Alpers as a Dutch "art of describing," wherein the science of optics gave mimesis an entirely new perspective.[12] It seems that the combination of bravura brushwork and a narrow conception of realism, manifested most prominently in the artistic attitudes of Hals and Velázquez, has overcome the caesura of modernity. It is now interpreted as its precursor. In retrospect, bravura seems to have been a much more promising path to success than the academic royal road because it is geared toward innovative practices that establish the future of painting instead of simply repeating and handing down past models.

THE AFTERLIFE OF BRAVURA

Instrumental to the genesis of modern art was an increasing disaffection at the end of the eighteenth century with the academy's pedagogical regimentation. One figure in particular proposed an alternative that incorporated bravura's quintessential anti-academic stance while investing it with renewed spirit and combativeness. Francisco de Goya, who became a member of the Real Academia de las Tres Nobles

Artes de San Fernando in 1780, laid out his position on the matter in a statement written on October 14, 1792, after a meeting held by the academy to discuss the implementation of new regulations. His open letter called for a liberalization of studies. By this he meant that students should not be required to adher to the academy's program of "mechanical precepts" (*preceptos mecanicos*) that followed in rigid sequence, but should have some flexibility in determining their course of study. The individual student, he argued, should be able to decide for themselves according to their affinities and talents at what point in their artistic development it would be appropriate to learn, for example, geometry and perspective. For Goya, there were no rules in painting. That said, compulsory uniformity in artistic education was "a great hindrance for youths that practice this difficult art" (*es un grande impedimento à los Jovenes que profesan este arte tan dificil*). The cultivation of individuality, which could only be done independently, presented a challenge not only for those receiving instruction, but even more so for their instructors, who must additionally contend with the fundamental problem of mediation. Those who had come closest to the secrets of art would, Goya thought, be hard pressed to come up with even a few laws to convey the profound understanding that was required (*podra dar pocas reglas delas profundas funciones del entendimiento*). He goes on to say that the artist cannot answer the question of what conspired to make him perhaps "more happy in a work of less caution than in one of greater effort" (*mas feliz tal vez en la obra de menos cuidado, que en la de mayor esmero*).[13] His position that any subservience in the student must be prevented lest the academy come to resemble an *escuela de niños* aimed directly at the axiom, often repeated in the Early Modern period, that learning the rules of painting was like learning the alphabet. For Goya, the "language of painters" could not be reduced to mandatory conventions or transmitted by the repetition or variation of models. The decidedly unacademic educational curriculum he proposed left artistic development up to the individual. It meant nothing less radical than redefining painting as a "liberal art," and it would become orthodoxy in the modern period.

"All the rules, all the canons of art vomit death," the painter James Ensor (1860–1949) proclaimed a good century later.[14] But once vomited out, this death seemed to drag art down along with it. Pablo Picasso (1881–1973) described to his lover and companion Françoise Gilot the precarious consequence of freeing art from the strictures of academic rules: "But as soon as art had lost all link with tradition, and the kind of liberation that came in with Impressionism permitted every painter to do what he wanted to do, painting was finished.... Painters no longer live within a tradition and so each one of us must recreate an entire language. Every painter of our times is fully authorized to recreate that language from A to Z."[15]

Picasso, whom Jean Cocteau likened to a tornado and declared a danger to young artists,[16] would identify the artful destruction of precedents as the guiding premise of the modern. His oft-quoted maxim—"One must kill modern art, which also means one must kill oneself if one wants to continue to be able to make anything"—only manifests its full lethal force when considered in tandem with another of his statements: "Because modern, once repeated, is no longer so" (*Car modern, une fois de plus, il n'est plus*). This death blow to the past served his declared intention to "rediscover painting."[17] Commenting on a still life by the father figure of

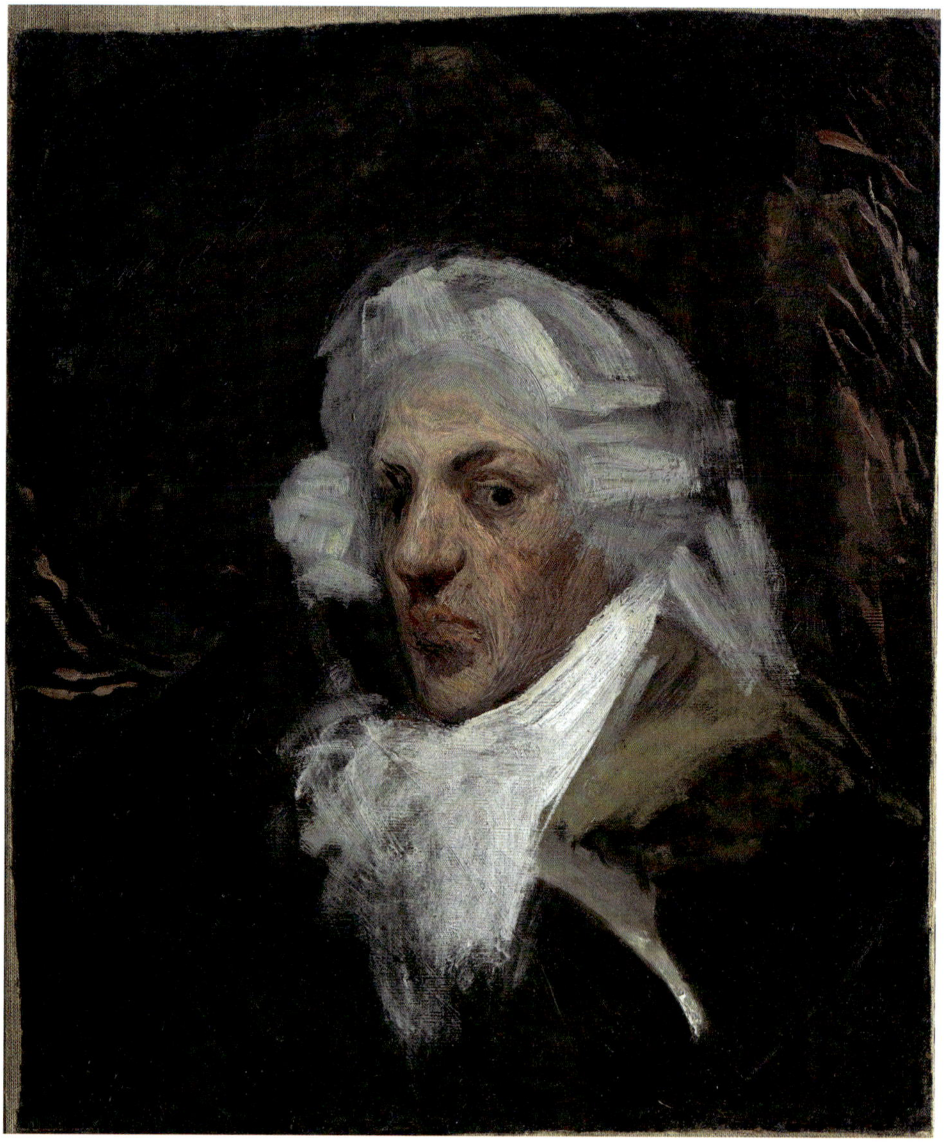

135
Pablo Picasso, *Self-Portrait with Wig*, ca. 1898–1900. Oil on canvas, 55.8×45.8 cm. Museu Picasso, Barcelona.

modern art, Picasso reveals how deeply he believed this antagonistic principle had permeated the pictorial process of modern painting: "The apples of Cézanne, they are also a battle painting [*une peinture de bataille*]. One line, one color, one painting, a perpetual battle."[18] Georges Braque seemed to share the sentiment of his friend and enemy when he compared Cézanne's achievements to a battle "waged against a large part of our knowledge, or what we had chosen to respect, to admire or to love.[...] Cézanne swept the idea of mastery off the table.[...] He opened us up to a taste for risk."[19]

In Picasso's opinion, this drive toward radical new beginnings resulted from a fundamental shortcoming: "[Cezanne] had absolutely no talent, no skill at mimesis."[20] There is a positive dimension to *gaucherie* in its being the artist's most particular expression of idiosyncrasy—of their individuality. That *gaucherie* itself can become a declared artistic goal is documented in Henri de Toulouse-Lautrec's joyful exclamation (as rumored by Henri Matisse): "At last I no longer know how to draw!" Matisse explained as follows: "This meant he had found his true line, his true drawing, his own draftsman's language."[21] Picasso would note accordingly in his sketchbook: "One should not learn to draw" (*il faut pas apprendre dessiner*).[22]

Bravura artists, as we have abundantly seen, continually confronted the accusation that their art was not based on the rules of *disegno* but rather on the caprices of practice. The radicalness of the modern artist's deliberate "de-skilling" is a novel take on bravura, but it was bravura's original martial spirit that paved the way for the combativeness of their art. According to Picasso, our museums are filled with "failed pictures" (*tableaux ratés*), for the artworks that are today considered "masterpieces" (*œuvres maîtresses*) were "those most distant from the rules dictated by the masters of their epoch. The best expose most clearly the stigmata of the artists who painted them."[23]

Throughout his lifetime, Picasso performed such signature bravura feats as single-line drawings and, in general, cultivated the playfully aggressive painterly disposition that would bring succeeding generations under his spell. It is therefore not surprising that one of his early works bears witness to the influence of seventeenth-century bravura. Picasso portrayed himself when he was fifteen years of age dressed as an "old master" wearing a white wig. In this painting, dashed down with excessively broad and vigorous brushstrokes, he seems once again to join in the old-fashioned but still fitting masquerade of the *bravo* in painterly terms (fig. 135).

Notes

INTRODUCTION

1 Félibien, *Entretiens*, vol. 3, 265. The source of this anecdote is Bellori, *Vite dei pittori, scultori ed architetti moderni*, 73.

2 Artistotle, *Nicomachean Ethics*, [book 2.4–5], 73.

3 "Indeed we see men of experience succeeding more than those who have theory without experience." Aristotle, *Metaphysics*, [book 1. 8–9], vol. 1, 5.

4 "A los que hazen las tales pinturas de simple imitacion, los venero como a medicos impiricos, que sin saber la causa hazen obras milagrosas: y es cierto que en el tribunal de los sentidos tendran aplauso grãde, y sus obras causaràn asombro, engañando tal vez el de la vista con la afectuosa imitacion, y de todos los que militan en este tribunal, no dudo se llevarã la voz y el victor." Carducho, *Dialogos de la pintura*, 53.

5 "Anzi i maestri eccellenti de'nostri tempi han posto in costume, ch'io chiamerò piú tosto abuso, di riserrarsi e chiudere ogni minima fessura quando lavorano, di maniera che apena li posson vedere coloro che li servono." Armenini, *De' veri precetti*, 12.

6 "E chi, senza essi, si mette per cosí lungo e faticoso viaggio, è forza che trabocchi, non altrimente che si faccia il cieco che camina senza il bastone in disusate maniere et intricati viluppi." Ibid., 13.

7 Lomazzo, "Tempio," *Scritti*, vol. 1, 245.

8 Ibid., 246–247.

9 "We assume that artists are wiser than men of mere experience [...]; and this is because the former know the cause, whereas the latter do not. For the experienced know the fact, but not the wherefore; but the artists know the wherefore and the cause." Aristotle, *Metaphysics* [book 1.I.8–11], vol. 1, 7.

10 "Thus the master craftsmen are superior in wisdom, not because they can do things, but because they possess a theory and know the causes. In general the sign of knowledge or ignorance is the ability to teach, and for this reason we hold that art rather than experience is scientific knowledge; for the artists can teach, but the others cannot." Aristotle, *Metaphysics* [book 1.I.13], vol. 1, 7. Cf. chapter 8, "Delle scienze necessarie al pittore," in Lomazzo, "Tempio": *Scritti*, vol. 1, 271.

11 Varchi, *Due Lezzioni*, 58, 61–62, 87.

12 Dempsey, *Annibale Carracci*, 52.

13 Adorno, *Ästhetische Theorie*, 317.

14 Reynolds, *Discourses on Art*, 194.

15 Polanyi, *Personal Knowledge*, 49.

16 Michael Polanyi here refers to musical performance, but his argument is also valid for the visual arts. Polanyi, *Personal Knowledge*, 50.

17 See Dempsey, *Annibale Carracci*, 52.

18 Giovanni Battista Agucchi, in Mahon, *Studies in Seicento Art*, appendix I, 254.

19 "La virtuosité ne cherche pas la pénombre pour s'y cacher, mais au contraire elle fait ses cabrioles sous les feux de la rampe et des projecteurs." Jankelevitch, *Liszt et la Rhapsodie*, 9.

20 Giovan Paolo Lomazzo, *Idea of the Temple of Painting*, 89–90.

21 Jean-Auguste Domique Ingres staged this legendary encounter in a painting that is part of a series celebrating legendary artists (*Aretin dans l'atelier du Tintoret*, Metropolitan Museum of Art, New York).

22 Ridolfi, *Le Maraviglie dell'arte*, vol. 2, 251f. The demonstration of artistic sovereignty in Tintoretto's prank is also evident on another occasion, where he used

27 De' Dominici, *Vite*, vol. 3, 1.

28 Walter K. Lang clarified Ribera's painting as being derived from Domenichino's version, and interpreted the meeting of blade and signature as a concetto. Lang, *Grausame Bilder*, 143, 148.

29 The intervention of the artist's signature in the space between these two pictorial elements may also be found in Ribera's earlier version of the same theme. The platter here is slightly raised, the bowl lies on top of the staff and sword blade, while the signature is inscribed between the two ends of the sword grip: "Jusepe de Ribera espanol / F. 1644" (Madrid, Museo de la Real Academia de Bellas Artes de San Fernando). See Spinosa, *Ribera*, 367, 369f.

30 Aristotle, *Poetics*, 15.

31 Ibid.

32 Wassiliwizky et al., "Tears Falling on Goosebumps," 7.

33 Letter written in 1604 to Bernardo Castello, in Marino, *Epistolario*, vol. 1, 37–42 (no. XXIII–XXIX). See Pericolo, "Le 'Fantasiette.'"

34 Letter to Bernardo Castello: "È intitolata la Galeria, e contiene quasi tutte le favole antiche. Ciascuna favola viene espressa in un disegno di mano di valent'uomo; e sopra ogni disegno io fo una breve elogio in loda di quel maestro, e poivo' scherzando intorno ad esso con qualche capriccio poetico." Marino, *Epistolario*, vol. 1, 133–134 (no. LXXIX).

35 Marino, *La Galeria*, 348. For the English translation of the poem and further discussion of the significance of this passage, see Cropper, "The Petrifying Art," 202–205. On the vivifying effect, see Stoichita, *The Pygmalion Effect*, 96–100.

36 "Crudel fu ben colui, / Che vivo e ver dal busto / La sacra testa al buon GIOVANNI sciolse, / Pietoso è ben costui, / Che finto in campo angusto / Nel' Opra istessa illustre tela accolse. / Quei già di vita il tolse, / Questi in atto più pio l'armi severe / Alza sì, ma non fère." Marino, *La Galeria*, 147.

37 "Qual cruda man commise il crudo scempio? E qual, pietosa dele membra sante, Ritrasse in vivo lino il caro essempio?" Marino, *La Galeria*, 146.

38 "Che fai Guido? che fai, / La man, che forme angeliche dipigne, / Tratta hor'opre sanguigne? / Non vedi tu, che mentre il sanguinose / Stuol de'fanciulli ravivando vai, / Nova morte gli dai?" Marino, *La Galeria*, 103.

39 "O nela crudeltate anco pietoso Fabro gentil, ben sai Ch'ancor Tragico caso è caro oggetto, E che spesso l'horror va col diletto." Marino, *La Galeria*, 102f.; Cropper, "The Petrifying Art," 207.

40 See Cropper, "Marino's 'Strage degli innocenti,'" 150.

41 Cropper, "Marino's 'Strage degli innocenti'," 161; Cropper, "The Petrifying Art," 207; Cropper and Dempsey 1996, esp. 276. See also a thorough analysis of the painting in Wimböck, *Guido Reni*, 169–196.

42 Cropper, "The Petrifying Art," 207.

43 "Alas! That neither my tongue nor my quill (*la mia lingua e lo mio stile*) / Cuts as deep as a crueler implement (*Non punge al par de le crudeli spade*) / To mark readers' hearts (*in ogni cor gentile*) with wounds that are filled / Full of pious and righteous sentiment! Why is that my unworthy pen (*la mia penna oscura e vile*) / Should prove but a useless instrument? / To paint the grim martyrdom of the Jews (*Ch'a ritrar tanti orror vien meno e cade, / Del gran martirio Ebreo l'istoria amara*)—What, Arpino, can I not learn from you? (*Arpin, dal tuo penello or non impar?*); Marino, *The Massacre of the Innocents*, 116. Interestingly, although Arpino seems to be the primary reference for Marino's imaginative tableau, the only painting that is referred to specifically is Arpino's lovely figure of Charity. Marino, *The Massacre of the Innocents* (stanza 59), 144.

44 Cropper, "The Petrifying Art," 205.

45 Hendrix, "The Repulsive Body," 89.

46 The authors assume a single written source, "a *discriptio* whether in poetry or in prose." Cropper and Dempsey, *Nicolas Poussin*, 259.

47 Ekaterini Kepetzis, "Der *Bethlehemitische Kindermord.*"

48 Ibid., 173.

49 Jaffé, *Rubens's Massacre of the Innocents*, 87.

50 "El del bel petto e del bel volto, / Come può meglio, al caro suo la scudo" (Engl. trans. mine). Marino, *The Massacre of the Innocents*, 134.

51 "Haveva uno dei Manasdieri presa una Donna per le chiome, & ravoltatosi al braccio i crini che'erano piu belli che le fila de l'oro: gliene svelleva à scosse. Et ella fattosi scudo del suo petto, si forzava di scampare il figlio, la semplicita delquale voleva prendere il ferro, che gli veniva contra." Aretino, *Humanità di Christo*, 23r.

52 Her gesture evokes the maiden who rescued the child Moses.

53 See Jaffé, *Rubens's Massacre of the Innocents*, fig. 136, 135.

54 Bust, Museo Altemps, Rome.

55 Jaffé, *Rubens's Massacre of the Innocents*, 138–139.

56 "Ne sono rotti nel muro. Se ne scagliano da i tetti. Se ne tuffano nelle acque che bollano.... Se ne strangola con le mani. S ne trafigge co i piedi. Se ne schiaccia co i pugni. Se ne gitta nelle latrine. Se ne sbravano, e se ne tagliano in pezzi." Aretino, *Humanità di Christo*, 21r.

57 Marino, *The Massacre of the Innocents*, 124.

58 Aretino compares the sentiment to that felt when watching a jousting tournament: "A così duro spettacolo era intento Herode; e piu ne godeva, che non gode il popolo de le battaglie, che fanno le fiere condotte dentro le sbarre ne i giuochi, che se gli dedicano." Aretino, *Humanità di Christo*, 22v-23r.

59 Jaffé, *Rubens's Massacre of the Innocents*, 94.

60 It seems at first glance that she touches his shoulder, but if so she would have to be much taller than the murderer. The height of the figures in general is not congruent with the space indicated by the grid of the floor.

61 Wittkower, "The Classical Models," 106. This association, as Yona Pinson discovered, is supported by the codified "scena tragica" of the painting's background. Pinson, "Un langage muet," 109–127. Pinson refers to Sebastiano Serlio's stage design in his *De architectura libri quinque* (1569).

62 Wittkower connects this gesture with King Croesus as depicted on a Median sarcophagus. Wittkower, "The Classical Models," 106.

63 Cropper, "Marino's 'Strage degli innocenti'," 162.

64 "The boy greeted him by smiling and calling out 'Daddy'!" Marino, *The Massacre of the Innocents*, 141.

65 Badt, *Die Kunst des Nicolas Poussin*, 448.

66 Ovid, *Fasti*, II, 795f.

67 Cropper, "Marino's 'Strage degli innocenti'," 162.

68 "Fanno forza maggiore / Ai dubbi affetti di chiunque vede / Le dispietate prede, / Ch'ai seni ignudi, et ale trecce sparte / Delle belle Sabine / Non fan vostre rapine, / O squadre rapacissime di Marte. / Ma non so di qual parte / Far maggior violenca altrui si crede, / La violata, e qui violatore: La pietate, o'l furore." Marino, *La Galeria*, 364.

69 "Pinge, il caso Artemisia, e lo rinnova: Già Roma il ferro insanginar ti vede: Hor più del ferro il suo pennel t'uccide." Toesca, "Versi in lode di Artesemia Gentileschi," 90. See Lang, *Grausame Bilder*, 93.

70 Toesca, "Versi in lode di Artesemia Gentileschi," 91.

71 Garrard, *Artemisia Gentileschi*, 230.

72 Ibid., 348.

73 "Finally, I think we *hear* the suspense of this scene, as we would in the theater." Ciletti, "Gran Macchina è Bellezza," 102.

74 Christiansen and Mann, *Orazio and Artemisia Gentileschi*, No. 70; 368–369. Judith and her Maidservant, here: 369.

75 Garrard, "Artemisia's Hand," 6.

76 Ibid., 6.

77 Locker, *Artemisia Gentileschi*, 20.

78 Ciletti speaks rightly of "a sudden, ominous, larger-than-life cessation of sound that we can hear." Ciletti, "Gran Macchina è Bellezza," 102.

79 Alessandro Tassoni, *Se il boia sia infame* (1608). Cited in Vazzoler, *La Maschera del boia*, 51–52.

80 "Di maniera che Boia viene a significar l'istesso che Bravo, titolo e nome che veramente li si conviene." Cited in Vazzoler, *La Maschera del Boia*, 49. Vazzoler notes that Tassoni probably invented this etymological derivation.

81 Preimesberger, "Caravaggio im *Matthäusmartyrium* der Cappella Contarelli," 140.

82 Philip Sohm also analyzes how Bellori exaggerated Caravaggio's facial characteristics to give him a signature sinister physiognomy that tellingly discloses his art and destiny. Sohm, "Caravaggio's Deaths," 452.

83 "Non però il Caravaggio con le occupationi della pittura, rimetetva punto le sue inquiete inclinationi; e dopo ch'egli haveva dipinto alcune hore del giorno, compariva per la Città con la spada al fianco, e faceva professione d'armi, mostrando di attendere ad ogn'altra cosa fuori che alla pittura." Bellori, *Vite*, 208.

84 Bellori, *Vite*, 214. See also Stone, "In Figura Diaboli," 21; Sohm, "Caravaggio's Deaths," 453.

85 "Oltre che egli abbassò anche l'arte medesima nel mettersi che e'fece per lo più a far vedere nelle sue tele atti di persone plebee, imitandone ogni gesto più vile... offende gli occhi, e la fantasia altresì de'più intendenti, l'arte medesima avvilisce e oscura. Ma che? Perdonisi al Caravaggio questo suo modo d'usare il pennello; mentre egli volle avverare in se medesimo quel proverbio che dice, che ogni pittore dipinge se stesso." Baldinucci, *Notizie*, vol. 3, 690. See also Stone, "In Figura Diaboli," 22.

86 For more on this, see Spike, "La fortuna critica di Mattia Preti," 24.

87 De' Dominici, *Vite*, vol. 3, 314–388.

88 Ibid., 333.

89 George Hersey believes De' Dominici's story of Preti committing murder to be fictional; the program of decorating the city gates was indeed carried out by Preti, but, as Capasso was already able to determine, the works were commissioned by the *eletti* or city officials for a typical sum as payment, without any evidence of this being a punishment (his source: Bartolommeo Capasso, "Sull'aneddoto riguardante il Cavalier Calabrese sopra le porte di Napoli," *Archivio storico di Napoli*, vol. 3, 1878, 597ff.). Hersey, "Mattia Preti," 87–88.

90 With continuing research on the artist biography as a literary genre—a primary result of the critical revision of Vasari's *Vite*, the foundational work of art history—a perspective has recently been established in Early Modern Studies that attributes a positive value to fictional elements in narrative structures, for example, those used to construct genealogies. These fabrications (previously misunderstood as deceptive falsehoods) show a premodern conception of history that was focused more on the plausibility of developments than on the correctness of facts. See Paul Barolsky: "Although for a long time art historians often misread Vasari, either misconstruing his fictions as facts or misidentifying them as errors, in recent years they have returned increasingly to Pater's point of view, recognizing the deeper truths of Vasari's poetic fabrications." Barolsky, "Vasari and the Historical Imagination," 286. See also Jürgen Müller's thought-provoking consideration on method in relation to Carel van Mander's biographies: "The primary interest of my research is not concerned with the question of whether we should trust Van Mander's information, but of how the biographies of the Rudolfinian court painters are staged and how insights for the reader are installed by means of this structure." Müller, *Concordia Pragensis*, 20.

91 Philip Sohm understands the artist's biography as a form of art critique that clarifies "why works of art look the way they look." Sohm, "Caravaggio's Deaths," 449.

92 See Paul Barolsky, who writes in the introduction to *Michelangelo's Nose*: "My purpose here is to show, on the contrary, that there is no separation between 'myth' and 'reality'—to show that Michelangelo created his own myth, which is central to his reality. Many of his fictions in the writing of his biographers and of those who wrote about him later are metaphorical exaggerations of the ways in which Michelangelo saw and thus formed himself. Michelangelo is, far more than has been recognized, responsible for his own myth." Barolsky, *Michelangelo's Nose*, xviii. This perspective is taken up by David Marshall Stone with regard to Caravaggio's self-representation in the head of Goliath. Stone, "In Figura Diaboli." See also Raulff, *Inter lineas*, 133.

93 Kris and Kurz, *Legend, Myth, and Magic*, 132.

94 "Volendo figurare un milito, con quelle qualità e bravure che se gli appartiene, convien che il detto maestro sia bravissimo, con buona cognizione dell'arme." Varchi, "Lettere," in Barocchi, *Trattati*, vol. 1 [Letter from January 28, 1547], 81.

95 "Tutte queste sono parole formali. Or non bisognerebbe qui gridare: Proh divûm numinam sancta! che sia un sì pazzo che dica cose sì stravaganti e che le si stampino?" Borghini, "Una selva di notizie," 132. See also Cole, "Am Werkzeug erkennen wir den Künstler," 43.

96 Spezzaferro, "Mattia Preti tra immagine letteraria e realtà documentaria," 32.

97 See also Hersey, *Mattia Preti*, 83. George Hersey emphasizes that both men belong to the same order as *cavaliere d'obbedienza*. Concerning the artist's quest for identity, Barolsky underscores the important guiding influence not only of the work of art, but also the biography, when he writes about Benvenuto Cellini: "Cellini not only modeled his works on Michelangelo's, but he modeled himself on Michelangelo, making himself Michelangelesque." Barolsky, *Michelangelo's Nose*, 141.

98 De' Dominici, *Vite*, vol. 3, 225.

99 Ibid., 226.

100 Ibid., 75.

101 Ibid., 74.

102 "Volentiere faceva delle bizzarrie, essendo animoso ed ardito, considato anche nella perizia di ben maneggiare la spada... il suo genio bizzarro, e per vero dire rissoso." De' Dominici, *Vite*, vol. 3, 77.

103 Saxl, "The Battle Scene without a Hero," 71.

104 "L'é 'l Rosa, valoroso in far batagie, / Pitor in Roma certo di gran conto / In tuto, ma in le istorie de bravura." Boschini, *La carta del navegar pitoresco*, 79f.

105 Scott, *Salvator Rosa*, 39.

106 On "Sarò" as Rosa's anagram see Patz, 64f. Scott, *Salvator Rosa*, 40.

107 See Fumagalli, "Napoli a Firenze nel Seicento," 43.

108 Ibid. Elena Fumagalli also impressively describes how the architecture enhances the impact of the Christian army, seemingly forming a bulwark. The motif of the cut-off arm had previously appeared at the lower edge of the image in Giulio Romano's *Battle of Troy*. Palazzo Ducale, Mantova.

109 Zeri, *Nascita della Battaglia*, IX–XXVII.

110 Farina, *Il giovane Salvator Rosa*, 37.

111 On Giovanni Contarini (1549–1605): "Di là dale finestre sopra il rio evvi una sanguinosa battaglia, che successe nella presa di Verona, nel mezzo della quale si vede un soldato con l'asta in mano, e braccia ignude, ch'è il ritratto di Giovanni Contarini autore dell'opera, ed evvi ancora il ritratto di Girolamo Magagnati suo amico, poeta, e chimico, che inventò il contrafare gioje, e perle. Zanetti, *Pittura Veneziana in cui osservarsi l'ordine del Busching*, vol. 1, 32. However, Ridolfi identified in the battle painting only the portrait of Contarini's friend, a producer of fake pearls and jewels: "E vi ritrasse Girolamo Magagnati, molto amico suo, con asta in mano, il quale affronta un cavaliere." Ridolfi, *Le Maraviglie dell'arte*, vol. 2, 284.

112 See Bristot, "Giovanni Contarini," *i*.

113 In one of these portraits, Rosa adopts the role of a soldier spoiling for a fight. With his right hand on the grip and his left on the scabbard, Rosa seems to be in the process of drawing his dagger. While he directs his piercing gaze over his shoulder at the beholder, the menace of the situation is at the point of climax: Directly next to his hand, a drum cord has caught on fire; a musket leaning against the wall signals battle readiness; a horn lying on a drum, whose opening is directed toward his hand, seems to further intensify the mood. In his reading of this self-portrait, Jonathan Scott bases his argument on Peter Tomory (1990), and sees Rosa's staging as soldier as an implicit critique of war. Scott, *Salvator Rosa*, 60f.

114 See Tintoretto's self-portrait as a centurion in his well-known *Crucifixion of Christ* in the Scuola di San Rocco, and Veronese's self-representations as a man in armor in *Christ and the Centurion from Capernaum* (Kansas City, Nelson Gallery) and as *Saint Menas* (1560, Modena, Galleria Estense). See also Weigel, "Ein Selbstbildnis Jacopo Tintorettos hoch zu Ross," 176; Garton, *Grace and Grandeur*, 94f.

115 See for example, a portrait by Nicolas Régnier from the Kunsthistorisches Museum in Vienna, which proves to be a self-portrait when compared with another painting ascribed to Régnier, *Self-Portrait with a Portrait on an Easel*. In the Vienna painting, the left hand is demonstratively laid upon the sword's crossguard.

116 On Giorgione's self-portrait, see Woods-Marsden, *Renaissance Self-Portraiture*, 117–119. Giorgione's Braunschweig self-portrait has come down to us in a reduced state that leaves out the head of Goliath and frames the scene more narrowly—it is cut off just below the shoulder that is emphasized by reflected light. Savoldo's spectacular *Portrait of Gaston de Foix* (1515, Paris, Louvre), which according to the latest research is a self-portrait, and another work, *The Archer* (Venetian School, sixteenth century, Edinburgh, National Gallery of Scotland), play with the motif of the hand reflected in armor as a display of the *bravuroso* command of mimesis.

117 Orlandi, *Abecedario*, 427.

118 Ibid., 203.

119 Ibid., 346.

120 Ibid., 132.

121 Ibid., 334.

122 "Stefano March...datosi a dipingere battaglie.... Poco dipigneva, e sol quando era forzato dalla necessità. Quando doveva farlo, si chiudeva nella sua stanza ch'era piena di armi, e quelle con grande fatica a maneggiar si metteva, fino che si stancava, ed allora prendeva i pennelli, ed a maraviglia esprimeva morti, semivivi e feriti." Orlandi, *Abecedario*, 465.

123 See Palomino, *El museo pictórico*, 973, 1132.

124 "Y en especial tuvo gran genio para batallas, las cuales hizo con superior excelencia. Erade genio algo lunático y atronado; y para poder pintar con propriedad algunos instrumentos bélicos, en las batallas, había recogido gran número de armas y arneses, los cuales tenía colgados en su obrador, hasta la caja de guerra, lanzas, alfanjes, y dardos: y poniéndose à discurrir el lance de batalla, que se le ofrecía pintar, se enfervorizaba de suerte, que tomaba la caja, o el clarin, y tocaba a embestír, y echando mano de una cimitarra, u otro instrumento, comenzaba a disparar golpes, y cuchilladas por todo el aposento; de suerte, que las paredes eran el blanco de sus iras, y aun los trastos no estaban seguros;...y en estando poseído de este furor, hacía maravillas en las batallas." Palomino, *El museo pictórico*, 888–889.

125 Ratti, *Vite*, vol. 2, 16.

126 Bellori, *Lives*, 267.

127 Ibid., 257.

128 Baldinucci, *Notizie*, vol. 5, 212f.

129 Pascoli, *Vite*, 112–114.

130 Vasari, *Vite*, vol. 5, 56.

131 Ibid.

132 Gramaccini, "Raffael und sein Schüler."

133 Baldinucci, *Notizie*, vol. 5, 212f.

134 Vasari, *Vite*, vol. 1, 134.

135 Pio, *Vite*, 52–53.

136 Kroschewski, *Über das allmähliche Verfertigen der Bilder*, 82–84.

137 Baglione, *Vite*, 138, 146. See also: Bellori, *Vite*, 205.

138 Orlandi informs us that Vignon was involved in the art trade and set the prices of paintings. Orlandi, *Abecedario*, 126.

139 Vignon's picture of *The Young Singer* (ca. 1622–1623; Louvre, Paris) belongs to a successful genre, developed by Caravaggio during his early years in Rome, depicting young, beautiful musicians. But whereas Caravaggio's works showcase a refined illusionism that supports their inviting eroticism, Vignon foregrounds the pastose application of paint, whose bulk, particularly in the rendition of the opulent gold and ocher sleeve, keeps the spectator at a distance.

140 De Piles, *Abrégé*, 497.

141 See Pacht-Bassani, *Claude Vignon*, 182–183.

142 Pascoli, *Vite*, 113.

143 Bellori, *Lives*, 183. See also, Kroschewski, *Über das allmähliche Verfertigen der Bilder*, 90.

144 Vasari, *Vite*, vol. 1, 118.

145 Leando Ozzòla, who describes Il Borgognone as a "pittore velocissimo," connects his style of painting "con colore colpeggiato e con pasta grossa" with the concept of *pittoresco*. Ozzòla, *I pittori di battaglie*, 42.

146 Da Vinci, *Trattato*, [145: "Come si deve figurare una battaglia"], 63–64.

147 Ibid.

CHAPTER TWO: THE FIGURAL TOUR DE FORCE

1 Martin S. Soria attributes this battle painting to Esteban March's son Miguel, an opinion not shared by the latest research. Soria, "Esteban March;" for the most recent review, see Doménesch, *Cinco siglos de pintura valenciana*, cat. no. 35, 84.

2 There are several drawings extant by March after

Tempesta's prints. See Espinós Díaz, "Modelos de A. Tempesta;" Angulo Iniguez, "Pintura del siglo XVII," 249; Pérez Sánchez, *Mostra di disegni spagnoli,* (no. 78) 76.

3 "I più spiritosi cavalli." Francesco Scannelli, *Il microcosmo della pittura,* 85.

4 In the vita of Ercole de' Robert (1451–1496), Vasari praised the representation of a rider on a horse whose forelegs were so powerfully suspended in the air that the group appeared to be three dimensional ("di rilievo"), Vasari, *Vite,* vol. 3, 421. Other striking and much admired representations of this stock image were produced by Il Pordenone in Venice—showing a horse leaping from the façade of the Palazzo d'Anna—and by Hans Holbein in his painting on the façade of the Haus zum Tanz in Basel (see Bätschmann, "Regeln und Erfindung," 95).

5 Esteban March's battle pictures, like those of Borgognone, were associated with Aniello Falcone and Salvator Rosa as formative prototypes. See Doménesch, *Cinco siglos de pintura valenciana,* cat. no. 34/35, 84.

6 On the demonstration of art in battle painting, see also Andreas Thielemann, who designates the mastery of *copia, varietà,* and *difficoltà* "as the quintessence of every battle representation." Thielemann, "Schlachten erschauen—Kentauren gebären," 58.

7 Vasari mentions that he gave it to Ottaviano de Medici as a present. Vasari, *Vite,* vol. 5, 473.

8 Marco Boschini, in accordance with Vasari, defines the subject of the painting more precisely as a "battle in which Charles V meets with Barbarossa," and interprets the commission as a recognition of Schiavone's talent. This however does not hinder him from also accusing Vasari of stifling "nostra gran Maniera Veneziana." Boschini, *La carta del navegar pitoresco,* 85. For the first comprehensive art-historical appraisal of Schiavone, see Fröhlich-Bum, "Andrea Meldolla, genannt Schiavone."

9 The other two represent allegories of *Priesthood* and *Empire.* Richardson, *Andrea Schiavone,* cat. no. 238, 239.

10 See also Artolni and Dal Pozzolo, *Andrea Schiavone,* cat. no. XVI, 5–7.

11 See Richardson, *Andrea Schiavone,* 146.

12 The famous painting is only documented through an engraving by Giulio Fontana (ca. 1569, Paris, Bibliothèque Nationale). Richardson, *Andrea Schiavone,* cat. no. 237, 147.

13 Ridolfi, *Le Maraviglie dell'arte,* vol. 1, 242.

14 Ibid.

15 "È un compendio di quanto può dare l'arte pittoresca." Zanetti, *Descrizione,* 252.

16 The extreme foreshortening of the fallen man is aptly reminiscent of the naked slave in Tintoretto's *Miracle of the Slave.*

17 Letter of Aretino to Tintoretto, 1550. Quote cited in Krischel, *Jacopo Tintorettos "Sklavenwunder,"* 99.

18 "The Salute paintings were greatly admired because Titian had succeeded in projecting powerful volumes overhead without the use of an elaborate perspective system." Friedlaender, "Titian and Pordenone," 119.

19 Félibien on ceiling paintings: "Il se trouve dans la pratique des difficultez que la theorie ne peut prévoir, & où les regles ne servent guéres, à cause que ceux qui regardent, ne peuvent pas toûjours êtres placez dans un même lieu, & ne voir les Tableaux qu'aux travers d'une pinulle, principalement dans les grands ouvrages qu'on ne peut voir d'un seul endroit." Félibien, *Entretiens,* vol. 3, 80. On foreshortening as a form of applied perspective and thus freehand technique that relies on dexterity as well as a competent eye, see Summers, *Michelangelo,* 369.

20 Ridolfi, *Le Maraviglie dell'arte,* vol. 1, 227f.

21 "Quel Antonio Vandich, sì valoroso, Ha fato notomia de sta Pitura, Col copiar sto desseno e sta bravura, E dir: sta volta me fazzo famoso." Boschini, *La carta del navegar pitoresco,* 191. Also related in this context is Rubens's sketch after *The Sacrifice of Isaac* (Vienna, Albertina); see Müller-Hofstede, "Rubens in Italien," 284.

22 A faithful reproduction of this figure is found in Niccolò dell'Abate's *Martyrdom of Saint Peter and Paul* (Dresden, Gemäldegalerie [destroyed]). See also Spagnolo, *Correggio,* 59, fig. 12.

23 Vasari, *Vite,* vol. 5, 169.

24 Armenini, *De' veri precetti,* 110.

25 Ibid.

26 Ibid., 111.

27 Ibid., 114.

28 Ibid., 117.

29 The presence of one Cyclops among the Giants seems to indicate that Giulio Romano did not discriminate between the two groups of Gaia's offspring; in the myth the Cyclopes supported Zeus in his fight against their brothers.

30 Dolce, *Dialogo,* 181.

31 See also Francesco San Gallo's *paragone* letter to Benedetto Varchi: "La scultura ha la difficultà del lavorare la materia, la pittura ha la difficultà delli scorci." Barocchi, *Trattati,* 77.

32 Pino, *Dialogo,* 107, 109. On the *figura sforzata* see Cole, "The 'Figura Sforzata.'"

33 See "Cap. XVII, De li scórti delle figure al di sotto insù e di quelli in piano," in Vasari, *Vite,* vol. 1, 122f.

34 Armenini, *De' veri precetti,* 110–112, 114.

35 Vasari, who emphasizes Michelangelo's performance, criticizes "i nostri vecchi" (our elders) for foreshortening by means of perspective lines. Vasari says that the most difficult *scorti* are the ones from "al di sotto insù," which have such power ("tanta forza") that they seem "to pierce the ceiling," and adds that this difficulty is only successfully mastered through a study "dal vivo" and "models hung in the air." Vasari, *Vite*, vol. 1, 122f.

36 Ridolfi, *Le Maraviglie dell'arte*, vol. 2, 174. Whether these words actually adorned Tintoretto's workshop wall or were merely Ridolfi's embellishment of the vita is debatable. It is, however, certain that he echoes an idea of perfection in painting that reaches back to Paolo Pino's formulation: "Se Tiziano, e Michiel Angelo fussero un corpo solo, over al disegno di Michiel Angelo aggiontovi il colore di Tiziano, se gli potrebbe dir lo dio della pittura." Pino, *Dialogo*, 122. Alessandro Guarini revered Tintoretto as the "Michelangelo of our time" because he knew how to "captivate the soul with his colors and the force of his art," and "in this way to tyrannize every single one of our emotions." Guarini, *Il frenetico savio*, 50ff.

37 See von Schlosser, "Aus der Bildnerwerkstatt der Renaissance," esp. 107; Rosenberg, *Beschreibungen und Nachzeichnungen*, 86.

38 Claus Virch associates the patchy character of the sketch with the fact that, as Ridolfi relates, Titian's drawing studies were done at night by lamplight. Virch, "A Study by Tintoretto after Michelangelo," 116.

39 In his *Diologo di pittura* (1557), the Florentine Giovan Francesco Fabrini criticizes the Venetian Sebastiano del Piombo, who "truly did not joust on a par with Raffael, even if he did hold in his hand the lance of Michelangelo, because he did not know how to use it." "Invero che Bastiano non giostrava di pari con Raffaello, se bene aveva in mano la lancia diMichelagnolo; e questo, perché egli non la sapeva adoperare." Dolce, *Dialogo*, 151.

40 De Hollanda, *On Antique Painting*, 134.

41 Condivi, *Life of Michelangelo*, 83.

42 Vasari, *Lives*, 465.

43 Armenini, *De' veri precetti*, 83. See Baldinucci, Vocabulario, 89: [Michelangelo:] "Questa mia maniera vuol fare dimolti goffi Artifeci."

44 See Schlitt, "Painting, Criticism, and Michelangelo's *Last Judgment*," 12.

45 Vasari, *Lives*, 465.

46 See Schlitt, "Painting, Criticism, and Michelangelo's *Last Judgment*," 126: "Although Nicolas Beatrizet included Michelangelo's name next to the skin in his 1562 engraving of the *Last Judgment*, thus suggesting at least some recognition among Michelangelo's contemporaries, it is curious that there are no other contemporary sources, written or verbal, that acknowledge the self-portrait."

47 Cited in Schlitt, "Painting, Criticism, and Michelangelo's *Last Judgment*," 126.

48 "And it appears to me that the artists who came before Michelangelo paid more attention to truth and devotion than to ostentation." Gilio, *Dialogue*, 160.

49 Gilio, *Dialogue*, 173.

50 Ibid., 157–160.

51 Matthew 4:19.

52 See the in-depth discussion of Leonardo's project and its artistic challenges: Farago, "Leonardo's Battle of Anghiari," 307. For a comprehensive account, see Pedretti, "Nuovi documenti," 53–78. Anne-Marie Logan offers a more detailed analysis of the copy after Leonardo's *Battle of Anghiari*. Although all of her conclusions cannot be presented here, suffice it to say that she considers the copy to be the work of three different hands. Anne-Marie Logan in Bambach, *Leonardo da Vinci*, cat. no. 135, 671–768. Michelangelo's study is located in the Windsor Collection (12326 r). See Dalli Regoli, "Leonardo e Michelangelo."

53 In this context, the question arises as to whether the passage cited here explains the incompleteness of *Hieronymus* (ca. 1482, Rome, Vatican Museum). The severe foreshortening of his body, which can be read as a posture of humility, was perhaps simply not understood.

54 "Ricordati, pittore, quando fai una sola figura, di fuggire li scorti di quella, sì delle parti come del tutto, perché tu avresti da combattere con l'ignoranza degl'indotti di tale arte; ma nelle istorie fanne in tutti i modi che ti accade, e massime nelle battaglie, dove per necessità accadono infiniti scorciamenti e piegamenti de'componitori di tal discordia, o vuoi dire pazzia bestialissima." Da Vinci, *Trattato*, [173.], 72. Vasari, *Vite*, vol. 4, 32.

55 See the drawing study in the Royal Collection, London: *Expressions of Fury in Horses, a Lion, and a Man*, ca. 1503–1504, 19.6 x 30.8 cm, pen and ink with wash and red chalk, RCIN 912326. On the juxtapositions in this sheet, see Arasse, *Leonardo da Vinci*, 74–75.

56 See Zöllner, "Rubens Reworks Leonardo," 184 (with references to secondary literature). In a further stage of development, Rubens rendered the model in color (Vienna, Gemäldegalerie der Akademie der bildenden Künste). See Müller-Hofstede, "Rubens in Italien," 150. Anne-Marie Logan assumes that Rubens retouched the drawing only later, ca. 1615–1616. Anne-Marie Logan, in Bambach, *Leonardo da Vinci*, 135; Logan and Plomp, "Rubens als Zeichner," 48.

57 Joannides, "Leonardo da Vinci, Peter-Paul Rubens," 80.

58 "Egli mostrò nelle forme e lineamenti de' cavagli, i quali Lionardo meglio ch'altro maestro fece di bravura, di muscoli e di garbata bellezza." Vasari, *Vite*, vol. 4, 33.

59 Ibid., 32.

60 Peter Meller describes the figure of field commander Niccolò Piccinino as "human, half demon, half animal." Meller also points out the close interrelationship between man and beast in the cavalry group: "Gli animali prendono parte alla battaglia, lottano come gli uomini, e gli uomini come le bestie." Meller, "La Battaglia d'Anghiari," 189.

61 Vasari, *Vite*, vol. 4, 33.

62 Rathe, *Die Ausdrucksfunktion extrem verkürzter Figuren*, 7. The tendency of a spatially projecting, extremely foreshortened figure to become an artistic exemplar, and therefore detached from the narrative context of the painting, is later observed by Boschini in Tintoretto's *Saint Roch in Prison*: "La veda quel incaenà per tera, che vien fuora coi piè tuto del quadro; No so se' l sia in preson per furbo o ladro, So ben che l'è un bel scurzo, e ha gran maniera." Boschini, *La carta del navegar pitoresco*, 109.

63 Vasari, *Vite*, vol. 4, 7.

64 Ibid.

65 "Nel disegno non v'erano gli estremi del fine suo, perché, se bene e' favecano un braccio tondo et una gamba diritta, non era ricerca con muscoli con quella facilità graziosa e dolce che apparisce fra 'l vedi e non vedi, come fanno la carne e le cose vive; ma elle erano crude e scorticate, che faveca difficoltà agli occhi e durezza nella maniera." Vasari, *Vite*, vol. 4, 5.

66 Varchi, "Della Maggioranza delle Arti: Disputa 1," in Barocchi, *Trattati*, vol. 1, 38.

67 Zöllner, "Rubens Reworks Leonardo," esp. 183–184.

68 Rubens added the right arm of the fallen man and altered the back of his attacker. See Logan, in Bambach, *Leonardo da Vinci*, 676.

69 Vasari, *Vite*, vol. 4, 7.

70 Along with Leonardo's *Battle of Anghiari*, Rubens also intensively studied Titian's *Battle of Cadore* and Raffael's *Battle of Constantine*. Copies by Rubens after all three of these masterpieces of battle painting are extant. See Jaffé, *Rubens and Italy*, esp. figs. 51, 52, 54; Wheelock, *Flemish Paintings*, 149.

71 Panofsky, "Die neoplatonische Bewegung und Michelangelo," esp. 283.

72 Wheelock, *Flemish Paintings*, 146; Georgievska-Shine, "Horror and Pity," 221.

73 Several of the figures developed for the first time in the *Fall of Phaeton* would prominently reappear in Rubens's later works.

74 Müller-Hofstede, "Rubens in Italien," 146.

75 The sarcophagus, today in the Galleria degli Uffizi, was already studied in the sixteenth century as Zuccari's drawing after the relief shows. See Brooks, *Taddeo and Federico Zuccaro*, 90, fig. 35.

76 Arthur K. Wheelock Jr. interprets the light by virtue of its power as a substitute for the physical presence of Jupiter. *Flemish Paintings*, 150.

77 Ovid, *Metamorphoses* [Book 2], vol. 1, 77.

78 Ibid., 65–67.

79 Ibid., 75.

80 Müller-Hofstede, "Rubens in Italien," 146.

81 Healy, "Losing Control of the Senses," 111.

82 "[Jupiter] hurled him from the car and from life as well, and thus quenched fire with blasting fire. The maddened horses leap apart, wrench their necks from the yoke, and break away from the parted reins. Here lie the reins, there the axle torn from the pole; in another place the spokes of the broken wheels.... Phaeton, fire ravaging his ruddy hair, is hurled headlong and falls with a long trail through the air." Ovid, *Metamorphoses* [Book 2], vol. 1, 81–83.

83 Huemer, "Rubens and Galileo," 192.

84 "Grant me a proof, my father, by which all may know me for thy true son, and take away this uncertainty from my mind." Ovid, *Metamorphoses*, [Book 2], vol. 1, 63.

85 Ibid., 65.

86 Ibid., 73.

87 The element of acceleration in the myth is the symptom of a "megalomanic techno-phanstasmagoria," which Hartmut Böhme characterizes as "wanting to take on a greater role than one could possibly endure or take responsibility for." Böhme, "Phaeton, Prometheus und die Grenzen des Fliegens," 40.

88 The missing Hora is indicated by the subsequently added fifth horse, which, as Fiona Healy convincingly demonstrates, elicits the ethical theme of the "chariot of the soul." Healy, "Losing Control of the Senses," 109–114.

89 Joachim von Sandrart performs this service for Rubens when he concludes his vita with the following words: "As long as the world lives, his name will always flourish and untiring *Fama* will proclaim his virtue from her trumpet to all four corners of the Earth." Von Sandrart, *Teutsche Academie*, vol. 1, part 2, book 3, 293.

90 Ibid.

91 Ibid.

92 Bellori, *Vite*, 232.

93 Ibid., 247.

94 "Regarding color, Rubens had stupendous freedom: he studied in Venice and looked always at Titian, Paolo Vernise, and Tintoretto, observing the chiaroscuro and the masses of hues.... He maintained such unity and resoluteness that his figures seem executed in one dash of the brush and infused with one breath." Bellori, *Lives*, 205.

95 "Tout ce qui dépend du Coloris est admirable dans Rubens, il a porté la Science du Clairobscur, plus loin qu'aucun Peintre, & il en a fait sentir la nécessité." De Piles, Abregé, 405.

96 De Piles, *Abregé*, 395. See the copy of *Psyche* in Jaffé, *Rubens and Italy*, fig. 114.

CHAPTER THREE: THE SPATIAL TOUR DE FORCE

1 Bellori, *Vite*, 214.

2 Ibid., 214.

3 Caravaggio seems to have looked at Raphael's *Urania* painted on the ceiling of the Stanza della Signoria. The goddess draws a similar version of the universe with her compass.

4 I want to thank Principessa di Piombino who brought my attention to this marginal but significant detail.

5 Bellori, *Lives*, 256.

6 Vasari, *Lives*, 449.

7 Condivi, *Life of Michelangelo*, 48.

8 Ibid.

9 Rossella Vodret, "Jupiter, Neptune, and Pluto," in Vodret Adamo and Cardiali, *Caravaggio: Opere a Roma*, 161–163; here 161.

10 Wallach, "An Iconographic Interpretation," 107.

11 As previously noted by Lechner, *Nuda Veritatis*, 210.

12 See Pugliesi, "Caravaggio's Life," 112. See also Maurizio Calvesi's interpretation of the painting as a visualization of the philosophy of alchemy. He compares Jupiter's gesture with that of God the Father separating light from darkness in Michelangelo's Sistine Chapel. Calvesi, *La realtà di Caravaggio*, 174.

13 Wallach, "An Iconographic Interpretation," 102.

14 Michelangelo Buonarroti was, as Rudolf Preimesberger has shown, key for Caravaggio's self-definition as artist. See Preimesberger, *Michelangelo da Caravaggio—Caravaggio da Michelangelo*, 243–260.

15 Cole Wallach, "An Iconographic Interpretation," 102.

16 Bellori, *Lives*, 84.

17 Ginzburg, *La Galleria Farnese*, [M/4] 218.

18 Lovén, "Too Many Levels of Reality," 327.

19 Bellori, *Lives*, 282; He begins with the statement: "His spirit and ability for painting were growing ever greater because he was fascinated by the manner of Correggio and would draw and paint his works."

20 Bellori, *Lives*, 288.

21 Ibid., 281.

22 Ibid.

23 Passeri, *Vite*, 125.

24 Bellori, *Lives*, 284.

25 Turner, "Ferrante Carlo's 'Descrittione,'" 321.

26 Bellori, *Lives*, 288.

27 Scannelli, *Il microcosmo*, 18, 44.

28 Ibid., 19.

29 Ibid., 44.

30 [July 8, 1713] Coypel, "Commentaire de l'Épître," 75.

CHAPTER FOUR: BRAVURA AS PAINTERLY STYLE

1 Scannelli, *Il microcosmo*, 19.

2 Ibid., 359.

3 Ibid., 22.

4 Ibid., 35.

5 Ibid., 12.

6 Ibid., 13.

7 Seneca, *Epistles*, 281.

8 Lebrun, "Recueuil des essaies," 767.

9 " [I]o mi servo di certa idea che mi viene nella mente." Bottari and Ticozzi, *Raccolta*, vol. 2, 24.

10 Bellori, *Lives*, 251.

11 Vasari, *Vite*, vol. 5, 140.

12 "È però dirassi coi soprascritto Castiglione essere la vera arte quella, che il tutto contiene in eminente grado, senzo punto dimostrarsi." Scannelli, *Il microcosmo della pittura*, 17.

13 Castiglione, *Il libro del cortegiano*, 61. On this subject, see Eduardo Saccone, who considers the concept of sprezzatura in light of Aristotle's *Nicomachean Ethics*: Saccone, "Grazia, Sprezzatura, Affettazione," esp. 54–63.

14 Castiglione, *Il libro del cortegiano*, 59.

15 Ibid., 59.

16 Ibid., 60–61.

17 Scannelli, *Il microcosmo*, 17.

18 Ibid., 17.

19 The phrase appears in a discussion of two landscapes by Francesco di Giovane. Scannelli, *Il microcosmo della pittura*, 255.

20 Castiglione, *Il libro del cortegiano*, 61.

21 Ibid., 63.

22 Zanetti, *Pittura Veneziana in cui osservarsi l'ordine del Busching*, vol. 2, 209. One person for whom Bassano's bravura remained inaccessible was the Bolognese diplomat Giovanni Battista Agucchi, who described Bassano as "un Pierico nel rassomigliare i peggiori." Cited after Mahon, *Studies in Seicento Art and Theory*, appendix 1, 256.

23 "Piace poi tanto più questo modo à gl'Intendenti, quanto che mirandolo da vicino scoprono maggiormente in esso la bravura, e la felicità dell'Artefice." Zanotti, *Nuovo fregio*, 102.

24 Concerning Tintoretto's method of working, Marco Boschini noted that before the execution of a work for a public space, he would first examine the location where it would be placed. Boschini, *La carta del navegar pitoresco*, 730.

25 Ridolfi, *Le Maraviglie dell'arte*, vol. 2, 202.

26 Boschini, *La carta del navegar pitoresco*, 731.

27 "Di colpi. Termine proprio di pittura: e diecesi, fatta di colpi quella pittura, la quale l'Artefice condusse, col posare con gran franchezza le tinte al luogo loro, o chiari, o scuri, e mezze tinte, o dintorni che si fussero, dando ad essa pittura un gran rilievo, e facendo in essa apparire una gran bravura e padronanza del pennello e de'colori; tutto il contrario di quelle pitture, che diremmo sfumate, o affaticate.... Franchezza f. Ardimento, bravura, l'esser franco." Baldinucci, *Vocabolario*, 48, 64.

28 Malvasia, *Felsina pittrice*, vol. 1, 279. The difference in style corresponds to the gender of the represented figure. On this subject, see Henry Keazor, who relates such considerations of appropriateness in the choice of style to the Reformation. Keazor, "*Il vero modo*," 67.

29 Scannelli, *Il microcosmo della pittura*, 255.

30 Ridolfi, *Le Maraviglie dell'arte*, vol. 1, 253.

31 "Spesso ancor nella pittura una linea non stentata, un sol colpo di penello tirato facilmente, di modo che paia che la mano, senza esser guidata da studio o arte alcuna, vada per se stessa al suo termine secondo la intenzion del pittore, scopre chiaramente la eccellenzia dell'artefice." Castiglione, *Il libro del cortegiano*, 63.

32 Ridolfi, *Le Maraviglie dell'arte*, vol. 2, 248.

33 On Odoardo Fialetti see Carlo Cesare Malvasia, who writes about Fialetti's military training and then continues: "Ora siccome quegli, tratto da spirito ardente e generoso non meno, che dagli esercizii cavallereschi, nei primi anni appresi, a fare il soldato, sentì poi da più potente genio lusingarsi al trattare i pennelli, sui fondamenti saldi del buon disegno." Malvasia, *Felsina pittrice*, vol. 1, 228. See also Marco Boschini's panegyric, which he prefaces with: "Odoardo Fialeti Bolognese, Ma Venezian per el so bravo inzegno." Boschini, *La carta del navegar pitoresco*, 502.

34 Ridolfi, *Le Maraviglie dell'arte*, vol. 2, 248; also cited in Delogu, *Drawings by Tintoretto*, 2. See also Rosand, "The Crisis of the Venetian Renaissance Tradition."

35 Odoardo Fialetti will go on to develop geometric templates as guides for the construction of faces and bodies in his textbook *Il vero modo e ordine per disegnare tutte le parti et membra del corpo humano* (Venice, 1608).

36 "Qu'il laisse aux Maîtres de l'Art ce style prompt & hardi, cet usage de faire passer sur le papier, en quatre coups élégans, tout l'esprit de la Nature! Ils se sont familiarisés depuis long-tems avec elle; ils la sçavent, pour ainsi dire, par cœur." Dandré-Bardon, *Traité de peinture*, vol. 1, 29.

37 "Dans la hardiesse nous comprenons la facilité à manier le crayon, le pinceau, l'ébauchoir, ou le ciseau. Cette facilité suppose la connoissance parfaite des formes, des tons, & des effets." Dandré Bardon, *Traité de peinture*, vol. 1, 126.

38 See Weigel, "Tintoretto und das Non-finito."

39 Malvasia, *Felsina pittrice*, vol. 1, 283. In contrast to his brother Agostino, Annibale's painterly style is characterized by Malvasia as generally untidy and sketch-like: "Annibale avea tirato giù con quel suo modo impaziente e poco pulito; onde quelle storie in tal guisa non ben terminate e finite, tenessero più dello schizzo e forma di primo sbozzo, che di veri quadri aggiustati e compiti." Ibid., 274. Malvasia says his works are modeled after Tintoretto's "op[e]re spaventose." Ibid., 264.

40 Tellingly, he seems to have little money for this work: "E per pochi denari al Marchese Angelelli una Madonna col Signorino, al quale fugge di mano una rondinella ad un filo appesa; lavorandole di botte, di tratti, con certa sprezzatura da gran maestro, creduta nuova, perchè non usata nella scuola di Roma e nella Lombarda; ma qualche volta praticata dal Tintoretto." Malvasia, *Felsina pittrice*, vol. 2, 17.

41 Von Sandrart, *Teutsche Academie*, vol. 1, part 2, book 2, 169.

42 Ibid., 167.

43 Watelet and Lévesque, *Dictionnaire*, vol. 5, entry: Lévesque, *Prestezze*, 175f.

44 Roland Krischel points to the formulaic element in this statement and quotes Bartolomeo da San Concordio's assertion from 1300: "Ne' vecchi ha luogo e si conviene gravezza di costumi e ne' giovani uomini accorgimento e prestezza." Krischel, *Jacopo Tintorettos "Sklavenwunder,"* 101, note 20.

45 "Ma non insuperbite, se bene è così, ché ciò sarebbe un non voler salire in maggior grado di perfezione. E beato il nome vostro, se reduceste la prestezza del fatto in la pazienzia del fare. Benché a poco a poco a ciò provederanno gli anni; conciosia ch'essi, e non altri, sono bastanti a raffrenare il corso de la trascuratezza, di che tanto si prevale la gioventù volonterosa e veloce." Aretino, *Lettere sull'arte*, 205.

46 Sansovino, *Delle cose notabili*, 18.

47 Boschini, *La carta del navegar pitoresco*, 223.

48 "The most terrible mind painting ever had, as one sees in all his works." Vasari, *Vite*, vol. 5, 468.

49 "JACOPO ROBUSTI, detto il TINTORETTO... Questo fu il più terribile pittore, che da questa scola sortisse, e veramente il Padrone, e disponitore della pittura possiamo chiamarlo." Zanetti, *Pittura Veneziana in cui osservarsi l'ordine del Busching*, vol. 2, 212, 214.

50 "Don Lelio Orsino ne riportò a Roma quello [ritratto] di Camiletta dall'Orto, dama veneta, tocco con maestrevole sprezzatura." Ridolfi, *Le Maraviglie dell'arte*, vol. 2, 238.

51 Zanetti, *Della pittura veneziana e delle opere pubbliche*, 91.

52 Castiglione, *Il libro del cortegiano*, 63.

53 "L'é 'l Rosa, valoroso in far batagie. Pitor in Roma certo de gran conto In tuto, ma in le istorie de bravura Con le so man l'ilustra Pitura." Boschini, *La carta del navegar pitoresco*, 79f.

54 "Eserciti ha formà quie gran Guerieri Dei nostri gloriosi Veneziani. Quei xe stai valorosi Capitani, Che ha fato in la Pitura ati sì fieri! Qua ghe xe piazza d'arme, e qua ressiede El Campo dei colori e dei peneli; Qua ghe xe la bravura e i Coloneli: Tuti sbassa la pica, e tuti ciede." Boschini, *La carta del navegar pitoresco*, 88.

55 "L'esser pien d'ardimento al improviso: Che l'omo al fin, che non ha sangue in viso, L'è giusto un schiavinon mal scartizà." Boschini, *La carta del navegar pitoresco*, 136.

56 "De gracia, in che consiste la Pitura? Se me puol dir: in cose purassae. E mi dirò: la xe la veritae; Ma el verbo principal xe in la bravura." Boschini, *La carta del navegar pitoresco*, 227.

57 "Non fu mai vista la mazor bravura, Che la fa spaventar ogni Bravazzo." Boschini, *La carta del navegar pitoresco*, 228.

58 Zanetti, *Pittura Veneziana in cui osservarsi l'ordine del Busching*, vol. 2, 212, 214.

59 "Maniera... resolute e veloce sul gusto di Tintoretto." Da Canal, *Vita di Gregorio Lazzarini*, XXXV.

60 See the passage on bravura in Grassi and Pepe, *Dizionario*, vol. 1, 82: "Significa abilità e destrezza nella pittura. Il termine concerne prevalentemente il modo di dipingere colpeggiato, alla veneta, di macchia, per cui v. anche *Borrón, Borrones*. La parola B.[ravura] ricorre in un importante esponente della critica d'arte barocca a Venezia: M. Boschini 1660." On Marco Boschini's martial rhetoric see Sohm, *Pittoresco*, esp. 152, 154–5; Rossi, "La Peinture Guerrière;" Rossi, "Maniera e Manierismi Veneti," 433–4.

61 "Chi no dà el primo liogo al Tentoreto In Guera, e no'l fa mistro e general De campo, no sa cosa sia l'azzal Del so robusto e forte corsaleto. Perché, quando se trata de bravura, Ogni sghero è depento; e in la so spada Sta la vita e la morte; e gran passada El fa con chi GUERIZA in la PITURA." Boschini, *La carta del navegar pitoresco*, 228f. The work was, however, largely a product of his workshop.

62 "Questa è dotrina e nobile artificio! Oh quante bele cose a l'ochio è pronte! Quando che arivo in sto salon de gloria, Par che senta una salva de periere, Trombe, tamburi e simil cose fiere, Per la Pitura segni de vitoria; Segni de gran dominio imperial; Segni d'una assoluta podestà; Segni, che qua Pitura impera e sta Col trono e col stendardo marcial.... Questo xe l'arsenal, dove Pitura Tien la moschetaria, tien i canoni; Qua se despensa peti e celadoni A chi brama rolarse in la bravura." Boschini, *La carta del navegar pitoresco*, 121f.

63 Boschini, *La carta del navegar pitoresco*, 227.

64 From the *Breve Istruzione*, Boschini, *La carta del navegar pitoresco*, 730.

65 Ridolfi, *Le Maraviglie dell'arte*, vol. 2, 202.

66 See Plesters and Lazzarini, "I materiali e la tecnica dei Tintoretto," 276. See also Ilchman, "Tintoretto as a Painter of Religious Narrative," 66.

67 See Echols, "Tintoretto the Painter," 155.

68 "El Tentoreto è un spirito divin, Che viense al Mondo con un torzo in man." Boschini, *La carta del navegar pitoresco*, 226.

69 Snakes winding their way through the tangled branches on the cliff face refer to the central panel on the ceiling, which portrays the Israelites' deliverance from the plague of serpents.

70 See Echols, "Tintoretto the Painter," 77–79; Dunkerton, "Tintoretto's painting technique," 155.

71 Antonio Manno, "La Sala superiore," in Romanelli, *Tintoretto*, 173.

72 Echols, "Tintoretto the painter," 79.

73 See Echols, "Tintoretto the Painter," 29.

74 Echols, "Tintoretto the Painter," 28–29.

75 To give just two examples: the eccentric bodily rotation of the youth "reiterates" the torsion in the body of Jonah, who on the ceiling of the Sala Superior emerges from the maw of the whale. In the central ceiling painting, *Worship of the Brazen Serpent*, the radiant female figure pointing at Moses "reiterates" his posture in *Moses Strikes Water from the Rock*.

76 Preliminary sketches were reused multiple times, as were wax models, which were primarily employed as aides for the design of flying bodies. For a thorough exploration of the subject, see Krischel, *Jacopo Tintorettos "Sklavenwunder*,*"* 65–66.

77 Zenkert, *Tintoretto*, 247.

78 Boschini, *La carta del navegar pitoresco*, 127–128.

79 Antonio Manno identifies the scene as the battle of the Israelites against the Amalekites (Exodus 17:8–16), in Romanelli, *Tintoretto*, 173. The background scene here, as in the *Baptism of Christ*, functions to provide a historical dimension.

80 "Me par veder quel'acqua a nascer viva, E me fa creder, che a star in sto posto, La sia per cascar certo qua sul pian, Sì che vogio tirarme da lontan, Se no me bagno certo, tosto, tosto." Boschini, *La carta del navegar pitoresco*, 128.

81 "Quanti mistri de scrimia vien stimai, Perché in Cademia i mostra gran bravura, Che par che a Marte i

meteria paura, Se i fusse aponto da lu disfidai! Ma quando ghe convien ziogar da seno, E che bisogna tior la spada bianca, Alora int'un istante el cuor ghe manca, E privi i resta de giudicio e seno." Boschini, *La carta del navegar pitoresco*, 87.

82 "Orsù passemo, per sta volta tanto, Per osservar la scrimia e la bravura Del nostro Tentoreto in la pitura, Dala Gesia ala Scuola de sto Santo." Boschini, *La carta del navegar pitoresco*, 118.

83 "Oh bravo scrimiador, che senza spada Colpisse in ogni parte la figura, Con sì agiustada e singular mesura, Che ogni feria resplende lumizada." Boschini, *La carta del navegar pitoresco*, 460. The artist referred to here is Antonio Vassilacchi, called l'Aliense.

84 David Rosand has pointed out that Venetian *colorito* is based on the brushstroke. Rosand, "Tintoretto e gli spiriti nel pennello," 133.

85 Compare also the following lines: "El Tentoreto è un bravo, che aterisse Tuti i Guerieri de tute le etae: El tira colpi, el destende stocae, E più che l'urta in duro, e più el ferisse. No gh'è nissun, che sia bon de star saldo Ala furia, al teror, al so spavento. El val più lu, che non ghe ne val cento; L'è un vero Paladin, in stampa d'Aldo. Se puol dir più de quele so fierezze? Che i vaga a veder le guere naval, Che le par giusto le furie infernal, Con schiopi, con bombarde, e spade, e frezze!" Boschini, *La carta del navegar pitoresco*, 227.

86 See Rossi, "La Peinture Guerrière," 82–83.

87 "Veloce così colla mano, come coll'ingegno, ma veloce come buon schermitore con arte, con due soli colpi di pennello tutto ciò meglio vivo e spirante fece apparire, che altri mille volte toccando e ritoccando, appena potrebbe adombrare." Guarini, *Il frenetico savio*, 51.

88 Compare also Marco Boschini's statement on Leandro Bassano comparing the painting style with swordsmanship: "Leandro il Fratello, degno Cavaliere, corre anch'egli la sua Lancia con ordinato ardimento, e prontissima azione; di modo che fa comparire nel campo di vaste tele il generoso suo sentimento, schermando con colpi di pennello tratti infiniti di legiadre attitudini e pronte positure, atte a difendersi dal Tempo e dalla Morte." Boschini, *La carta del navegar pitoresco*, 729.

89 Sansovino, *Delle cose notabili*, 18.

90 "Egli accompagna la mano col suo veloce intelletto." Ibid.

91 Alberti, *On Painting*, 103.

92 Ibid., 102.

93 Quintilian, *The Orator's Education*, book 10.1 (106.), 311.

94 "But we, let us not forget, stand armed in the front line, fight for high stakes, and strive for victory. And I should not wish our weapons to be foul with neglect and rust; they should have the brilliance that strikes terror, the brilliance of steel that dazzles both mind and eye, not that of gold and silver, which is unwarlike and more dangerous to its possessor than to the foe." Quintilian, *The Orator's Education*, book 10.1 (30.), 267.

95 Quintilian, *The Orator's Education*, Book 10.1 (33.), 269.

96 Aristotle, *Metaphysics* [book 1.IV.2–3], vol. 1, 29.

97 "[W]hat has been said of the sword and sword and dagger also applies to all of those weapons that follow—for I have said, and say now, and will always say, that a sword alone, provided it is skillfully wielded and governed by the principles I have given, will give you the ability to use all other weapons just as an author uses all of the letters of the alphabet." Agrippa, *Fencing*, 83.

98 "I would have those who begin to learn the art of painting do what I see practised by teachers of writing. They first teach all the signs of the alphabet separately." Alberti, *On Painting*, 97.

99 "I wish [the painter] above all to have a good knowledge of geometry." Alberti, *On Painting*, 95.

100 "Chap. 2: Concerning a Geometrical Figure. As I stated previously, this pursuit is ultimately governed by points, lines, measures, and so forth, and comes from thinking in a mathematical—which is to say, a geometrical—fashion." Agrippa, *Fencing*, 10 [*Trattato*, 3r, 38r].

101 Agrippa, *Fencing*, 14–5 [Agrippa, *Trattato*, 6r].

102 "Abbassando la punta de la spada in terra presso al pie dritto gli interrumperebbe ogni disegno." Agrippa, *Trattato*, 12v. The English translation gives: "and so spoil his plans." Agrippa, *Fencing*, 24.

103 See the introduction of John Michael Geer, Thibault, *The Academy of the Sword*, esp. 1–3.

104 Thibault, *The Academy of the Sword*, 49.

105 Ibid., 15.

106 Ibid., 15, 50.

107 "Deux hommes adroits faisant ensemble, combattont plus de tête que de la main." Labat, *L'Art en fait d'armes*, 117.

108 Thibault, *The Academy of the Sword*, 15.

109 Ibid., 82.

110 Ibid., 152.

111 Ibid., 15.

112 Ibid., 152.

113 Ibid., 177.

114 Ibid., 168.

115 Ibid., 15.

116 Ibid., 205.

117 "Most of those who set out to learn about cutting attacks do this with the intention of apprehending in one or two months, as they say, as much as is necessary to defend against them.... Familiarity cannot be acquired without a firm understanding of the rules, which cannot be had without study, nor study without patience, nor patience without time, hard work, and modesty." Thibault, *The Academy of the Sword*, 237, 278.

118 Thibault, *The Academy of the Sword*, 278–279.

119 Ibid., 278.

120 Ibid., 237.

121 "C'est avec raison qu'on nomme la vitesse & le tems, l'ame des armes, puis que tous les coups doivent leur reüssite à cette qualité, ne pouvant donner que par surprise, & ne pouvant surprendre sans vitesse." Labat, *L'Art en fait d'armes*, 134.

CHAPTER FIVE: COMMUNICATING ARTIFICE

1 "La forza del gran talento di Giacomo Tintoretto." Scannelli, *Il microcosmo della pittura*, 250.

2 Scannelli, *Il microcosmo della pittura*, 252.

3 "[Michelangelo:] Eu vos direi: fazer com grande ligeireza e destreza qualquer coisa é muito proveitoso e bom; e dom é recebido do imortal Deus que aquilo que outro (que) stá pintando em muitos dias se faça em poucas horas." De Hollanda, *Quatro Dialogos*, 46.

4 Continuing from the passage cited above: "Que se assim não fora, não trabalhara tanto Pausia Siciónio por num dia pintar a perfeição de um menino em uma tábua. Assim que o que, pintando depressa, não deixa por isso de pintar tão bem como o que pinta vagarosamente, merece por isso muito mor louvor." Ibid.

5 Pliny the Elder, *Natural History*, book 35 [124], 353.

6 "E disse che nel picciolo, e nel finito bisognava andar piano, e sospendere il lavoro di quando in quando, e perciò vi si consumava il tempo; ma nel grande il pennello ha campo di sfuggire, e correr velocemente." De' Dominici, *Vite*, vol. 3, 246. The question of painting formats and their various implications is a topic that has yet to be explored in art history. The art-theoretical dimension of small formats was first introduced by Alberti when he promoted painting in large formats as a demonstration of artistic skill und knowledge: "The man who has learned to make or paint large figures would at once do small things of this kind easily and well; whereas the man who has accustomed his hand to these tiny jewels, will easily go wrong in larger works." Alberti, *On Painting*, 101.

7 De Hollanda, *On Antique Painting*, 215.

8 Ibid.

9 Plutarch, "The Education of Children," 29.

10 Alberti. *On Painting*, 105.

11 Lomazzo, "Tratto," 419. David Summers directly connects Giovanni Paolo Lomazzo's statement to the Sala dei Cento Giorni. Summers 1981, 64.

12 Pino introduces this legend with the information that Apelles criticized himself for being "troppo diligente": "Il contrario poi si dice d'un altro pittore, il qual dimostrò una sua opera ad Apelle, gloriandosi averla fatta prestissimo, al che rispose Apelle, senza che tu me lo dica l'opera lo manifesta da sé stessa." Pino, *Dialogo*, 113.

13 Pino, *Dialogo*, 113.

14 "E anco quest'empiastrar, facendo il pratico, come fa il vostro Andrea Schiavone, è parte degna d'infamia, e questi tali dimostrano saperne puoco." Pino, *Dialogo*, 113.

15 Alberti, *On Painting*, 105.

16 "The painter will never apply his brush or style to his work before he has clearly decided in his own mind what he is going to do and how he will do it." Alberti, *On Painting*, 101–103.

17 Von Sandrart, *Teutsche Academie*, vol 1, part 1, book 3, 66–67.

18 "The means of perfecting art will be found in diligence, study, and application." Alberti, *On Painting*, 97.

19 Alberti, *On Painting*, 103.

20 There is a particularly expressive testament in art literature to the widespread legend of the one-day work: "OPERA D.VN GIORNO DEL CAVALIER TROPPA" is inscribed on the foremost plane of the *Vision of St. Hieronymus* by Gerolamo Troppa. The hermit Hieronymus assailed by the sound of the trumpets of the Last Judgment was a commonly represented subject in Troppa's time. His version of the theme is not particularly original, but what is surprising is the foregrounded level of meaning established by the inscription; the religious subject is effectively privatized. Written prominently and in blatantly large letters into the book of his saintly namesake, the self-confident, oversized signature of the art-historically insignificant Troppa (ca. 1635–1710) stretches the limits of decorum. The *alla prima* technique and poor quality of this painting seem to verify the inscription's claim, and its shortcomings are also why it is today relegated to the depot of the Vienna Kunsthistorisches Museum. I am grateful to Gudrun Swoboda for bringing this work to my attention.

21 "È a opera maravigliosa, di grande studio, e fatica, e degna di somma lode per essere ingegnosa nell'invenzione, copiosa nel componimento, studiosa, e in un atto mirabile, abbondante, e vaga nell'ornamento, e condotta con tal maestria del pennello, che pare tutta dipinta in un giorno." Passeri, *Vite*, 412.

22 "Brio of the brush, a good handling of color, impact, and vividness."

23 Zanetti, *Della pittura veneziana e delle opere pubbliche*, 519.

24 "Fu solito operare poco più che alla prima, cioè abbozzando, ed immediatamente terminando." Baldinucci, *Notizie*, vol. 4, 656f.

25 Baldinucci, *Notizie*, vol. 4, 656–657.

26 Ibid., 657.

27 "Il peignoit extrêment vîte; souvent il commençoit un tableau de moyenne grandeur & le finissoit dans le même jour." Dézallier d'Argenville, *Abrégé*, vol. 1, 352.

28 "Maffeo Verona fù molto pronto d'ingegno, e dipinse con tal prestezza, che ne'giorni dell'estate soleva nel bel mattino abbozzare le figure, & asciugatele al sole, prima di notte dava loro compimento." Dal Pozzo, *Vite*, 151.

29 "Mémoire historique des principaux ouvrages de M. Vignon le père, Conseiller-Professeur de l'Académie royale de peinture et de sculpture," in *Conférences de l'Académie royale de Peinture et de Sculpture*, part 2, vol. 1 (1682–1699), 316–325, here 318–320.

30 Bellori, *Lives*, 215–216.

31 Hermitage, St. Petersburg, 116.5 x 93.5 cm, oil on canvas.

32 Bellori, *Lives*, 220.

33 "[Ad loc. Van Dyck] Après le diné, il reprenoit son ouvrage, & travailloit avec une telle promtitude & une si grande intelligence, qu'il auroit fait deux portraits par jour, ne faisant plus ensuite que les retoucher pour les finir." Félibien, *Entretiens*, vol. 3, 448.

34 Bellori, *Lives*, 220.

35 "Ove gli altri seguivano una abbreviatura, e un certo facile Tintoresco, e risoluto insinuato loro da' maestri, egli al contrario, trovandosi già di questa pratica possessore, dilettavi di una più esatta ricercata d'ogni minutissima parte, d'ogni muscolo, all'uso quasi de'Passerroti, ma raddolcendo poi tutto, e coprendolo d'una certa facilità e sprezzatura maravigliosa." Malvasia, *Felsina pittrice*, vol. 2, 8.

36 "Proposto perciò il premio d'una collana d'oro a chi fra loro fosse stato il primo a dar la sua parte finita; che sproposito, diceva Guido? siam noi cavalli barbari, maggior dei quali, e più bravo si stimi che prima giunge al palio?" Malvasia, *Felsina pittrice*, vol. 2, 16.

37 On the Accademia dei Virtuosi al Pantheon, a congregation of those who have made extraordinary achievements in the arts and sciences, see Brugnoli et al., "L'Accademia dei Virtuosi"; Haskell, *Patrons and Painters*, 126.

38 Houbraken, *De groote schouburgh*, vol. 2, 224f.

39 "Filippo Roos, chiamato anche Rosa di Tivoli, per avere lungamente studiato in Roma ed in Tivoli, fu buon pittore di animali e paesaggi, quali toccò con franco e spedito pennello.... E ben potea servire a contentare ognuno, usando grande speditezza nell'operare." Orlandi, *Abecedario*, 170, 171.

40 Houbraken explains the artist's nickname "Markurius" as inspired by the quickness of his thoughts and brush: "Vlugtig van gedachten en vaardig met het penceel." Houbraken, *De groote schouburgh*, vol. 2, 219.

41 "Fu huomo di gran spirito, di bell'aspetto, di buona partata, e di gran bravura nel suo pennello, che per la sua velocità nell'operar e toccar le sue cose con tanta franchezza e risoluzione, gli fu dall'ambasciador Cesareo Lambergh, che lo tenne per qualche tempo in sua casa, posto il cognome di fulmine." Pio, *Vite*, 147.

42 Ticozzi, *Dizionario*, 195.

43 "Il tutto però gli era permesso dalla gran velocità del suo pennello; poichè mille volte fu osservato aver dipinta una mezza figura in meno d'un'ora, bella, e finita, ed alcuna fiata una Madonna col Bambino." Bellori, "Vita Luca Giordano," 100.

44 "In somma sì vedeva in quest'opera tutto il componimento, la bizzarria e lo studio, che si ammira nel Veronese, nel Tintoretto ed in Tiziano." Bellori, "Vita Luca Giordano," 65f. On this subject see Finocchi Ghersi, "Luca Giordano a Venezia."

45 "Carlo Cignani, Carlo Lotti e Carlo Maratta lo chiamavano il Veronese, e'l Tintoretto de'moderni tempi." Bellori, "Vita Luca Giordano," 133.

46 But according to Luigi Lanzi, sprezzatura instigates a "degeneration" of style because when other painters try and fail to imitate this practice, which abolishes the old rules in order to make new ones, they end up producing works that look like preparatory sketches. His critique specifically refers to the school of the Dandini, which Lanzi examines in his book's section on the "Fifth Epoch." Lanzi, *Storia pittorica*, vol. 1, 248.

47 "LUCA GIORDANO Napolitano. Tante e sì belle sono le opera, che di questo pittore in Venezia si veggono, che sebbene Viniziano non non sia, deesi discorrere anche di lui tra I Viniziani. Ebbe egli un particular suo modo di dipingere con un maneggio di pennello così franco e inteso, che spaventa I professori." Zanetti, *Della pittura veneziana in cui osservarsi l'ordine del Busching*, vol. 2, 227.

48 See Kris and Kurz, *Legend, Myth, and Magic*, 95.

49 "LUCA GIORDANO, Napoletano, detto *Luca Fapresto*, per la volontà del pennello nel dipingere, nel concepire, e nel partorire in un fiato medesimo." Orlandi, *Abecedario*, 351.

50 "Non si niega già per noi che questa via del far presto non sia di mestieri per qualche urgente bisogno, sí come per archi trionfali, per feste, per scene e per tali cose improvise ordinate spesse volte dalle republiche e da' gran signori, con molta sollecitudine e prestezza; e da esse se ne suole appresso de'popoli acquistar fama di valentissimi uomini e con premii onorati di quelli, le quali opere poi non durano però molto a vedersi." Armenini, *De' veri precetti*, 88.

51 Baldinucci, *Vocabolario*, Appendix, 185.

52 See for example: "[ad loc. Fragonard] On a de lui, dans ce genre, des tours de force, des merveilles, des figures où il se revèle comme un prodigieux *Fa presto*." Goncourt and Goncourt, *L'Art du XVIIIe siècle*, vol. 2, 344.

53 De' Dominici, *Vite*, vol. 3, 416f.

54 Palomino, *El museo pictórico*, 1095.

55 De' Dominici, *Vite*, vol. 3, 421f.

56 Ibid., 422.

57 "No es creíble la liberalidad, y agrado con que fué recibido nuestro Velázquez de un tan gran Monarca, mandándole tuviese obrador dentro de su Real Palacio, en la galería, que llaman del Cierzo; de la cual tenía Su Majestad la llave, y silla, para verle pintar despacio." Palomino, *El museo pictórico*, 903–904.

58 "Así como lo hizo el magno Alejandro con Apeles, e quien muy de ordinario iba a ver pintar a su oficina, honrándole con tan singulares favores, como los que refiere Plinio en su Historia Natural. Y como la Majestad Cesárea del señor Emperador Carlos Quinto, aunque ocupado en tantas guerras, gustaba de ver pintar a el gran Ticiano. Y el católico Rey Filipe Segundo iba muy frecuentemente a ver pintar a Alonso Sánchez Coello, favoreciéndole con singulares muestras de amor." Ibid.

59 Ibid.

60 "...que deseando Su Majestad verle pintar." Palomino, *El museo pictorico*, 1094.

61 See, for example, Bartholomäus Spranger at the court of Rudolph II: "From then on the Emperor did not want Spangher to work at home any more as before, but in the chamber that His Majesty was wont to use for relaxation; thus Spangher began to work in the presence of the Emperor, to the great pleasure and satisfaction of His Majesty.... He merely applied himself to satisfy and pleasing his Emperor by working in his chamber, where His Majesty was often present—and that lasted about seventeen years." Van Mander, *Lives*, vol, 1, 350.

62 See the first sentence in the quotation above, note 494.

63 Dolce, *Dialogo*, 157f.

64 De Piles, *Abregé*, 397.

65 "Stavasi egli una mattina in camera di un gran principe, che, trovandosi in letto alquanto indisposto, lo avea chiamato a operare presso di sè per proprio divertimento." Baldinucci, *Notizie*, vol. 5, 488.

66 "Pittore maraviglioso, fatto da Dio per soddisfare a'principi." De' Dominici, *Vite*, vol. 3, 406.

67 "In memoria della stupenda velocità con cui era stata fatta." De' Dominici, *Vite*, vol. 3, 406, 407. See also Giannini, "Luca's 'Macchie,'" 237.

68 De' Dominici, *Vite*, vol. 3, 438.

69 Vasari, *Vite*, vol. 5, 101f.

70 Ibid., vol. 4, S. 10.

71 De' Dominici, *Vite*, vol. 3, 438.

72 Pierre-Jean Mariette gives Antwerp as the journey's destination. Mariette, *Abecedario*, vol. 3, 36.

73 Houbraken, *De groote schouburgh*, vol. 1, 133.

74 Houbraken, *De groote schouburgh*, vol. 1, 133. See also the two seminal studies on Raymond Lafage, which both mention Houbraken's anecdotes: Whitman, *The Drawings of Raymond Lafage*; Arvengas, *Raymond Lafage: Dessinateur.*

75 "Peu de personnes ont eu une imagination plus féconde; il étoit toujours prêt, sur quelque sujet qu'on luy demandât, et ce qui luy étoit de particulier, ce qu'il exécutoit avec le plus de promptitude et le moins de préparation, étoit infiniment préférable à ses ouvrages les plus terminés, et où il avoit donné toutes ses réflections." Mariette, *Abecedario*, vol. 3, 31.

76 Mariette, *Abecedario*, vol. 3, 37.

77 Nicola Pio reports that during his stay in Rome Lafage had studied the works of the Carracci. Pio, *Vite*, 174. See Suthor, "Drawing a Line and Questioning Art."

78 Pliny, *Natural History*, book 35, 323 (lat.: 320).

79 Pascoli, *Vite*, 74f.

80 Mariette, *Abecedario*, vol. 3, 37f.

81 "Car La Fage sçavoit parfaitement l'anatomie, et, tout praticien qu'il étoit, il formoit toutes ses parties avec beaucoup de précision." Mariette, *Abecedario*, vol. 3, 32.

82 "Il fit souvent cette épreuve en présence des maîtres de l'art, qui, surpris de sa facilité de dessiner, n'admiroient pas moins la science profonde qu'il mettoit dans son dessein." Mariette, *Abecedario*, vol. 3, 32.

83 Kris and Kurz, "Legend, Myth, and Magic," 92; Van Mander, *Lives*, 441. Also cited in Cordellier, "Martin Fréminet," 59.

84 Van Mander, *Lives*, 441. On Toussaint Dubreuil, see also Félibien, *Entretiens*, vol. 3, 125–126. The *Portrait Henri IV en Hercule terrassant l'hydre de Lerne* (ca. 1600, Paris) is today in the Louvre.

85 Van Mander, *Lives*, 441.

86 "Son principal séjour fut à Rome, où il demeura sept ans, & ses principales Etudes furent d'aprés Michelange; en sorte que tout ce qu'il a fait depuis, tient beaucoup de la maniére de ce grand Peintre." De Piles, *Abregé*, 460.

87 "Mais pourtant il s'attacha principalement à étudier les ouvrages de Michel-Ange, & prit de lui cet air fier, & cette forte maniere de dessiner, qui fait que l'on voit dans ses figures les nerfs & les muscles, comme ils paroissent dans celles de Michel-Ange." Félibien, *Entretiens*, vol. 3, 314.

88 Félibien *Entretiens*, vol. 3, 314.

89 "Ma dove ha maggior forza, in questo, o in quello O la spada, o'l pennello? Là velo, e sangue, e qui tela, e colore L'uno è del'Arte, e l'altro fu d'Amore." Marino, *La Galeria*, 18f.

90 "Cependant vous serez obligé de m'avouër, dit Pymandre, qu'il n'y a guéres eu de Peintres dont la reputation ait si peu duré que celle de Freminet. Car je n'entends point parler de lui; je ne vois aucun de ses ouvrages dans les Cabinets; & si j'ose vous parler librement, je vous dirai qu'ayant consideré plusieurs fois la Chapelle de Fontainebleau, je n'ai rien trouvé qui m'ait pû plaire, quoique je tâchasse de me conformer en quelque sorte au jugement de ceux qui en faisoient état, à cause, peut-être, que l'ouvrage n'étant fait que pour le sçavans, j'ai trop peu de connoissance pour en découvrir les beautez.... Ainsi il est certain que ce qu'il y a dans les Peintures de Freminet de plus à estimer, n'est pas connu de tout le monde, parce qu'il s'est éloigné de la nature, & c'est aussi ce qui les a renduës si peu recherchées.... Or il est vrai que Freminet n'avoit pas une maniere de peindre qui pût plaire à tout le monde. Elle étoit, comme je vous ai dit, fiére & terrible, donnant à ses figures des mouvemens trop forts, & marquant tellement les muscles, qu'ils paroissent jusques sous les draperies. De sorte que ses ordonnances sont presque toûjours d'actions étudiées & recherchées à la maniere des Florentins, & non pas naturelles & aisées." Félibien, *Entretiens*, vol. 3, 316–319.

91 De' Dominici, *Vite*, vol. 3, 453.

92 Malvasia, *Life of the Carracci*, 282.

93 Boschini, *La carta del navegar pitoresco*, 99–101.

94 "Sei in Pitura un Capitan spavento.... Questo xe un colpo veramente bravo! Questi è quei colpi che fa i Veneziani!" Boschini, *La carta del navegar pitoresco*, 101.

95 On the self-portrait of Niccolò Cassana (ca. 1683) see also, (coll. cat.) Caneva, *Il Corridoio vasariano agli Uffizi*, cat. no. 29, 203.

96 "Tanto era intesa la sua premura di riuscir più che bene." Ratti, *Vite*, vol. 2, 16.

97 Cited in Prinz, *Die Sammlung der Selbstbildnisse*, 107. Niccolò Cassana would eventually become a business competitor to Del Teglia; beginning in 1698, he acted as Grand Prince Ferdinand de' Medici's art agent in Venice. On this subject, see Haskell, *Patrons and Painters*, 232.

CHAPTER SIX: ECONOMIES OF PRACTICE

1 Roger de Piles names the second mistake as "falling into gray;" the third is painting shaded portions with a brush that was previously used with a color containing white, thereby ruining the quality of the shadow's darkness. De Piles, *Elémens*, 113, 119.

2 "In Carlo impareggiabile diligenza; ed in Giordano la maravigliosa speditezza del pennello." Baldinucci, *Notizie*, vol. 5, 359.

3 Baldinucci, *Notizie*, vol. 5, 336. See also Watelet and Lévesque, *Dictionnaire*, vol. 3, entry by Lévesque, "Oeconomie," 632: "L'œconomie d'un tableau est la même chose que son ordonnance."

4 "Il fondo di sì gran tristezza era il persuadersi al suo solito di non essere nell'arte sua più buono a nulla." Baldinucci, *Notizie*, vol. 5, 359, 360. See Wittkower and Wittkower, *Born under Saturn*, 122–124.

5 See, for example, the legendary death of Antonio del Castillo, who, according to Palomino, exclaimed, "Castillo is now dead!" (*¡Ya murió Castillo!*) when he first saw a beautiful painting by Murillo. He fell into such a depression that he died soon after. Palomino, *El museo pictórico*, 953.

6 "E perciò invitollo, che a capo di pochi giorni si portasse a veder terminata la Galleria del Riccardi, che già avea veduta cominciata.... In vederla il buon vecchio di Carlino, fece questa una sì vive impressione nel di lui animo, che riflettendo al breve tempo, che vi era stato impiegato, e al molto da lui speso invano nell'opere sue, per la soverchia finitezza, anche de'pelami ne'panneggiamenti, si lasciò così opprimere della malinconia, che in pochi giorni finì di vivere." Bellori, "Vita Luca Giordano," 40.

7 Baldinucci, *Notizie*, vol. 5, 354.

8 See Vasari, *Vite*, vol. 4, 302, 303.

9 This interpretation had been earlier formulated by Giuseppe Gallasso. Entry no. 103 in (exhib. cat.) *Luca Giordano 1634–1705*, 310.

10 See Bellori, "Vita Luca Giordano," 50f., 102, 103.

11 "Debbono le figure, così di rilievo come dipinte, esser condotte più con il giudicio che con la mano, avendo a stare in altezza dove sia una gran distanza; perché la diligenza dell'ultimo finimento non si vede da lontano... perché nella semplicità del poco si mostra l'acutezza dell'ingegno." Vasari, *Vite*, vol. 1, 84.

12 Richardson, "On the Art of Painting," 90.

13 Bellori, "Vita Luca Giordano," 100. Tintoretto is also said to have been flexible about his commissions: "Ha dipinto quasi di tutte le sorti pitture a fresco, a olio, ritratti di naturale, et ad ogni pregio, di maniera che con questi suoi modi ha fatto e fa la maggior parte delle pitture che si fanno in Vinezia." Vasari, *Vite*, vol. 5, 469.

14 In the vita of Giordano's student Paolo de Matteis, Cavaliere Farelli rejects the excuse that a painting may be poorly executed if the artist is not paid well, on the grounds that those who look at the work know nothing of the price: "Che chi vedeva l'opera nulla sapea del prezzo." De' Dominici, *Vite*, vol. 3, 525.

15 De' Dominici, *Vite*, vol. 3, 411.

16 Baldinucci, *Notizie*, vol. 5, 358.

17 Tom Nichols identifies the unnamed painter in Dolce's *Dialogo di pittura* (1557) as Tintoretto. Nichols, "Tintoretto, prestezza," 72.

18 "[Ad loc. Veronese] Riveriva Tiziano come padre dell'arte, ed apprezzava molto il vivace ingegno del Tintoretto, spiacendogli solo ch'egli apportasse danno a' professori col dipingere ad ogni maniera, ch'era per appunto un distruggere il concetto della professione e le proprie sostanze." Ridolfi, *Le Maraviglie dell'arte*, vol. 2, 79.

19 De' Dominici, *Vite*, vol. 3, 411. See: Bellori, "Vita Luca Giordano," 48f.

20 "Ma per dir vero questa suo soverchia prestezza fu spesso cagione del giusto biasimo che si dà a molte opere sue, poichè il far bene, e'l far troppo presto hanno del contrario: e soleva egli dire, che aveva tre sorti di pennelli, uno d'oro, un di argento, ed un altro di rame, con i quali soddisfaceva a' Nobili, a' Civili, ed a' Plebei, e che a tutti tre questi ceti corrispondeva col merito dell'opera proporzionata al prezzo." De' Dominici, *Vite*, vol. 3, 433.

21 In Dézallier d'Argenville's version the anecdote is likewise preceded by an accusation of poor quality: "Une fougue dont il n'étoit pas le maître lui a fait peindre des tableaux médiocres & rien n'est plus inégal que ce peintre. On disoit à Vénice qu'il avoit trois pinceau, 'il penello d'oro, il penello d'argento, e l'altro di ferro' qu'il employoit suivant son caprice." Dézallier d'Argenville, *Abrégé*, vol. 1, 167.

22 See Brusati, *Artifice & Illusion*, 218–258.

23 "Ik en kan geen behaegen krijgen in't geene de Ridder P.C. Hoost, van Mr.Dirk Barentszoon, des vermaerden Titiaens leerling, zegt: dat hy dryderley penseelen, als goude, zilvere, en kopere hadt, en hy yder berichte nae zijn gelt." Van Hoogstraten, *Inleyding*, 235.

24 "En schoon alle stukken niet even zorgvuldelijk tot den eynde toe worden uitgevoert, zoo zullen mooglijk die geene, die met een wakkere toezicht als ter vlucht overloopen schijnen, meer gouts uit het penseel hebben, als daer de laetste hand aen gehouden is." Van Hoogstraten, *Inleyding*, 235.

25 Von Sandrart, *Teutsche Academie*, vol. 1, part 2, book 3, 292. Cited in De Piles, *Abregé*, 401; Houbraken, *De groote schouburgh*, vol. 1, 57f.

26 "Luca Giordano figlio d'Antonio Giordano mediocre Pittore, il quale fu Scolaro del Ribera detto il Spagnoletto." De' Dominici, *Vite*, vol. 3, 541. Concerning Ribera's anecdote see De' Dominici, *Vite*, vol. 3, 18f.

27 De' Dominici, *Vite*, vol. 3, 18f.

28 Ibid., 18.

29 "E poi la notte se ne stavano in casa a dipingere a gran lume artificiale; per lo quale esercizio Carlo Coppola ne restò cieco." De' Dominici, *Vite*, vol. 3, 226.

30 Scaramuccia's recommendation is found in his maxims, *Massime, o siano ricordi*, under the maxim "Della solitudine, o ritiramento": "Porrai adunque ogni tua applicatione (à causa d'approfittarti) nell'hore più notturne, overo in quelle dell'Aurora, dissegnando, schizzando, e ponendo giù pensieri &c. e tutto ciò per poterti mettere nell'immaginativa quello pretendi fare." Scaramuccia, *Le finezze de'pennelli*, 201.

31 De' Dominici, *Vite*, vol. 3, 245f.

32 In his monograph on the artist, Jonathan Scott sheds light on this seemingly outrageous behavior toward a potential client by pointing out Baldinucci's explanation in his vita of Salvator Rosa: "I can find few, in fact, I cannot find any, artists either before or after him or among his contempories, who can be said to have maintained the status of art as high as he did." Scott, *Salvator Rosa*, 136.

33 "Ho promesso più di una volta al Signor de Rosis di servir Vostra Signoria Illustrissima ma perch'io non depingo per arrechire ma solamente per propria sodisfazione è forza il lasciarmi trasportare dagl'impeti dell'entusiasmo et esercitare i pennelli solamente in quel tempo che me ne sento violentato." Rosa *Lettere*, 342f.; cited in Haskell 1980, 22.

34 Vasari, *Vite*, vol. 4, 127f.

35 See Vasari, *Vite*, vol. 3, 211f. A comic tale of Donatello's destructive rage is also reported in Poliziano's *Bel Libretto*. He relates that Donatello, under extreme pressure to complete a head of the mercenary leader Gattamelata, smashed it in anger. Threatened by his patrons, the Signoria of Venice, to be beheaded if he ever fell into their hands, he replied that unlike them he could restore the head of Gattamelata, while they could not reattach the decapitated heads of those they executed. Poliziano, *Polizianos Tagebuch*, 27f. The reverberation of this storied response throughout Early Modern art writing is shown in its repetition by Vasari in his vita of Andrea Verocchio: "Rispose che se ne guarderebbe, perché spiccate che le avevano, non era in loro facultà rapiccare le teste agl'uomini, né una simile alla sua già mai, come arebbe saputo lui fare di quella ch'egli avea spiccata al suo cavallo, e più bella." Vasari, *Vite*, vol. 3, 541.

36 Malvasia, *Scritti*, 129.

37 See Warwick, "Caravaggio in History," 16.

38 "E così sosteneva egli i gran prezzi; onde avveniva, che a chi volea suoi quadri, bisognava pagarli quel ch'e'voleva." Baldinucci, *Notizie*, vol. 5, 483f.

39 The price politics of artists, always viewed with a critical, if not moralizing, eye in art history, has been freed from the stigma of avarice by Svetlana Alpers. Based on the example of Rembrandt, she identifies the speculative inflation of price as a justified obligation to render due tribute to art. Alpers's argument is founded on that of Thomas Hobbes, the "prophet of market economics," who in his *Leviathan* (1651) captures the logical connection between commerce and homage in the formula: "The Value, or WORTH of man, is as of all other things, his Price." Alpers, *Rembrandt's Enterprise*, 106.

40 Scott, *Salvator Rosa*, 136.

41 Vasari, *Vite*, vol. 6, 23.

42 De Hollanda, *On Antique Painting*, 206–207. See also Buscaroli, *Il concetto dell'arte nelle parole di Michelangelo*, 14–15.; Clements, "Michelangelo on effort and rapidity in art." Michelangelo was renowned for his virtuoso draftsmanship. In the shortest amount of time he was able create a drawing that looked as if it were the result of a month's work ("Era un stupore grande a quelli cge ciò avevano veduto fare in cosí poco tempo, che altri vi avrebbe giudicato dentro la fatica di un mese."). Armenini, *De' veri precetti*, 93.

43 De' Dominici, *Vite*, vol. 3, 246.

44 Palomino, *El museo pictórico*, 1106. See Nichols, "Tintoretto, prestezza."

45 Bellori, "Vita Luca Giordano," 42.

46 Tintoretto's act was not completely unselfish, however. With this gift he sought, among other things, to acquire his *sansaria*, a brokerage patent for painters. See Krischel, *Jacopo Tintorettos "Sklavenwunder,"* 93–101.

47 "La finale è quella cagione che invita e sforza l'artefice a farla, il quale può essere così il disiderio della gloria, come il bisogno o la voglia di guadagnare." Varchi in: Barocchi *Trattati*, vol. 1, 23.

48 "Era Paolo feracissimo nell'inventare, ma molte volte (volendo anche in tal parte emulare il gran Luca Giordano) non erano tutte le figure egualmente studiate nel medesimo quadro; perchè voleva ad un tratto partorire e dipingere." De' Dominici, *Vite*, vol. 3, 540.

49 "[Paolo de Matteis] dicea, che in questa parte della velocità avea superato Luca Giordano." De' Dominici, *Vite*, vol. 3, 526.

50 Palomino, *El museo pictórico*, 1114.

51 De' Dominici, *Vite*, vol. 3, 530.

52 Ibid., 529, 540.

53 "Paul Mattei, qui avoit été si fort vanté, fut fort mal accueilli à Paris, et l'on sçait qu'en sortant il ne put s'empêcher d'en témoigner du dépit." Mariette, *Abecedario*, vol. 3, 291. See Brejon de Lavergnée 1990.

54 "Quanto meglio avrebbe fatto ad impiergarvi 66 mesi, e col debito studio farla buona, che il farla presto sol per la vanagloria di farsi vedere sollecito senza profitto." De' Dominici 1724, vol. 3, 527.

55 "Ciò spesso volte avveniva a cagion della troppa velocità usata da Paolo, a solo fine di farsi vedere maraviglioso nell'operar con prestezza.... Sicchè oscecato dall'interesse, e dalla stessa vanagloria, non badava a porvi quello studio, e diligenza che si conveniva." De' Dominici, *Vite*, vol. 3, 532f.

56 "E molte volte cominciava l'opere senza nemmeno averne fatto un abozzo in carta; anzi senza averci nemmen pensato.... Piantandovi certe figure a caso, come gli venivano partorite dalla mano, e non dalla riflessione! tutto effetto di una temeraria opinione di se stesso." De' Dominici, *Vite*, vol. 3, 532f.

57 "Paolo de Mattei, Napoletano, detto Paoluccio, velocissimo nel dipingere, creare, e partorire in un subito opere grandi tanto a fresco, quanto a olio." Orlandi, *Abecedario*, 407.

58 "Mattei (Paul), surnommé Paoluccio, avoit un génie extrêmement vif et facile; il inventoit et peignoit au premier coup, tant à fresque qu'à huile, les plus grands ouvrages.... J'ajouterai qu'il est vray que ce peintre avoit beaucoup de génie, mais il n'avoit aucun fond de science. C'étoit un praticien, et puis c'est tout. Il avoit renchéri pour la célébrité de ses opérations sur le Giordano; mais il n'avoit point dans son pinceau ce brillant séducteur qui fait réussir les ouvrages de son maître. Il avoit, au contraire, un coloris fade et languissant." Mariette, *Abecedario*, vol. 3, 289.

59 De Caylus, "De la légèrté de l'outil," 151.

60 "Je crois même qu'on ne pourrait tomber dans cette erreur pour le plus grand nombre des tableaux du Tintoret lequel est peut-être le premier des modernes qui a donné l'exemple d'une facilité qui a autorisé et perdu un si grand nombre d'artistes, d'autant plus qu'ils étaient incapables de l'imiter dans les ouvrages arrêtés qu'il a produits." De Caylus, "De la légèrté de l'outil," 151–152.

61 Reynolds, *Discourses*, 214.

62 "Paolo de Matteis, il cui celebre nome va la Fama dappertutto spargendo, e le sue rinomate opere si veggono in quantità prodigiosa, non solo in Napoli, ove al presente fa sua dimora, ma in Roma, in Lombardia, in Genova, in Firenze ed in Francia; e'l valore del cui pennello sarà impresa di più dotta, e fortunata penna il descriverlo, perocché nell'angusto confine di poche righe non può restringersi; non essendo bastevole qualunque laude se l'intessa, l'esprimere i fastiosi sui vanti." Bellori, "Vita Luca Giordano," 122–123. See also Brejon de Lavergnée, "Plaidoyer pour un peintre 'de pratique.'"

63 De' Dominici, *Vite*, vol. 3, 531. See Pestilli, "Lord Shaftesbury e Paolo de Matteis," 103.

64 "Tuvo Lucas Jordán innumerables discípulos, pero pocos, que aprovechasen; porque era más práctico, que teórico, y los discípulos se dejaban llevar de aquella facilidad, con que veían pintar a su maestro, y queriendo seguir lo mismo, se perdián, por faltarles aquellos fundamentos de estudio, con que fué dirigido Jordán en sus principios por José de Ribera, y Pedro de Cortona sus maestros." Palomino, *El museo pictórico*, 1114.

65 "Era también Don Claudio muy agudo, y satírico en sus dichos; y así sucedió un diá, que Don Cristóbal Ontañón le dijo: 'Ahora vendrá Jordán a enseñarles a ustedes a ganar mucho dinero.' Y le respondió Claudio: 'Sí señor, y a absolvernos de muchas culpas, y quitarnos muchos escrúpulos.'" Palomino, *El museo pictórico*, 1065.

66 "Cercando d'imitare la magia de'suoi colori, senza pescar nel profondo sapere del loro maestro." De' Dominici, *Vite*, vol. 3, 520.

67 Ridolfi, *Le Maraviglie dell'arte*, vol. 1, 336: "E fu senza dubbio un de' migliori coloritori della Scuola Veneziana."

68 Baldinucci, *Notizie*, vol. 2, 479: "A questo pittore da' professori dell'arte è dato luogo fra gli ottimi coloritori della veneta scuola; e non è forse a notizia d'alcuno, che altri, avanti o dopo, l'abbia avanzato nella felicità, facilità e bravura con che maneggiò il pennello." See also Ridolfi, *Le Maraviglie dell'arte*, vol. 1, 336: "Il cui bel modo di dipingere fu sempre ammirato da' professori, stendendo egli i suoi colori con tale felicità, che rende maraviglia."

69 Baldinucci, *Notizie*, vol. 2, 479. "Ma Tiziano, che bene aveva posto l'occhio al suo modo di colorire, cioè con una bravura, di pannello da mettere spavento in ognuno che maneggiasse colori." Baldinucci, *Notizie*, vol. 2, 477.

70 Baldinucci, *Notizie*, vol. 2, 476.

71 "Andrea Schiaon, vien qua con la to forza, Vien qua con la bravura to infinita, Con quel impasto, che ha calor e vita." Boschini, *La carta del navegar pitoresco*, 344f.

72 Boschini, *La carta del navegar pitoresco* (in: *Breve Instruzione*), 754.

73 "Spaventerà la furia Dalmatina De quel Schiaon teribile e feroce, Penelo veramente più veloce Che frezza, trata da man sarasina." Ad loc. Convento del Carmine: "Son capità zà ziorni in quel Convento, Per veder del Schiaon le penelae, Pronte cusì, da quele man formae, Chele rende teror, le fa spavento. Con furia tal del machia e colorito, E ressoluta pratica e maniera, Che non fu vista mai cosa sì fiera; Né ghe xe muodo da portarla in scrito." Boschini, *La carta del navegar pitoresco*, 62, 310f.

74 Ridolfi, *Le Maraviglie dell'arte*, vol. 1, 321f.

75 "Le pitture d'Andrea, benchè di buona maniera e tocche con molt'arte, più dilettavano i pittori che l'universale." Ridolfi, *Le Maraviglie dell'arte*, vol. 1, 322.

76 "La cognizione poi di quest'arte non è conceduta ad ognuno, ma riservata solo a coloro che col lungo studio hanno di così difficile e laboriosa materia i termini appresi." Ridolfi, *Le Maraviglie dell'arte*, vol. 1, 322.

77 "E lo sa il mirabile Tiziano... lo in che maniera io ho sempre laudato la prestezza saputa del vostro fare intelligente. Anzi il sì degno pittore se è talora istupito de la pratica che dimostrate nel tirare giuso le bozze de le istorie, sì bene intese e sì bene composte che, se la fretta del farle si convertisse ne la diligenzia del finrle anche voi confermareste il mio ricordo per ottimo." Aretino, *Lettere sull'arte*, 221.

78 Ibid.

79 "Accostumando egli di porre in opera le mischie, che per alcun giorno lasciava allestite sopra la tavolozza, formandone poi le carni così morbide e fresche, sichè pajon vive." Ridolfi, *Le Maraviglie dell'arte*, vol. 1, 336.

80 Boschini, *La carta del navegar pitoresco*, 724.

81 "Quindi sopra il gran canale, nelle case de'signori Zanni, colorì quattro istorie, ed a piedi una Galatea ignuda sopra un delfino, cosi morbida e vezzosa che par veramente sen vadì trastullando fra le acque; ed un Tritone che suona un corno ritorto di carne arsciccia dal sole; paesi ed altre figure con molta vaghezza." Ridolfi, *Le Maraviglie dell'arte*, vol. 1, 324. Mythological sea creatures seem to have been Schiavone's specialty: Marco Boschini reports that Schiavone painted Neptune on the façade of the Palazzo Zen in Campo ai Gesuiti: "Terribile Pitor xe'l to Schiaon, A segno tal, che'l Dio Neturno istesso L'Ha rapì." Boschini, *La carta del navegar pitoresco*, 668.

82 Boschini, *La carta del navegar pitoresco*, 711.

83 "Qual via di fare ha dato materia ai professori di trarne bellissime osservazioni, avendo in uso di velar le parti dell'ombre d'alcune teste d'ocria, di lacca e d'aspalto, che fa in vero maraviglioso effetto, componendo in quella guisa un misto casuale di tinte, che, ben praticate dall'intelligente pittore, fanno mirabile riuscita: il che proviene principalmente dallo sprezzo ed arditezza del pennello." Ridolfi, *Le Maraviglie dell'arte*, vol. 1, 336.

84 "Soleva perciò dire Jacopo Tintoretto, ch'era degno di riprensione quel pittore che non tenesse in sua casa un quadro d'Andrea, ma che meritava ancora non lieve castigo che non procurasse meglio disegnare, essendo in questa parte talor difettoso per lo breve studio che fatto aveva; ma egli ricoperse gli errori del disegno col vago suo colorito." Ridolfi, *Le Maraviglie dell'arte*, vol. 1, 320.

85 "Fu però degno di scusa, mancandogli quel comodo che faceva di mestieri per istudiare, essendo il di lui padre poverissimo e mal atto al proprio sovvenimento, non che del figliuolo, sì che fu necessitato prima del tempo a procurarsi co'pennelli il pane. E benchè la natura somministri la prontezza all'ingegno, fa però di mestieri l'erudirlo con lo studio, per incamminarsi con buoni fondamenti all'acquisto dell'arte." Ridolfi, *Le Maraviglie dell'arte*, vol. 1, 320.

Zanetti echoes this critique when he begins his passage on Schiavone with the remark: "If Andrea had been able to thusly comprehend and draw, or to phrase it better, if his contrary talent had allowed him to study design in precisely the same way that he keenly painted and invented, then he would have been counted without a doubt among the premier masters." Zanetti thus adopted Vasari's critique of Venetian painting. Zanetti, *Pittura veneziana in cui osservarsi l'ordine del Busching*, vol. 2, 207.

86 Cf. "Zà avemo dito, che'l Vasari oprime Sta nostra gran Maniera Veneziana, Se ben d'ogni altra la xe sempre anziana; E strapazza el Schiaon, pitor sublime." Boschini, *La carta del navegar pitoresco*, 84.

87 Boschini, *La carta del navegar pitoresco*, 62.

88 "Quel povero Schiaon el mel strapazza, Col dir che'l fava ben, ma per desgrazia: Ché de dir mal de lu mai no 'l se sazia, Co' se 'l fusse una fezza, una scoazza. La senta si se puol ofender più In general la strada Veneziana!... El dise che quel far de Andrea Schiaon Xe fato d'una pratica, che s'usa Far a Venezia; come a dir, confusa, De abozzi e machie, senza conclusion. Oh machie senza machia, anzi splendori, Che luse più de qual se sia lumiera!" Boschini, *La carta del navegar pitoresco*, 67.

89 "Sprezzando la diligenza, anzi calpestandola." Boschini, *La carta del navegar pitoresco*, 725.

90 "La diligenza di questo artefice fu sempre in procurar di fuggire la diligenza, ed in quella vece servirsi d'un maraviglioso e non più da altri usato ardire." Baldinucci, *Notizie*, vol. 2, 479.

91 Pino, *Dialogo*, 113.

92 Ibid., 123.

93 "Guido Reni lo stimò assaissimo e soleva dire che non aveva mai conosciuto un altro che fosse nato veramente pittore come il Mastelletta che, con tanta rissolutezza, assaliva una quadro di smisurata grandezza e lo rissolveva in pochi giorni come fece ne'duoi quadroni dell'Arca di S. Domenico." Malvasi, *Scritti*, 125. On Giovanni Andrea Donducci, called Il Mastelletta, see Coliva, *Il Mastelletta*; Sohm, *Pittoresco*, 158–159; Coliva, "La decorazione della Cappella dell'Arca in San Domenico;" Benati, "Un outsider di Genio."

94 Malvasia, *Scritti*, 119.

95 Malvasia, *Felsina pittrice*, vol. 2, 68.

96 "Adoprò il nero assai e il verderame che in breve tempo gli fece smontare i quadri e li fece neri tanto più che, subito imprimito, si poneva a dipingere onde l'imprimatura di poco tempo asciuttava e si beveva tutto il colore onde che non si copriva bene due e tre volte, ma lavorava alla prima non di corpo ma di colore liquido." Malvasia, *Scritti*, 119.

97 Malvasia, *Felsina pittrice*, vol. 2, 67.

98 "Ammirarono bene anch'essi a principio e lodarono que'gran maestri un tant'animo, ed una sì formidabile prestezza, ma non poterono successivamente non condannarne l'impazienza alla fatica, atrettanto nemico egli di ben raffinare e digerire i suoi parti, quanto pronto e veloce in iscaricarne i pensieri." Malvasia, *Felsina pittrice*, vol. 2, 67.

99 "Ma che vi dirò di Francesco Parmigiano? Diede costui certa vaghezza alle cose sue, che fanno inamorar chiunque le riguarda." Dolce, *Dialogo*, 199.

100 Malvasia, *Felsina pittrice*, vol. 2, 69.

101 Coliva, *Mastelletta*, 71, 92.

102 The shadow's delicacy consists in its *scansione cromatica* (chromatic decomposition). Ibid.

103 Malvasia *Scritti*, 119.

104 "Fu il suo fare una maniera furbesca; perchè non altro meggiormente adoprando che il nero, cacciando il tutto in ombra, veniva a scansare non solo le difficoltà, ma a confondere, e a perdere entro quelle oscurità i contorni, onde sopra di essi non si potessero fare i conti; ed ascondendo in tal guisa le scorrezioni e gli errori quando ve ne potessero essere stati, e su que'scuri poi maravigliosamente spiccando le prime piazze de'chiari, che alla prima ferivano la vista, e con estrema vaghezza appagavano il gusto." Malvasia, *Felsina pittrice*, vol. 2, 67f.

105 "Vedendosi di sua mano nelle Chiese teloni che spaventano, da lui che avea gran fuoco e tutto bolliva, così presto, ed a sì vil prezzo intrapresi e finiti, ch'è stupore e vergogna." Malvasia, *Felsina pittrice*, vol. 2, 68.

106 "Ma che poi in ultimo fu da lui stesso conosciuta e confessata necessaria pratica e fondamento, prima d'ingolfarsi al dipingere, per non caminar poi sempre al buio e a tentone." Malvasia, *Felsina pittrice*, vol. 2, 67.

107 Von Sandrart, *Teutsche Academie*, vol. 1, part. 1, book 3, 58.

CHAPTER SEVEN: ARTE-FACTUM

1 "Sono infinite le cose appertinenti al colorire e impossibil è isplicarle con parole, perché ciascun colore o da sé o composito può far più effetti, e niun colore vale per sua proprietà a fare un minimo dell'effetti del naturale, però se gli conviene l'intelligenza e prattica del buon maestro." Pino, *Dialogo*, 111.

2 Plato, *The Dialogues*, 68b, 489f.

3 De Piles, *Dialogue*, 45.

4 "C'est-à-dire, qu'il faut parler en premier lieu, des couleurs qui s'employent, soit à l'huile, soit à détrempe, qui sont des materies réelles & terrestres. En second lieu, de celles qui paroissent dans les objets de la nature." Félibien, *Entretiens*, vol. 3, 7.

5 Félibien *Entretiens*, vol. 3, 45.

6 "Les couleur étrangeres qui peuvent paroître parmi les véritables & naturelles, & qui les peuvent changer." Félibien, *Entretiens*, vol. 3, 45.

7 Félibien, *Entretiens*, vol. 3, 29.

8 Vasari, *Vite*, vol. 6, 373. On the motif of reflected light on armor as a painterly tour de force, see also Campbell, "Il ritratto del duca Alessandro de'Medici," 347f.; Spagnolo, "Vasari e le 'difficultà dell'arte,'" 92; Bodart, "Le reflet"; Bodart, "Le prince miroir," 123.

9 Vasari, *Vite*, vol. 6, 373. A similar story was told by Bernini, with Michelangelo and Daniele da Volterra as the protagonists of the art lesson. The work in question was a Pallas Athene. See De Chantelou, *Journal de voyage*, 139f.

10 "Tutti questi lumi feriscono gagliardamente i corpi, in modo che non lasciano a pena scorgere altro che quella parte che è direttamente allumata, o per forza di riflessi, all'incontro del lume; il che avviene nei metalli et altri corpi lustri e chiari." Lomazzo, *Trattato*, 194.

11 "Maniera forte, o gagliarda; è di quel Pittore, che a forza di profondi scuri, e vivi chiari, con mezze tinte appropriate, fa spiccare, e molto relevare le sue figure sopra il piano della tavola." Baldinucci, *Vocabolario*, 88.

12 See for example Leonardo's definition of painting: "La pittura è tenuta arte eccellente, cioè del far rilevare quel ch'è nulla in rilievo.... Solo la pittura si rende ai contemplatori di quella per far parere rilevato e spiccato dai muri quel che non lo è...il quale rilievo è l'importanza e l'anima della pittura." Da Vinci, *Trattato*, [56], [120], [121], 38, 56, 57. On *rilievo* as a categorical term in art theory see Freedman, "'Rilievo.'"

13 De Piles, "De la disposition," 112.

14 Ibid., 115.

15 De Piles, *Dialogue*, 13.

16 Félibien *Entretiens*, [*preface*], vol. 1, 85.

17 Ibid.

18 Ibid.

19 Félibien, *Entretiens*, vol. 3, 15.

20 "Nel disegno non v'erano gli estremi del fine suo, perché, se bene e' facevano un braccio tondo et una gamba diritta, non era ricerca con muscoli con quella facilità graziosa e dolce che apparisce fra 'l vedi e non vedi, come fanno la carne e le cose vive; ma elle erano crude e scorticate, che faceva difficoltà agli occhi e durezza nella maniera, alla quale mancava una leggiadria di fare svelte e graziose tutte le figure, e massimamente le femmine et i putti con le membra naturali come agli uomini, ma ricoperte di quelle grassezze e carnosità che non siano goffe come li naturali, ma arteficiate dal disegno e dal giudizio." Vasari, *Vite*, vol. 5, 12.

21 Vasari, *Vite*, vol. 6, 159, 162, 164, 166.

22 Vasari, *Vite*, vol. 6, 156. See also Sohm, *Pittoresco*, 107.

23 "C'est, répondit Pamphile, qu'ils commencent par où il faut finir; ils se jettent dans le Coloris avant que d'être suffisamment fondez dans le Dessein, & que l'ignorance de celuy-cy les embarassant dans la pratique de l'autre, fait qu'ils n'en attrapent pas un. C'est encore parce que les jeunes gens ayant pris d'abord une méchante maniere, ils s'en font une habitude, dont, pour l'ordinaire, ils ne se retirent jamais. Ils n'ont pour modeles que les Ouvrages de leurs Maîtres & ceux qui sont publics; ils estiment naturellement les premiers, & se nourissent insensiblement l'esprit par la veuë des autres. Et cela se fait avec d'autant plus de facilité, que ces ouvrages sont les objets qui se presentent les premiers à leurs yeux & à leur esprit. C'est enfin cette premiere liqueur, laquelle étant mise dans un vaisseau tout neuf, y communique tellement son odeur, que quoy qu'on puisse faire pour l'en ôter, elle y demeure treslong-temps." De Piles, *Dialogue*, 53–54.

24 De Piles, *Dialogue*, 47.

25 Vasari, *Vite*, vol. 6, 166.

26 Boschini, *La carta del navegar pitoresco*, 712. See also Sohm, *Pittoresco*, 117.

27 Boschini, *La carta del navegar pitoresco*, 327f.

28 Vasari, *Vite*, vol. 6, 166.

29 Boschini, *La carta del navegar pitoresco*, 711f. Full quotation in the next note.

30 "Altre volte con una pennellata di biacca, con lo stesso pennello, tinto di rossi, di nero e di giallo, formava il rilievo d'un chiaro, e con queste massime di Dottrina faceva comparire in quattro pennellate la promessa d'una rara figura, e in ogni modo questi simili abbozzi satollavano i più intendenti, di modo che da molti erano così desiderati, per tramontana di vedere il modo di ben incaminarsi ad entrare nel Pelago della Pittura." Ibid.

31 The painting came into Philip II's possession in 1562. See Goffen, *Titian's Women*, 267–273; Fehl, *Decorum and Wit*, 88. The following is a shortened version of the chapter "Manu-factur: Velázquez' Hommage an Titian," in Suthor, *Augenlust*, 165–187.

32 Other copies after Titian made by Rubens include *Diana and Actaeon*, *Venus and Adonis*, *Venus and Cupid*, *Adam and Eve*, etc. See Pacheco, *El Arte de la Pintura*, vol. 1, 153.

33 See Perez Sanchez, "Presencia de Tiziano," 141, 146ff.; Mena Marques, "Titian, Rubens, and Spain," 72.

34 "Y nuestro Filipo III, siguiendo el exemplo de su padre y abuelo, cuando se quemó la casa del Pardo, ano de 1604, donde perecieron en el fuego muchas pinturas originales, sólo preguntó por un cuadro de Ticiano, diciendo que importaba poco que se quemase lo demás." Pacheco, *El Arte dela Pintura*, vol. l, 107.

35 Brown and Garrido, *Velázquez*, 195. Later additions

to the canvas along the upper margin and both sides are not shown in the illustration.

36 Justi, *Diego Velázquez*, 428.

37 See e.g., Angulo Iniguez, "Las Hilanderas."

38 Ovid, *Metamorphoses* [book 6], vol. 1, 297.

39 See for instance a similar conception, Velázquez's costumed "Mars," which, following Caravaggio's example, looks like a live model because essential signs of fictionality are missing.

40 See Justi's comment: "At first glance the picture in the background might be taken for some theatrical performance." Justi, *Velázquez*, 428.

41 Bach, "Metamorphosen Ovids in Velázquez Malerei," 49f.

42 See also Moffitt, "Painting, music and poetry," 78.

43 Ibid.

44 Ovid, *Metamophoses* [book 6], vol. 1, 291.

45 Perez Sanchez, "Presencia de Tiziano," 145.

46 Palomino, *El museo pictórico*, 893. See also McKim-Smith, *Examining Velázquez*, 23.

47 Palomino, *El museo pictórico*, 913.

48 "Hizole con pinceles, y brochas, que tenía de astas largas, de que usaba algunas veces, para pintar con mayor distancia, y valentía; de suerte, que de cerca no se comprendía, y de lejos es un milagro." Palomino, *El museo pictórico*, 905.

49 Boschini, *La carta del navegar pitoresco*, 75f.

50 Ibid., 76f.

51 Ibid., 77. See also Marques, "Titian, Rubens, and Spain," 72.

52 Boschini, *La carta del navegar pitoresco*, 79.

53 See Nebrija's *Vocabulario* published in 1492, where *borron* is derived from *borra*, and the verb *borror* is translated as "to wipe off," "to blot out." Cited in McKim-Smith, *Examining Velázquez*, 17.

54 Bach, "Metamorphosen Ovids in Velázquez Malerei," 56.

55 "Otra objeción más fuerte que la primera, es afirmar que la pintura a borrones, hecha para de lexos, tiene su particular artificio y acuerdo, en los que la exercitan bien; y tiene mayor fuerza y relievo que la acabada y suave. Tambien ponen otra fortísima, que parece imposible impugnarla, con el exemplo de Ticiano, uno de los más excelentes coloridores que ha tenido Italia, y cabeza de la Academia Veneciana, y casi de todos confesado por el mayor; pues se tiene por adagio cuando la pintura no es acabada, llamarla 'borrones de Ticiano,' con que se califica sumamente este camino." Pacheco, *El Arte dela Pintura*, vol. 1, 478. See also Marques, "Titian, Rubens, and Spain," 73.

56 McKim-Smith, *Examining Velázquez*, 15–27.

57 According to McKim-Smith, the sermon was printed in 1638, so Velázquez certainly could have been aware of it. McKim-Smith, *Examining Velázquez*, 22.

58 "Pues no mirada a su luz una tabla de Ticiano, no es mäs que una batalla de borrones, un golpe de arreboles mal asombrados. Y vista a la luz que se pintó, es una admirable y valiente uniön de colores, una animosa pintura que aun sobre autos de vista de los ojos, pone pleytos a la verdad." Cited in McKim-Smith, *Examining Velázquez*, 137, n. 111. First printed in Perez Sanchez, "Presencia de Tiziano," 144f.

59 "Y por ti el gran Velázquez ha podido, diestro, cuanto ingenioso, ansi animar lo hermoso, ansi dar a lo mórbido sentido con las manchas distantes; que son verdad en el, no semejantes." Cited in McKim-Smith, *Examining Velázquez*, 17.

60 Ovid, *Metamorphoses* [book 6], vol. 1, 289–291.

61 Brown & Garrido, *Velázquez*, 199–200.

62 Alpers, *The Vexations of Art*, 146.

63 Palomino, *El museo pictórico*, 900–901.

64 Moffitt, "Painting, Music, and Poetry," 78, 76. According to Moffitt the string instrument emblematically supports, in line with the ladder leaning on the wall next to it, the idea of the "scala sapientis" evoked, as already mentioned, in the steepness of the steps.

65 De Hollanda, *Quatro Dialogos*, 17, 39.

66 Ibid., 11.

67 Palomino, *El museo pictórico*, 895.

68 "Talche siano tinti e carichi di corpo—si come usavano di fare già alcuni pittori—, il disegno ne viene ad essere offeso di maniera che le figure restano più presto dipinte dal colore, che dal pennello." Vasari, *Vite*, vol. 1, 124f.

69 Ibid., 126.

70 "Pero, bien sabemos que la excelencia y ventaja de la pintura a olio es poderse retocar muchas veces, como hacía Ticiano. Otros labran el bosquexo y, al acabado, usan de borrones, queriendo mostrar que obran con más destreza y facilidad que los demás y costándoles esto mucho trabajo lo dissimulan con este artificio, porque?" Pacheco, *El Arte dela Pintura*, vol. 2, 78–79. "Esta parte tuvo Ticiano, come tan grande artifice, y sus borrones no se toman en el sentido que suenan, que mejor se dirian golpes dados en el lugar que conviene, con gran destreza." Pacheco, *El Arte dela Pintura*, vol. 1, 480. See also Boschini: "Veramente là bate tuto el ponto De intender el mestier con gran giudicio; E che'l Pitor possieda l'artificio; E con el so cervel tegnirlo sconto. Ghe xe tanti balordi che se pensa, Che quei colpi sia fati in pressa in pressa; E si ghe xe la diligenza istessa, E forsi fati con fadiga imensa. La vede se in quei colpi gh'e pacienza, Che un omo tuta la so vita mena Con molta

assiduità tra studio e pena, Per arivar a quela inteligenza." Boschini, *La carta del navegar pitoresco*, 86–87.

71 On Goya's version of the exchange of gender roles in *Hercules and Omphale* as one of the motifs for the "world turned upside down," see Stoichita and Coderch, *Goya*, 38ff.

72 "The scene suggests a sophistical joke, a puzzle picture painted to amuse a patron, or perhaps the artist himself." Wilson-Bareau and Marqués, *Goya*, 154.

73 Manuela B. Mena Marqués identifies the Hercules figure as Manuel Godoy, who met Maria Teresa in 1784. Rumors that they were having a love affair were a contemporary topic of speculation. In (exh. cat.) *Goya*, cat. no. 10, 58.

74 Wilson-Bareau and Mena Marqués identify the standing figure as Omphale. Wilson-Bareau and Mena Marqués, *Goya*, 154.

75 Águeda, "Sul Rapporto tra Mengs e Goya," 22.

CHAPTER EIGHT: ENDANGERING THE YOUTH

1 "Anzi presso alcuni sistima, haver' esso rovinata la pittura, poiché molti giovani ad esempio di lui si danno ad imitare una testa del naturale, e non studiando ne'fondamenti del disegno, e della profondità dell'arte, solamente del colorito appagansi; onde non sanno mettere due figure insieme, nè tessere historia veruna, per non comprendere la bontà di sì nobil arte." Baglione, *Vite*, 138. It should be mentioned that at this time Giovanni Baglione was the target of Caravaggio's withering criticism and he felt physically threatened by him; he even sued Caravaggio in court for slander. Caravaggio responded during his examination that Baglione's *Resurrection of Christ* for the Il Gesù Church in Rome was "absurd"; he furthermore stated he knew of not one single painter who considered Baglione a good artist. In the trial documents from September 13, 1603, Caravaggio gives his definition of good art: "Quella parola valent'huomo appresso di me vuol dire che sappi far bene, cioè sappi far bene dell'arte sua così in pittura valent'huomo che sappi depingere bene et imitar bene le cose naturali." Macioce, *Michelangelo Merisi da Caravaggio* [*I DOC 145, ASR, TCG, Processi, sec. XVII, Vol. 28Bis, cc. 398v-401r*], 127–128; see also [*II DOC 309/b*], 208.

2 "Diedesi a voler' imitare la maniera del Caravaggio, & abbandonare gli studii, che l'haverebbono fatto eccellente maestro, si come anche ad altri è succeduto." Baglione, *Vite*, 146.

3 "Sur les Ouvrages de Michelange de Caravage. Les Idées du Caravage ressemblent à son tempérament, elles étoient fort inégales, & jamais fort élevées. Ses Dispositions étoient bonnes, son Dessein d'un méchant Goût, & il n'en savoit pas assez pour bien choisir, ou pour bien corriger la Nature. Toute son application étoit dans le Colorit & et il y a merveilleusement réüssi." De Piles, *Abregé*, 342f.

4 "Deve molto questa età a Michelangelo da Caravaggio, per il colorir che ha introdotto, seguito adesso assai communemente." Mancini, *Considerazioni*, vol. 1, 223.

5 See Scott, *Salvator Rosa*, 5.

6 Bellori, *Lives*, 180; Bellori, *Vite*, 203.

7 Bellori, *Lives*, 181.

8 Mancini, *Considerazioni*, 108f.

9 Bellori, *Lives*, 180.

10 Ibid., 185.

11 Ibid., 180.

12 Bellori, *Vite*, 201; Bellori *Lives*, 179.

13 See Morselli, "La fortuna critica," 32.

14 The correspondence between Manfredi's *Midas* and Caravaggio has been repeatedly noted. See for example, Papi, *Bartolomeo Manfredi*, cat. no. 22, 162; Nicole Hartje, *Bartolomeo Manfredi*, 118.

15 Bellori, *Vite*, 207: "Nella Chiesa della Madonna del Popolo entro la Cappella dell'Assunta dipinta da Annibale Carracci, sono di mano del Caravaggio li due quadri laterali, la Crocifissione di San Pietro, e la Conversione di San Paolo, la quale historia è affatto senza attione." See Pericolo, *Caravaggio*, 257.

16 Cherubino Alberti, after Taddeo Zuccari, *The Conversion of Saint Paul*, etching, 46.5 × 34 cm, Rijksmuseum, Amsterdam.

17 See Pericolo, *Caravaggio*, 257–259

18 Marcia Hall, *The Sacred Image*, 253.

19 Friedlaender, *Caravaggio Studies*, 7.

20 Pericolo, *Caravaggio*, 262.

21 "The model for the horse, Duerer's Large Horse, the most phlegmatic animal Caravaggio could have found, would not dream of rearing or running away even in the face of startling lights and sounds." Friedlaender, *Caravaggio Studies*, 28.

22 Bardon, *Caravage*, 108.

23 Von Sandrart, *Teutsche Academie*, vol. 1, part 2, book 2, 189. The "taking up" of Saint Paul mentioned here by von Sandrart seems to be a misremembering of the painting.

24 Paleotti, *Discourse on Sacred and Profane Images* [book 1, chap. 1: "The main intention of the present treatise concerning the abuse of images"], 57.

25 Paleotti, *Discourse on Sacred and Profane Images* [book 1, chap. 32: "Whether the same cult is owed to a sacred image as the cult suitable to its 'imaged' prototype, and whether this is a single act, and how"], 136–137.

26 Friedlaender, *Caravaggio Studies*, 28.

27 Ibid., 31.

28 "We look straight into the lower right angle, so that by a curious trompe l'oeil the transverse bar on which the left arm of St. Peter is nailed, appears to be almost a continuation of the main bar, which is covered with his body." Friedlaender, *Caravaggio Studies*, 32.

29 Bardon, *Caravage ou l'expérience de la matière*, 102.

30 "En nuestros tiempos se levantò en Roma Michael Angelo de Carabaggio, en el Pontificado del Papa Clemente VIII. con nuevo plato, con tal modo, y salsa guisado, con tanto sabor, apetito y gusto, que pienso se ha llevado el de todos con tanta golosina y licencia, que temo en ellos alguna apoplexia en la verdadera doctrina: porque le siguen glotonicamente el mayor golpe de los Pintores, no reparando si el calor de su natural (que es su ingenio) es tan poderoso, ò tiene la actividad que el del otro, para poder digerir simple tan recio, ignoto, è incompatible modo, como es el obrar sin las preparaciones para tal accion? Quien pintò jamas y llegò a hazer tan bien como este monstruo de ingenio, y natural, casi hizo sin preceptos, sin doctrina, sin estudio, mas solo con la fuerça de su genio, y con el natural delante, a quien simplemente imitava con tanta admiracion?" Carducho, *Diálogos*, 89–90. Due to Caravaggio's affected and superficial imitation ("con su afectada y exterior imitacion"), which "turns its back on the true way to make itself everlasting" (que han buelto las espaldas al verdadero modo de eternizarse), Vicente Carducho concludes by designating the artist as the "AnteMichaelAngel."

31 De Piles, *Abregé*, 466.

32 Perrault, *Les hommes illustres*, 90.

33 De Piles, *Abregé*, 466, 467, 468.

34 De' Dominici, *Vite*, vol. 3, S. 3.

35 Bellori, *Lives*, 185.

36 Félibien *Entretiens*, vol. 3, 194.

37 Dézallier d'Argenville, *Abrégé*, vol. 1, 260.

38 Bellori, *Lives*, 184.

39 Orlandi, *Abecedario*, 76.

40 Dézallier d'Argenville, *Abrégé*, vol. 1, 374.

41 Strinati, "Pittore bravissimo," 59.

42 Others classified by Giustiniani as working "di maniera" were Barocci, Romanelli, and Passignano. On Vincenzo Giustiniani, see Haskell, *Patrons and Painters*, 94–95; and Cropper and Dempsey, *Nicolas Poussin*, 64–105.

43 Giustiniani, *Discorso*, 43.

44 Félibien, *Entretiens*, vol. 3, 289.

45 Van Mander, *Appunti*, 196f.

46 Ibid., 196.

47 See Baglione, *Vite*, 368. See also Judges 16:3.

48 It makes sense to read this explosive potential as a "preview" of Sampson's final act of strength: "Then Samson reached toward the two central pillars on which the temple stood. Bracing himself against them, his right hand on the one and his left hand on the other, Samson said, 'Let me die with the Philistines!' Then he pushed with all his might, and down came the temple on the rulers and all the people in it. Thus he killed many more when he died than while he lived." Judges 16:29–30.

49 Röttgen, *Il Cavalier Giuseppe Cesari d'Arpino*, 8.

50 Bellori, *Vite*, 20.

51 Ibid., 3–13. See Gründler, "Gloriarsi della mano e dell'ingegno."

52 Félibien, *Entretiens*, vol. 3, 248.

53 See (exhib. cat.) Manning and Manning. *The Genovese Renaissance*, fig. 18, 43.

54 "Fu un certo Luchetto da Genova, il quale al mio tempo dipingeva in San Mateo... egli dipinge con tutte due le mani, tenendo un pennello per mano pien di colore e si vede esser tanto esperto e rissoluto, che fa le opere sue con incredibil prestezza.... Simile fare è quasi quello di Giacomo Tintoretto veneziano." Armenini, *De' veri precetti*, 133, 134.

55 Ridolfi, *Le Maraviglie dell'arte*, vol. 2, 253.

56 Van Mander, *Lives*, 370; see also Galley, *De l'original à l'excentrique*; Warnke, "Der Kopf in der Hand," 58.

57 Galley, "Cornelis Ketel," 89.

58 De' Dominici, *Vite*, vol. 3, 426.

59 Vasari, *Vite*, vol. 5,15.

60 Van Mander, *Lives*, 370.

61 Pliny the Younger, *Letters*, vol. 2, book 9, chap. XXVI, 129. The letter is cited in Junius *De pictura veterum*, 249f. See also Cropper, *The Ideal of Painting*, 165.

62 Watelet and Lévesque, *Dictionnaire*, vol. 3, entry: Lévesque, "Main," 365f, "Manœuvre," 379.

63 Watelet and Lévesque, *Dictionnaire*, vol. 3, entry: Lévesque, "Manœuvre."

64 Von Sandrart, *Teutsche Academie*, vol. 1, part. 1, book 3, 89.

65 "Ma che poi in ultimo fu da lui stesso conosciuta e confessata necessaria pratica e fon- damento, prima d'ingolfarsi al dipingere, per non caminar poi sempre al buio e a tentone." Malvasia, *Felsina pittrice*, vol. 2, 67.

66 Alberti, *On Painting*, 97.

67 Leonardo, *Trattato*, [77.], 45.

68 Boschini, *La carta del navegar pitoresco*, 187.

69 Von Sandrart, *Teutsche Academie*, vol. 1, part 1, book 3, 66–67.

70 "A dire il vero non evea sodisfatto il Testa con questa sua opera il gusto de' Professori, e quella bravura, che mostrava colla penna, e collo stile, si convertiva in altrettanta feddaturo nel pennelli, e nel colore." Passeri, *Vite*, 182.

71 Alberti, *On Painting*, 93.

72 "Quelle arti che più partecipano delle mattematiche

sono più nobili perché hopera[no] con più vere ragioni." Quoted in Cropper, *The Ideal of Painting*, 229.

73 Quoted in Cropper, *The Ideal of Painting*, 206.

74 Cropper, *The Ideal of Painting*, 229.

75 "VOLONTÀ... sarà cieca, sporgendo ambedue le mani avanti una più dell'altra in atto di volersi appigliare ad una cosa.... La cecità le conviene, perche non vedondo per se stessa cosa alcuna, và quasi tentone dietro al senso, se è debole, & ignobile, ò dietro alla ragione, se è gagliarda, & di prezzo." Ripa, *Iconologia*, vol. 2, 249–250.

76 Dürer, *Schriftlicher Nachlass*, vol. 3, 297.

77 "Aber so du kein rechten grund hast, so ist es nit müglich, das du etwas gerechtz vnnd gutz machst, vnd ob du gleych den grösten gebrauch der welt hettest in freyheyt der hand. Dann es ist mer ein gefencknus, so sie dich verfürt. Darumb sol kein freyheit on kunst, so ist die Kunst verborgen on den gebrauch. Darumb muß es bey einander sein, wie oben gesagt." Ibid.

78 Du Fresnoy, *De l'art de peinture*, 7.

79 Ibid.

80 Ibid., 20.

81 Ibid., 68.

CHAPTER NINE: THE ACADEMIC RESPONSE

1 Coypel, "Commentaire," [Discours I: Les fautes des grands hommes] 72–75.

2 Coypel, "Commentaire," [Discours III: Ce qu'on appelle le pinceau, en quoi consiste la plus excellente pratique de la peinture, 82–89] 83.

3 "Cette habitude de la main, qu'on l'appelle parmi les peintres le pinceau, s'acquiert par la pratique, mais quand cette pratique est dénuée de la partie de l'esprit, elle est assez commune et souvent plus pernicieuse qu'utile." Ibid.

4 Coypel, "Commentaire," 84.

5 Coypel buttresses Molière's pithy statement by citing another proverb: Horace's "Festina lente." Coypel, "Commentaire," 85.

6 Coypel, "Commentaire," 83.

7 Montaiglon, *Procès-verbaux*, vol. 6, 205f.

8 The head added by Coypel was retouched in 1830. See Gould, *The Paintings of Correggio*, 194f. (with sources).

9 "Le Corrège dis-je, trouva des charmes dans le maniment de la brosse; il prenoit plaisir à empâter, à fondre, & savourait l'amusement *de se perdre & de se retrouver* dans la couleur sans se rendre esclave des formes, ni s'occuper de leur choix. Un *pinceau* si hardi, *si amou- reux*, si caressant, communiqua le plaisir & l'ivresse dont son auteur savoit sûrement jouir, à tous ceux qui virent ses ouvrages." Watelet and Lévesque, *Dictionnaire*, vol. 5, entry: Robin, Pinceau, S. 64.

10 De Caylus, "De la légèrté de l'outil," 149.

11 De Piles, *Dialogue*, 59.

12 "L'exemple du Dominquin nous doit suffire. Grand, précis pour le dessin, et moins touché de la couleur, la légèrté de l'outil ne l'a point affecté." De Caylus, "De la légèrté de l'outil," 152.

13 Desportes, "Sur l'utilité des conférences," 120.

14 Bellori, *Lives*, 239.

15 Ibid.

16 "L'étude de leurs ouvrages me persuaderait que la légèreté d'outil n'excède point la superficie, qu'elle est cette dernière touche qui fait le plus d'impression sur l'esprit du spectateur, celle qui le séduit et, dans ce dernier cas, elle est la dernière main de la facilité dont elle est dependant.... Enfin la légèreté d'outil me paraît le dernier degré de ces parties essentielles." De Caylus, "De la légèrté de l'outil," 152.

17 Zanetti, *Descrizione*, 11.

18 "Tiziano era solito di condurre le cose sue con grande accuratezza ed amore; ma condotte che l'aveva presso a lor fine, dava loro sopra aleuni colpi, come noi diremmo strapazzati,e questo faceva per coprire la fatica, e farle parere più maestrevoli."Baldinucci, *Notizie*, 264.

19 De Caylus, "De la légèrté de l'outil," 157.

20 "Les tableaux de ce maître sont dignes d'admiration: mais l'imitation en pourroit être dangereuse." Michel, *Le Voyage d'Italie*, 354. It is interesting to note that for Sebastiano Ricci, Raphael's style was dangerous. Pierre-Jean Mariette reports that after Ricci began studying Raffael's frescoes, he immediately wanted to return to Venice: "Disant que la manière de ce grand homme étoit capable de corrompre la sienne." Mariette, *Abecedario*, vol. 4, 393.

21 "Si aggiunse circa a questi tempi un costume di lavorare con certa sprezzatura, come alcuni lo chiamano, e la commendano nel Giordano e in alcuni veneti. Si provarono in Firenze ancora vari maestri ad imitargli, e fecer opere che sentono dell'abbozzo." This critique refers to the school of the Dandini family, which Luigi Lanzi examines in his book, in its section on the "fifth epoch." See Lanzi, *Storia pittorica*, vol. 1, 195.

22 *Il newtonianismo per le dame ovvero dialoghi sopra la luce e i colori.* (1737, German transl. 1745).

23 Algarotti, *Saggio*, 52.

24 Massé, "Connaître l'antique et l'anatomie," 390, 401.

25 Coypel, in: Montaiglon, *Procès-verbaux*, vol. 6, 215.

26 "Il me reste à faire quelques réflexions sur les dangers que préparent aux jeunes artistes les attraits de ce genre de composition. La marche ordinaire de l'art de la peinture est telle que le temps de la jeunesse, qui doit être destiné à l'exercice fréquent des parties de la pratique de l'art, est celui dans lequel il semble qu'on soit plus porté

aux charmes qui naissent de la partie de l'esprit. C'est en effet pendant le cours de cet âge que l'imagination s'echauffe aisément. C'est la saison de l'enthousiasme, c'est le moment où l'on est impatient de produire, enfin c'est l'âge des *esquisses*; aussi rien de plus ordinaire dans les jeunes élèves, que le desir & la facilité de produire des *esquisses* de composition, & rien de si dangereux pour eux que de se livrer avec trop d'ardeur à ce penchant. L'indecision dans l'ordonnance, l'incorrection dans le dessin, l'aversion de terminer, en sont ordinairement la suite, & le danger est d'autant plus grand, qu'on est presque certain de séduire par ce genre de composition libre, dans lequel le spectateur exige peu & se charge d'ajouter à l'aide de son imagination tout ce qui y manque. Il arrive de-là que les défauts prennent le nom de beautés. En effet que le trait par lequel on indique les figures d'une *esquisse* soit outré, on y croit démêler une intention hardie & une expression mâle; que l'ordonnance soit confuse & chargée, on s'imagine y voir briller le feu d'une imagination féconde & intarissable." Watelet and Lévesque, *Dictionnaire*, vol. 2, entry: Watelet, *Esquisse*, 208.

27 Vasari, *Lives*, 417f.

28 Vasari, *Lives*, 362. See also Held, "The Early Appreciation of Drawings," 86.

29 This understanding of the sketch as an expression of artistic inspiration or frenzy is found as a note in Vasari's vita of Luca della Robbia: "La sperienza fa conoscere che tutte le cose che vanno lontane—o siano pitture o siano sculture o qualsivoglia altra somigliante cosa—hanno più fierezza e maggior forza se sono una bella bozza che se son finite; et oltre che la lontananza fa questo effetto, pare anco che nelle bozze molte volte, nascendo in un sùbito dal furore dell'arte, si sprima il suo concetto in pochi colpi, e che per contrario lo stento e la troppa diligenza alcuna fiata toglia la forza et il sapere a coloro che non sanno mai levare le mani dall'opera che fanno." Vasari, *Vite*, vol. 3, 51f. The passage concerns Donatello's cantoria, whose illusionistic effect in comparison to Robbia's is more convincing. Vasari takes up this argument again in the vita of Palma il Vecchio: "Per la quale opera merita Iacopo Palma grandissima lode e di esser annoverato fra quegli che posseggono l'arte et hanno in poter loro facoltà d'esprimere nelle pitture le difficoltà dei loro concetti, con ciò sia che in simili cose difficili a molti pittori vien fatto nel primo abbozzare l'opera, come guidati da un certo forore, qualche cosa di buono e qualche fierezza, che vien poi levata nel finire, e tolto via quel buono che vi aveva posto il furore." Vasari, *Vite*, vol. 4, 551.

30 See also Claude Henri Watelet's entry "Esquisse" in Watelet and Lévesque, *Dictionnaire des arts de peinture, sculpture et gravure*, according to which the spirit inevitably loses its fire through the tediousness of the means it is forced to employ in order to express and preserve its ideas. Watelet & Lévesque, *Dictionnaire*, vol. 2, entry: Watelet, *Esquisse*, 204.

31 "Ce grand feu fait qu'en général le *Tintoretto* est moins admirable quand il est plus fini; son imagination se refroidit pendant le temps de l'exécution; & comme il n'a pas la correction du dessein, & le sçavoir de détail, qui est la perfection de l'exécution finie, il lui reste peu de beautés." Cochin, *Le Voyage d'Italie*, 343; see also Ivanoff 1966.

32 Félibien, *Entretiens*, vol. 2, 187.

33 Watelet and Lévesque, *Dictionnaire*, vol. 2, entry: Lévesque, "Feu," 275.

34 Ibid.

35 In one of his lectures, Reynolds described the steps a "clever imitator" would need to take to study coloring: After the student has analyzed compositional layout, the placement of chiaroscuro, the interplay between advancing and receding elements in the pictorial ground, and the inner logic of the color arrangements, he should then be able to more closely examine the juxtaposition of tones in the paints. From this method of imitation and intensive study, the painter will be able to develop their own principles. Reynolds's demand that imitation be governed by reason and divided into stages, each of which operates according to different artistic perspectives, does not belie the fact that coloring is the portion of art that cannot be translated from the example of a single work to a discretionary set of rules. Coloring was therefore never part of the academic training program—completely in contrast to drawing, which is the medium for studying nature or the art of antiquity.

36 Reynolds, *Discourses*, 151.

37 Du Fresnoy, *De l'art de peinture*, 68.

38 Reynolds, *Discourses*, 17.

39 Ibid., 43.

40 Ibid., 18.

41 Ibid., 64.

42 Ibid., 67.

43 Ibid., 63.

44 Ibid., 64.

45 Füssli, *Lectures on Painting*, vol. 1, 231.

46 "I say in part, for Tiziano perhaps never, Paolo and Tintoretto, though by much too often, yet not always, spread the enchanting nosegay, which is the characteristic of this style, with indiscriminate hand.... But perhaps it is not to Tiziano, but to Tintoretto and Paolo Cagliari, that the debaucheries of Colour and blind submission to fascinating tints, the rage of scattering flowers to no purpose, are ascribed." Füssli, *Lectures on Painting*, vol. 1, 231f.

47 Füssli, *Lectures on Painting*, vol. 1, 66.

48 Ibid., 66f.

49 Ibid., 186.

50 Reynolds, *Discourses*, 215f.

51 See Constable's letter from May 29, 1802, to Dunthorne, in Leslie. *Constable*, 40.

52 Reynolds, *Discourses*, 18.

53 Ibid., 191.

54 On the inferiority complex of nineteenth-century English artists vis-à-vis their French colleagues, see *Ausstellungskünstler*, 48.

55 Reynolds, *Discourses*, 224.

56 "C'est une bergère debout, qui tient d'une main une couronne, et qui porte de l'autre un panier de fleurs: elle est arrêtée devant un berger assis à terre, son chien à ses pieds. Que'est- ce que cela dit? Rien." *Salons*, vol. 2, 82.

57 "Cet homme est la ruine de tous les jeunes élèves en peinture.... Ils n'en ont que les défauts." Diderot, *Salons*, vol. 1, 205.

58 The identification of the child as Boucher is purely speculative because we have no other image of Boucher as a child to prove it, but Melissa Hyde points out evidence that goes beyond questions of similarity and is related to the structure of the image: The colors on the palette, matching not the landscape but the boy, and the identification of the landscape as a *paysage Boucher* speak for a self-portrait with a fictional element. Hyde, "Getting into the Picture," 17–19. For a more guarded view see Aspinwall et al., *Boucher 1703–1770* [cat. no. 22], 150: "We cannot, however, deduce from this that the figure of the artist is a self-portrait, since he is patently a young student, whereas Boucher would have been around thirty at the time this was painted."

59 See for example Restout, *Charles-Nicolas Cochin*, vol. 1, 133f.; Hyde, "Getting into the Picture," 21.

60 Watelet and Lévesque, *Dictionnaire*, vol. 3, entry: Watelet, "Manièré," 375.

61 Diderot, *Salons*, vol. 4, 67, 68.

62 Reynolds, *Discourses*, 225.

63 Diderot, *Salons*, vol. 1, 112.

64 Goncourt and Goncourt, *L'Art du XVIIIe siècle*, vol. 1, 209.

65 Ibid., 218.

66 Reynolds, *Discourses*, 18.

67 Ibid., 18.

68 Marigny in a letter to Charles-Joseph Natoire, October 11, 1759, in Montaiglon, *Correspondance des directeurs*, vol. 11, 313.

69 Goncourt and Goncourt, *L'Art du XVIIIe siècle*, vol. 3, 214.

70 "On a de lui, dans ce genre, des tours de force, des merveilles, des figures où il se revèle comme un prodigieux Fa presto. On voit dans la galerie La Caze quatre portraits de grandeur naturelle à mi-corps. Au dos de l'un je lis ceci écrit, me semble-t-il de sa main: Portrait de M. de La Bretèche, peint par Fragonard en 1769, en une heure de temps." Goncourt and Goncourt, *L'Art du XVIIIe siècle*, vol. 3, 246.

71 Ibid.

72 See Rosenberg, *Fragonard*, cat. no. 133, 276. On the *Portraits de Fantaisie* as a group see also Ashton, *Fragonard*, 117–133.

73 This process-centered attitude is qualified as "heroic *franchezza*" in the vita of Alessandro Magnasco (1667–1749): "Egli aveva in ciò una franchezza sì prode, ed una non curanza sì particolare; che talvolta lasciava scoperta ne'quadri l'imprimitura, e in alcuni luoghi facea servire al suo bisogno la tinta di quella." Ratti, *Vite*, vol. 2, 157.

74 Here I follow Mary D. Sheriff's interpretation: "While pondering this masquerade, however, we recognize the artist as the real hero of these portraits. This realization clarifies the persistent questions because we understand that their posing is part of Fragonard's invention, his ability to play cleverly with traditions, conventions, and definitions of genre." Sheriff, "Invention, Resemblance," 84.

75 See Sheriff, "Invention, Resemblance," 86.

76 Thuillier, *Fragonard*, 87.

77 Rosenberg, *Fragonard*, 282 (cat. no. 136).

CHAPTER TEN: REENACTMENTS AND ECHOES

1 "Le détail, il l'a en horreur, et c'est dans une belle pâte fluide et rutilante qu'il noie les traits de ses modèles par un large maniement de pinceau." Portalis, *Honoré Fragonard*, 132.

2 "C'est du Franz [*sic*] Hals enragé!" Ibid.

3 "Gy moet maar stout toesmeeren: als gy vast in de Konst wort zal de neitheit van zelf welkomen." Houbraken, *De groote schouburgh*, vol. 2, 165.

4 Houbraken, *De groote schouburgh*, vol. 3, 193.

5 For an in-depth analysis of this painting, see Slive, "On the Meaning of Frans Hals' 'Malle Babbe'"; Von Zitzewitz, *Frans Hals: Malle Babbe*.

6 "Nu moet 'er het kennelyke van den meester noch in." Houbraken, *De groote schouburgh*, vol. 1, 73. On Hals's virtuosity of the brushstroke see Atkins, "Frans Hals's Virtuoso Brushwork," esp. 286.

7 Bürger, "Frans Hals," 438. Theophile Thoré's most important art-historical achievement is the discovery of Jan Vermeer.

8 Bürger, "Frans Hals," 439.

9 Fromentin, *Les Maîtres autrefois*, 251f.

10 "Un sentiment subit de la substance des choses, une mesure sans la moindre erreur, l'art d'être précis sans trop

expliquer, de tout faire comprendre à demi-mots, . . . le mot juste, et rien que le mot juste, trouvé du premier coup . . . Jamais on n'a mieux peint, on ne peindra pas mieux." Fromentin, *Les Maîtres autrefois*, 255.

11 De Hollanda, *On Antique Painting*, 180.

12 Alpers, *Art of Describing*.

13 Cited after Held, "Goyas Akademiekritik," 214.

14 "Toutes les règles, tous les canons de l'art vomissent la mort. . . ." Ensor, *Mes Écrits*, 127.

15 Gilot and Lake, *Life with Picasso*, 74–75.

16 "Je n'ignore pas que la tornade Picasso représente un danger pour la jeunesse." Cocteau, *Picasso*, 85.

17 Parmelin on Picasso: "It was during this period that he declared himself ready to kill modern art, and thus art itself, in order to rediscover painting." Parmelin, *Picasso says*, 84.

18 "Les pommes de Cézanne, était aussi une painture de bataille. Une ligne, une couleur, un tableau, une perpétuelle bataille." Verdet, *Entretiens*, 139.

19 "Je n'étais pas seul à avoir subi le choc. Une bataille à livre contre une grande partie de notre savoir, de ce que nous avions tendance a respecter, à admirer, à aimer. . . . Il a balayé la peinture de l'idée de maîtrise. . . . Il nous a ouvert le goût du risque." Verdet, *Entretiens*, 16, 12.

20 Steinberg, "Resisiting Cezanne," 124.

21 Flam, *Matisse on Art*, 213.

22 Picasso's sketchbook: *Barcelona Carnet 1917*.

23 Jaime Sabartés, in Bernadac and Michael, *Picasso*, 166.

Bibliography

Adorno, Theodor W. *Ästhetische Theorie.* Frankfurt: Suhrkamp, 1970.

———. *Quasi Una Fantasia: Essays on Modern Music*, translated by Rodney Livingstone. London: Verso, 2002.

Agrippa, Camillo. *Trattato di scienza d'arme et un dialogo in detta materia.* Venice, 1604.

———. *Fencing: A Renaissance Treatise*, translated with an introduction by Ken Mondschein. New York: Italica Press, 2009.

Águeda, Mercedes. "Sul Rapporto tra Mengs e Goya." In *Goya*, edited by Mercedes Villar, Felipe Llombart, and Lorenza Onori, 13–26, Rome: Edizioni De Luca, 2000. Exhibition catalog.

Alberti, Leon Battista. *On Painting and On Sculpture: The Latin Texts of De pictura and De statua*, edited and translated by Cecil Grayson. London: Phaidon, 1972.

Algarotti, Francesco. *Il newtonianismo per le dame ovvero dialoghi sopra la luce e i colori.* 1737.

———. *Saggio sopra la pittura.* Livorno, 1763. Reprint, edited by William Spaggiari. Rome: Archivio Guido Izzi, 2000.

Alpers, Svetlana. *The Art of Describing: Dutch Art in the Seventeenth Century.* Chicago: University of Chicago Press, 1983.

———. *Rembrandt's Enterprise: The Studio and the Market.* London and Chicago: University of Chicago Press, 1990.

———. *The Vexations of Art: Velázquez and Others.* New Haven, CT: Yale University Press, 2005.

Angelo, Sydney. *The Martial Arts in Renaissance Europe.* New Haven, CT: Yale University Press, 2000.

Angulo Íñiguez, Diego. "Las Hilanderas." *Archivo español de arte* 21 (1948): 1–19.

———. *Pintura del siglo XVII.* Madrid: Plus Ultra, 1971.

Arasse, Daniel. *Leonardo da Vinci: The Rhythm of the World*, translated by Rosetta Translations. Old Saybrook, CT: Konecky & Konecky, 1998.

Aretino, Pietro. *I quattro libri di humanità di Christo.* Venice, 1540.

———. *Lettere sull'arte*, edited by Ettore Camesasca. 3 vols. Milan: Edizioni del Milione, 1957

Aristotle. *Nicomachean Ethics*, translated by H. Rackham. Loeb Classical Library. Cambridge, MA: Harvard University Press, 1926.

———. *Metaphysics.* Volume 1, books 1–9, translated by Hugh Tredennick. 2 vols. Loeb Classical Library 271. Cambridge, MA: Harvard University Press, 1933.

———. *Poetics*, translated by Stephen Halliwell. Loeb Classical Library 199. Cambridge, MA: Harvard University Press, 1995.

Armenini, Giovan Battista. *On the True Precepts of the Art of Painting*, edited and translated by Edward J. Olszewski. New York: B. Franklin, 1977.

———. *De' veri precetti della pittura.* Ravenna, 1586. Reprint, edited by Marina Gorreri. Turin: Enaudi, 1988.

Arslan, Edoardo. *I Bassano.* 2 vols. Milan: Ceschina, 1960.

Artoni, Paola, and Enrico Maria Dal Pozzolo, eds. *Andrea Schiavone: ventuno dipinti in infrarosso.* Treviso: ZeL Edizioni, 2016.

Arvengas, Jeanne. *Raymond Lafage: Dessinateur.* Paris: Chez l'auteur, 1965.

Ashton, Dore. *Fragonard in the Universe of Painting.* Washington, DC: Smithsonian Institution Press, 1988.

Aspinwall, Margaret, Zachary R. Leonard, Ann Lucke, and Jean Wagner, eds. *François Boucher, 1703–1770.* New York: Metropolitan Museum of Art, 1986. Exhibition catalog.

Bal, 63–105. Chicago and London: University of Chicago Press, 2005.

Clements, Robert J. "The Authenticity of de Hollanda's 'Dialogos em Roma,'" *Transactions and Proceedings of the Modern Language Association of America* 61, no. 4 (1946): 1018–1028.

———. "Michelangelo on Effort and Rapidity in Art," *Journal of the Warburg and Courtauld Institutes* 17 (1954): 301–310.

Cocteau, Jean. *Picasso*. Paris: L'École des loisirs, 1996.

Cole, Michael W. "The 'Figura Sforzata': Modeling, Power and the Mannerist Body," *Art History* 24 (2001): 520–551.

———. "Am Werkzeug erkennen wir den Künstler": Waffen und Wappen in der Zeit Cellinis." In *Benvenuto Cellini: Kunst und Kunsttheorie im 16. Jahrhundert*, edited by Alessandro Nova and Anna Schreurs, 39–58. Cologne: Böhlau, 2003.

Coliva, Anna. *Il Mastelletta: Giovanni Andrea Donducci 1575–1655*. Rome: Multigrafica, 1980.

———. "La decorazione della Cappella dell'Arca in San Domenico." In *Furore e Bizzarria: I quadroni restaurati del Mastelletta per la Cappella dell'Arca in San Domenico*, edited by Jadranka Bentini, 13–25. Bologna: Minerva, 2001.

Colton, Judith. "The Fall and Rise of Bernardo De Dominici." In *A Taste for Angels: Neapolitan Painting in North America, 1650–1750*, 57–68. New Haven, CT: Yale University Art Gallery, 1987. Exhibition catalog.

Condivi, Ascanio. *Life of Michelangelo*, translated by Alice Sedgwick Wohl, edited by Hellmut Wohl. Baton Rouge: Louisiana State University Press, 1976.

———. *Vita di Michelangelo Buonarroti*. Rome, 1553. Reprint, edited by Giovanni Nencioni. Florence: SPES, 1998.

Cooper, Anthony Ashley, Earl of Shaftesbury. "A Notion of the Historical Draught or Tablature of the Judgement of Hercules, printed first in the Year M.DCC.XIII." In *Characteristicks of Men, Manners, Opinions, Times*, vol. 3, 345–391. London, 1737–1738.

Cordellier, Dominique. "Martin Fréminet, 'aussi scavant que judicieux': À propos des modelli retrouvés par la Chapelle de la Trinité à Fontainebleau," *Revue de l'art* 81 (1988): 57–72.

Coypel, Antoine. "Commentaire de l'Épître à son fils. Le coloris et le pinceau." In *Conférences de l'Académie royale de peinture et de sculpture: Tome 4, 1712–1746*, vol. 1, edited by Jacqueline Lichtenstein and Christian Michel, 75–89. Paris: Beaux-Arts de Paris, 2010.

Cropper, Elizabeth. *The Ideal of Painting: Pietro Testa's Düsseldorf Notebook*. Princeton, NJ: Princeton University Press, 1984.

———. "The Petrifying Art: Marino's Poetry and Caravaggio," *Metropolitan Museum Journal* 26 (1991): 193–212.

———. "Marino's 'Strage degli innocenti': Poussin, Rubens, and Guido Reni," *Studi Secenteschi* 33 (1992): 137–166.

Cropper, Elizabeth, and Charles Dempsey. "The State of Research in Italian Painting of the Seventeenth Century," *The Art Bulletin* 69, no. 4 (December 1987): 494–509.

———. *Nicolas Poussin: Friendship and the Love of Painting*. Princeton, NJ: Princeton University Press, 1996.

Cropper, Elizabeth, Charles Dempsey, Francesco Solinas, Anna Nicoló, and Francesca Consagra. *Pietro Testa (1612–1650): Prints and Drawings*. Philadelphia: Philadelphia Museum of Art, 1988. Exhibition catalog.

Da Canal, Vincenzo. *Vita di Gregorio Lazzarini*. Venice: Dalla stamperia Palese, 1809.

Dalli Regoli, Gigetta. "Leonardo e Michelangelo: Il 'Tema della 'Battaglia,'" *Academia Leonardi Vinci* 7 (1994): 98–106.

Dal Pozzo, Bartolomeo. *Le vite de' pittori degli scultori et architetti veronesi*. Verona, 1718.

Dandré-Bardon, Michel François. *Traité de peinture suivi d'un essai sur la sculpture pour servir d'introduction à une histoire universelle, relative à ces beaux-arts*. 2 vols. Paris: Chez Desaint, 1765.

Daprà, Brigitte. "I ritratti di Salvator Rosa." In *Salvator Rosa: tra mito e magia*, 58–65. Naples: Electa, 2008. Exhibition catalog.

Da Vinci, Leonardo. *Trattato della pittura de Leonardo da Vinci: condotto sul cod. Vaticano Urbinate 1270*, edited by Gaetano Milanesi. Rome: Unione Coop, 1890.

De Caylus, Comte. "Reflexion sur la peinture: Conférence de 1747." In *Vies d'artistes du XVIIIe siècle*, 130–137. Paris: Librairie Renouard, 1910.

———. "De la légèrté de l'outil." In *Vies d'artistes du XVIIIe siècle*, 149–159. Paris: Librairie Renouard, 1910.

De Chantelou, Paul Fréart. *Journal de voyage du Cavalier Bernin en France*, edited by Milovan Stanić. Paris: Macula-Insulaire, 2001.

De Covarrubias, Sebastián. *Tesoro de la lengua castellana o española*. Madrid: Luiz Sanchez, impressor del Rey N.S., 1611.

De' Dominici, Bernardo. *Vite de' pittori, scultori ed architetti napoletani*. 3 vols. Naples, 1742–1743.

De Hollanda, Francisco. *Quatro dialogos da pintura antigua*, edited by Joaquim de Vasconcellos. Porto: Renascença Portugueza, 1896.

———. *Dialoghi di Roma*. Reprint. Edited by Rita Biscetti. Rome: Bagatto, 1993.

———. *On Antique Painting*, translated by Alice Sedgwick

Wohl, edited by Hellmut Wohl. University Park: Pennsylvania State University Press, 2013.
De Lairesse, Gerard. *Het groot schilderboek*. Haarlem, 1740.
D'Elia, Una Roman. "Tintoretto, Aretino, and the Speed of Creation," *Word & Image* 20 (2004): 206–218.
Delogu, Giuseppe. *Drawings by Tintoretto*. New York: Dover, 1969.
Dempsey, Charles. *Annibale Carracci and the Beginnings of Baroque Style*. Glückstadt: Augustin, 1977.
———. "Some Observations on the Education of Artists in Florence and Bologna during the Later Sixteenth Century," *The Art Bulletin* 62, no. 4 (December 1980): 552–569.
De Piles, Roger. *Cours de peinture par principes*. Paris, 1708. Revised edtion by Charles-Antione Jombert. Paris, 1766.
———. *Elémens de peinture pratique par de Piles, nouvelle édition entièrement refondue, & augmentée considérablement par Charles-Antoine Jombert*. Revised edition, edited by Charles-Antoine Jombert. Amsterdam, 1776.
———. *Abregé de la vie des peintres: avec des reflexions sur leurs ouvrages, et un traité du peintre parfait, de la connoissance des desseins, & de l'utilité des estampes*. Paris, 1699. Reprint. Hildesheim: Olms Verlag, 1969.
———. "Dialogue sur le Coloris." In *L'Art de peinture de C. A. Du Fresnoy, traduit en Français enrichi de Remarques, augmenté d'un Dialogue sur le Coloris*. Paris, 1673. Reprint. Geneva: Minkoff, 1973.
———. "De la disposition." In *Conférences de l'Académie royale de peinture et de sculpture: Tome 3, 1699–1711*, edited by Jacqueline Lichtenstein and Christian Michel, 111–120. Paris: Beaux-Arts de Paris, 2009.
Derrida, Jacques. *Mémoires d'aveugle: L'autoportrait et autres ruines*. Paris: Réunion des musées nationaux, 1991.
Desportes, Claude-François. "Sur l'utilité des conférences." In *Conférences de l'Académie royale de peinture et de sculpture: Tome 5, 1747–1752*, vol. 1, edited by Jacqueline Lichtenstein and Christian Michel, 75–89. Paris: Beaux-Arts de Paris, 2012.
Dézallier d'Argenville, Antoine. *Abrégé de la vie des plus fameux peintres avec leurs portraits gravées en taille-douce*. vols. 1 and 2. Paris, 1745; vol. 3. Paris, 1752.
Diderot, Denis. *Salons*. Reprint, edited by Jean Seznec. 4 vols. Oxford: Clarendon, 1957–1967.
Dolce, Lodovico. "Dialogo di Pittura." In *Trattati d'arte del Cinquecento: fra Manierismo e Controriforma*, edited by Paola Barocchi, vol. 1, 143–206. Bari: G. Laterza, 1960.
Doménesch, Fernando Benito, ed. *Cinco siglos de pintura valenciana: obras del Museo de Bellas Artes de Valencia*. Madrid: Fundación Central Hispano, 1996.
Dubos, Jean Baptiste. *Réflexions critiques sur la poésie et sur la peinture*. 3 vols. Paris, 1770.
Du Fresnoy, Charles-Alphonse. *De l'art de peinture traduit en Français et avec des remarques de Roger de Piles*. Paris: N. l'Anglois, 1668.
Dunkerton, Jill. "Tintoretto's Painting Technique." In *Tintoretto*, edited by Miguel Falomir, 139–158. Madrid: Museo Nacional del Prado, 2008. Exhibition catalog.
Dürer, Albrecht. *Vier Bücher von menschlicher Proportion*. Nuremberg, 1528.
———. *Schriftlicher Nachlass*, edited by Hans Rupprich. 3 vols. Berlin: Deutscher Verein für Kunstwissenschaft, 1956.
Ebert-Schifferer, Sybille. "Il teatro filosofico della vanità: Le iconografie di Salvator Rosa." In *Salvator Rosa tra mito e magia*, 66–82. Naples: Electa, 2008. Exhibition catalog.
Echols, Robert. "Tintoretto the Painter." In *Jacopo Tintoretto*, edited by Miguel Falomir, 25–62. Madrid: Museo Nacional del Prado, 2007. Exhibition catalog.
Ekserdjian, David. "Correggio disegnatore." In *Correggio e l'antico*, edited by Anna Coliva, 77–83. Milan: F. Motta, 2008. Exhibition catalog.
Ensor, James. *Mes écrits, ou les suffisances matamoresques*. Reprint, edited by Hugo Martin. Belgium: Labor, 1999.
Ersch, Johann Samuel, and Johann Georg Gruber. *Allgemeine Encyclopädie der Wissenschaften und Künste in alphabetischer Folge*, vol. 12. Leipzig: Gleditsch, 1824.
Espinós Díaz, Adela. "Modelos de A. Tempesta en la obra de Esteban March," *Archivo español de arte* 53, no. 212 (1980): 499–501.
Faccio, Paolo. *Nuova guida per forestieri amatori delle belle arti per conoscere facilmente le cose più notabili che si trovano in Padova*. Padua, 1818.
Falomir, Miguel, ed. *Jacopo Tintoretto*. Madrid: Museo Nacional del Prado, 2008. Exhibition catalog.
Farago, Claire J. "Leonardo's Battle of Anghiari: A Study in the Exchange between Theory and Practice," *Art Bulletin* 76, no. 2 (June 1994): 301–330.
Farina, Viviana. *Il giovane Salvator Rosa, 1635–1640 circa*. Naples: Paparo, 2010.
Fehl, Philipp P. *Decorum and Wit: The Poetry of Venetian Painting: Essays in the History of the Classical Tradition*. Vienna: IRSA, 1992.
Fehrenbach, Frank. "Much ado about nothing: Leonardo's Fight for the Standard." In *BILD/GESCHICHTE: Festschrift für Horst Bredekamp*, edited by Philine Helas, Maren Polte, Claudia Rückert, and Bettina Uppenkamp, 397–412. Berlin: De Gruyter, 2007.
Félibien, André. *Entretiens sur les vies et les ouvrages des plus excellents peintres, anciens et modernes*. 6 vols. Paris, 1725.
———. *Entretiens sur les vies et sur les ouvrages des plus excellents peintres anciens et modernes, I et II*. Paris, 1725. Reprint, edited by René Démoris. Paris: Les Belles Lettres, 1987.

Felton, Craig, and William B. Jordan, eds. *Jusepe de Ribera: Lo Spagnoletto. 1591–1652*. Seattle: University of Washington Press, 1982. Exhibition catalog.

Ferrari, Oreste. "La fortuna (e sfortuna) critica del 'bozzetto' nel Settecento." In *Studi in onore di Giulio Carlo Aragan*, 253–258. Scandicci: La Nuova Italia, 1994.

Finocchi Ghersi, Lorenzo. "Luca Giordano a Venezia e la moda dei 'tenebrosi.'" In *"Napoli e tutto il mondo": Neapolitan Art and Culture from Humanism to the Enlightenment*, edited by Livio Pestilli, Ingrid Rowland, and Sebastian Schütze, 227–241. Pisa: Fabrizio Serra, 2008.

Flam, Jack. *Matisse on Art*. Revised edition. Berkeley: University of California Press, 1995.

Freedman, Luba. "'Rilievo' as an Artistic Term in Renaissance Art Theory," *Rinascimento* 29 (1989): 217–247.

Friedlaender, Walter. *Caravaggio Studies*. Princeton, NJ: Princeton University Press, 1955.

———. "Titian and Pordenone," *Art Bulletin* 47, no. 1 (March 1965): 118–121.

Fröhlich-Bum, Lili. "Andrea Meldolla, genannt Schiavone," *Jahrbuch der Kunsthistorischen Sammlungen in Wien* 31 (1913–14): 137–220.

Fromentin, Eugène. *Rubens et Rembrandt: les Maîtres d'autrefois*. Paris, 1876. Reprint. Brussels: Éditions Complexe, 1991.

Fumagalli, Elena. "Napoli a Firenze nel Seicento." In *"Filosofico umore" e "meravigliosa speditezza": Pittura napoletana del Seicento dalle collezioni medicee*, edited by Elena Fumagalli, 27–135. Florence: 2007.

Füssli, Johann Heinrich. *Lectures on Painting: Das Modell der Antike und die moderne Nachahmung*, edited by Gisela Bungarten. 2 vols. Berlin: Gebrüder Mann, 2005.

Galley, Nicolas. "Cornelis Ketel: A Painter without a Brush," *Artibus et Historiae* 25 (2004): 87–100.

———. "De l'original à l'excentrique: L'emergence de l'individualité artistique au nord des Alpes." PhD diss., Universtiy of Freiburg (CH), 2005. http://ethesis.unifr.ch/theses/downloads.php? le=GalleyN.pdf.

Garrard, Mary D. *Artemisia Gentileschi: The Image of the Female Hero in Ialian Baroque Art*. Princeton, NJ: Princeton University Press, 1989.

———. "Artemisia's Hand, " in *The Artemisia Files: Artemisia for Feminists and Other Thinking People*, edited by Mieke Bal, 1–31. Chicago and London: The University of Chicago Press, 2005.

Garribaldi, Vittora, and Francesco Federico Mancini, eds. *Perugino: Il divin pittore*. Milan: Silvana Editoriale, 2004. Exhibition catalog.

Garton, John. *Grace and Grandeur: The Portraiture of Paolo Veronese*. London: Harvey Miller, 2008.

Georgievska-Shine, Aneta. "Horror and Pity: Some Thoughts on the Sense of the Tragic in Rubens' 'Hero and Leander' and 'The Fall of Phaeton,'" *Marburger Jahrbuch für Kunstwissenschaft* 30 (2003): 217–228.

Giannini, Cristina. "Luca's 'Macchie' for the Riccardi and the Late-Baroque Taste for the 'INACCOMPLI.'" In *Stanze segrete: gli artisti dei Riccardi: i "ricordi" di Luca Giordano e oltre*, edited by Cristina Giannini and Silvia Meloni Trkulja, 235–249. Florence: L.S. Olschki, 2005.

Gilio, Giovanni Andrea. *Dialogue on the Errors and Abuses of Painters*, translated by Michael Bury and Lucinda Byatt. Los Angeles: The Getty Institute, 2018.

Gilot, Françoise, and Carlton Lake. *Life with Picasso*. New York: McGraw-Hill Book Company, 1964.

Ginzburg, Silvia. *La Galleria Farnese: Gli affreschi dei Carracci*. Milan: Electra, 2008.

Giustiniani, Vincenzo. "Discorso sopra la pittura." In *Discorsi sulle arti e sui mestieri*, edited by Anna Banti, 37–45. Florence: Sansoni, 1981.

Gludovatz, Karin. "Caravaggios Blutsbrüderschaft: Der Subtext der Signatur in der Enthauptung des Johannes von 1608," *Kunsthistoriker: Mitteilungen des Österreichischen Kunsthistorikerverbandes* 15/16 (1999/2000): 141–147.

———. *Fährten legen, Spuren lesen. Die Künstlersignatur als poetische Referenz*. Munich: Wilhelm Fink, 2011.

Goffen, Rona. *Titian's Women*. New Haven, CT: Yale University Press, 1997.

———. *Renaissance Rivals: Michelangelo, Leonardo, Raphael, Titian*. New Haven, CT: Yale University Press, 2003.

Goldstein, Carl. *Visual Fact over Verbal Fiction: A Study of the Carracci and the Criticism, Theory, and Practice in Renaissance and Baroque Italy*. Cambridge: Cambridge University Press, 1988.

———. *Teaching Art: Academies and Schools from Vasari to Albers*. Cambridge: Cambridge University Press, 1996.

Gombrich, Ernst. *Norm and Form: Studies in the Art of the Renaissance*. London: Phaidon, 1966.

Goncourt, Edmond de, and Jules de Goncourt. *Journal: Mémoires de la vie litteraire*, edited by Robert Ricatte. 4 vols. Paris: Fasquelle,1956.

———. *L'Art du XVIIIe siècle*. 3 vols. Paris: G. Charpentier, 1906.

Gould, Cecil. *The Paintings of Correggio*. London: Faber, 1976.

Goya. (exhib. cat.) Rome: Galleria Nazionale d'Arte Antica, Palazzo Barberini, 2000.

Gramaccini, Norberto. "Raffael und sein Schüler—eine gemalte Kunsttheorie," *Georges Bloch-Jahrbuch des Kunsthistorischen Seminars der Universität Zürich* 2 (1995): 45–55.

Grassi, Luigi, and Mario Pepe. *Dizionario della critica d'arte.* 2 vols. Turin: Unione tipografico-editirice torinese, 1978.

Groen, Karin, and Ella Hendriks. "Frans Hals: A Technical Examination." In *Frans Hals*, edited by Seymour Slive, 114–120. London: National Gallery of Art, 1989. Exhibition catalog.

Gründler, Hana. "'Gloriarsi della mano e dell'ingegno': Hand, Geist und pädagogischer Eros bei Vasari und Bellori." In *Begrifflichkeit, Konzepte, Definitionen: Schreiben über Kunst und ihre Medien in Giovan Pietro Belloris Viten und der Kunstliteratur der Frühen Neuzeit*, edited by Elisabeth Oy-Mara, Marieke von Bernstorff, and Henry Keazor, 77–103. Wiesbaden: Harrassowitz, 2014.

Guarini, Alessandro. *Il franetico savio ovvero il Tasso.* Ferrara, 1610. Reprint, edited by Ferdinando Ronchetti. Città di Castello, 1895.

Günther, Antje. *Ölskizzen und Skizzenbilder: Untersuchungen zur Bedeutung und Wertung des sichtbaren Pinselstrichs im 16. und 17. Jahrhundert.* Marburg: Tectum, 1999. Microfilm.

Hall, Marcia. *The Sacred Image in the Age of Art.* New Haven, CT: Yale University Press, 2011.

Harris, Ennquetta. *The Prado: Treasure House of the Spanish Royal Collections.* London: Studio Publications, 1940.

Hartje, Nicole. *Bartolomeo Manfredi (1582–1622): ein Nachfolger Caravaggios und seine europäische Wirkung: Monographie und Werkverzeichnis.* Weimar: Verlag und Datenbank für Geisteswissenschaften, 2004.

Hartt, Frederick. *Giulio Romano.* 2 vols. New Haven: Yale University Press, 1958.

Haskell, Francis. *Patrons and Painters: Art and Society in Baroque Italy.* New Haven, CT: Yale University Press, 1980.

Healy, Fiona. "Losing Control of the Senses: The Fifth Horse in Rubens's Fall of Phaeton." In *Von Kunst und Temperament: Festschrift für Eberhard König*, edited by Caroline Zöhl and Mara Hofmann, 105–118. Turnhout: Brepols, 2007.

Held, Julius. "The Early Appreciation of Drawings." In *Latin American Art and the Baroque Period in Europe: Studies in Western Art: Acts of the Twentieth International Congress of the History of Art*, vol. 3, 72–95. Princeton, NJ: Princeton University Press, 1963.

Held, Jutta. "Goyas Akademiekritik." *Münchner Jahrbuch der Bildenden Kunst* 17 (1966): 214–224.

Hendrix, Harald. "The Repulsive Body: Images of Torture in Seventeenth-Century Naples." In *Bodily Extremities: Preoccupations with the Human Body in Early Modern European Culture*, edited by Florike Egmond and Robert Zwijnenberg, 68–91. Aldershot: Ashgate Publishing, 2003.

Hersey, George. "Mattia Preti, 1613–1699." In *A Taste for Angels: Neapolitan Painting in North America, 1650–1750*, 83–110. New Haven, CT: Yale University Art Gallery, 1987. Exhibition catalog.

Houbraken, Arnold. *De groote schouburgh der Nederlantsche konstschilders en schilderessen*, edited by P. T. A. Swillens. 3 vols. Maastricht: Leiter-Nypels, 1943–1953.

Huemer, Frances. "Rubens and Galileo, 1604: Nature, Art, and Poetry," *Wallraf-Richartz-Jahrbuch* 64 (1984): 175–196.

———. *Rubens and the Roman Circle: Studies of the First Decade.* New York: Garland, 1996.

Hüttinger, Eduard. "Tintorettos Bilderzyklen in der Scuola di S. Rocco." In *Licht und Farbe: Zur Kunstgeschichte Italiens*, 131–148. Zurich: Schweizerisches Institut für Kunstwissenschaft, 2001.

Hyde, Melissa. "Getting into the Picture: Boucher's Self-Portraits of Others." In *Rethinking Boucher*, edited by Melissa Hyde and Mark Ledbury, 13–38. Los Angeles: Getty Research Institute, 2006.

———. *Making the Roccoco: François Boucher and His Critics.* Los Angeles: Getty Research Institute, 2006.

Ilchman, Frederick. "Tintoretto as a Painter of Religious Narrative." In *Jacopo Tintoretto*, edited by Miguel Falomir, 63–94. Madrid: Museo Nacional del Prado, 2008. Exhibition catalog.

Ivanoff, Nicola. "Charles-Nicolas Cochin et la peinture vénitienne," *L' information d'histoire de l'art*, vol. 11, no. 3 (May–June 1966): 93–105.

Jacoby, Brigitte. "Studien zur Ikonographie des Phaetonmythos." PhD diss., Universität Bonn, 1971.

Jacquot, Dominque. "La licence de l'esquisse." In *L'Apothéose du geste: l'esquisse peinte au siècle de Boucher et Fragonard*, edited by Hélène Charbonnier, 13–23. Paris: Hazan, 2003. Exhibition catalog.

Jaffé, David. *Rubens and Italy.* Ithaca, NY: Cornell University Press, 1977.

———. *Rubens's Massacre of the Innocents.* Ottawa: Skylet Publishing, 2009.

Jankelevitch, Vladimir. *Liszt et la rhapsodie.* Paris: Plon, 1979.

Joannides, Paul. "Leonardo da Vinci, Peter-Paul Rubens, Pierre-Nolasque Bergeret, and the 'Fight of the Standard.'" *Academia Leonardi Vinci* 1 (1988): 76–86.

Jowell, Frances Suzman. "Thoré-Bürger and the Revival of Frans Hals," *The Art Bulletin* 56, no. 1 (March 1974): 101–117.

Jucker-Scherrer, Ines. *Der Gestus des Aposkopein: Ein Beitrag zur Gebärdensprache in der antiken Kunst.* Zurich: Juris-Verlag, 1956.

Junius, Franciscus. *De Pictura Veterum, Libri Tres.* Rotterdam,

1694. Reprint, edited by Colette Nativel. Geneva: Librairie Droz, 1996.

Justi, Carl. *Diego Velázquez und sein Jahrhundert.* 2 vols. Bonn: Cohen, 1988.

Keazor, Henry. *"Distruggere la maniera?" Die Carracci-Postille.* Freiburg im Breisgau: Rombach, 2002.

———. *"Il vero modo": Die Malereireform der Carracci.* Berlin: Gebrüder Mann, 2007.

Kecks, Ronald G. "Die Virtuosität des Malers und die italienische Kunstliteratur des 14. bis 16. Jahrhunderts." In *"Bedeutung in den Bildern": Festschrift für Jörg Träger zum 60. Geburtstag,* edited by Karl Möseneder and Gosbert Schüssler, 121–145. Regensburg: Schnell & Steiner, 2002.

Kemp, Wolfgang. "Disegno: Beiträge zur Geschichte des Begriffs zwischen 1547–1607," *Marburger Jahrbuch für Kunstwissenschaft* 19 (1974): 219–240.

Kepetzis, Ekaterini. "Der Bethlehemitische Kindermord in der Kunstliteratur: Vasari, van Mander und die Darstellungen des Rubens," *Zeitschrift für Kunstgeschichte* 69 (2006): 169–193.

Knox, George. *Giambattista Piazzetta, 1682–1754.* Oxford: Clarendon, 1992.

Koerner, Joseph Leo. *The Moment of Self-Portraiture in German Renaissance Art.* Chicago, IL: University of Chicago Press, 1993.

Krieger, Verena. "Arachne als Künstlerin: Velázquez' 'Las Hilanderas' als Gegenentwurf zum neuplatonischen Künstlerkonzept," *Zeitschrift für Kunstgeschichte* 65 (2002): 545–561.

Kris, Ernst. "The Image of the Artist: A Psychological Study of the Role of Tradition in Ancient Biographies." In *Psychoanalytic Explorations in Art,* 64–84. New York: International Universities Press, 2000.

Kris, Ernst, and Otto Kurz. *Legend, Myth, and Magic in the Image of the Artist: A Historical Experiment.* New Haven, CT: Yale University Press, 1979.

Krischel, Roland. *Jacopo Tintorettos "Sklavenwunder."* Munich: Scaneg, 1991.

———. *Tintoretto.* Hamburg: Rowohlt, 1994.

Kroschewski, Nevenka. *Über das allmähliche Verfertigen der Bilder: Neue Aspekte zu Caravaggio.* Munich: Scaneg, 2002.

Krüger, Klaus. *Das Bild als Schleier des Unsichtbaren: Ästhetische Illusion in der Kunst der frühen Neuzeit in Italien.* Munich: Wilhelm Fink, 1997.

Kusch-Arnhold, Britta. "Zur Bedeutung der Praxis für die künstlerische Virtus." In *Die Virtus des Künstlers in der italienischen Renaissance,* edited by Joachim Poeschke, Thomas Weigel, and Britta Kusch-Arnhold, 173–195. Munich: Rhema, 2006.

Labat, Jean-François. *L'Art en fait d'armes, ou de l'épée seule, avec les attitudes.* Toulouse, 1696.

Lang, Walter K. *Grausame Bilder: Sadismus in der neopolitanischen Malerei von Caravaggio bis Giordano.* Berlin: Reimer, 2001.

Lanzi, Luigi. *Storia pittorica della Italia.* 3 vols., edited by M. Capucci. Florence: Sansoni, 1968–1974.

Lebensztejn, Jean-Claude. "Florilège de la nonchalance." In *Annexes—de l'œuvre d'art,* 225–262. Brussels: Part de l'œil, 1999.

Lebrun, Pierre. "Recueuil des essaies des merveilles de la peinture de Pierre Lebrun, peintre." In *Medieval and Renaissance Treatises on the Arts of Painting: Original Texts with English Translations,* edited by Mary P. Merrifield, 766–841. Mineola, NY: Dover, 1999.

Lechner, Sonja. *Nuda Veritatis. Caravaggio als Aktmaler. Rezeption und Revision von Aktdarstellungen der römschen Reifezeit.* Munich: Scaneg, 2006.

Lemoine, Annick. "Nicolas Régnier, zugeschrieben, Porträt des Marquese Vincenzo Giustiniani." In *Caravaggio in Preussen: Die Sammlung Giustiniani und die Berliner Gemäldegalerie,* edited by Silvia Danesi Squarzina, 200. Milan: Electa, 2001. Exhibition catalog.

Leslie, Charles Robert. *John Constable d'après les souvenirs recueillis de C. R. Leslie,* translated by Léon Bazalgette. Paris: H. Floury, 1905. Reprint. Paris: École nationale supérieure des beaux-arts, 1996.

Lessing, Maria. "Leonardo da Vinci's Pazzia Bestialissima," *The Burlington Magazine* 64, no. 374 (May 1934): 219–231.

Leuschner, Eckhard. *Antonio Tempesta: Ein Bahnbrecher des römischen Barock und seine europäische Wirkung.* Petersberg: M. Imhof, 2005.

Levine, David A. "The Bentvueghels: 'Bande Académique.'" In *Essays Honoring Irving Lavin on his Sixtieth Birthday,* edited by Marilyn Aronberg Lavin, 207–226. New York: Italica, 1990.

Lichtenstein, Jacqueline, and Christian Michel, eds. *Conférences de l'Académie royale de Peinture et de Sculpture.* vols. I-VI. Paris: Beaux-Arts de Paris éditions 2006–2015.

Locker, Jesse M.. *Artemisia Gentileschi: The Language of Painting.* New Haven, CT: Yale University Press, 2015.

Logan, Anne-Marie, and Michiel C. Plomp. "Rubens als Zeichner." In *Peter Paul Rubens,* edited by Klaus Albrecht Schröder and Heinz Widauer, 21–80. Ostfildern-Ruit: Hatje Cantz, 2004.

Lomazzo, Giovan Paolo. "Idea del tempio della pittura." In *Scritti sulle arti,* edited by Roberto Paolo Ciardi, vol. 1, 241–373. Florence: Marchi & Bertolli, 1973.

———. "Trattato dell'arte della pittura, scoltura et architettura." In *Scritti sulle arti,* edited by Roberto Paolo Ciardi, vol. 2, 9–589. Florence: Marchi & Bertolli, 1974.

———. *Idea of the Temple of Painting*, edited and translated by Jean Julia Chai. University Park: Pensylvania State University Press, 2013.

Longhi, Roberto. "L'inizio dell'abbozzo autonomo," *Paragone* 17 (1966): 25–29.

Loughman, Thomas J., ed. *Fierce Reality: Italian Masters from Seveneenth Century Naples.* Milan: Skira, 2006. Exhibition catalog.

Lovén, Christian. "Too Many Levels of Reality: An Almost Abandoned Idea in Pietro da Cortona's Barberini Ceiling," *Konsthistorisk tidskrift* 83 (2014): 319–330.

Macioce, Stefania. *Michelangelo Merisi da Caravaggio: fonti e documenti, 1532–1724*. Rome: Ugo Bozzi, 2003.

Mahon, Denis. *Studies in Seicento Art and Theory.* London: Warburg Institute, 1947.

Malvasia, Carlo Cesare. *Felsina pittrice: vite de' pittori bolognesi*, edited by Giampietro Zanotti. 2 vols. Bologna: Guidi all'Ancora, 1841.

———. *Scritti originali del Conte Carlo Cesare Malvasia spettanti alla sua Felsina Pittrice*, edited by Lea Marzocchi. Bologna: Alfa, 1984.

———. *Malvasia's Life of the Carracci*, commentary and translation by Anne Summerscale. University Park: Pennsylvania State University Press, 2000.

Mancini, Giulio. *Considerazioni sulla pittura*, edited by Adriana Marucchi. 2 vols. Rome: Accademia nazionale dei Lincei, 1956.

Manning, Bettina Suida, and Robert Manning, eds. *The Genovese Renaissance, Grace and Geometry: Paintings and Drawings by Luca Cambiaso from the Suida Manning Collection.* Houston: Museum of Fine Arts, 1974. Exhibition catalog.

Mariette, Pierre-Jean. *Abecedario et autres notes inédites de cet amateur sur les arts et les artistes.* 6 vols. Paris: J.B. Dumoulin, 1854–1856.

Marin, Louis. *Détruire la peinture.* Reprint. Paris: Flammarion, 1997.

Marino, Giambattista. *Epistolario*, edited by Angelo Borzelli and Fausto Nicolini. 2 vols. Bari: Scrittori d'Italia, 1911–1912.

———. *La Galeria.* Dual Language Edition, Italian-German. Translated by Christiane Kruse and Rainer Stillers. Mainz: Dietrich, 2009.

———. *The Massacre of the Innocents*, translated by Erik Butler. Cambridge, MA: Wakefield Press, 2015.

Massé, "Connaître l'antique et l'anatomie," in: In *Conférences de l'Académie royale de peinture et de sculpture: Tome 5, 1747–1752*, vol. 2, edited by Jacqueline Lichtenstein and Christian Michel, 75–89. Paris: Beaux-Arts de Paris, 2012.

McKim-Smith, Grindley, Greta Andersen-Bergdoll, and Richard Newman. *Examining Velázquez.* New Haven, CT: Yale University Press, 1988.

Meller, Peter. "La Battaglia d'Anghiari." In *Leonardo: La Pittura*, edited by Giulio Carlo Argan, 187–194. Florence: Martello-Giunti, 1977.

Mena Marques, Manuela B. "Titian, Rubens, and Spain." In *Titian and Rubens: Power, Politics and Style*, by Hillard T. Goldfarb, David Freedberg, and Manuela B. Mena Marques, 69. Boston: Isabella Stewart Gardner Museum, 1998. Exhibition catalog.

Michel, Christian. *Le Voyage d'Italie de Charles-Nicolas Cochin, 1758.* Rome: École Française de Rome, 1991.

Moffitt, John. "Painting, Music, and Poetry in Velàzquez's Las Hilanderas," *Konsthistorisk tidskrift* 54 (1985): 77–90.

Montaiglon, Anatole de. *Procès-verbaux de l'Académie royale de peinture et de sculpture 1648–1793.* 11 vols. Paris: J. Baur, 1875–1909.

Montaiglon, Anatole de, and Jules Guiffrey. *Correspondance des directeurs de l'Académie de France à Rome avec les surintendants des bâtiments.* 17 vols. Paris: Charavay frères, 1887–1908.

Morselli, Raffaella. "La fortuna critica." In *Dopo Caravaggio: Bartolomeo Manfredi e la Manfrediana Methodus*, 32–41. Milan: Mondadori, 1987.

Mucchi, Ludovico. *Caratteri radiografici della pittura di Giorgione.* Florence: Alinari, 1978. Exhibition catalog.

Müller, Jürgen. *Concordia Pragensis: Karel van Manders Kunsttheorie im Schilder-Boeck: Ein Beitrag zur Rhetorisierung von Kunst und Leben am Beispiel der rudolfinischen Hofkünstler.* Munich: Oldenbourg, 1993.

Müller-Hofstede, Justus. "Rubens in Italien." In *Peter Paul Rubens 1577–1640*, edited by Gerhard Bott, 13–354. Cologne: Wallraf-Richartz Museum, 1977. Exhibition catalog.

Neuner, Stefan, and Wolfram Pichler. "Tintorettos Schwellenkunde." In *Ikonologie des Zwischenraums: Der Schleier als Medium und Metapher*, edited by Johannes Endres, Barbara Wittman, and Gerhard Wolf, 243–286. Munich: Fink, 2005.

Nichols, Tom. "Tintoretto, Prestezza and the Poligrafi: A Study in the Literary and Visual Culture of Cinquecento Venice," *Renaissance Studies* 10 (1996): 72–100.

———. *Tintoretto: Tradition and Identity.* Revised and expanded 2nd edition. London: Reaction Books Ltd., 2015.

Nougaret, Pierre Jean-Baptiste. *Anecdotes des beaux-arts*, 3 vols. Paris, 1776–1780.

Orlandi, Pellegrino Antonio. *Abecedario pittorico*, Venice, 1753.

Ovid. *Metamorphoses.* 2 vols, translated by Frank Justus

Miller. Loeb Classical Library 42–43. Cambridge, MA: Harvard University Press, 1916.
——. *Fasti.* Translated by James G. Frazer. Loeb Classical Library 253. Cambridge, MA: Harvard University Press, 1931.
Ozzòla, Leandro. *I pittori di battaglie nel Seicento e nel Settecento.* Mantua: Tipografia A.L.C.E., 1951.
Pacheco, Francisco. *El Arte de la Pintura.* 1638. Reprint, edited by F. J. Sánchez Cantón. 2 vols. Madrid: Instituto de Valencia de Don Juan, 1956.
Pacht-Bassani, Paola. *Claude Vignon, 1593–1670.* Paris: Arthena, 1993.
Paleotti, Gabriele. *Discourse on Sacred and Profane Images,* translated by William McCuaig, Los Angeles: Getty Publications, 2012.
Pallucchini, Rodolfo. "Miscellanea Piazzettesca," *Arte Veneta* 22 (1968): 106–130.
Pallucchini, Rodolfo, and Adriano Mariuz. *L'opera completa del Piazzetta.* Milan: Rizzoli, 1982.
Palomino De Castro y Velasco, Antonio. *El museo pictórico y escala óptica,* edited by Juan Agustín Ceán y Bermúdez. Madrid: Aguilar, 1947.
Panofsky, Erwin. "Die neoplatonische Bewegung und Michelangelo." In *Studien zur Ikonologie: humanistische Themen in der Kunst der Renaissance,* 251–326. Cologne: DuMont, 1980.
Papi, Gianni. *Bartolomeo Manfredi.* Soncino: Edizioni dei Soncino, 2013.
Parmelin, Hélène. *Picasso says…,* translated by Christine Trollope. London: George Allen & Unwin, 1969.
Pascoli, Lione. *Vite de' pittori, scultori, ed architetti moderni,* vol. 2. Rome: Antonio de Rossi, 1736.
Passeri, Giovanni Battista. *Vite de' Pittori Scultori ed Architetti che anno lavorato in Roma morti dal 1641 fino al 1673.* Rome: Gregorio Settari, 1722.
Patz, Kristine. "Sub Rosa: Verschwiegende Beredsamkeit im Londoner Selbstporträt von Salvator Rosa." In *Diletto e Maraviglia: Ausdruck und Wirkung in der Kunst von der Renaissance bis zum Barock,* edited by Christine Göttler, Ulrike Müller-Hofstede, Kristine Patz, and Kaspar Zollikofer, 61–73. Emsdetten: Edition Imorde, 1998.
Pedretti, Carlo. "Nuovi documenti riguardanti la 'Battaglia d'Anghiari.'" In *Leonardo da Vinci inedito: tre saggi,* 53–78. Florence: G. Barbèra, 1968.
Pérez Sánchez, Alfonso E. *Mostra di disegni spagnoli.* Florence: Olschki, 1972.
——. "Presencia de Tiziano en la España del Siglo de Oro," *Goya* 135 (1976): 140–159.
Pericolo, Lorenzo. "Le 'Fantasiette' di Nicolas Poussin per Giovan Battista Marino," *Critica d'arte* 12 (2001): 12, 35–45.
——. *Caravaggio and Pictorial Narrative: Dislocating the Istoria in Early Modern Painting.* London: Harvey Miller Publishers, 2011.
Perrault, Charles. *Les hommes illustres qui ont paru en France pendant ce siècle avec leurs portraits au naturel.* Paris, 1700.
Perruzzi, Andrea. *Idee delle Muse.* Naples, 1695.
Pestilli, Livio. "Lord Shaftesbury e Paolo de Matteis: Ercole al bivio tra teoria e pratica," *Storia dell'arte* 68 (1990): 95–121.
Pevsner, Nikolaus. *Academies of Art, Past and Present.* Cambridge: Cambridge University Press, 1940.
Pichler, Wolfram. "Schmincke/Leinwand—Caravaggio/Goya: Selbstreflexion und Untergang des Illusionismus in Farbe." Unpublished PhD diss., University of Vienna, 1999.
Pino, Paolo. *Dialogo di pittura.* 1548. Reprint, edited by Susanna Falabella. Rome: Lithos, 2000.
Pinson, Yona. "Un langage muet: métaphore et morale dans les éléments architecturaux et scénographiques de Nicolas Poussin," *Artibus et Historiae* 18 (1997): 109–127.
Pio, Nicola. *Le vite di pittori scultori et architetti (cod. ms. Capponi 257),* edited by Catherine Enggass and Robert Enggass. Vatican City: Biblioteca Apostolica Vaticana, 1977.
Plackinger, Andreas. *Violenza: Gewalt als Denkfigur im michelangelesken Kunstdiskurs.* Berlin: De Gruyter, 2016.
Plato. *The Dialogues of Plato,* vol. 3, edited and translated by Benjamin Jowett. London: Oxford University Press, 1931.
Plesters, Joyce, and Lorenzo Lazzarini. "I materiali e la tecnica dei Tintoretto della Scuola di San Rocco." In *Quaderni di Venezia Arti (Jacopo Tintoretto nel qurto centenario della morte)* 3 (1996): 275–280.
Pliny the Elder. *Natural History,* vol. 9, books 33–35, translated by H. Rackham. Loeb Classical Library 394. Cambridge, MA: Harvard University Press, 1952.
Pliny the Younger. *Letters,* vol. 2, books 8–10, translated by Betty Radice. Loeb Classical Library 59. Cambridge, MA: Harvard University Press, 1969.
Plutarch. "The Education of Children." In *Moralia,* vol. 1, translated by Frank Cole Babbitt. Loeb Classical Library 197. Cambridge, MA: Harvard University Press, 1960.
Polanyi, Michael. *Personal Knowledge: Towards a Post-Critical Philosophy.* New York: Routledge, 2002.
Poliziano, Angelo. *Polizianos Tagebuch (1477–1479),* edited by Albert Wesselski. Jena: E. Diederichs, 1929.
Portalis, Roger. *Honoré Fragonard: sa vie et son œuvre.* Paris: Rothschild, 1889.

Posner, Donald. "Concerning the 'Mechanical' Parts of Painting and the Artistic Culture of Seventeenth-Century France," *The Art Bulletin* 75, no. 4 (December 1993): 583–598.

Pousão-Smith, Maria-Isabel. "Sprezzatura, Nettigheid and the Fallacy of 'Invisible Brushwork' in Seventeenth-Century Dutch Painting," *Nederlands kunsthistorisch jaarboek* 54 (2003): 259–279.

Poussin, Nicolas. *Lettres*, edited by Pierre du Colombier. Paris: À La Cité des Livres, 1929.

———. *Lettres, précédées de la vie du Poussin par Félibien*. Paris: J. & R. Wittmann, 1945.

Preimesberger, Rudolf. "Tragische Motive in Raffaels 'Transfiguration,'" *Zeitschrift für Kunstgeschichte* 50 (1987): 89–115.

———. "Caravaggio im 'Matthäusmartyrium' der Cappella Contarelli." In *Zeitenspiegelung: Zur Bedeutung von Traditionen in Kunst und Kunstwissenschaft*, edited by Peter K. Klein and Regine Prange, 135–149. Berlin: Reimer, 1998.

———. "Michelangelo da Caravaggio—Caravaggio da Michelangelo: zum 'Amor' der Berliner Gemäldegalerie." In *Der stumme Diskurs der Bilder*, edited by Valeska von Rosen, 243–260. Munich: Deutscher Kunstverlag, 2003.

Prinz, Wolfram. *Die Sammlung der Selbstbildnisse in den Uffizien: Geschichte der Sammlung mit Regesten zur Tätigkeit der Agenten und Dokumentaranhang*. Berlin: Gebrüder Mann, 1971.

Pugliesi, Catherine. "Caravaggio's Life and Lives over Four Centuries." In *Caravaggio: Realism, Rebellion, Reception*, edited by Genevieve Warwick, 23–35. Newark: University of Delaware Press, 2006.

Puttfarken, Thomas. "La reconstruction de la pensée de Poussin par les théoriciens de l'Académie," *Revue d'esthétique* 31/32 (1997): 133–147.

Quintilian. *The Orator's Education*. Volume IV, books 9–10, edited and translated by Donald A. Russell. Loeb Classical Library 127. Cambridge, MA: Harvard University Press, 2002.

Rathe, Kurt. *Die Ausdrucksfunktion extrem verkürzter Figuren*. London: Warburg Institute, 1938.

Ratti, Carlo Giuseppe. *Delle vite de' pittori, scultori, ed architetti genovesi*. 2 vols. Genoa, 1743.

Raulff, Ulrich. "Inter lineas oder Geschriebene Leben." In *Der unsichtbare Augenblick: Zeitkonzepte in der Geschichte*, 118–142. Göttingen: Wallstein, 1999.

Rearick, W. Roger. "From Drawing to Painting: The Role of Disegno in the Tintoretto Shop." In *Quaderni di Venezia Arti (Jacopo Tintoretto nel Quarto Centenario della Morte* 3 (1996): 173–181.

Restout, Jean-Bernard. *Charles-Nicolas Cochin, Jean-Thomas Hérissant, Galerie françoise; ou, Portraits des hommes et des femmes célèbres qui ont paru en France*. 2 vols. Paris, 1771.

Reynolds, Sir Joshua. *Discourses on Art*, edited by Robert R. Wark. New Haven, CT: Yale University Press, 1997.

Richardson, Francis Lee. *Andrea Schiavone*. Oxford: Clarendon Press, 1980.

Richardson, Jonathan. "On the Art of Painting." In *Works*, 20–123. London, 1773.

Ridolfi, Carlo. *Le Maraviglie dell'arte*. 1648. Reprint. 2 vols. Bologna: Arnaldo Forni Editore, 2002.

Ripa, Cesare. *Iconologia*. Padua, 1618. Reprint, edited by Piero Buscaroli. 2 vols. Turin: Fògola, 1986.

Romanelli, Giandomenico. *Tintoretto: La Scuola Grande di San Rocco*. Milan: Electa, 1994.

Rosa, Salvator. *Lettere*. Collected by Lucio Festa, edited by Gian Giotto Borrelli. Bologna: Il mulino, 2003.

Rosand, David. "The Crisis of the Venetian Renaissance Tradition," *Arte* 11–12 (1970): 5–53.

———. "Tintoretto e gli spiriti nel pennello." In *Quaderni di Venezia Arti (Jacopo Tintoretto nel Quarto Centenario della Morte)* 3 (1996): 133–137.

Rosenberg, Pierre, ed. *Fragonard*. New York: Metropolitan Museum of Art, 1988. Exhibition catalog.

Rosenberg, Raphael. *Beschreibungen und Nachzeichnungen der Skulpturen Michelangelos: Eine Geschichte der Kunstbetrachtung*. Berlin: Deutscher Kunstverlag, 2000.

Rossetti, Giovambattista. *Descrizione delle Pitture, Sculture, ed Architetture di Padova*, 2 vols. Padua: Stamperiadel Seminaria, 1780.

Rossi, Massimiliano. "La Peinture Guerrière." In *La Jérusalem délivrée du Tasse: poésie, peinture, musique, ballet; Actes du coloque, Musée du Louvre, 1996*, 69–108. Paris: Musée du Louvre, 1999.

———. "Maniera e Manierismi Veneti." In *Da Bellini a Veronese: temi di arte veneta*, edited by Gennaro Toscano and Francesco Valcanover, 411–441.Venice: Istituto veneto di scienze, lettere ed arti, 2004.

Rossi, Paola. "I soffitti veneziani da Pordenone a Tintoretto." In *Da Bellini a Veronese: Temi di Arte Veneta*, edited by Gennaro Toscano and Francesco Valcanover, 509–536. Venice: Istituto veneto di scienze, lettere ed arti, 2004.

Röttgen, Herwarth. *Il Cavalier d'Arpino*. Rome: De Luca, 1973. Exhibition catalog.

———. "Eine Persönlichkeit in Bild und Wort: Giuseppe Cesari d'Arpino und seine Selbstbildnisse." In *Kunst und Geschichte: Festschrift für Karl Arndt zum siebzigsten Geburtstag*, edited by Marion Ackermann, 159–172. Munich: Deutscher Kunstverlag, 1999.

———. *Il Cavalier Giuseppe Cesari d'Arpino.* Rome: Ugo Bozzi, 2002.

Rubin, Patricia. "Signposts of Invention: Artists' Signatures in Italian Renaissance Art," *Art History* 29:4 (2006): 563–599.

Saccone, Eduardo. "Grazia, Sprezzatura, Affettazione in the Courtier." In *Castiglione: The Ideal and the Real in Renaissance Culture*, edited by Robert W. Hanning and David Rosand, 45–67. New Haven, CT: Yale University Press, 1983.

Saint Girons, Baldine. "Un nouveau 'Discours de la méthode': La première conférence de Roger de Piles à l'Académie, juillet 1699," *Revue d'esthétique* 31/32 (1997): 83–98.

Sansovino, Francesco. *Delle cose notabili che sono in Venezia.* Venice, 1561.

Saxl, Fritz. "The Battle Scene without a Hero: Aniello Falcone and His Patrons," *Journal of the Warburg and Courtauld Institutes* 3 (1939–1940): 70–87.

Scannelli, Francesco. *Il microcosmo della pittura.* Cesena, 1657. Reprint. Bologna: Nuova Alfa, 1989.

Scaramuccia, Luigi. *Le finezze de' pennelli italiani ammirate e studiate da Girupeno sotto la scorta e disciplina del genio di Raffaello d'Urbino.* Padua, 1674. Reprint, edited by Guido Giubbini. Milan: Labor, 1965.

Schaefer, Scott. "New Drawings by Martin Fréminet (1567–1619)," *Gazette des Beaux-Arts* 101 (1983): 137–140.

Schlitt, Melinda. "Painting, Criticism, and Michelangelo's 'Last Judgment' in the Age of the Counter-Reformation." In *Michelangelo's "Last Judgment,"* edited by Marcia B. Hall, 113–149. Cambridge: Cambridge University Press, 2005.

Scott, Jonathan. *Salvator Rosa: His Life and Times.* New Haven, CT: Yale University Press, 1995.

Seneca. *Epistles*, vol. 2, epistles 66–92, translated by Richard M. Gummere. Loeb Classical Library 76. Cambridge, MA: Harvard University Press, 1920.

Sennett, Richard. *The Craftsman.* New Haven, CT: Yale University Press, 2008.

Shearman, John. *Mannerism: Style and Civilization.* Harmondsworth: Penguin, 1967.

Sheriff, Mary D. "Invention, Resemblance, and Fragonard's Portraits de Fantaisie," *The Art Bulletin* 69, no. 1 (March 1987): 77–87.

———. *Fragonard: Art and Eroticism.* Chicago: Chicago University Press, 1990.

Slive, Seymour. "On the Meaning of Frans Hals' 'Malle Babbe,'" *The Burlington Magazine* 105, no. 727 (October 1963): 432–436.

———. *Frans Hals.* 3 vols. London: Phaidon, 1970–1974.

———, ed. *Frans Hals.* London: National Gallery of Art, 1989. Exhibition catalog.

Socrate, Mario. "'Borrón' e la pittura 'di macchia' nella cultura letteraria del 'siglo de oro,'" *Dialoghi di storia dell'arte* 4/5 (1997): 262–280.

Sohm, Philip. "Affectation and 'Sprezzatura' in 16th- and early 17th-century Italian Painting, Prosody and Music." In *Akten des 25. Kongresses für Kunstgeschichte*, edited by Hermann Fillitz, 23–40. Vienna: Böhlau, 1984–1986.

———. *Pittoresco: Marco Boschini, His Critics, and Their Critiques of Painterly Brushwork in Seventeenth- and Eighteenth-Century Italy.* Cambridge: Cambridge University Press, 1991.

———. "Gendered Style in Italian Art Criticism from Michelangelo to Malvasia," *Renaissance Quarterly* 48 (1995): 759–808.

———. "Baroque Piles and Other Decompositions." In *Pictorial Composition from Medieval to Modern Art,* edited by Paul Taylor and François Quiviger, 58–90. London: Warburg Institute, 2000.

———. *Style in the Art Theory of Early Modern Italy.* Cambridge: Cambridge University Press, 2001.

———. "Caravaggio's Deaths," *Art Bulletin* 84, no. 3 (September 2002): 449–468.

Soria, Martin S. "Esteban March: Baroque Battle and Portrait Painter," *The Art Bulletin* 27, no. 2 (June 1945): 109–123.

Soussloff, Catherine M. *The Absolute Artist: The Historiography of a Concept.* Minneapolis: University of Minnesota Press, 1997.

Spagnolo, Maddalena. "Vasari e le 'difficultà dell'arte.'" In *Percorsi vasariani: Tra le arti e le lettere. Atti del Convegno di Studi*, edited by Maddalena Spagnolo and Paolo Torriti, 89–108. Montepulciano: Le Balze, 2004.

———. *Correggio: geografia e storia della fortuna (1528–1657).* Milan: Silvana, 2005.

Spezzaferro, Luigi. "Mattia Preti tra immagine letteraria e realtà documentaria." In *Mattia Preti: Il Cavalier Calabrese*, edited by Giorgio Ceraudo, Claudio Strinati, and Luigi Spezzaferro, 31–44. Naples: Electa, 1999. Exhibition catalog.

Spike, John T. "Mattia Preti cavaliere e pittore dell'Ordine Gerosolimitano." In *Mattia Preti e l'Ordine di San Giovanni tra la Calabria e Malta*, 22–29. Naples: Electa, 1999. Exhibition catalog.

———. "La fortuna critica di Mattia Preti." In *Il Cavalier calabrese Mattia Preti tra Caravaggio e Luca Giordano*, 21–26. Milano: Silvana Editoriale, 2013. Exhibition catalog.

Spinosa, Nicola. *Ribera.* Naples: Electa, 2006.

———. *Dipinti del XVII secolo: la scuola napoletana.* Naples: Electa, 2008.

Spinosa, Nicola, Silvia Cassani, and Wolfgang Prohaska, eds.. *Barock in Neapel: Kunst zur Zeit der österreichischen Vizekönige.* Naples: Electa, 1993. Exhibition catalog.

Spinosa, Nicola, Andrea Rich, and Wilfried Seipel, eds. *Luca Giordano 1634–1705.* Castel Sant'Elmo, Naples: Museo di Capodimonte, 2001. Exhibition catalog.

Steinberg, Leo. "Resisting Cézanne: Picasso's *Three Women.*" *Art in America* 66, no. 6 (November–December 1978): 114–33.

Sterling, Charles. "Quelques Imitateurs et Copistes de Poussin." In *Nicolas Poussin: Colloque international 19.–21. September 1958*, edited by André Chastel, 264–276. Paris: Centre National de la Recherche Scientifique, 1960.

———. "An Unknown Masterpiece by Fragonard." In *Portrait of a Man (The Warrior)*, n.p. Williamstown, MA: Sterling and Francine Clark Art Institute, 1964. Exhibition catalog.

Stigliani, Tommaso. *Dello occhiale: opera difensiva al cavalier Gio. Battista Marini.* Venice, 1627.

Stoichita, Victor. *The Pygmalion Effect: From Ovid to Hitchcock.* Chicago: University of Chicago Press, 2008.

Stoichita, Victor, and Anna Maria Coderch. *Goya: The Last Carnival.* London: Reaktion, 1999.

Stone, David Marshall. "Theory and Practice in Seicento Art: The Example of Guercino." PhD diss., Harvard University, 1991.

———. "In Figura Diaboli: Self and Myth in Caravaggio's David and Goliath." In *From Rome to Eternity: Catholicism and the Arts in Italy, ca. 1550–1650*, edited by Pamela M. Jones and Thomas Worcester, 19–42. Leiden: Brill, 2002.

Strinati, Claudio M. "Pittore bravissimo, il più bravo di tutti ma non un grande artista," *Il Giornale dell'Arte* 21 (2003): 59.

Summers, David. *Michelangelo and the Language of Art.* Princeton, NJ: Princeton University Press, 1981.

Susinno, Francesco. *Le vite de' pittori messinesi.* Messina, 1724.

Suthor, Nicola. *Augenlust bei Tizian: Zur Konzeption sensueller Malerei in der Frühen Neuzeit.* Munich: Wilhelm Fink, 2004.

———. "'Il pennello artificioso': Zur Intelligenz der Pinselführung." In *Instrumente in Kunst und Wissenschaft: Zur Architektonik kultureller Grenzen im 17. Jahrhundert*, edited by Helmar Schramm, Ludger Schwarte, and Jan Lazardzig, 114–136. Berlin: De Gruyter, 2006.

———. "Schnitt=Strich in Albrecht Dürers Stereometrischen Zeichnungen." In *Linea I: Gra e di imagini tra Quattrocento e Cinquecento*, edited by Marzia Faetti and Gerhard Wolf, 87–109. Venice: Marsilio, 2008.

———. "Drawing a Line and Questioning Art." In *Image, Improvisations, Sound, and Silence from 1000–1800—Degree Zero*, edited by Babette Hellemans and Alissa Jones Nelson, 91–112. Amsterdam: Amsterdam University Press 2018.

Thibault d'Anvers, Gérard. *Académie de l'epee, ou se dimonstrent par reigles mathématiques sur le fondement d'un cercle mysterieux....* Leyden, 1628.

———. *The Academy of the Sword.* 1628–1630. Reprint, translated by John Michael Greer. London: Aeon Books, 2017.

Thielemann, Andreas. "Schlachten erschauen—Kentauren gebären: Zu Michelangelos Relief der Kentaurenschlacht." In *Michelangelo: Neue Beiträge*, edited by Michael Rohlmann, 17–92. Munich: Deutscher Kunstverlag, 2000.

Thuillier, Jacques. *Fragonard. A Biographical and Critical Study*, translated by Robert Allen. Geneva: Skira, 1967.

Ticozzi, Stefano. *Dizionario dei pittori.* 2 vol. Milan, 1818.

Toesca, Ilaria. "Versi in lode di Artesemia Gentileschi," *Paragone* 22 (1971): 89–92.

Tomory, Peter. "Battles, War and Soldiers: Salvator Rosa as Moralist," in *Storia dell'arte* 68, (1990): 256–267.

Turner, Nicholas. "Ferrante Carlo's 'Descrittione della Cupola di S. Andrea della Valle depinta dal Cavalier Gio. Lanfranchi': A source for Bellori's Descriptive Method," *Storia dell'arte* 12 (1972): 297–325.

Vaes, Maurice, ed. "Appunti di Carel van Mander su vari pittori italiani suoi contemporanei," *ROMA* 9 (1931): 193–208.

Van Hoogstraten, Samuel. *Inleyding tot de hooge schoole der schilderkonst.* Rotterdam, 1678.

Van Mander, Karel. *Appunti di Carel van Mander su vari pittori italiani suoi Contemporanei*, ed. by Maurice Vaes, in: *ROMA*, vol. 9, 1931, 193–208.

———. *The Lives of the Illustrious Netherlandish and German Painters, from the first edition of the* Schilder-boek *(1602–1604)*, edited by Hessel Miedema. Vol. 1: The Text. Doornspijk, 1994.

Varchi, Benedetto. *Due Lezzioni.* Florence: Lorenzo Torrentino, 1550.

Vasari, Giorgio. *Le Vite de' più eccellenti pittori scultori e architettori*, edited by Rosanna Bettarini and Paola Barocchi. 6 vols. Florence: Sansoni, 1966–1987.

———. *The Lives of the Artists*, translated with an introduction and notes by Julia Conaway Bondanella and Peter Bondanella. Oxford: Oxford University Press, 2008.

Vazzoler, Franco. *La Maschera del Boia: testi letterari italiani del XVI e XVII secolo sul carnefice.* Genua: Herodote, 1982.

Verdet, André. *Entretiens, notes et écrits sur la peinture:*

Index

Note: Page numbers in italic type indicate illustrations.

Photo Credits

Permission to reproduce illustrations is provided by the owners and sources as listed in the captions. Additional copyright notices and photography credits are as follows. Numbers refer to figure numbers.

(1) The Picture Art Collection / Alamy Stock Photo; (2) Scala / Art Resource, NY; (3) Author; (4) Gabinetto Fotografico delle Gallerie degli Uffizi; (5) Scala / Art Resource, NY; (6) Album / Alamy Stock Photo; (7) Framed Art / Alamy Stock Photo; (8) Rogers Fund, 1922; (9) Art Gallery of Ontario; (11) Purchased with the Rogers Fund, transferred from the Library, 1941; (12) Bequest of Alexandrine Sinsheimer, 1959; (14) Purchased with the Elisha Whittelsey Fund, 1949; (15–16) Author; (17) Heritage Image Partnership Ltd / Alamy Stock Photo; (19) British Museum; (21) The Picture Art Collection / Alamy Stock Photo; (22) Detroit Institute of Arts, USA, Gift of Mr. Leslie H. Green / Bridgeman Images; (23) Purchased with the Harris Brisbane Dick Fund, 1941; (24) © Photographic Archive Museo Nacional del Prado; (26) Gabinetto Fotografico delle Gallerie degli Uffizi; (28–29) Author; (32) © Rijksmuseum Amsterdam; (33) Herzog Anton Ulrich-Museum Braunschweig, Kunstmuseum des Landes Niedersachsen Foto: Museum; (35) © Collection musée Réattu; (38) Scala / Art Resource, NY; (39) © RMN-Grand Palais / Art Resource, NY; (40) Per gentile concessione delle Gallerie Nazionali di Arte Antica Bibliotheca Hertziana—Istituto Max Planck per la storia dell'arte / Enrico Fontolan; (42) © Museu de Belles Arts de València; (43) © Rijksmuseum, Amsterdam; (44) Author; (45) © Rijksmuseum, Amsterdam; (46) Cameraphoto Arte, Venice / Art Resource, NY; (47) HIP / Art Resource, NY; (48–52) Author; (53) Purchased with the Roger Fund, 1954; (54) Author; (55) Vatican Museums and Galleries, Vatican City Artothek / Bridgeman Images; (57) The Elisha Whittelsey Collection, purchased with the Elisha Whittelsey Fund, 1959; (58) © DeA Picture Library / Art Resource, NY; (59) The Royal Collection © 2019, Her Majesty Queen Elizabeth II; (60) © RMN-Grand Palais / Art Resource, NY; (61) Patrons' Permanent Fund; (62) © Rijksmuseum Amsterdam; (66) The Elisha Whittelsey Collection, purchased with the Elisha Whittelsey Fund, 1974; (70) Scala / Art Resource, NY; (71) Author; (73–78) Author; (79) Alinari / Art Resource, NY; (80–81) Author; (82) Scala / Art Resource, NY; (83) © DeA Picture Library / Art Resource, NY; (84–85) Author; (86) The Elisha Whittelsey Collection, purchased with the Elisha Whittelsey Fund, 1959; (87) Author; (88) Gift of Allen Evarts Foster, B. A. 1906; (89) Erich Lessing / Art Resource, NY; (90) Author; (91) Scuola Grande di San Rocco, Venice, Italy, Cameraphoto Arte Venezia / Bridgeman Images; (93) classicpaintings / Alamy Stock Photo; (95) National Central Library of Rome; (96) Purchased with income from the Jacob S. Rogers Fund; (97) Purchased with the Jules Bache Collection, 1949; (98) Harvard Art Museums / Fogg Museum, Gift of Mrs. Eric Schroeder; (99–100) Gabinetto Fotografico delle Gallerie degli Uffizi; (101) © Staatsgalerie Stuttgart; (102) DeA Picture Library / Art Resource, NY; (104) Isabella Stewart Gardner Museum, Boston; (106) © Photographic Archive Museo Nacional del Prado; (108) The History Collection / Alamy Stock Photo; (109) Adoc photos / GETTY IMAGES; (110) Santa Maria del Popolo, Rome, Italy / Bridgeman Images; (112) Rogers Fund, 1962; (113) Vatican Museum; (114) Kunstpalast/ARTOTHEK; (116) Bert Freidus Fund; (126) © National Portrait Gallery, London; (127) © RMN-Grand Palais / Art Resource, NY; (128) The Elisha Whittelsey Collection, purchased with the Elisha Whittelsey Fund, 1955; (129) © RMN-Grand Palais / Art Resource, NY; (130) Gift of Mrs. Mellon Bruce in memory of her father, Andrew W. Mellon; (131) bpk Bildargentur/ (Gemaeldegalerie / SMB / Joerg P. Anders) Art Resource, NY; (135) © 2019 Estate of Pablo Picasso / Artists Rights Society (ARS), New York